The Globalisation of War

Volume 1

Nicholas Browne

First published in 2023 by:
Nicholas Browne

© Copyright 2023
Nicholas Browne

The right of Nicholas Browne to be identified as the author of this work has been asserted by him in accordance with the Copyright, Designs and Patents Act 1988.

All Rights Reserved

No reproduction, copy or transmission of this publication may be made without written permission. No paragraph of this publication may be reproduced, copied or transmitted save with the written permission or in accordance with the provisions of the Copyright Act 1956 (as amended).

ISBN: 978-1-7391210-0-6

Printed and bound in Great Britain by:
Book Printing UK Remus House, Coltsfoot Drive, Woodston, Peterborough PE2 9BF

Dedicated to my wife Henrietta

The bells of hell go ting a ling a ling

For you but not for me

O death where is thy sting a ling a ling

Or grave thy victory?

Great War Song

Contents

Foreword 7

A Word on Statistics 20

List of Maps 22

The World Before 1914 24

Rising Nations 32

Other Key Developments Before 1914 45

The First World War Commences 52

The War Continues 1915–1916 73

The War on Land at Sea and in the Air 92

Talk of Peace 110

The First World War 1917 119

The Central Powers Advance 134

The Allies Strike Back 158

The Peace Conference 178

The Russian Revolution 201

Boom, Depression and the League of Nations 219

Changing Times in Germany 237

Other Rising World Powers 248

The Changing World Scene 266

Developments in the Far East 285

Nations Seeking Advantage 294

This is a summary of the 6 books and will be omitted from future publications. MWB.

Foreword

The six volumes, after an introductory prelude, cover the time between the start of the Great War and the Second World War. The Great War is now termed the First World War. It was only a world war in part as the fighting took place in Europe, the Atlantic Ocean and the Middle East. South America, the Pacific Ocean and Asia were hardly involved. Many thought the war would be short but it became a war of attrition with enormous casualties at Verdun, the Somme and the Brusilov offensive. The latter was the most successful in terms of territory gained but the Russians lost a million men and they and the Austro-Hungarians never recovered.

Towards the end of 1916 there were people seeking peace after such slaughter, which resolved nothing. Churchill wrote that the only chance of a peaceful settlement was at the end of 1914. By the end of 1916 there was stalemate. The last two years of the war saw the collapse of Russia, the development of the tank and aircraft, and the involvement of the United States. Economics was beginning to dominate and the United States was funding Britain just as Britain and France were funding the rest of Europe, including Russia, which collapsed economically. The American role in the fighting war was not significant, more soldiers dying of flu than were killed on the battlefield, but the tired Germans and Austro-Hungarians perceived the great potential of the United States. That and the Allied use of the tank and aircraft, plus the debilitating effect of the flu pandemic determined the ending of the war.

When the fighting stopped a peace conference was convened. Russia was in chaos and at war with Poland, which was forced back to its borders, but the Russian civil war continued and it ignored the peace conference where there were endless problems. The break-up of the Ottoman Empire saw the formation of fragile nation states. The Austro-Hungarian Empire also disintegrated into nation states and the problem of reparations became solely a

German problem. The United States was influential and wanted to stop future wars through the formation of the League of Nations. The failures of the peace conference were many but provided a blueprint for the world, which endures.

Peace was celebrated. Radio came into being and the motor car was mass produced. The war had diminished the wealth of the major participants and its cost had to be paid for. The depression led to severe unemployment and suffering, and politics revolved around the means of solving this. Many of the men who would lead their countries through the next war were in power. Stalin, Hitler, Roosevelt and Mussolini were leaders in the 1930s. Churchill was ignored and France could not find a dominant personality. Japan had an emperor who presided over a government repeatedly threatened by a coup d'état. China had warlords and was not united.

A war took place between fascism and communism in Spain but was localised. A more significant war took place in China with Japan conquering the eastern littoral. Further north, in 1940, the Soviets and the Japanese conflicted at the Battle of Nomonhan and Japan's failure was a factor in it looking south for conquests. September 1939 is regarded as the start of the Second World War, although the United States, the Soviet Union and Japan were not involved. In Western Europe, the brilliant German army knocked France, the Netherlands and Belgium out of the war and sent the British back to their homeland. The French decided to fold and would not continue the fight from North Africa.

Germany's attempts to neutralise Britain by air and sea failed and, with Italy entering the war as an Axis partner, the fighting continued in North and East Africa. The Germans were only partially interested in the Italian Empire, their eyes being on the Soviet Union, and on 22 June 1941 they attacked. Hitler thought that the Soviet Union, at the Archangel–Astrakhan line, would be conquered by Christmas. There was a magnificent capture of territory until the Wehrmacht was stopped by the weather, desperate defences and stretched supply lines in December 1941.

Nevertheless, it seemed to the Japanese that Germany would win and the Germans and Italians honoured the pact with Japan and declared war on the United States. In December 1941 Japan decided to go south and attacked Pearl Harbor with aerial torpedoes, a brilliant technological breakthrough but the achievement was limited. Japan's submarines were failures and the American aircraft carriers were elsewhere. At the same time, Japan attacked Malaya and the Philippines, which soon succumbed, as did the Dutch East Indies. The Japanese were masters of the west Pacific, their objective to limit

American infiltration of the east Pacific. In May 1942 a great fleet of aircraft carriers, battleships, cruisers, destroyers, oilers and assorted ships set out to capture Midway Island and what followed was one of the most significant naval battles in history. It shattered Japanese morale even though Japan would hold out for a further three years.

With the Battle of Britain, the British had limited German expansion. The Luftwaffe had gone to the Soviet Union via Yugoslavia, Greece and Crete. Hitler was determined, once the Soviet Union was beaten, to bomb Britain into submission. The Germans had overcome the Balkans but made no headway in Syria and Iraq, while the Italians had lost East Africa. The fighting coalesced around Libya, Egypt, the Mediterranean Sea and Malta. There were fluctuating fortunes dictated by leadership, tank and aircraft qualities. In the Atlantic, the Kriegsmarine tried to break the British supply lines. It was a long battle dictated by intelligence appreciations and air and sea battles. The British counter-attack by bombing Germany started inefficiently but became more aggressive and successful.

Churchill and Roosevelt met at Casablanca and determined that the defeat of Germany was the prime objective. Moreover, Roosevelt wanted American troops to be bloodied in North Africa. The British had won a great and decisive victory at El Alamein and the Allied invasion of West Africa provided a pincer movement of the Axis forces, which eventually led, seven months later, to the surrender of 350,000 soldiers in Tunisia. This was a great victory, which led to the invasion of Sicily and the southern part of Italy. However, the Americans were very keen to take the direct route to Berlin. The British were less keen and it would remain a point of difference. The United States wanted to invade the mainland of Europe from Britain in 1943, which would have pleased Stalin but a lack of shipping prevented this.

In the summer of 1942 mobility returned to warfare in the Soviet Union. The Germans ignored Moscow and moved south into the Caucasus. Their objective was oil. The Soviets had learned to retreat, which caused the Germans to split their army. The move into the Caucasus was a partial success until they reached country that would not take tanks and was forested. The small amount of captured oil was difficult to extract and transport. This was failure. The other part of the Wehrmacht tried to control the Volga through the capture of Stalingrad. Here was the key battle where the Soviets would not give ground. Although the Germans had air superiority, it was not very effective as the two antagonists were so close together. The Germans suffered a great defeat, one of the most significant of the war. It forced them back into the western part of Ukraine, where Von Manstein, the victor of the Crimea, stabilised the situation.

In the Pacific, battles raged. At Guadalcanal in the Solomon Islands, the United States wanted control of the airfield and the island, plus the sea around it. Air supremacy would guarantee control of the route to Australia. It was a long battle, which Nimitz and the US Navy would control. Further west was New Guinea where air supremacy was also of cardinal importance. MacArthur controlled this area and he had his difficulties. He was scathing about the splitting of the commands in the Pacific.

In the Atlantic there was a cyber war between Germany and Britain. At first the Germans had the advantage as they penetrated British codes and knew when the convoys sailed. But they failed to perceive that the British could penetrate their very sophisticated codes with the use of computers. Again Allied air supremacy started to extend over the Atlantic, and U-boats, which had to surface from time to time, were bombed or depth-charged. In the end Dönitz had to take his U-boats out of the Atlantic. They would not return as a major attacking force, so food and oil would get through to Britain. Enormous amounts of oil turned into aviation fuel were needed for the bombing of Germany. In 1943 the RAF was causing huge damage to industry in the Ruhr. It was difficult to bomb accurately because of industrial haze and resourceful German defence. After the Ruhr the next target was Hamburg, the second city of Germany. The city was hit so hard that it suffered from firestorms. Albert Speer said that Germany could not take too much of this. Up until this point, the US air force had not been fully operational but it was increasing its resources.

Germany was now fighting on four main fronts, of which the Soviet one was the most important. Stalingrad was a great victory but the Soviets needed a victory with tanks and aircraft, which was what they got at the Battle of Kursk. Soviet tank resources were greater, with parity in the air. Soviet tanks broke the Wehrmacht tank army, a defeat from which the Germans would not recover as they needed tanks on three fronts. At the same time, the Allies landed on the Italian mainland and made slow progress. Italy was not a good place to make war.

The air war in Europe was developing. The Americans wanted to bomb industrial sites and they targeted ball bearing and oil installations. They bombed by daylight, while the British went at night and targeted cities, including Berlin. The German defence system was very good and caused lots of casualties but it was focusing on Berlin, much to the benefit of the Allies when they decided to land in Normandy.

The Japanese now dominated Burma and had ambitions in India. There were Japanese generals who supported this and others who thought it could lead to a loss of control. The Japanese army lived off the land and what they could capture but they met their match at Kohima and Imphal, where they found their supply lines had become too attenuated and their fight became heroic but futile.

The Americans believed that their gradual move forward in the Pacific was the correct strategy against Japan. They could not understand that the British wanted to go south and capture Sumatra prior to retaking Malaya. They had a point. The Americans were always direct but they had their problems. Nimitz was recapturing islands such as Guam, Tinian and Saipan. They were important as this brought aircraft within striking distance of mainland Japan. MacArthur wanted to capture the Philippines and ignore Formosa (Taiwan). Roosevelt agreed to this. He feared Mac Arthur's political ambitions.

The British and the Americans also had divergent views on Europe. The Americans wanted a cross-channel operation and to take a direct route to Berlin. Churchill and Alan Brooke, in addition to the landing in France, wanted to attack Germany through its soft underbelly and take Vienna. The cross-channel operations (Overlord) took the majority of resources and it has claim to be the most brilliant operation of the war. It could be said that to land in Normandy and to fight through the bocage country was absurd. If the Germans could bring their overwhelming tank advantage into the fight, the invasion could be stopped. The Allies needed a port and created an artificial one. False intelligence caused the Germans to keep their tanks around Calais. The big advantage to the Allies was the control of the air and sea. The Luftwaffe was busy defending Berlin and Allied control of the air over Normandy and the sea landings was decisive.

The fighting in Normandy was attritional but, if the Allies broke through, both Montgomery and Rommel knew that France would quickly fall. When that happened it became a matter of the allocation of resources. The Soviets had promised to attack in the east and their resources, especially in manpower and tanks, allowed them to press on. Italy, despite the fall of Rome, was forgotten by the Allies but not by Hitler, who took great pride in the weak Allied advance. To hope to win on three fronts, having lost control of the Atlantic and the air over Germany, was ridiculously optimistic. The Germans were relying on a secret weapon. They were producing pilotless aircraft whose payload of bombs was not large. They also had missiles to which there was no defence. They were very destructive and dangerous but lacked accuracy. In the United States, the development of the atomic bomb was proceeding and the scientists were optimistic about its production and efficacy.

In the east there were great sea battles to defend the invasion of the Philippines. Battleships were still used, despite their vulnerability to air and submarine attack. The Americans had created the greatest navy in the world and, with aircraft carriers and superior planes, they had control. The fight in the Philippines was subject to Japanese fanaticism in difficult terrain. Manila, which MacArthur had ceded to Japan in 1942, incurred vicious fighting. In the Pacific Islands, airfields were being prepared for the bombing of Japan.

In Western Europe the question of logistics determined where the Allies attacked. Patton demanded fuel to go via Metz. Montgomery wanted to end the war in 1944 via Arnhem and the north. Even if Arnhem was captured this was not possible as supplies could not be provided via Antwerp. Hitler had organised a system of port defences that held up the Allies. The Germans created an army in the Ardennes, which aimed to split the British and the Americans and take Antwerp. The surprised Americans were forced to retreat in what was called the Battle of the Bulge. The failed attack was the last great action of the Wehrmacht.

The Soviets moved slowly forward. Their armies were formidable but did not have great mobility. They used trucks from the United States, delivered under lend-lease. They had good artillery, vastly superior manpower and, because of the defence of Berlin and the rest of the Reich, the Germans lacked aircraft on the Soviet front. The leadership of the Soviet army was first class. In Zhukov they had a soldier, albeit a butcher, who had a great strategic feeling for war. The chief of staff, Shaposhnikov, was exceptionally able and they both acted in tandem. The generals directing the armies also had great talent. The dross had been removed.

It could be said that the Philippines could have been bypassed and Formosa captured, but taking the Philippines cut the supply lines from the south and the sea battles were triumphant and destroyed the Japanese navy. The big land battles were in Burma. The Japanese, in retreat after the great battles in Bengal, had a logistical nightmare in supplying their troops, while the British had the good fortune to be supplied by the magnificent Dakotas, one of the great aircraft of the war. Even for the British, provisions were sparse. As they moved on past Mandalay and on to Rangoon a great leader had made his reputation. Slim had not only military matters to engage him but also political ones. The Burmese army was changing sides and it was a most delicate challenge in man-management. Slim managed this with some finesse. Moreover, his army was largely Indian and, as a Gurkha, he took great pride in the prowess and achievements of the Indians.

In the middle of 1944 there was a meeting at Bretton Woods, on the east coast of the United States, of economic representatives of the free world. An interesting fact was that the Germans took a great interest in the proceedings. The two most influential representatives were Harry Dexter White for the United States and John Maynard Keynes for the British Empire. Prior to the meeting there had been a disagreement between the two of them about what should be the unit of account. Keynes wanted a neutral unit and called it the bancor. White countered by suggesting it be called unitas and then rejected neutrality and advocated the dollar, which was accepted. There were fixed exchange rates, which lasted for a quarter of a century, but the flaw in the agreement was making the dollar the world's reserve currency. One might call it a flaw but it has lasted a long time to the benefit of the world; however, it hugely benefits the United States and it has created a rift between the empire states of the Soviet Union, China and the United States.

In September 1944 Roosevelt and Churchill met at Quebec. Roosevelt was accompanied by Morgenthau, his secretary of state. Morgenthau was a Jew and obviously affected by what had happened to the Jews. He wanted the Germans punished and suggested that post-war it should become an agrarian state with no industrial base. Surprisingly, Roosevelt agreed with this but it shocked Churchill. Moreover, it was used in negotiations. If Churchill did not accept this, lend-lease would end with the European war. Britain was in a financial mess and, without lend-lease, it could not maintain its position in the world. It was Anthony Eden who persuaded the Americans that an agrarian German state was not feasible and Roosevelt had second thoughts about lend-lease.

The invasion of Germany necessitated the crossing of the Rhine, a wide river in many places with many bridges, and Patton managed to capture one. His passionate attacking always threatened to lead to success. His way of operating was different to that of Montgomery, who encouraged the enemy to confront him and, once he had sucked in the reserves and beaten the opposition, the way was open to Berlin. This is what happened in Normandy. Montgomery made great use of paratroopers, who descended in their thousands, but once on the ground were very dependent on the ground forces. The significance of the use of paratroopers in this war was hard to discern. They were usually elite troops and easy targets in the air. Montgomery crossed the Rhine and was ready to move on Berlin. Meanwhile, Patton had recorded a great victory in the Ruhr, with a large German surrender. Hitler used Model as a general who could restore fortunes but this defeat was too much for him and he committed suicide.

How would the Germans end the war? Hitler was always contemptuous of the Soviets and thought they could be counter-attacked and driven back. In this he was wrong. He feared the western Allies but they were in a dilemma. British influence was not significant and the Americans had a president who was dying and incapable of much work. There were plenty of able people around him but they did not have authority to make decisions. Roosevelt had just been elected for a fourth term and he and the Democratic Party had taken care in the selection of a vice-president. Roosevelt ignored Harry Truman and did not take him to Yalta.

Roosevelt, overall, was the greatest leader of his time and his distinction has not been diminished. However, his treatment of De Gaulle and Truman was dire. This weakness was small but all men have their weaknesses. The dying man had no strategic vision for the ending of the war in Europe and allowed Marshall and Eisenhower to deal with the problem of the southern redoubt. Hitler was wedded to Berlin and would never leave it, although many tried to persuade him. Eisenhower had to agree with the Soviets where they would meet. The Soviets were intent on the capture of Berlin and did not want interference from their western Allies. Eisenhower stopped at the Elbe, with Patton, Montgomery and Churchill straining at the leash and wanting to go further.

The meeting of the 'Big Three' at Yalta was very revealing. Stalin was in a state of insecurity and would not leave the Soviet Union. The cachexic Roosevelt behaved with great bravery and travelled to Yalta. He believed that, as the head of a great country that had a contiguous empire, he could make an accommodation with Stalin, the head of another contiguous empire. Roosevelt was obsessed with the legitimacy of power, which is why he was contemptuous of De Gaulle, who had little legitimacy. Both Stalin and Roosevelt saw the weakness of Britain, with a near bankrupt and dissolving empire made up of non-contiguous countries.

The war in Europe started with Poland and ended with the same problem. The Soviets thought it was their problem to solve and objected to any interference from Britain. As a quid pro quo they gave Britain a free hand in Greece and stopped the communists from making civil war. The Soviet solution was to move Poland westwards, obliterating East Prussia, which Churchill opposed. Roosevelt was not much interested in Poland but pursued agreement on the setting up of the United Nations.

There was also the matter of the break-up of Germany, where France posed a problem. At first, Germany was divided into three parts but Churchill wanted France to be allocated a part. He was deeply worried as to how Western Europe could face the Soviets, especially as Roosevelt wanted the United States to leave Europe after two years. Roosevelt was always worried about the isolationists in American politics. Stalin had a wonderful time provoking his very able generals, such as Konev, and with Zhukov, who was in the front line, not excepted. In the end the Soviets captured Berlin, the western Allies remained on the Elbe and there was no fighting in the southern redoubt.

The battle against Japan continued and few on the Allied side thought it would end quickly. The Americans dominated the Pacific Ocean in a magnificent display of power but they were still a long way from Japan. When the Mariana islands were captured they were 1,500 miles from Tokyo but they were in flying distance with the superb B-39s. This aircraft had a long gestation and many teething problems and it was not until late 1944 that they were ready to bomb Japan. The B-39s, like the American submarines, had air conditioning, a perk totally unknown to the Lancasters.

It was not effortless basing the B-39s at Saipan. Airfield runways had to be extended and the crews had to have stamina as the flight to Japan and back was fifteen hours. They could be attacked by Japanese fighters from bases such as Iwo Jima, which was 700 miles from Tokyo. That is why the Americans were determined to capture this tiny island with three airfields and no natural harbour. It was a natural defensive haven with hills and plenty of caves. In a sense it was like a repeat of Guadalcanal but the Japanese navy was out of the argument. It was thought that Iwo Jima would be taken in a fortnight but it went on much longer, with the Japanese taking terrible casualties. Few surrendered. The Americans lost 7,000 killed. It was an important victory and a staging post for the aircraft on their way to Japan.

Japan's policy was for sacrifice and for the United States to sustain attrition, which would persuade it to negotiate and not invade the main islands. The Japanese were pleased with the battle at Okinawa, with the attritional ground conflict causing great sacrifices on both sides. Although the Japanese navy was weak, their kamikaze pilots caused grief among the American navy, which the Japanese thought might make them reluctant to invade. They had hopes of a reasonable negotiated peace. The Japanese wanted the kokutai to remain in place, which meant that the emperor remained as head of state and would retain certain powers. In a way it was a sensible solution. Monarchies have their limitations but they are important.

They provide continuity in a country, which the kaiser and none of the Romanovs understood.

The invasion of the islands was not necessary after the dropping of the atomic bombs, which there was much discussion about in the United States. Stimson was very reluctant to do so and he was influential. Curtis LeMay reckoned area bombing would make the Japanese surrender. However, the enormous energy put in to create the bombs demanded that they should show their efficacy, as Japan, to the very end, was reluctant to surrender. It was only the emperor's casting vote that brought peace to Asia.

Peace may have come but there is no end to the problems created by such intense wars. The problems posed by the atomic bomb will never be satisfactorily sorted. All mankind can do is to live in fear of its deliverance. Now that it has been created it will never go away. But its power is too great. Even conquerors want territory that is alive and viable but the conquered might want to let loose devastating bombs as a death wish.

The United States was the great winner of the war and was looking to the future. At Bretton Woods the Americans planned the world's economic future. They tried to encapsulate all nations, including the Soviets, and even with that important failure, the dollar was made a universal reserve currency with privileges that last to this day. They also formed the International Monetary Fund (IMF) and the World Bank, while the ground rules were established for the United Nations. Such institutions were the bedrock for world government but their effectiveness depended on the inspiration of able people. The great thing is that institutions transcend the lives of men and women and create a tradition that is modified by events. The United Nations is a too large collection of delegates, which begs the question: what is a nation? The veto powers still lie with the victors of 1945 but it is still a viable institution looking for someone to inspire it.

The differences between Roosevelt and Churchill were only mildly overt. Roosevelt believed in the future of China as a great power, while Churchill saw China as a chaotic nation without coherence. Roosevelt believed that China would become a capitalist nation, which did not happen, but he respected such a large nation with such a long history and so many people. He hoped it would mould Asia, with Japan defeated, in its traditional way.

The second way Roosevelt differed to Churchill was in his opposition to the British Empire. Here he was very subtle. Churchill did not understand that in forming the Atlantic Charter there was a direct attack on the British Empire. The Charter said that all people should be given the right to forge their own destiny. Churchill did not believe it applied to his own empire. It should not have done as the empire was subject to evolution. Canada, Australia, New Zealand and South Africa were independent states within the empire. India and Burma were negotiating independence. Malaya was not too bothered but did not want the Chinese communists. West Africa was backward, East Africa more so. It was Canada's relationship with the United States that broke the empire.

Canada was dominated economically by the United States, which the Canadian dollar symbolised. When India and Egypt left the sterling area, it was seriously weakened but it could have continued. Canada, Australia, New Zealand and South Africa covered an enormous territorial area, which made the United States look insignificant, but the United States economically controlled Canada, and Britain had lost too much wealth during the war. Canada had been made into a country that was placid and had innocuous politics. Roosevelt was adamant that North America was under the control of the United States. When it was mooted that King George would establish the monarchy in Canada if Britain was invaded, Roosevelt vehemently opposed it.

The Soviet Union, the great empire builder, established the Slav line in Europe. It moved Poland eastwards, obliterating East Prussia, and made Konigsberg a Soviet city so that it had all-weather links to the rest of the world. Although it wanted world domination through its ideology of communism, its ambitious expansion was in Europe. The British tended to think of empire in terms of India when they should have confronted the United States over Canada, which was the key to the British Empire.

The defeated Japanese empire was controlled by the United States and it used its power to exclude Britain from any influence. Britain, with the help of the United States, had beaten the Japanese in Burma and its small navy had served in the Okinawa battles and controlled the Indian Ocean. ANZAC (Australian and New Zealand Army Corps) navies had been active in the Pacific, and Malaya had been important in the struggle; the Australians had fought well in New Guinea, yet Britain was excluded.

France was another loser. Conquered, humiliated and unable to find a role, it redeemed itself through De Gaulle, who maintained that the state was still coherent and had been only temporarily overrun. This was shown when Roosevelt wanted to impose a military currency on France in 1944. De Gaulle insisted that the franc should not be replaced, and won.

Real power was in the hands of empires with formal and informal powers. The United States relinquished the Philippines but retained informal power over the whole of North and South America. The United States bound other countries to it through trading links and would not tolerate military threat to the Americas. The Soviet Union was powerful through the influence of communist parties. Within the Slav line, European nations were enslaved. Outside this line the communist parties were loyal to the Soviet Union, which had to be confronted and the hundreds of years of imperial expansion stopped.

Turkey had been very clever in keeping out of the Second World War. It had also been very clever in maintaining the integrity of the nation after the Great War. Where it had failed was in the break-up of the Ottoman Empire, which disintegrated into nation states without a unifying factor. Because of its oil it could have become a great power.

Few thought of the distinctions between empires, nation states and nations. The United States and the Soviet Union were not nation states, they were empires. The British built India into an empire but it soon became dismembered and a weak empire. Roosevelt helped China to become an empire and it absorbed nations around it.

Europe, the wider Europe that included Russia to the Urals, was deeply under the influence of Christianity until the bombshell of the Great War and the rise of scientific truth. At its end, the Russian Orthodox Church was all but obliterated. In Western Europe the divided Christian churches held on to the faithful but the divinity of Christ, the lynchpin of belief, was being questioned even by those who were subject to Christian inspiration, such as Tolstoy and Smuts.

War put the Christian churches on the defensive. Communion could be given to those about to go into battle, the dead could be buried with the ritual of believing in the afterlife, but it did not add up. The finality of death was disturbing. The authority of the churches in defining life was undermined by the two great wars and the increasing revelations of scientific enquiry. We are but a tiny fertile planet in a great cosmos.

The ancient world had many gods but they were usurped and supplanted by the one God. The Christians gave their God divinity through his son Jesus Christ. The Muslims had no such instrument. The break-up of belief in the ancient world revolved around the Greek investigation into the nature of mankind. The playwrights were instrumental in this. It was Goethe who proclaimed the genius of Shakespeare, who presented mankind as it was in all its tragic, comic and historical roles. Some treat Shakespeare as a pre-eminent playwright. Some, such as Tolstoy, do not like him at all, but he is without peer in the history of all civilisations. It is he who guides us all.

The Christian Church ignores war, as does the Sermon of the Mount, which so inspired Tolstoy, who understood war but ignored it at the end of his life. Shakespeare treats war as part of the human condition. There will always be wars and rumours of wars, which demand ritualisation. There will always be atomic bombs, big or small, floating around. Shakespeare did not have to deal with atomic bombs but he always dealt with people and conditions as they were.

After God, Shakespeare has created most.[1]

A Word on Statistics

Statistics figure widely in these volumes. Some are authoritative, many are not, but they are always interesting. The Battle of Crete is a good example of the perils of taking statistics too seriously. Paul Freyberg, the son of General Lord Freyberg, wrote a biography of his father Bernard and tried to account for the German dead from this battle. Soon after the battle had ended, the Germans supplied a figure of 1,350 killed. Only they could query this but it hid the fact that the paratroop attack had been a fiasco.

After the war, Bernard Freyberg requested the figures of the number of Germans killed at this battle and a figure of 5,000 was suggested. New Zealander General Kippenberger, who had fought in the battle, counted 4,400 graves at Maleme and Galatas, with an addition of 2,000 graves at Rethymno and Heraklion. The seriously wounded who were flown back to Greece and later died were buried in Loukinia cemetery, plus there were those killed at sea, putting the figure in excess of 7,000.

The Germans hid the tragedy of the paratroop attack by crack troops but gave the Iron Cross to every paratrooper who survived. A consequence of this attack was that Hitler became reluctant to make a similar attack on Malta. To this day there is no definitive figure for the number of Germans killed. Anthony Beevor, who wrote perhaps the best account of the battle, produces the figure of 3,986 killed and missing and 2,594 wounded. The latter figure is unusual in warfare as the ratio of killed to wounded tends to be one to three.

This was just a small battle but larger ones were even more difficult to evaluate. However, one of the most interesting statistics was the lack of a statistic. The Germans did not adequately count the casualties at the Third Battle of Ypres (Passchendaele). The British managed to provide a figure and the lack of German data occupied Lloyd George for the rest of his life as he wished to prove that British sacrifices were greater than those of the enemy.

Aircraft statistics were notoriously inaccurate. The claims for aircraft shot down by the British and Germans were far too high during the Battle of

Britain. It continued with British claims over France in 1941/42. The Americans were no better when they started bombing Germany; their claims for enemy aircraft destroyed was fanciful.

Macro figures are very unreliable. How many dead in the wars is subject to intelligent guesses but they vary widely. I have yet to find a figure for those in the British armed forces who died in the flu pandemic of 1918. The Americans did produce figures and the number of men in their forces who died roughly equated to the number killed during that war.

The imprecision of statistics is well known but, when presented, they have a power of their own and tend to be believed. I ask the reader to be sceptical of all the figures that are produced in these volumes. Some are true, others pertain to the truth and are useful, while some may well be wrong. They are inserted in good faith but all statistics should be treated with care.

Nicholas Browne

List of Maps

1. Entente and Central Powers before and during the First World War (p53)
2. The Ottoman Empire during the First World War (p65)
3. Front lines early in the First World War (p69)
4. Situation in the Dardanelles in 1915 (p71)
5. The lines at Verdun, 1916 (p88)
6. The Battle of Jutland, 1916 (p98)
7. Front lines of the Brusilov Offensive, 1916 (p101)
8. Front lines at the Somme, 1916 (p104)
9. Relative positions at the Third Battle of Ypres, 1917 (p130)
10. Relative positions at the First Battle of Cambrai, 1917 (p143)
11. The route to the capture of Jerusalem, 1918 (p148)
12. The advancing German front lines, 1918 (p152)
13. The Allied front line advance, 1918 (p159)

Chapter 1

The World Before 1914

Introduction

There are always wars and rumours of wars. Their effect on nations, empires or continents is often profound and they often remain unresolved from century to century. Napoleon changed the face of Europe but with his final defeat in 1815 there was exhaustion and Europe knew peace for some years, although the threat of revolution remained. Europeans regard the period between then and the start of the Great War of 1914 as a period of relative peace but it is only partly true as there were several wars, among them the Crimean and Franco–Prussian wars, not all of short duration.

Many of these wars were colonial, where the application of power was lopsided, or European rivalries, which led to more prolonged bloodshed as in the Boer War. Outside Europe there was a civil war in the United States, which for the combatants had a proportional mortality as great as the First World War.

At the same time, before and after the momentous civil war and lasting for at least forty years, the invading Europeans in North America fought the Native Americans as they moved to the west, defining the ownership of land by force. In China, a Christian insurgency led to a war lasting thirteen years. The casualties rivalled that of either world war and the existing order's pyrrhic victory sealed the fate of the Manchus and heralded the rise of Japan. In Europe itself, war solved problems and caused even more intransigence but they were not fights to the death and usually had limited objectives. Nevertheless, these disputes choreographed the two world wars.

The Chinese Civil War 1851–1864

The civil war in China, also known as the Taiping Rebellion, had a slow genesis and started from the coastal regions of the south. Although Christianity had briefly entered China in the eighth century, it rapidly expired and it was not until the middle of the nineteenth century that it became influential. It rapidly gained adherents in 1851 when Hong Xiuquan announced the formation of the Taiping Heavenly Kingdom and proclaimed himself the new emperor of China with the title of Heavenly King. Having lost the Opium Wars, many Chinese had turned to Christianity and the Taiping rebels had embraced it. There was widespread missionary activity in China that was coming face to face with Confucianism, although not necessarily into conflict with it. The texts of Confucius were being translated into English and the philosophy was respected but the missionaries wanted the inspiration of Christianity to supplant it. On a more prosaic level, the aim of the rebels of the Heavenly Kingdom was to stop the Manchus ruling China.

For two years, Hong Xiuquan fought his way to the Yangtze and picked up half-a-million followers who converted or paid lip service to Christianity but were grateful for the security of being part of a strong army. Hong moved up the Yangtze and eventually captured Nanjing, which he established as his capital. The response of the Qing officers of the Manchus was drastic, murdering entire families who had any connection with the Taiping Heavenly Kingdom. As they still controlled most of China, the loss of life in the south was horrendous.

The West, through the influence of Christianity, may have been interfering in the affairs of China but, overall, was neutral and mainly interested in securing trading rights. The British and French, with the Americans in the background, were trying to figure out what was happening in this civil war. They wanted to trade and to reach the magnificent tea and silk producing areas via the Yangtze.

With the Chinese ambivalent about these adventurers, it was not always straightforward sailing up the Yangtze in the chaos of civil war, where no one knew who controlled what and for how long. The one advantage the Westerners had was their gunboats, which they used to force treaties with the Manchus. Ostensibly, the British and French were neutral in the civil war but, inevitably, they took a view where their interests were concerned. For instance, the Taiping Heavenly Kingdom was keen to capture Shanghai but the Europeans did not want the city involved in the war and defended it against Taiping encroachment. But they also fought the Manchus at Taku

Forts, their gunboats receiving a beating.

It was a complicated war, and like all Chinese wars there was scant regard for the right to life. Eventually, the Heavenly Kingdom reached the peak of its conquest and set up its capital at Nanjing, but by 1864 the Heavenly King was having trouble recruiting men to protect his territory. The Manchus of the Qing dynasty had found leaders from the family of Zeng Guofan, who besieged Nanjing and captured it soon afterwards. Guofan had China in the palm of his hand. Because he was not a Manchu, they were very suspicious of him but he had no ambition to become emperor. He had restored peace to the nation. The suffering had been immense and it is surmised that twenty to thirty million died. China was ravaged and would not recover for a long time. The beneficiary, in a sense, was Japan because it had signed trading treaties with the Europeans and the Americans and had learned from them.

It says much for the vastness of China and its multitudes that this civil war, with its human sacrifices on a great-war scale, did not have more impact on Europe. For the most part, the Europeans did not take sides except where it interfered with their trading rights, nor were they much concerned that Christianity was taking on Confucianism. They wanted peace and the right to trade, while the missionaries wanted peace in order to convert. If the Chinese wanted to fight each other that was their business. The Europeans used their gunboats to protect their trade routes and enclaves so, while there was a lot of killing, the European contribution to this was not significant.

The Crimean War 1853–1856

There was an increase in warfare in Europe during the second half of the nineteenth century, with two localised, significant wars in the 1850s. Empires are always waxing and waning, and one of the great empires of the time, the Ottoman, was on the wane, while the Russian Empire was predatory. The British feared Russian encroachment into India, while the Turks feared it on their borders with Europe and Asia and the seas they controlled.

The British and French did not want Russia to become a major power in the eastern Mediterranean, so they sided with the Turks in what became the Crimean War. Their limited objective was to subdue Russian naval power in the Black Sea by destroying the dockyard at Sebastopol. After much bungling and incompetence, and with several land battles, they achieved their aim.

The Austro-Hungarian Empire

The rise of nationalism was weakening the appeal of the complex multinational, multi-ethnic Austro-Hungarian Empire and gave intimations of its decline. It still flaunted its power and in the northern part of a yet-to-be-united Italy, which it controlled, they confronted the French in June 1859 at the battles of Magenta and Solferino. These battles were indecisive and the two emperors shied away from further bloodshed and made peace. However, it was clear that the defects in the dual monarchy side were greater than those of the French. The latter had made repeated frontal attacks, making large dents in the Austro-Hungarian forces, and the success of these tactics would be influential when the Austro-Hungarians met the Prussians in 1866.

The American Civil War 1861–1865 and the Move West

Away from Europe, several states in the southern slave-owning plantocracy of the United States wanted to secede from the Union, which the elected government forbade. When the southerners announced that they would secede, war was declared between north and south. This was the great war of the second half of the nineteenth century and many aspects of it would be reproduced in the two world wars.

The southern Confederacy was economically weak compared with the north. It depended on the export of cotton to Europe but had no real navy and the Union navy blockaded it along the eastern seaboard. However, the north's Federal Army, which was bigger and backed by the Union's industrial strength, could not achieve a result by destroying the Confederate army. In the end it had to break the Confederacy by economic means. A mean, ruthless army led by General William Sherman marched through Georgia and the Carolinas, living off the land, cutting communications and sacking cities. The casualties on both sides were horrific in proportion to the population and this attrition, together with the economic warfare, mirrored the two world wars to follow.

There were two influential developments from this war. One was the idea of unconditional surrender, which put the defeated at the mercy of the victor, who could then determine the rights they would accord the vanquished. Although the slave-owning plantation aristocracy was broken and a new economic order formed, every man and woman regained their rights as US citizens. With this came the principle of the democratic rights of individuals within the Union, whereby there was a government of the people, by the people and for the people. The wounds and scars took a long time to heal but the American Civil War became a monument to American idealism. The tragedy of war was there in full panoply but the death of men and women was somehow hallowed by the feeling that they did not die in vain, that war had been cathartic in the formation of a great nation.

The war continued for another fifteen years until the Native Americans were herded into reservations where the land was of dubious quality and the bison could not roam free. This is how empires are established, the great precedent being the Russian Empire. While the Americans went west, the Russians had gone east.

The Prussians

The Prussians, too, were eager for a territorial empire but the land they coveted was occupied and other nations stood in their way. Prussia's first major conflict was with the Austro-Hungarians in 1866 when its professional army won a victory that both sides came to accept. In territorial terms it was not of much moment but the fulcrum of power in the German-speaking world had passed from Vienna to Berlin. The victory owed much to the professionalism of the Prussian army and the use of the breech-loading Dreyse rifle. The Prussian army was very disciplined and represented a nation at arms. Service in the army was compulsory but for most was of short duration, which created trained reserves. The permanent army corps was directed by a general staff that studied the theory and science of war, which was being transformed by using railways and the telegraph.

The French were still regarded as having the greatest army in Europe, the heirs of the great Napoleonic army. However, when attacked in 1870, the French elan and courage could not match that of the Prussians, whose army manoeuvred, attacked and defended with cohesion. French rifle power was greater and more effective but the firm of Krupp was making its mark and mass-producing breech-loading artillery with percussion fuses, which was superior to the French artillery.

Sedan, on 1 September 1870, was the key battle of the conflict, after which the Prussians advanced on Paris, leading to the fall of Emperor Napoleon III, who was replaced by a republican government. In November there was a small French victory at Coulmiers but the siege of Paris was not lifted and the Prussians were able to negotiate an advantageous peace. Alsace and Lorraine were incorporated into a German empire and the financial indemnities forced on the French were such that they proved greater than they would get from the Germans at the end of the First World War. The Franco–Prussian War was a bitter struggle between mass armies but was limited. In technological terms it signalled the decisive influence of artillery.

The Russo–Turkish War

Turkey still had command of the Black Sea as a result of the Crimean War but Russian and Turkish enmity persisted and Russia was becoming an ally of Christian nations in the Balkans. The Muslims were persecuting the Bulgarian Christians, whom they ruled, and the Russians decided to come to their aid. They had to do this by land because of Turkish control of the Black Sea. It was difficult for the Russians going through Romania with its poor railways and having to cross the bridges of the Danube but they managed to establish a salient 180 miles across with its head at the Shipka Pass. They thought this would be a sufficient show of power for the sultan to recognise their might and retreat from Bulgaria but this did not come to pass. Osman Pasha, the Ottoman field marshal, marched from Vidin to Pleven and threatened the Danube bridges and the existence of the Bulgarian Christians because, for many people in this area, as now, ethnic cleansing was a way of life. The Turks dug in at Pleven and held out against Russian attacks but were starved out by December 1877. The Russians created a momentum and occupied most of Bulgaria, forcing the Turks to flee by sea. However, the Russians did not occupy the whole of Bulgaria as they thought it prudent to agree terms, while the Turks occupied some territory.

Egypt

Egypt had for a long time been part of the Ottoman Empire but very much a self-governing part with its own Khedive. However, with the indebtedness of the Ottoman Empire, Egypt also suffered. The French and English helped Egypt financially by providing two ministers to look after their own interests but in 1879 the Khedive rejected them.

The French and English governments appealed to the sultan, who deposed the Khedive and replaced him with his son. He was not a strong personality and Egyptians in the army revolted with nationalistic cries of Egypt for the Egyptians. Although they were mollified by a measure of power, the atmosphere was not good, Christians were made scapegoats and fifty were massacred in Alexandria. Prime Minister William Gladstone did not wish to interfere and recognised the sultan's sovereignty but felt that this massacre was going too far.

The British and French consulted with the sultan in Istanbul but found him devious and an arch prevaricator who was unwilling to restore order. The British wanted to restore order in conjunction with the sultan to avoid overriding his sovereignty but he procrastinated to such an extent that they put an army into Egypt in September 1882, fighting a decisive battle and earning the grateful thanks of the Khedive, whose power was restored.

Britain had no ambitions for control of Egypt but did want a stable regime under Turkish sovereignty. In 1887, the Turks and British were about to agree to Egyptian neutrality with the British leaving in three years provided there was stability. However, the French opposed this and the sultan sided with France, so the British stayed. The Suez Canal was now becoming more important than ever as it was the most direct link with India. As British money was now propping up Egypt, the sultan's sovereignty was ignored and his influence was diminishing.

The Boer War 1899–1902

The Boer War was profound in an unexpected way. Although the fight was between the British and the Afrikaners of Dutch extraction, two other major races were numerically in the ascendancy. Indians had been recruited as labourers for work that the Africans were unable to do and had been followed by small traders, usually Muslims, who catered for their needs. At this time, the Indian population may have just exceeded the combined white population. The African population was vastly more than this but lacked skills and the power that comes from these skills.

The war between the Afrikaners and the British could not be quickly resolved as it was fought over a large territory and the Afrikaners were very resourceful. At the time, this southern part of Africa was divided into four self-governing units: Cape Province, the Transvaal, Natal and the Orange Free State. Cape Province was predominantly British, the Orange Free State overwhelmingly Afrikaner and the other two provinces more equally divided.

The war came down to a costly British intervention and, in the end, they cut the logistical support of their opponents by taking Boer families from their homes and concentrating them in camps. Although these camps were often insanitary and resulted in deaths, they were only the harbingers of the concentration camps of the future. Peace came when the Boers realised that they could not sustain their participation in the war.

Out of this came a remarkable solution. The British and the Boers were conciliatory towards each other. On the Boer side there were two remarkable men in Luis Botha and Jan Christian Smuts. Botha was a farmer and bucolic by nature and temperament. He was not as clever as Smuts but had a warmth and understanding of people that disarmed all but fanatics. Botha's first language was Afrikaans, English was his second, unlike Smuts who had been to Cambridge University and was equally at home in both languages.

In the great language debate that would forever dominate the identity of this part of Africa, Botha sided with Smuts, who believed that English should be the dominant language as it was used in commerce and politics and had an intellectual hinterland that was lacking in the Afrikaans dialect of Dutch. Other Boer politicians opposed this and the lack of unity on the Boer side would continue to dominate South African politics and limit the power of Smuts.

Although the British had won the war and were in the ascendancy, democracy was difficult as the Boers were numerically greater. Botha and Smuts understood that this gave them an advantage, but they wanted to be part of the British Empire with its trading and defensive capability. After all, German West Africa was next door and if Germany increased its power in Europe and produced a powerful navy, it might become predatory. Thus, to Botha and Smuts it was sensible for the four provinces of South Africa to become a unit and an integral part of the British Empire. With this came true reconciliation and an ability for the newly formed nation to move forward, although it was not entirely to the liking of many of the Boers. Botha and Smuts, however, understood the realpolitik of the time.

Chapter 2

Rising Nations

Germany as a Great Power

At the beginning of the nineteenth century, Germany was not a nation as such but part of the Holy Roman Empire. Its power was diffused into small units, of which Prussia was the largest, but it was not able to defend itself against Napoleon's predations. This inability to confront large nations and form a nation of their own had preoccupied Germans for centuries.

What was a nation and what were its parameters? Language over time became regarded as a major factor. Germans, led by Luther, initiated the great split in religion at the beginning of the sixteenth century, which resulted in Germany being broadly divided into a Protestant north and a Catholic south. This was not a cohesive result for a nation but Luther's genius led him to translate the Bible into demotic German, which appealed to the masses despite the fact that they could not afford to buy the Bible.

At this time Germany was divided by language into the High German of the south and the Low German of the north, which were distinct dialects, although there was understanding between the two. The great majority spoke one or the other but Luther, a Saxon, spoke both and in his translation of the Bible he integrated the two. This written work was accepted as standard German. The language was beginning to be unified; however, this did not create a nation, rather a people with common interests, which is a precursor to becoming a nation.

It was language again, in the mighty form of Goethe, which would help propel Germany towards nationhood. Although there was a form of unification, the language was under French influence, which tended towards the refined and accentuated the difference between the learned and the demotic use of language. Goethe sensed this but it was not until he read Shakespeare that he became inspired. He described it thus: 'The first page I read made me a slave to Shakespeare for life. I jumped high in the air and, for the first time, I felt that I had hands and feet.'[2]

In 1771, at the age of twenty-two, Goethe arranged a festival celebrating Shakespeare's work. He rhapsodised on how natural the Bard's work was. These were real people saying what they felt. The upshot was a novel, *The Sorrows of Young Werther*, with its violence and agonies of love that thrilled the youth of Germany. Communication was direct and vivid but Goethe knew the world was wide.

When he was thirty-seven, he was drawn to the south and went to Rome. This was his next love affair and he waxed lyrical about Italy, saying that his visit there was the happiest time of his life. His interests ranged wide and embraced the whole world. He created a collection of plants and minerals, Newtonian optics fascinated him and he produced his own theory of colour.

Then, of course, there was his great work, *Faust*, which can be interpreted in many ways. It was representative of a growing nation and could be used as inspiration by autocratic, democratic, fascist and communist regimes but, overall, its humanity transgresses them. This was the emblem of high civilisation that propelled Germany to the forefront of Europe, not as a nation but as a people who spoke German.

Towards the end of Goethe's life, with Napoleon holding sway in Europe, Crown Prince Ludwig of Bavaria, with the break-up of the Holy Roman Empire, created Valhalla. Germany was creaking politically and Ludwig wanted to create a pantheon of great Germans, choosing a site near Regensburg, which was where the Holy Roman Empire had assembled its delegates to form a parliament. Valhalla is the place where the Valkyries placed their heroes. In his Valhalla, Ludwig placed sculptures of great Germans who had to be of German origin and speak the language.

This criterion of language was all-important. Dutch and Flemish were regarded as dialects of Low German and those speaking them qualified for inclusion in the pantheon. Catherine the Great, the ruler of Russia, was included and there were many great cultural figures; however, as in any collection of this sort, there were idiosyncratic absences. Catholic Bavaria did not look kindly on the disruption that Luther caused and he, one of the greatest Germans, was omitted until 1848 when Ludwig lost popularity and abdicated.

It was still a Christian pantheon and there were no Jews until Albert Einstein was admitted in 1990. To this day there is debate and dispute as to who should be in this pantheon but it is a heroic memorial to greatness in the German nation and its diaspora and made the German people aware of their common heritage while the nation was formed in the nineteenth century.

The creativity and energy of the new German nation spilled out all over mainland Europe and was mirrored elsewhere. The wealth created by the Industrial Revolution in Britain had found a natural outlet in its empire, while in the United States there was this great move westwards. Russia and Japan were modernising in their own ways, as was France, which had produced a nation of great beauty. However, its dynamism was muted by the lack of resources, especially coal and the psychological reverses suffered in the Napoleonic era, while it was the one country whose population did not increase greatly.

Coal was the great shaper of industrial might in the late nineteenth and early twentieth centuries. Its production in Germany increased from 30 million tons in 1871 to 70 million by 1890, 110 million by 1900 and 190 million by 1913. The smoking furnaces produced unparalleled wealth and Germany dominated Continental Europe to such an extent that it was the industrial star and all other nations were part of its constellation. There was the peripheral European nation of Great Britain, which was still a greater power but only because of its past and the potential of its empire. In many respects it was being overtaken and if its empire were taken away it would be dwarfed in terms of territory and population.

In terms of population, Europe had exploded. Malthus's predictions had been swept aside and the people, although multiplying greatly, were being fed. Germany's population in 1870 was about forty million and by 1892 had risen to fifty million, then in the next twenty-two years it rose to sixty-eight million. In Britain, there was a substantial increase in population but this was reduced by emigration, which was negligible in Germany. The Austro-Hungarian Empire grew less rapidly, from forty million in 1890 to fifty million in 1914 but emigration was significant. The biggest increase, however, was in European Russia, which grew from 100 million in 1890 to 150 million by 1914. This was a significant figure if the energies of the people could be harnessed. Russian manpower always worried Germany.

With an abundance of coal, an expanding population and sound political and educational foundations, Germany became the focal point of Europe and the chief trading partner of its neighbours. It was also the second most important trading partner of Britain, India having a greater share of exports and the United States being more important for imports. With Russia and the Austro-Hungarian Empire, Germany's share was more than a quarter of its total trade. With that went an export of capital and skills, which increased the industrial efficiency of these empires.

The use of capital was fundamental to all expansion. During the first decade of the twentieth century, all corners of the world were becoming accessible if people were determined enough to get there. The physical impediments to movement were being rapidly overcome. Large numbers of motor cars were being produced, aerial flight was in gestation, the railways traversed continents and were even beginning to open up the interior of Africa, and ships were powered by coal rather than wind.

Soon oil would replace coal. Trade routes criss-crossed the world's oceans and all the major nations could import or export their goods by rail or ship. Germany, with a sparse coastline and maritime tradition, had a modern and efficient railway system but it also had a substantial merchant marine, which traded primarily with its colonies and the Americas. These colonies were the recipients of much capital and were emerging as nations themselves.

All over Europe, this surplus capital was being used to develop the rest of the world, including the United States. The surplus was the result of capital being in very few hands. The very rich and the middle class were small in numbers, but it was they who owned the surplus capital, while the working class had a subsistence economy.

There were seeming advantages in the garnering and release of this excess capital by the few but it was already creating envy and a demand that it be released to a wider base, which helped to propagate the ideas of socialism. It would not triumph but socialism would shape the structure of Europe for the next hundred years.

The Territorial Power of Russia

Although Germany was the powerhouse of Europe, Britain the worldwide maritime empire and the United States the burgeoning expanding industrial power of another continent, Russia and its empire was the territorial giant of the world. In its western part it met Europe, to the east it faced Asia and to its south was both Asia and the Middle East. It was vast, a magnificent forbidding land empire, which in total area dwarfed the United States, even if large areas were seemingly of no use to anyone. Not only were its inhabitants fecund at the time but its wealth was increasing too.

Although it was not at the forefront of wealth-producing nations, Russia was not far behind. There was a sublime cultural flowering in literature, music and the theatre, as fine as anything in the world at the time but there was less genius in the government and the organisation of its people. It was plagued by inefficiencies exacerbated by political inadequacy and moral corruption, not helped by the country's size and climate.

Russia was a predator, like all great powers, and in Asia both Japan and China were watching it closely. In 1891, the Trans-Siberian Railway was started and those to the east feared that, when it was finished, Russia would be able to conquer Mongolia, extend its influence in Manchuria and threaten Peking. The Chinese were having enough trouble dealing with European maritime traders and did not want a land threat from Europe, while the Japanese coveted such areas as Korea, which the Russians were also eyeing.

To counteract this, the Japanese needed a strong army and navy, which existed in embryo and it strengthened. When Japan's army was put to the test against the Chinese in Korea in 1895, it was not to be found wanting and the Chinese capitulated, which was reflected in the subsequent treaty under which Japan became sovereign in Formosa, the Liaotung Peninsula, which included Port Arthur, and the Pescadores.

This was a tough treaty, which the Chinese saw as unequal, so they looked to the west for allies. The French, Germans and Russians confronted the Japanese about their position on the Liaotung Peninsula, which threw the Japanese off balance, so they sought support from Britain and the United States, who recommended that they be conciliatory. The emperor advised his people to endure the unendurable and give up Southern Manchuria.

The Japanese were humiliated, especially when Western influence and concessions grew apace on the mainland. The Chinese allowed the Russians to construct a railway across North Manchuria, 925 miles long, thus cutting 600 miles off the line to Vladivostok. With this trade route, Russia was granted timber and mining rights in Korea and challenged Japanese power.

The Armenian Massacres

No one suffers more than those at the confluence of empires and in this Armenia was a great loser. The Russian, Ottoman and Persian empires controlled the territory where the Armenians lived and Armenia had not been a nation in its own right for 500 years. It considered itself European and its people were Christians of predominantly Catholic sympathies amid the Russian Orthodox and Muslims.

There were 2.5 million Armenians, of which 1.5 million were in six eastern provinces of Turkey. However, they were not in a majority in any of these provinces. With the growth of nationalism in the Balkans and elsewhere in the Ottoman Empire, they felt themselves as a coherent unit whose time had come and, at the Congress of Berlin, they requested a Christian governor general. Sultan Abdul Hamid did appoint a Christian sub-governor to each of the six provinces but his power and influence was limited.

The Ottoman government was undoubtedly tough on the Armenians and especially harsh and discriminatory in the way they taxed them. They also turned a blind eye to Kurdish persecution. This gained the interest of European powers, led by Britain, but Otto von Bismarck, the Prussian statesman, was not prepared to support European representation on the Armenian question. The Armenians now realised that they had to defend their own rights with an armed organisation. This alarmed the sultan, who started to support a Kurdish militia that in 1892 was formalised into a force of 15,000 men. The Kurds not only confronted the militant Armenians but tried to blackmail their businesses. The Turks, with a double whammy, increased taxes and the Armenians had reason to feel persecuted.

This inflammatory situation led the Kurds to kill Armenians, which Britain, France and Russia noted, protesting to the sultan. His sympathies were with the Kurds but he promised Armenian reform, which he initiated in a dilatory way while his agents kept up the killing in eastern Turkey. It was a systematic massacre, initiated and finished by bugle calls. Turkish troops would enter a town and commence the massacre, followed by the Kurds, who were allowed to plunder. It was often started on a Friday while the Muslims were at prayer, being told that the Christians were about to slaughter them. Coming from the mosque, the inflamed Muslims would carry out their nefarious work. In the winter of 1895, between 50,000 and 100,000 Armenians lost their lives.

Gladstone made a speech of great impact, deploring Turkish behaviour and describing them as a disgrace to civilisation and a curse to mankind. He suggested that they should be erased from the map. There were thoughts in Britain of forcing the Dardanelles and making Turkey see sense but Prime Minister Lord Salisbury thought better of it and limited himself to a moral condemnation of the sultan and the Ottoman Empire.

The Rise of Japan

Between 1899 and 1901, the Boxer Rebellion reflected Chinese anger at their humiliation, directed at their rulers. However, the Manchus cleverly finessed this into hatred of foreigners, especially Christians, in China. The culmination of this unrest came in 1900 when troops helped the mob attack the foreign legations in Peking. This triggered an international response led by the Japanese. When this intervention achieved its goal, the indemnity requested increased the Chinese humiliation.

At the same time, Russia marched into Manchuria and demanded that China acknowledge it as a Russian protectorate. The Manchus were tottering and the Japanese were becoming fearful of Russian power in Asia, which they wanted to diminish. For millennia, China had been the great power in Asia, with peripheral nations acknowledging the grandeur of its civilisation and suzerainty. Japan sensed that this power was evaporating and there was an opportunity for legitimate imperial ambitions in Asia to fill the vacuum. This ambition was not necessarily against the Chinese or for the eclipse of their power but rather the acknowledgement of the reality of Japanese power and its civilisation.

Over the next five years, Japan showed the world that it was a formidable power in the East. It was aware of its weaknesses and recognised that it needed allies and should not alienate too many powers at the same time. The difficulty was with whom to ally, a conundrum that would remain for the next forty years.

There were advocates of a German alliance as the Japanese constitution and army had been modelled on that country. Others said that Russia was a natural ally, while there were advocates of an alliance with Britain, acknowledging the physical similarities of an island with maritime interests off a continental land mass. It was the latter that materialised, with the Anglo–Japanese Alliance signed in 1902. For the British it was important to repair the image of empire tarnished by the Boer War and to counteract possible Russian imperial ambitions towards India.

This alliance troubled the Russians, so with the French they reconsidered their position. The balance of power in Asia had altered, which led to the Russians and Chinese forming an accord and for Russian troops to leave Manchuria. The Russians still wanted an ice-free winter port to the east and, as their troops left the north of Manchuria, they poured troops into the south. The Japanese, British and United States governments protested and, when they could not resolve the matter diplomatically, Japan gave an ultimatum to the Russians.

Japan and Russia at War

In February 1904 Japan struck at the Russian fleet at Seoul and Port Arthur. Some thought this to be a dastardly deed, but surprise had been the norm in wars throughout the world in the preceding 200 years. The war escalated and was fought on land and at sea, with Russia regarded as a great power with substantial reserves who would easily overcome Japan. The Russians, however, had logistical problems with the single-line Trans-Siberian Railway, so the Japanese were able to deploy their forces more economically.

Although Japan had done great damage to the Russian fleet, they had not destroyed it and they had to blockade Port Arthur and invade the peninsula. The battles on land were ferocious, with the Japanese scorning death and showing great self-sacrifice. However, they were also merciful to the captured and their medical services were first class compared to the Russians. The battles on land were inconclusive but, in August 1904, a Russian fleet came from Vladivostok determined to reassert Russian power. Makarov, the Russian commander, had fought an admirable battle, pursuing the Japanese when they attacked and retreating to Port Arthur when necessary. It was on one of these retreats that his flagship struck a mine and within a few minutes sank.

Makarov's ultimate strategy had been to take his fleet to Vladivostok. It was a blow to the Russians that they had no other admiral of his quality and were now bottled up in Port Arthur. This led to Japanese command of the sea around Manchuria and Korea, while their ground troops were well supplied. However, Russia had the advantage in manpower, which the Japanese acknowledged. Despite this, the Japanese were successful on land and captured the high points near Port Arthur and sank the remaining ships in the harbour with artillery. The Japanese fleet returned home but it had been in a fight and had suffered casualties that it could ill afford.

It was not the end of the war, though. Russia felt the humiliation of its defeat in the Far East and decided on revenge through its substantial fleet in Europe. The only problem was how to get it to the other side of the world in fine fighting order. The Japanese had so far won because of their superior training and the quality of their ships, most of which had been built in Britain. All ships at this time were coal-fired and the coal had to be of good quality. Japan's ships were fired by Welsh coal, which Japan had in abundance, while Russia was supplied from Hamburg and coalers had to accompany the fleet from the Baltic to Vladivostok.

There were modern ships in the Russian fleet but they were not well handled and they had not eradicated faults. The higher command was weak, illustrated by a nervousness at the start of their long journey, fearing that Japan's torpedo boats had reached the North Sea. This resulted in the might of the Russian fleet attacking several British trawlers with fatal consequences.

Japan was Britain's ally and, although Britain held no real animosity towards Russia, this pushed it further into the Japanese camp. The Royal Navy shadowed the Russian fleet and showed feats of seamanship of which the Russians were not capable. The Russian fleet's move to the Far East took months and coaling problems continued, with most ships having coal covering their decks. There was poor maintenance below the sea line, which caused drag and a lessening in speed. Rozhestvensky, who had taken his fleet 18,000 miles, was a martinet who ruled by fear. He had sailed around South Africa but there was a lesser squadron that went through the Suez Canal. However, his relations with its commander were poor, which increased the odds against success in the Far East.

Meanwhile, the battle continued on land, with Russia able to increase its manpower more easily than Japan through the railway, but these battles proved indecisive. The Russians, nevertheless, retreated along the railway and, in March 1905, a brilliant encirclement forced them back from Mukden. However, Japan's victory proved of no significance as they had lost 86,000 dead, which was considerably more than the Russians. The war had exhausted them.

At sea it was different. Russia had felt the humiliation of losing sea power in the east and determined that its fleet, which had now reached the Far East, would regain it. The crunch came in May 1905 at the Battle of Tsushima, where the Japanese showed superior seamanship and gunnery. This was a naval battle of great might, with 12-inch guns projecting 850-pound shells over 8 miles and with gun sights weighing 50 tons. This was a new kind of warfare. Japan's ships were significantly faster at 15 knots to Russia's 9 knots, enabling them to cross the T and destroy the Russian fleet. They sank or captured eight Russian battleships and sank seven of twelve cruisers and five of nine destroyers. Japan lost just three torpedo boats.

Russia acknowledged defeat and US President Teddy Roosevelt mediated an armistice. The peace settlement acknowledged the paramountcy of Japan's interests in Korea and transferred to it territory on the Liaotung Peninsula, including Port Arthur. Manchuria was acknowledged as Chinese and returned to China's administration but Japan took over Russia's rights to patrol the South Manchurian Railway. The Chinese did not like this but the Manchus had to yield.

A second Anglo–Japanese Alliance in 1905 acknowledged Japan's interests in Korea and Britain's in India. This made Britain feel more secure in its Indian Empire and its possessions in the Far East. Japan now became de facto ruler in Korea, the Russians departed and this was formally recognised in

1910. In the following year, the Anglo–Japanese Alliance was again modified because it could have involved Britain in a war with the United States if there had been a dispute between the latter and Japan. The alliance reorientated itself around any German threat, which meant that Japan would join the allies in a future world war. In the same year, 1911, the Qing dynasty fell and a successor dynasty attempted to unite China, which had reached a low point in its fortunes. Japan was now the great power in the Far East and wanted that to be acknowledged.

Revolution in Russia, 1905

Russia's humiliation in the Far East spilled over into revolution in European Russia, for which the extreme revolutionaries were unprepared. It was a spontaneous uprising that linked the peasants, university students, liberals and the bourgeois. There were strikes, riots and assassinations

On 22 January 1905 there was a massacre of peaceful demonstrators in front of the Winter Palace in St Petersburg. Tsar Nicholas II responded by proposing an elected assembly to advise the government but the least that would satisfy the various factions was an elected assembly with real powers, so the strikes continued. The autocratic tsar did not realise that he had to cede power and become a constitutional monarch. The army was now in revolt, as was the navy, with the famous mutiny on the battleship *Potemkin* at Odessa. Meanwhile. the strikes spread through Russia into most of the big cities and along the Trans-Siberian Railway. They also affected the outposts of the empire, Poland, Finland, the Baltic states and Georgia, while the extreme revolutionaries were now forming soviets to direct the workers in their strikes.

By October 1905, the tsar was concerned, so he agreed to an elected legislature under the presidency of Sergei Witte, which attracted a measure of support. The revolutionaries were striving for a republic but, just as this revolution broke spontaneously, so it resolved itself. The workers went back to work, the army came to heel, as did the railway workers, who were crucial for the transport of food and raw materials that kept the cities functioning.

The tsar's government rounded on the revolutionaries, arresting the leaders of the St Petersburg soviet and sending military expeditions to the outposts of the empire to put down their revolts. As time went by, the reforms promised were attenuated but there was now a constitution and a Duma, which led to the formation of parties. The issues of the day could be debated but any real power was only grudgingly given.

The Ottoman Empire

The break-up of the Ottoman Empire was visible to all. The Turks were feudal overlords who made their money out of land and ignored the new industrial world. Business thrived in these territories but it was usually in the hands of other races such as the Greeks and the Armenians.

The Turks, however, were great absorbers of capital but used it badly and did not generate reasonable surpluses, so they were increasingly in debt and vulnerable to their creditors. If they had realised that they controlled most of the oil reserves of the world, which would enrich them beyond belief, they might have behaved differently. The sultans believed emphatically in the greatness of their empire and the inspiration that their religion provided. They believed that the great nations of Europe were but heirs of Muslim inspiration and creativity. They knew that they were weak economically and sought allies to correct this weakness.

Many nations courted Turkey but it was Germany, especially under Kaiser Wilhelm, who won its favour. Germany would not speak ill of Turkey and, in return, expected privileges. One of these privileges was the building of the Baghdad railway, which Germany hoped would continue to Basra. Britain, too, while critical of certain matters such as the Armenian massacres, wished to trade and was respectful of the sultan's power and sovereignty as long as the trade route through the Suez Canal was protected.

But it was the two forces of democracy and nationalism that were usurping the sultan's power. The European part of the Ottoman Empire was highly nationalistic, with Romania, Serbia and Montenegro becoming independent in 1878, while Bosnia and Herzegovina became part of the Austro-Hungarian Empire at the same time. In 1897, Crete became independent.

Democracy, the other force, was inexorably making the sultan, like the tsar, into a constitutional monarch, although both foolishly resisted the diminution of their powers. However, by degrees, the sultan was forced into the opening of the Turkish parliament in December 1908. Previously, the sultan had appointed all officials but now his power was circumscribed and the new leaders tried to integrate all religions and races and to industrialise. Because of this, it was more secular in outlook than the sultan's regime.

Everyone who could was taking advantage of Ottoman weakness. Italy coveted Libya and its traders settled there. By 1911, the Italians believed they needed protection so they took over the running of the country and there was nothing Sultan Mehmed V could do because his navy was weak. In the Balkans, Greece, Serbia, Bulgaria and Montenegro assembled an enormous army of 700,000 men and went to war over Macedonia and other parts of Europe controlled by Turkey. In 1912, the Turks were driven out of Europe, although in 1913 they did regain some territory from Bulgaria, which foolishly wanted to continue the fight on its own.

With a greater war a possibility, Russia had an agreement that it would respect Turkey's borders if it were on the winning side, in exchange for free access to the Mediterranean. Britain was friendly and was building two large ships for the Turkish navy but the Germans were there as advisers to what was now the great power base of the new constitution, the Turkish army. This would be crucial to the fate of Turkey. Above all, the Turks feared the Russians, therefore their natural allies were Russia's opponents.

The Response to German Power

Kaiser Wilhelm II was the all-important figure in Germany's constitution. Despite a democratically elected Reichstag, the kaiser appointed the chancellor and all ministries were part of the chancellery. When Wilhelm II became kaiser, there was a shift in policy, which became more pronounced through the 1890s and into the next century. Relations with Russia deteriorated, Bismarck and Russia did not renew their treaty and a rivalry formed over the weak and decaying Ottoman Empire. Russia coveted Constantinople so that it could control access to the Mediterranean and the oceans of the world, while Germany wooed the Ottomans with the prospect of modernisation in the form of the Baghdad railway, which would link the Middle East to Europe. The Ottomans were keen to have a counterweight to Russian ambitions, so German influence increased.

For many years, Russia, France and Britain had been imperial rivals but this rivalry became more muted as time passed and Germany's power increased. Russia had formed an alliance with France in 1892, which became more important as it counterbalanced German competition in the Middle East and reacted to the debacle of 1905. There was a feeling in both countries that Germany could only be contained on land if they stuck together. France and Britain also recognised a community of interest and in 1904 sealed it with the Entente Cordiale. This developed into the Triple Entente with Russia in 1907. Britain was concerned about the balance of power in Europe but was more worried about its role as a sea power. Germany's ambitions under Kaiser Wilhelm II included being a great sea power, with Grand Admiral Alfred von Tirpitz the engineer of this, starting a great shipbuilding programme.

At the turn of the century, Tirpitz felt that Britain was vulnerable because its empire was so far flung and needed to be defended against the predations of the Russian and French fleets, which would enable Germany to concentrate its naval power in the North Sea, which it hoped to dominate. This plausible scenario disappeared as Britain, France and Russia became diplomatic allies, and Britain modernised its navy.

Although Tirpitz's ambitions had seemingly been foiled, Germany still had great ambitions on land, embodied by the Schlieffen Plan. This was based on a quick knockout blow to France and, once it had folded, Germany's war machine would use its full weight against Russia. Britain was discounted as a land power but one problem for Germany was that to knock out France it needed to go through Belgium. The one thing that Britain would not tolerate was any ports in the Low Countries being under German control. This would threaten British domination of the North Sea and the links with France. A violation of Belgian or Dutch neutrality could cause Britain to enter a war and Germany knew this.

Chapter 3

Other Key Developments Before 1914

Gandhi

Gandhi was born in Gujarat and this was his core loyalty, although in time he extended this to India and the people who inhabited the subcontinent. His other core loyalty was his native language, Gujarati, and it vexed him greatly when he was in his home state that political meetings were held in English.

Language preoccupied him, just as it did the Dutch, but he was much more a realist than they were. His upbringing in Gujarat, which was a princely state and as such was slightly separate from British India, was traditional and he was married at the age of thirteen. Sustained by the knowledge that he possessed significant gifts, his ambition led him to study law in London and become a barrister. This enabled him to work within the British Empire, choosing South Africa, which had a large Indian population that needed defending through the law.

Gandhi was exceptionally broad-minded and friendly, having the capacity to view problems from all angles. While in London, his Christian friends drew him into religious discussions and were keen for him to accept the wisdom of the Bible. He was moved by the 'Sermon on the Mount' but, on reading the Bible from the beginning, he found the Old Testament very turgid. In his autobiography he wrote:

> Thus if I could not accept Christianity either as a perfect or the greatest religion, neither was I then convinced of Hinduism being such. Hindu

defects were pressingly visible to me. If untouchability could be a part of Hinduism, it could but be a rotten part or an excrescence. I could not understand the raison d'etre of a multitude of sects and castes. What was the meaning of saying that the Vedas were the inspired Word of God? If they were inspired, why not also the Bible and the Koran?[3]

Gandhi never became an adherent of an established religion, although he absorbed their teachings when he thought they were appropriate. Nor was he a disciple of the British Empire but he acknowledged that it had virtues. Who to support in the Boer War was a dilemma, as Gandhi felt that the Afrikaners had reason for their battle, but he also felt that the Indians were beneficiaries of the British Empire and, as such, should be loyal. He therefore became part of an ambulance corps on the British side.

With the war at an end, the Indians took pride in having given service. Later, in the Zulu Rebellion of 1906, Gandhi organised an ambulance service and was horrified by the violence that the British inflicted. At that time, he was seeking a philosophy to guide him through life but a belief in *ahimsa* (non-violence) was very much a natural part of his make-up. On the other hand, he was not much interested in the sufferings of the native Africans or in their development of skills. He was an Indian nationalist at heart.

It was not until 1908 that *satyagraha* developed into a coherent part of his philosophy. Most Indian philosophical terms are difficult to translate but, literally, *satyagraha* means 'holding to the truth'. However, Gandhi used it to imply 'passive resistance' and it became political in its use. At this time, he started to take vows, and with those vows he felt a sense of liberation. Being an arch puritan, he rejected most things that related to pleasure and health such as milk, which he would no longer drink because of the suffering cows endured in India. Celibacy, *brahmacharya*, was another vow to which his wife consented, although she did not always agree with him.

During his time in South Africa, Gandhi practised as a barrister and was an active politician, helping to create the Natal Indian Congress. This was instrumental in getting a deal for the indentured labourers who were the first Indians to come to South Africa to work in the sugar plantations.

The problem was that the Indians were thriving in this new environment. Their indenture was for five years but most wanted to stay. If they returned to their native land after five years or signed on for another two years, all was well. However, if they remained, they would be subject to an annual tax of £25, which was a substantial sum (over £3,000 today). Congress appealed to the Viceroy of India and the £25 was reduced to a poll tax of £3, including boys over sixteen and girls over thirteen. This was felt to be unsatisfactory and there was considerable agitation, with people being killed and 10,000 imprisoned before the tax was remitted.

Smuts and Gandhi met for the first time in 1908, after Gandhi had been imprisoned for civil disobedience in the Transvaal. Both men recognised their mutual conciliatory natures, Smuts admiring and acknowledging Gandhi's spiritual dimension, while Gandhi acknowledged the backwardness of the Indian compared to the European and wanted no impediment to their improving their status.

The Death of Tolstoy

On 7 November 1910, Count Tolstoy died at Astapovo station. His imminent death had been telegraphed to the world and there were Pathé cameras to record the event amid worldwide interest and adulation. However, those who ruled Russia, from whom he was estranged, did not share this adulation. First and foremost, Tolstoy was an aristocrat who embraced the privileges and responsibilities of his class before spending his mature years shedding them, finally seeking peace and martyrdom as a 'holy fool', a quintessential Russian concept best represented in English literature by the later years of King Lear. Tolstoy's life was littered with inconsistencies that do not belittle his genius, for he produced in *War and Peace* and *Anna Karenina* two great novels that he could not have written without his experience as an aristocrat.

Tolstoy inherited Yasnaya Polyana at nineteen, including 300 serfs, but gambled away much of his inheritance. He paid his debts by selling villages, along with their serfs, and even selling his grand house. His sexual appetite was immense; he seduced village girls and was a regular user of brothels. To put order into his life, he joined the army, fighting in the Caucasus and then the Crimea, facing the French at Sevastopol and feeling the humiliation of defeat. It stoked his sympathy for what the ordinary soldier had to endure.

It was a while before Tolstoy married but having settled on Sofia Behr the most creative part of his life followed. She was the copyist of his two great novels and they shared their experiences through reading each other's diaries. She also bore him many children, although not without trauma, as after the fifth child she had puerperal fever and nearly died. However, to Tolstoy childbearing was a woman's function and she went on to have twelve children in all.

The Russian aristocracy was, on the whole, immensely rich, far richer than their peers in the West. However, the wealth was all in land and serfs and the ownership of vast tracts of land in Russia's extensive empire. In the 1870s, when Tolstoy was in his forties, he was attracted to an area of Samara province, 500 miles to the east of Yasnaya Polyana. There was a six-day trip to reach it, which included two days by train and two days by boat on the Volga.

In the 1880s, Tolstoy thought deeply about his position. He was in his fifties and undergoing a change of life. His wife had become less of an emotional inspiration, so he sought a soulmate, finding one in Vladimir Chertkov, twenty-six years younger than himself, immensely rich and close to the court of Tsar Alexander II. The freedom that Chertkov's riches gave him allowed him to follow his own inclinations and, after serving for a short time, he rejected a career in the army. The bond that he formed with Tolstoy was the belief that war and armies were not compatible with Christianity.

Chertkov translated Tolstoy's *What I Believe* into English. There was no trouble in having it published in England but getting it past the censor in Russia was another matter. Tolstoy decided to publish fifty copies at an exorbitant price, of which eight were sent to the censor and thirty-nine were confiscated. Such was Tolstoy's fame that everyone wanted to read what he had written, so copies were soon circulating around St Petersburg. They found that he had rejected the divinity of Christ, the lynchpin of Christian belief, but his beliefs were based on the Sermon on the Mount: live in peace with all men, show the other cheek to those with evil intentions and do not lust, swear or hate. If all were to follow these precepts, there would, in Tolstoy's opinion, be no need for armies and war.

Of course, Tolstoy's rejection of the divinity of Christ put him at war with the Orthodox Church and led to his excommunication. As he was against all organised religion, this mattered little to him as he was on a pathway to martyrdom. However, the authorities of the Orthodox Church would be at war with him for the next twenty-seven years of his life.

Although they had watched Tolstoy for some time, the tsarist secret police began to take a more serious interest in his activities from 1883. It was reported from Samara that he was encouraging the peasantry to reject the idea of private property and to ignore the government and the Church. The secret police's interest increased in intensity over the ensuing years and, although they did not touch Tolstoy, they incarcerated many of his followers and searched for subversive material at Yasnaya Polyana.

For the last thirty years of his life, Tolstoy gradually divested himself of his worldly wealth, offering land to the serfs, helping the peasantry through the famine of 1891 and not accruing money from his publications during those years. Overall, Chertkov controlled this, although it was Sofia who controlled Tolstoy's great works from before 1880, which were constantly reprinted. There was tension between Chertkov and Sofia because of their differing views on money. Sofia had children to feed, a publishing business to run and married children who were producing the next generation.

Tolstoy had two spells in Western Europe when he was a young man and enjoyed them. However, the West did not have a great pull with him and in his later years he never returned. He was, however, not indifferent to the literature of the West, the works of Charles Dickens giving him much pleasure. What had little appeal was Shakespeare, of whom he was disparaging and critical.

A highly religious man, religion guided Tolstoy's life, especially in his later years. However, it was religion of his own creation, which denied the divinity of Christ and had its followers, known as Tolstoyans. They were the bane of Sofia's life at Yasnaya Polyana and she regarded them, at best, as misfits.

The tensions in Tolstoy's final years were acute and unresolvable. He gained solace from being in correspondence with Gandhi the year before he died and, among the intelligentsia and the peasantry that knew about him, he was regarded as the greatest living Russian. However, he was at war with his wife, to whom he denied the love of old age; he was at war with the government, whose secret police hounded him; he was at war with the Orthodox Church, which wanted him to recant on his deathbed; and his children were divided in their devotion. He was craving martyrdom.

One night, he took off with a friend without telling anyone else and was forced to stop at Astapovo station through illness, pursued by his family and the world's press. Sofia commissioned a private train but, when she arrived, she was not allowed to see her husband before he died. Family did not matter, Tolstoy wanted to die as a homeless wanderer.

The Divinity of Christ

Gandhi, Smuts and Tolstoy were all exceptionally religious and all three rejected the divinity of Christ. This was not a new concept, although not widely held, but it led to the questioning of authority of the Christian churches and the laws and customs of nations, which continues to this day.

The Romanovs had a symbiotic relationship with the Russian Orthodox Church, which gave them their divinity and legitimacy. Who would have thought in 1914 that this relationship would disintegrate and disappear within three years? The result elsewhere was not as extreme but there was a crumbling disintegration of belief that could not be stopped. A new world beckoned.

Militarism and War

The soldier was everywhere in Europe at the beginning of the twentieth century. It was a career that could lead to great prestige in its higher echelons and, in certain regiments, conferred great social status. Numerous families, by tradition, sent their sons into the army and navy. Military manpower was considerable and, as such, there was great political influence.

This varied from nation to nation. In Britain, the armed forces were subservient to the state but this was not so in Germany and Japan. The armed forces in these two countries were the dominating influences in the state and it was to prove detrimental to their place in the world. The landed families of Prussia needed an outlet for their talents and found it in militarism, which fused with the imperial ambitions of the state. To Prussians, war was a legitimate expression of their creativity and an indicator of the greatness of their nation. Other European nations felt these sentiments but they were never the dominant feelings of the political class or of the people.

Instability continued in the Balkans, only needing a catalyst for war to materialise, which came following the assassination of Archduke Franz Ferdinand, the heir to the dual monarchy, at Sarajevo on 28 June 1914. A Serbian fired the shot, so Serbia was seen as the culprit and, according to those in power in Vienna and Budapest, it was the nation that needed to be humiliated if the southern part of the Empire were to stick together. With German backing, the Austro-Hungarians imposed humiliating terms on Serbia, which it surprisingly accepted, but the Austro-Hungarians still declared war. It was a gamble by the Central Powers as they knew that Russia would support Serbia but felt that Britain might stay out as it had done in the Balkan fracas two years earlier.

Partial Russian mobilisation on 24 July 1914 did not frighten the Austro-Hungarians, who did the same. On 30 July Russia ordered full mobilisation and the die was cast. The French could have ignored this but feared that Russia could be beaten if left on its own and this would lead to a German–Russian alliance, which would be the end for France as a great land power.

Britain was more circumspect. Although the current action was in the Balkans, Germany's Schlieffen Plan required it to attack France first, while the ponderous Russian war machine moved towards East Prussia, Austria and Hungary. Britain, having an entente with France, was all but in the war. Being with France and Russia in the Triple Entente, with Germany attacking through Belgium, Britain had an imperative reason for war.

The tragic events had begun. It was a European adventure, even when Turkey and its empire entered the fray. Although the Turks had been virtually banished from Europe, they had been the dominant power in the Balkans for centuries and had links with European countries to the west to stop the encroachment of Russia. This was not a world war, although this was its designation in the West, this was a European war.

Chapter 4

The First World War Commences

Introduction

Most of the nations of Europe were ready for war and their culture embraced it with fervour. These outbursts of fervour and enthusiasm contributed to the hope that glory could be won on the field of battle and the war would soon be over. Germany was the best prepared to do battle and would attack to resolve the matter quickly in the west. However, the east was another matter, but few felt that the war would be long and most believed it could well be over by Christmas 1914.

Since the Franco–Prussian War, Germany had been thinking in terms of conquest. Its general staff had influenced its government in the building of railway lines and there were thirteen dual lines going to the border in the west. There was now hyperactivity along these lines and, from 6 August 1914, 550 trains crossed the Rhine bridges, deploying 1.5 million men plus equipment.

By 12 August Germany was ready to implement the Schlieffen Plan. This plan was based on the premise that Russia would be slow to mobilise and would not be a factor for about forty days. Thus, there would be a window of opportunity for a quick win in the west, with the attack coming from the north through Belgium into northern France and culminating in a decisive battle near Paris in the sixth week. Germany would then turn to the east, believing it could decisively beat Russia. Despite the quality of the German army and its superiority to that of Russia, Germany's leaders were concerned about Russia's manpower. The Russian army had 114.5 divisions to Germany's 96, plus an advantage of 6,720 mobile guns to 6,004. Moreover, it was predicted that, by 1917, Russia would have a hundred divisions in place

The First World War Commences | 53

for war within eighteen days, through the planned improvements in its railways. This was only three days more than it would take the Germany to achieve the same and much quicker than the forty days suggested in the Schlieffen Plan.

1. *Entente and Central powers before and during the First World War*

Belgium was neutral, so its army had to withstand the Germans alone. Although Belgium had good defences, with many rivers and a system of forts at key points such as Liège and Namur, its army was no match for Germany. The French waited on the border, while the British, who did not want Germany to capture the Belgian ports, could only mobilise a small army, which was linked to the French forces. The forts were the only obstacle that worried the Germans, although they had the Krupp 420 gun, which could pulverise them. However, due to its size, it was difficult to get into position and only a few could be transported by road.

The Germans had reached Liège by 5 August and, with great boldness, Ludendorff forced the city to surrender with its river bridges intact. However, it was not until 12 August that a Krupp 420 was brought up to destroy the forts and it took a further four days for them to surrender. The Krupp 420 was then taken to Namur, where three days of bombardment silenced its forts by 24 August.

Thus, the Belgian defences crumbled and the Germans were at the frontier with France. The reliance on forts had been shown to be of little use, which the French noted, as they had similar systems at Verdun.

Battle of the Frontiers

The French now had to bear the brunt of the German attack. While the Germans had been attacking through Belgium, the French crossed the frontier into Lorraine and tried to recapture the lost province. The Germans, for tactical reasons, allowed them to move forwards and, as they did so, the French 1st and 2nd Armies lost contact with each other and the German 6th and 7th Armies, under more cohesive command, counter-attacked and pushed the French back to the Meurthe river.

Further to the north-west, the French 3rd and 4th Armies were attacking the Ardennes region and southern Belgium, not expecting substantial opposition, but the Germans were using aerial reconnaissance and confronted the 3rd Army, parts of which disintegrated. This led to the French retreating behind the Meuse on 24 August. They were, though, in good defensive positions, which suited them, and gave them confidence to pare the manpower of their armies to form a reserve. Meanwhile, the Germans were happy that the front was quiet, for it had always been their intention that this area would be a holding operation until the decisive battle.

The French 5th Army was also on high ground and had a good defensive position but it was in a region of rivers crossed by bridges. The bridges were treated as outposts held by strategic garrisons but some were not manned, so the Germans captured them. This led to a disastrous French counter-attack, with three German divisions forcing nine French divisions to retreat 7 miles and to lose contact with the French 4th Army on their right and the British on their left.

The British occupied a 20-mile front and went into battle on 23 August with four divisions fighting against six from Germany. The British troops had been hardened in colonial wars and were adept at firing fifteen rounds a minute from their Lee-Enfield rifles. It was a fierce battle, with the British holding ground and incurring approximately 1,600 casualties to 5,000 for the Germans. The two sides fought to exhaustion but the situation of the French 5th Army forced the British to retreat on 24 August, which became the great general retreat masterminded by Marshal Joseph Joffre, commander-in-chief of the French forces, who wanted the retreating armies to confront and hold the Germans on ground of their own choosing while a new army was formed near Amiens.

The retreat tested the men of both sides to the utmost. Sometimes they would cover 25 miles or more in a day, complete with horses and the impedimenta of war, plus the simple things such as food and water. The attacking army was at a disadvantage in the sense that it was advancing into unknown enemy territory, while the French could retreat and plan a rendezvous where they would be welcomed with food and drink. There were many battles during the retreat, including one at Le Cateau where the British suffered 8,000 casualties. This led to a battle fought by the French 5th Army at Guise, where the commander of I Corps, General Louis d'Espèrey, established his reputation by leading a counter-attack that temporarily halted the Germans, although not for long, as the retreat continued for the next week.

The Russians

The Russians were far from inept in the arts of war and the Germans respected them. Russia's army was no more class-bound than any other European army. In fact, its officer class was very broad and did not have great prestige, with 40 per cent of its officers below the rank of colonel being of peasant or lower middle-class origin. There were, of course, class fissures in the army, with the wealthiest echelons of society staffing the cavalry. Above the rank of colonel, money mattered, as those who wanted high command had to pay to attend the requisite college.

Nevertheless, the fighting generals in the army were Russian in only varying degrees. Many had German names and were originally from the Baltic states. Of the sixteen generals involved in the early part of the war, seven were of German origin, one of Dutch, one of Bulgarian, while of the seven Russians, two had Polish antecedents. Russia's high command, the Stavka, was essentially men from St Petersburg, Moscow and Warsaw.

After the disasters of 1906, Russia recognised that a coordinating general staff was of fundamental importance, so one was formed. However, it was not given overriding authority, as the Stavka tried to hold on to its power, which increased considerably with the onset of war. Thus, there was a split between General Vladimir Sukhomlinov of the war ministry and Grand Duke Nicholas of the Stavka. Sukhomlinov subordinated the general staff into his ministry and was the great moderniser of the army, promoting talent, introducing six-gun artillery batteries where he could and providing enough shell. He also recognised that the great fortresses were vulnerable and could not be relied on for defence.

Just as the Russian army was a formidable force with plenty of weaknesses, a similar description pertained to the Russian economy. Russia was not yet confident in its own powers as it derived much of its strength from foreign investment and control. However, it was a prosperous economy moving by degrees towards the efficiencies of the West.

Russia's essential problem was linking all the components of a vast land so that they worked together coherently. It was making great strides and the economy was booming but there was danger in this because in booms wealth tends to be distributed unequally. The seeds of revolution were sprouting from a large expanding population in a state of flux, which was increasing in wealth but with a creaking and autocratic political system that could not react to these economic problems or to the problems that war caused.

The general staffs of Russia and France liaised and believed the war would be resolved within six weeks. Germany's plans were well known and Russia realised it would have to mobilise quickly. Thus, it kept a proportion of its troops in forward positions in Poland, thinking that the Germans would keep sixteen to twenty-five divisions in the east. This was an overestimate but Russia promised France it would help as soon as it could, believing it could get 800,000 men into the field three weeks after announcing mobilisation.

The Austro-Hungarians

In a sense, the Austro-Hungarians, with their Serbian dispute, were the cause of all that subsequently happened. Russia was the protector of Serbia and once it mobilised so did Germany, who rightly feared that Russia would eventually attack. The Austro-Hungarians, on the other hand, feared three states: tiny Serbia, which they despised, mighty Russia, which they feared, and Italy, to which they would give no quarter.

At this stage, Italy was not a factor but the Austro-Hungarians were in a dilemma about Serbia. Did they go for a knockout blow or not? They reflected this in the deployment of their army, which they divided into three: A-Staffel of thirty divisions to confront the Russians, a Balkan grouping of seven divisions to confront Serbia in an offensive or defensive role, and B-Staffel of twelve divisions to use offensively against the Serbs or the Russians. The problems came with deployment. The railway system into the Balkans could not take these troops and their equipment with speed and ease.

The Hapsburgs were tempted to deal with the Serbs by deploying twenty divisions against the Serbs' eleven and to go for a quick victory, as Germany was doing in the west. Then they could confront the mobilising Russians. B-Staffel was meant to go to Galicia but General Franz Conrad von Hötzendorf, the Hapsburg chief of staff, changed his plans at the start of the war, rerouted it to Serbia and sent railway planning into a spin. At this point, Germany intervened at the highest level and pleaded with its ally to not split its forces.

By this time, 132 troop trains had started to move towards Serbia and, if the orders were changed, there would be chaos. Moreover, the troops had marched and departed to the cheers, encouragement and plaudits of huge crowds. To return within a few hours would appear ridiculous, so the trains went to the Balkans, then over a period of a few weeks the troops were rerouted to Galicia. There was, however, an attack in the Balkans, with the Austrians advancing into Serbia with much confidence, whereupon the hardy Serbs attacked their flanks and supply lines and pushed them back and out of Serbia.

The Germans in the East

In the early part of the war, Germany was on the offensive in the west and on the defensive in the east. The Germans feared being hemmed in and squeezed by two fronts, so went for a quick victory in the west to be able to then concentrate resources in the east. Germany considered that it had not initiated the war in the east, as its defence of East Prussia was in response to a Russian attack. However, its mistake was that it had undoubtedly attacked in the west through both Belgium and France and the Entente's propaganda machine was busy highlighting the German army's cruelty and gratuitous killing as it moved through those countries.

An army moving through enemy territory always overreacts if it thinks that civilians are taking part in the fight or are hindering progress. In such cases, its soldiers will plunder and rape, which is what happened in East Prussia. This was a small enclave of two million inhabitants, of which 80 per cent were Germans, most of the remainder of Polish extraction, with a sprinkling of Lithuanians. There was no overt opposition to the German overlords in East Prussia but, with the majority of the German army being in the west, France demanded that Russia attack in East Prussia so that the paltry German defence of ten divisions would require reinforcement from the west.

Russia's mobilisation had been quicker than the Germans thought possible and it attacked with a manpower advantage of more than 50 per cent. East Prussia was a salient on one side of the Russian-administered Congress Poland. On the other side was Hapsburg-administered Galicia, consisting of a mélange of ethnic nationalities, among them Ruthenes, whom the Russians considered to be Ukrainians and, in Russian eyes, the Ukrainians were basically Russians, which the Ruthenes disputed.

The Russians were like any invading army trying to establish its legitimacy over hostile inhabitants, however passive they might be. They imagined spies to be everywhere and any man caught with an item of military clothing, however old, was immediately suspected and often murdered on the spot. There were few bicycles in Russia and they were regarded as war-related in Prussia and immediately destroyed, together with the cyclist. The invaders were convinced there was a civilian resistance, primed to kill, and they blamed the civilians for anything untoward, which led to overkill and the burning of villages. The plunder of food and the prevalence of rape made life hazardous for those who remained but there was an enormous exodus of 800,000, about 40 per cent of the population. They escaped the invaders, whose Cossack cavalry were the worst offenders against the accepted rules of war.

No German was safe once Russia overran East Prussia and thousands were deported to the Russian interior. All this was well reported in Germany so the Germans feared the Russians, whose behaviour was well beyond normal conventions. This is something the Germans never forgot. However, the German press failed to counterbalance such reports with mention of the atrocities that its own army committed in Belgium and France, although these were not as bad. So began the difference in making war between the eastern and the western Europeans. Germany was fighting a defensive war against a predatory aggressor who had a plan of conquest and had extended its empire, on average, by tens of miles every day for 300 years. East Prussia was small and most of the Russian army opposed the Hapsburg army in Galicia, an ethnically complex area that was an important food producer for the Hapsburg Empire. Of Galicia's population of eight million, 3.8 million were Ruthenes belonging to the Uniate Church, 3.2 million were Catholic Poles, while the remaining million were made up of 90,000 Germans and many Jews.

For the Hapsburgs, Russia's invasion was catastrophically destructive, as its army overran swathes of agricultural land, which affected Austria and its ability to feed its people. This would continue throughout the war. Russia was serious in its predation and, in April 1915, Tsar Nicholas proclaimed, 'There is no Galicia, rather a Great Russia to the Carpathians.'[4] A moderate governor, compared with his peers, was installed who did not want to disrupt the ethnic balance or make great changes until the end of the war, although he was constantly overruled.

Russia took Lvov in September. This city was Polish in character but the street names were changed and the tsar's birthday was compulsorily celebrated, although the law courts and local government were left alone. However, the Poles fared much better than the Ruthenes, whose language and religion were outlawed in eastern Galicia. Ruthene hostages were taken to Russia and all Ruthene schools were closed, although Russia allowed a few Polish ones to function. Uniate churches were either shared with the Russian Orthodox clergy or they were taken over. There was forcible conversion to orthodoxy and land was taken from any who tried to resist. But the greatest disruption to Galicia was the exodus caused by Russian conquest. The small number of Germans fled, the larger number of Jews fled, while many Poles and Ruthenes did likewise.

In East Prussia, the exodus had an ethnic homogeneity, which enabled people to be welcomed despite the inconvenience. Those fleeing from Galicia were not welcome in the ethnically diverse Austro-Hungarian Empire. The Jews were not welcome anywhere, not even in Vienna, where there was a large Jewish community in a population of a million. Vienna was a magnet for the refugees, of whom 200,000 reached the city, the majority being Jews. The tensions that such a large influx created showed itself in overt anti-Semitism and discrimination.

The rest of Austria was not much better and Hungary was worse. With food problems, extra mouths to feed caused strains, which ethnic diversity exacerbated. The Jews were in an awful dilemma. Those remaining in Galicia were subject to humiliation, persecution, appropriation of their property and deportation, which the Polish civil servants appointed by the Hapsburgs often aided. It was tsarist policy to rid Galicia of the Jews, something to which the remaining ethnic communities were not averse.

The break-up of the empire was being telegraphed and the Hapsburg military illustrated this when it took over the administration after the Russian retreat in 1915. General von Colard was put in charge, who before the war had accused the Poles of supporting Russian-sympathising Ruthenes rather than the Ukrainian nationalists. He now started a witch hunt against the Poles, whom he accused of still being sympathetic to the Russians, at the same time forcibly recruiting every Pole of military age into the army. This caused such a ferment in Lvov that there was an uprising. The Hapsburgs, unwisely, used Hungarians to police the city. They were not popular, nor were the Czechs who replaced them.

It has been suggested that the smuggling of food from Hungary saved Galicia from starvation. However, the Hungarians did not welcome refugees from Galicia, did little to help them and claimed it was an Austrian problem, which says little for the integration of the Austro-Hungarian empire.

The Battle of Tannenberg, August 1914

Russia started its invasion of East Prussia on 17 August 1914 with two separate armies, one led by General Rennenkampf, the other by General Samsonov, who General François opposed on a 35-mile front. François, showing great ability, fought a minor battle against orders, taking 3,000 Russian prisoners before retreating to a suitable defensive position. Rennenkampf advanced, which caused the German commander-in-chief, General Prittwitz, to lose confidence and declare that he should retire to the Vistula. This meant that Germany lost East Prussia to Russia and Prittwitz was not too optimistic that the line could be held on the Vistula, as it might be fordable.

Having lost his nerve, Prittwitz was recalled despite having a brilliant staff officer in Colonel Hoffmann, who wanted to confront the Russians so that the Germans could retreat in good order. Hoffmann requested a defensive capability to attack both Russian armies and had to put this to two new commanders: General Paul Hindenburg, who had been recalled from retirement aged sixty-seven to replace Prittwitz, and General Erich Ludendorff, his chief of staff.

The Russians were now deep into East Prussia and threatening its capital, Konigsberg. Ludendorff recognised Hoffmann's capabilities but, feeling the peril in this war, lost confidence in Hoffmann's plan to encircle the Russian armies at the battle on 27 August, although Hindenburg supported Hoffmann. Ludendorff, however, wanted General François to take his troops to a weakened sector but again François disobeyed his superior and successfully attacked the Russians where he was. This ultimately led to victory within a few days as the Russians lost their cohesion, could not rely on food or ammunition supplies and were not able to retreat or attack. Samsonov admitted defeat on 30 August and, feeling he had let down the tsar, shot himself and was found on the field of battle amid his dead soldiers.

The Battle of Tannenberg was henceforth celebrated as the symbol of Prussian military genius and a great defence of the Fatherland against the barbarians from the east. Five days at the end of August 1914 had elevated Hindenburg and Ludendorff to the pantheon of great military heroes. For thirty years the Germans would celebrate this battle with great fanfare until muted by the defeat of 1945 when the battle honours retreated with the Russian invasion.

The Battle of the Marne, September 1914

All plans have a weakness and the Schlieffen Plan was necessarily vague on where the decisive battle would be fought. Germany had the option to go east or west of Paris. If they went west and their lines attenuated, they would be susceptible to attack from the Paris garrison. If they went east, they would be running back into themselves and would be vulnerable to a flank attack. It was an unresolved dilemma with no firm strategic control from the chiefs of staff.

Von Moltke let the commanders on the spot lead the direction of the attack and they went east of Paris. Moreover, III Corps was occupied in Belgium, mainly around Antwerp, as the Belgian army was not yet defeated. With II Corps sent as reinforcements to East Prussia, Germany was not in a position to succeed, as it needed a more powerful attack and Joffre was cleverly marshalling a substantial reserve.

By 4 September 1914, the thirty-fifth day, the Germans knew they had to fight the decisive battle within the next week. The object was to encircle the French armies, while the French aim was to do the same to the Germans. The Germans attacked first, on 5 September, in response to French deployment. However, the Germans had a problem on their right flank with the 1st Army, which needed to be strengthened, so they took troops from the centre, which weakened that position. Joffre's reserves had come primarily from forces in the east and the defensive positions that had been set up on the Moselle and the Meuse were holding and not causing alarm. The battle that raged was in the region of the river Marne. The German 1st Army was north of the river, the right flank of the 2nd Army south of the river, while the left flank and the right of the 3rd Army were in the marshes of St Gond. Opposite the German 2nd Army was General Ferdinand Foch's new 9th Army, with orders to drive General Karl von Bulow's 2nd Army beyond the Marne.

The battle of 5–9 September on a 250-mile front showed little favour to either side. There were minor breakthroughs that were unexploited and often revealed cracks elsewhere. The German 1st Army, in trying to turn the French flank, widened a gap between itself and the 2nd Army to 40 miles, which the British Expeditionary Force, being too far to the rear, belatedly marched into and took the pressure off the French 5th and 6th Armies. Nevertheless, the 6th Army was still outnumbered and, on 9 September, Germany's 1st Army succeeded in turning a part of the French flank, the prerequisite for success of the Schlieffen Plan. On the German right flank, the way to Paris was open but the German general staff called a halt and retreated. The Germans realised that they could not fight a decisive battle on this 250-mile front with the present supply lines and the incoherent positions of the 1st, 2nd and 3rd Armies. The decision was irrevocable and the retreat a lengthy one over hard-won territory where the German armies dug in on the heights above the Aisne and its tributaries.

The retreat marked the demise of the Schlieffen Plan. In hindsight it was the worst defeat that Germany suffered until 1918, yet it was not a defeat. Some say that the Battle of the Marne was not even a battle. Although lacking in coherence, there were plenty of engagements along a wide front, which in aggregate made it one but the German retreat was voluntary and not due to defeat, more to prudence. The tragedy for the Germans was that they did not have the manpower on the right flank. The French had anchored them on the Moselle and Meuse and, far away in East Prussia, the Russian demands had led to two vital corps being moved there. These would have been invaluable in capturing the Channel ports.

Bands of German Uhlans wandered unchallenged around north-west France, while a worried Britain had plans to abandon the Channel ports and reroute its new divisions and supplies via Saint Nazaire. However, the key ports went unmolested and the Germans worried that their flanks were vulnerable and unsustainable if they fought a large battle. The problems of supplying mass armies on the move were at this time insuperable.

The First World War Commences | 63

The Battle of the Masurian Lakes, September 1914

After the Battle of Tannenberg, what remained of Russia's 2nd Army retreated beyond the borders of East Prussia but its 1st Army remained. Germany deployed as much of its 8th Army as possible against it and Ludendorff attempted to encircle the 1st Army. The Russian's had brought up the 10th Army to protect the left flank but were preparing for an orderly retreat.

By this time, Germany had two corps from the Western Front, which provided a numerical advantage. For about two weeks in September 1914 there were attacks, retreats and counter-attacks, with astute defence resulting in casualties, while advances created supply problems. During the Battle of the Masurian Lakes, the Germans managed to rid the territory of Russians and capture 30,000; however, they suffered 100,000 casualties. With the Russians expelled from German territory, it was a German victory but, in this sector, it was not overwhelming.

The Austro-Hungarians Attack

The Battle of Tannenberg had a galvanising effect on Conrad, the Austro-Hungarian commander, who craved that his soldiers could match the Germans with a great victory. His attacks on the Russians had started at the end of August 1914 during a battle in Galicia. He arranged his forces in a semi-circle running from a western flank, which could link up with the Germans, and an eastern flank, which bordered Russia. He had good intelligence but the problems of attacking were severe in that the Russians had more divisions and guns in most places and Conrad needed to concentrate his forces to attack. If he could achieve a breakthrough, it would be difficult to exploit on the eastern flank, as communications were primitive.

Russia's mobilisation had proceeded well and, although its overall command was weak, the aim was to disrupt the Hapsburg railway system and to cut the Austro-Hungarians off from the Germans by confronting them in eastern Galicia. On the western flank, forces were about equal in strength but the Russians had superiority to the east.

Initially, the Austro-Hungarians had small successes, pushing the Russians back towards Lublin, but this brought supply problems and Russia built up its forces and counter-attacked. The battles went on intermittently over a loose front of 250 miles, which had many gaps. Gradually, Conrad realised that he would not achieve a victory and appealed to the Germans for help, but none was forthcoming. He had to retreat and, in some areas, had to do so for 150 miles.

In territorial terms it was a Russian victory but not one of great significance. For the Austro-Hungarians, casualties were tragically high, losing 400,000 men to 250,000 Russians. Of these casualties, 100,000 became prisoners as opposed to 40,000 Russians, while the loss of guns was 300 to 100. The Austro-Hungarians now acknowledged the need for help from Germany.

The Ottoman Empire

With hindsight, it can be said that the Ottoman and Russian empires connived at their own downfall. Even in 1914, Turkey was prepared to do a deal with Russia whereby the straits would be closed to all enemy intrusion and Russia would guarantee Turkey's borders. This was to stop German control of the straits and would have served Russia well. However, the Triple Entente was fully operational and France would not agree because of Ottoman territorial ambitions in the Balkans, while Britain was purblind as to Turkey's intentions and felt that it was in Turkey's self-interest to remain neutral.

Britain did not recognise the possibility that an empire might not pursue policies that it construed to be in its self-interest; therefore, British diplomacy was half-hearted and tragedy ensued. It became a deep and bitter tragedy for every contestant in the war, even for the British, the eventual victors, as it was one of the key strategic areas.

In 1914, two Turkish ships, *Sultan Oman* and *Rashadiye*, were in British shipyards. Britain had the right to take the ships and pay compensation once it was at war, which hurt Turkey as its navy was weak. In trying to strengthen it there had been a public subscription, with men in public positions agreeing to cuts in salary to make donations. To Turkey, Britain was breaking international law and was guilty of theft.

As it happened, two German ships, *Goeben* and *Breslau*, were in the Mediterranean at the outbreak of war. Although the British were pursuing them, they did make it to the straits and sought sanctuary. German diplomacy achieved this, although breaking international treaties, especially as orders were given to fire on the British if they pursued them up the straits. Germany then transferred these ships to a grateful Turkey. They were renamed and the crews donned fezzes. The British, as advisers to the Ottoman fleet, were usurped, the British naval mission was dissolved and discreetly retired.

2. The Ottoman Empire during the First World War

Turkey did not immediately declare war but it was obvious now where its sentiment lay. The Triple Entente was prepared to guarantee Turkish territorial integrity in return for neutrality. There were plenty of individual Turks, even in the cabinet, who favoured neutrality, but war was in the air and the triumphs of war were influential. Germany and Austria were goading Turkey into action and, with the bribe of a large capital loan and a bellicose fleet in the Black Sea, the Turks recklessly attacked the Russians. On 5 November the Triple Entente declared war on the Ottoman Empire.

The Race to the Sea and First Ypres, October to November 1914

In the first week of September 1914, the Germans acknowledged the death of the Schlieffen Plan by replacing their chief of staff, Von Moltke, with General Erich von Falkenhayn. Joffre, the French chief of staff, satisfied with his fine defensive battle, pursued the enemy and engaged them when he could. He did not want them to settle but Von Falkenhayn, confident in the potential of his defensive position on the Aisne, saw an opportunity to turn the French flank in the open space between the Aisne defences and the sea. The German 6th and French 10th armies confronted each other in this space, while to the north the Belgians and a British naval division confronted the Germans at Antwerp. While the French held the Germans, on 10 October the Germans took Antwerp.

After two months of war, men of the belligerent nations, who had joined in that euphoric moment when war was declared, reached the front lines. The British Expeditionary Force was growing, with six infantry and three cavalry divisions, plus another infantry division on the way, together with four infantry and two cavalry divisions from the Indian Army.

Sir John French wanted to attack and recapture Brussels. General Foch, who was establishing his reputation as one of the outstanding commanders of the war, encouraged him. The British attacked from a 35-mile line with its fulcrum at Ypres. Directly opposing the British army were eight divisions composed of neophytes with only two months' training, many of whom were university students. The battle included the remnants of the Belgian army, a contingent of French, plus the British army in France, totalling nineteen divisions against Germany's twenty-four.

The battle was one of great intensity and sacrifice, with 25,000 German students being buried in one mass grave at Langemarck, while the British incurred more than 80,000 casualties. By the end of November there was stalemate as the fighting became desultory and the trench system became established. The armies faced each other from the Channel to the Swiss border, some 475 miles. This suited the Germans, who wanted a defensive position so that they could solve their problems in the east. In four months, there were 306,000 French dead, 30,000 British and 30,000 Belgians, while the German figure was 241,000. Thus, the first phase of the war ended, and mobility yielded to stasis.

The Winter of 1914–15 in the East

It was easy to gain tactical victories in the east as there were always gaps in the front line and flanks to be turned; however, the winter to come would show that this did not count for very much. Artillery was still the key to warfare and soldiers had to dig trenches to mitigate its effect. Earth and keeping one's head down were the best defences against anything but a direct hit. Russia's superiority in in numbers was not now as significant, as it needed to defend the Baltic and Black Sea coasts. It would not be until 1916 that Russia would create a marked superiority in manpower on the Eastern Front.

To attack in rain or snow with its concomitant mud was not the most sensible approach but all armies in the east did it. The Russians wanted to capture Przemysl, a great fortress that barred the way to Cracow and ultimately Budapest. The Germans, in turn, wanted to capture Lodz and Warsaw. They started in that direction but the Russians thwarted them, while the Austro-Hungarians retreated and left Przemysl surrounded with 120,000 men inside. Armies marching forward created their own problems and were usually held. The Germans expected to capture Lodz and Warsaw but were disappointed, as were the Russians with Cracow. There was extensive fighting in the Carpathians, with one side or the other either succeeding or blundering in foul conditions made worse by altitude.

Germany was worried by a possible link-up of the Anglo–French via the Dardanelles, which could bring in Greece, Bulgaria and Romania, while Italy could be encouraged to make a strike. To Germany, this latter intervention could be crucial. Von Falkenhayn believed the problem could be solved if Germany defeated France but, if this did not happen immediately, a Balkans campaign would be necessary. Conrad, his Austrian counterpart, took a different view, believing that a Russian defeat would profoundly influence the neutral states.

Von Falkenhayn was in an impossible position. The Eastern Front needed more men to overcome the Russians. Conrad said he was too weak in the Carpathians to do anything but defend; however, he gave Von Falkenhayn five divisions and said he would attack. If Conrad attacked, Ludendorff believed he had to attack on his flank from East Prussia as the Austro-Hungarian attack would only attract reserves and would not be strong enough on its own. The Russians, on the other hand, felt that decisive action would see the fall of Przemysl, with the Austro-Hungarians potentially making a separate peace.

As it happened, 1915 started with a German attack on the plains near the Vistula, with the first gas attack of the war, which blew back to the German lines. The Austro-Hungarians attacked in the Carpathians but made meagre progress and now wanted an attack to relieve Przemysl. The Germans could not help and, in March, the fortress with its 120,000 men fell to the Russians. Ludendorff, to the north, had been attacking since the end of January and on

21 February claimed a substantial victory over the Russians, although it was merely of tactical significance.

Russia's dilemma was just as acute as that of the Central Powers. It feared invading East Prussia because its railway system gave Germany a good advantage, while on the Turkish front, supply problems precluded any deep penetration. It was in the Carpathians that Russia was doing well and hoped for an Austro-Hungarian collapse. Already there was talk that the Slavs, such as the Czechs, did not have their heart in the fighting and the Russians captured thousands of prisoners in the mountains.

3. *Front lines early in the First World War*

The stress of war was widening the fissures in the Austro-Hungarian Empire. There was a good arms industry led by Skoda and Steyr but a lack of standardisation hampered the production of guns and shells, while there was the need and scope for greater productivity. Hungary was agrarian and its increasing prices affected the rest of the empire. The officer class had been decimated but there was also a language problem. The empire had fifteen languages, of which Conrad spoke seven, and there was a consequent inflexibility as to where officers could be selected and placed, added to which their defeats were tempting Italy to intervene. It wanted Austrian territory on the Adriatic coast and, with Turkey on the side of the Central Powers, Italy coveted territory in the Balkans.

The irony was that Italy would come in a couple of months later because Russia was being defeated and Italy thought the Central Powers were too strong. On 1 April, however, Conrad told Von Falkenhayn that a separate peace was possible and that he would rather lose Galicia to Russia than Trieste to Italy. Von Falkenhayn wanted to appease Italy by making concessions and, because the Austro-Hungarians were reluctant to do this, the Germans became reluctant to support their armies.

It was obvious that if Germany were to win the war in the east it would be through its own efforts. On 2 May the Germans attacked on a north-south line about 60 miles long and 50 miles west of the San river. Although, like most battles in this war, there was no element of surprise, the Russians were ill-prepared and had no defence in depth. On the Western Front, armies became adept at arranging reserves to plug areas where the enemy had become concentrated and was attacking. The Germans concentrated on the gap to be exploited, hit it with artillery and followed up with mortars. They would move through with difficulty because of the devastation but they would progress.

Russia was unable to respond with sufficient strength and, by 10 May, Ivanov's chief of staff acknowledged his troops' lack of mobility and inability to stop the German surge. The Russians retreated to the San and 250,000 were cut down to 40,000 fit men. They were mainly deployed on the western bank of the San but, when they were forced back, many died in the river. A German component now moved south to cut the communications to the rear of Przemysl, which the Russians parried, but on 4 June the Germans recaptured the fortress.

The Dardanelles and Aid to Russia

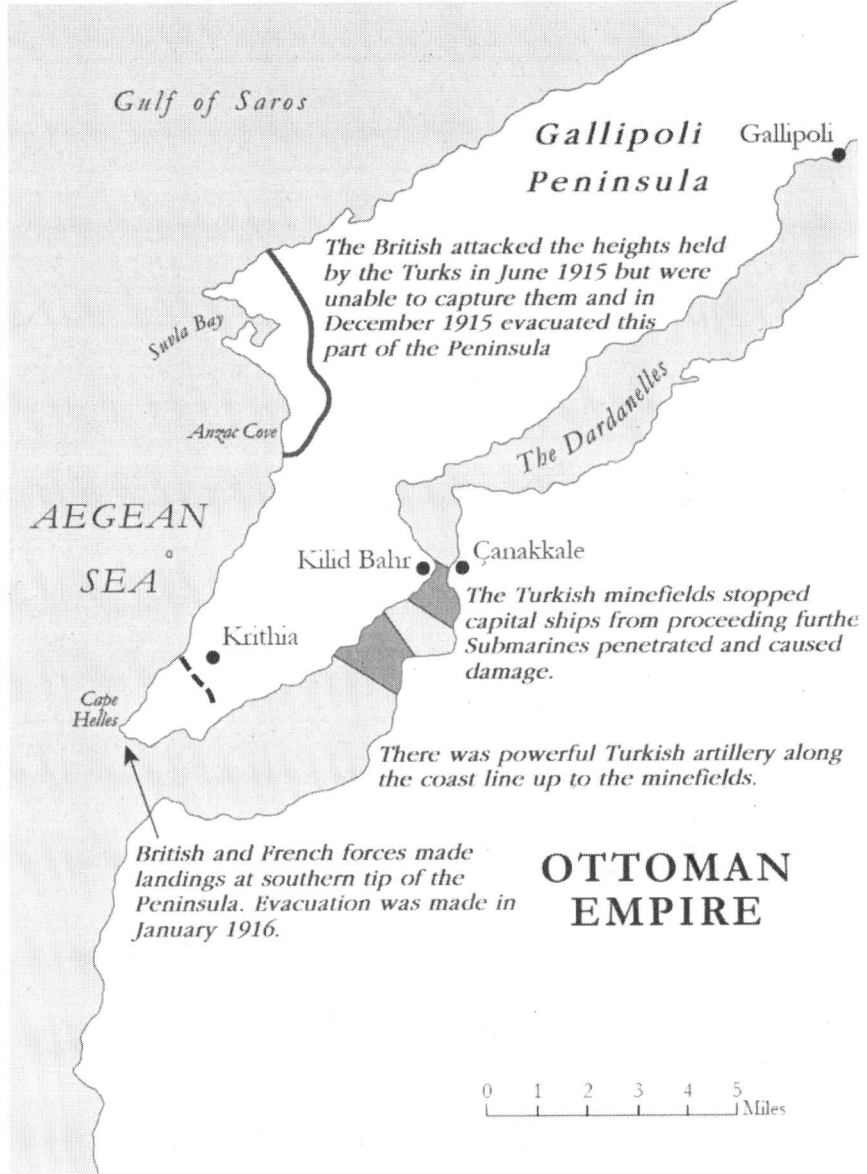

4. *Situation in the Dardanelles in 1915*

In January 1915 Russia persuaded Britain that there was an advantage in coming to its aid via the Dardanelles. Firstly, it was having trouble with the Turks in the Caucasus and, secondly, it needed munitions from Britain, especially shells. In return Russia wanted to export its surplus wheat. Britain thought that, with French naval help, although with a second-class fleet, it could force the Dardanelles, capture Constantinople and link up with the Russians. This strategic concept interested Churchill and on 18 March the operation started with a naval attack.

Italy Enters the War

Italy entered the war in May 1915 but there was not much initial activity. Despite the Austrians only having 100,000 men to defend the border against 800,000 Italians, the border passes were easy to defend and the Italians did not have the most modern of armaments. It was the Russian rout that worried the Italians and propelled them into war but they did not at first draw off any troops.

During June, Germany consolidated its successes by capturing Lvov and pushing the Russians out of Galicia. Cracks in the Russian Empire were beginning to appear. There was a shell and rifle shortage, a lack of proper training nullifying the advantage of greater manpower and a continuing obsession with cavalry regiments. The cavalry had the advantage of giving greater mobility to the army and was useful in reconnaissance in a front line where there were large, unmanned gaps, but it was counterproductive in large numbers.

In short, the Russian cavalry was a supply nightmare. It needed sixty trains of fifty wagons each per day to deliver food supplies, of which 60 per cent was for the horses. In defeat, men need something to blame, so they blamed shell shortage.

It is true that the Germans had greater shell resources but, on the Western Front, the Allies' shell superiority, which was about equivalent to German shell superiority in the east, did not lead to breakthrough. In the east, the front was less cohesive and longer and there were fewer reserves, as men were needed in the front line, and this was the breaking point.

Chapter 5

The War Continues 1915-1916

Winston Churchill

Churchill was almost forty when the war started and had been first lord of the admiralty for three years. As an army officer he had experienced the skirmishes and minor battles of colonial wars. As a journalist he had been captured by the Boers and found fame with a daring escape. He knew about war and revelled in its danger and capriciousness. He was also in a powerful position because the defence of Britain hinged on its navy, while its army was contemptibly small in Europe and its air force was still a fledgling without independence.

As the inevitability of war consumed Europe, Churchill recalled how the Russians had been surprised at Port Arthur and was determined that the Royal Navy would not be subject to such a coup. By the end of July 1914, after a review at Portland, a large part of the navy was dispersed to defensive positions in the North Sea, ports were prepared defensively and Churchill pleaded for mobilisation, which Prime Minister Herbert Asquith granted before war was declared. The navy was primed and ready and the troops of the small army could be transported across the Channel.

Churchill had a strategic genius for war. The drama of the conflict stimulated his energy, enthusiasm and imagination. Within a month, his popularity had surged as three German cruisers were sunk in the Heligoland Bight, contrasting with the Allied armies' dismal retreat in France. At the same time, he was asked to organise Britain's air defence. He also arranged for three squadrons to be sent to France. Later, airfields were formed near the front lines defended by Rolls-Royce cars with armoured plating, an early forerunner of the tank, the development of which Churchill would play a major part in. This was indeed the pupa of modern warfare.

Churchill's bellicosity did not appeal to all, however. King George V thought him vulgar when he declared that if the German fleet did not come out to fight, they would be 'dug out like rats in a hole'. In October Churchill got his chance for action as the Belgians were having trouble holding Antwerp and, if it fell, the Germans could come down the coast and threaten Dunkirk and Calais. Churchill, along with Field Marshal Herbert Kitchener, Secretary of State for War, deployed naval troops to the defence of Antwerp and went to the city. With his imagination inflamed with thoughts of combat and glory, Churchill offered to resign as first lord so that he could be given authority to command the troops. Kitchener was prepared to make him a lieutenant general but Asquith overruled this and ordered Churchill back to England.

It is a moot point as to whether Churchill was a good selector of men. Without doubt, he could be imaginative in his choice and, two months into the war, he planned, connived and even threatened resignation to get Admiral of the Fleet Lord Fisher installed as first sea lord. In the end he won, to the misgiving of some, as Fisher was a powerful personality, seventy-four years old and capable of taking as independent a line as Churchill. It did not help that Fisher's return coincided with the Battle of Coronel, when two cruisers were lost. This stung the navy into revenge at the Battle of the Falkland Islands, which ended German surface fleet influence in the Atlantic and Pacific Oceans.

With stalemate in France, an alternative method of beating Germany was sought. The Russians were under pressure, with the Turks threatening them. To ease the pressure, the Allies needed to link up with Serbia or attack Turkey so that it had to defend Constantinople. Thus, the Dardanelles campaign formed as a strategic possibility. It was initiated as a purely naval endeavour to be achieved by second-division ships.

The Ottoman Empire was not an insubstantial power and had organised a system of forts on both sides of the Dardanelles stretching to Constantinople, with a comprehensive mining of the waters, especially the Narrows. Churchill and Fisher were united in wishing to force the Dardanelles, destroy the forts and sink *Goeben* and *Breslau*, which were bottled up in Constantinople, thus hopefully forcing Turkey out of the war. It was decided that a modern battleship and some older ships should be sent to the Aegean to reinforce the fleet but this caused Fisher to threaten resignation, although he was persuaded out of it.

While this was going on, Churchill was trying to develop his armoured cars with guns so that they could overcome the defensive system of the trenches. Designs were developed for a land ship but, wishing to disguise their use, they were called water carriers for Russia; however, as the initials WC designated a lavatory, they were named water tank. So, these metal monsters became known as tanks. The designs of the first tanks, based on a tractor, were submitted to Churchill, who gave £70,000 from Admiralty funds for a prototype.

The first attack in the Dardanelles was on 18 March 1915. Naval gunfire silenced the first forts but there were plenty more all the way up the narrow sea. Ten British and French battleships proceeded up the straits but the mines were deadly. A French battleship was sunk and three British battleships struck mines but still the minefields could not be fully swept. The admiral was given discretion as to whether he should continue the attack. At first it was thought he would do so but caution prevailed, despite Churchill and Fisher's encouragement. The Admiralty had the cabinet's support but Admiral de Robeck cautiously held back as he thought that a purely naval enterprise was foolhardy and that the army should recapture the forts.

Once the Gallipoli landings occurred, the navy's role was lessened. The land battles on the Gallipoli peninsula dominated all and they did not go well. With the army in a bad way, Churchill wanted to help with a naval action to force the Narrows but Fisher was against it. In the middle of May Fisher unexpectedly resigned. It was an inappropriate decision in the middle of war and with it he took down Churchill.

The notion that Churchill was too brilliant for his own good and a loose cannon was the perception that prevailed. The nation wanted someone to blame for the fiasco of the Dardanelles and Churchill was the perfect fall guy at the time. With great injustice, the one man to show any imagination and genius for war, who recognised the crucial position of the navy and had it ready, who sensed the potential of air power and even wanted to exploit it in the Dardanelles, and who was one of the chief progenitors of the tank, was unjustly felled and taunted for decades with its failure.

Demoted to a minor post in the cabinet, his talents in the conduct of war ignored, Churchill was almost a political outcast as the Conservatives grew more powerful and a coalition government came into being. The Conservatives could not forget that Churchill, in political terms, was a traitor who had changed parties and they wanted their pound of flesh. Disloyalty was a heinous political offence and they had waited for ten years and were ready to pounce. He still had friends but they could not protect him in a meaningful way, so with great courage he re-joined the army. He was difficult to place but, in the end, he was given a battalion and the rank of lieutenant colonel. He had hoped for at least a brigade as a prelude to commanding a division but went into the line as the commander of a battalion of the Royal Scots Fusiliers in the 9th Division.

Churchill's mind was in ferment. The Dardanelles would not go away and he was defending himself against the malign accusations of his enemies. Once in the line, Germany's control of the air infuriated him. If he had been given the job of controlling the air force after he left the Admiralty, this might never have happened. And then there was the danger. It was a quiet part of the line in Belgium, with occasional shelling, which brought casualties and, over time, added up.

Churchill occasionally returned to London on leave and he plotted with his friends in parliament. Having been passed over for promotion, his ambition to be an army general waned and parliament looked more attractive. By May 1916 his battalion had diminished in the attrition of war, although in no major action, and was incorporated in the 15th Division. Churchill sought no new post but returned to parliament with a determination that there should be no more futile advances and that air superiority should be restored. This was after Verdun had started but before the Somme.

In December 1916, Asquith fell, and David Lloyd George became prime minister. It was a coalition government with considerable Conservative influence. Lloyd George wanted to appoint Churchill to the Air Board but the Dardanelles Commission Report had yet to be published and was used as an excuse to exclude him. He was out in the cold.

Gallipoli and Kut

Lack of resources blighted the Allied attacks on the Turks. The Western Front was of such importance that all necessities were sent there, while the landings on the Gallipoli peninsula were subject to much improvisation. It was not, however, a superfluous theatre of war. If the Allies were successful, Germany recognised the strategic implications in that Romania, Bulgaria and Greece could join the Allies, Russia would be strengthened, Turkey neutralised and Austria-Hungary would become more vulnerable. Turkey, with Germany's help, had to hold the straits and the peninsula.

The Allies had two objectives: the first was to capture Constantinople and knock Turkey out of the war; the second was to reinstate the trade route to Russia and allow its farming surpluses to reach the market to the west so that Russia could buy armaments. The Russians produced 100 million tons of wheat each year and most of it would go to waste unless exported. Russia was, therefore, keen for Britain and France to get through to the Black Sea.

With the strategic idea being regarded as sound, there was little controversy in Britain about the concept and they had France's support. It was the practicalities of amphibious warfare, something that would not be solved until the middle of the next world war, which would hamper success. There was an innocence about the Dardanelles campaign and a necessary improvisation as problems arose, such as the provision of troops to help the navy and, in turn, many of the troops had to be provided with drinking water from Egypt, 700 miles away.

The complications of this amphibious gamble were immense. Admiral Fisher was adamant that his first duty was to protect Britain and he could not spare any dreadnoughts for this expedition. Therefore, they would use battleships of the second division, some of which were due to be scrapped. Moreover, Fisher maintained from the beginning that an army would be necessary to help the navy.

His opinion was soon proved correct, but the army's high command was reluctant to let any division move from France. However, there were two Antipodean divisions training in Egypt, which were diverted to the Dardanelles. Britain and France wanted three Greek divisions to take part, which they eventually agreed to do, but Russia came into the equation and vetoed this because it wanted Constantinople without any Greek claims to the city. Greece was therefore excluded and could concentrate on the Salonika front, which would have increasing importance.

The great attack on the Narrows took place on 18 March 1915. The ten British battleships and four French ships had the sea to themselves, but when they arrived at Chanak, with its five defensive forts, the four British battleships in the van joined battle with a good deal of damage on both sides. These four ships then gave way to the four French ships, which did their best but then retired, with *Bouvet* receiving a direct hit on its magazine. Within two minutes it had sunk, losing over 600 sailors.

This was a reverse, with the Narrows, defended by mines, yet to be penetrated. With the forts quiet, the minesweepers were called into action and started to sweep; however, once they came under fire, four of them turned and fled, while two others did not arrive. These minesweepers were really trawlers manned by fishermen, not inculcated with the strong discipline of the Royal Navy. Soon, two battleships were in a bad way and another was sunk. The British could not believe what was happening and did not know about a row of mines that had been planted ten days previously, even though they were using aircraft to detect them.

The Turks were in an equally bad way and thought that the Royal Navy would sweep the mines the next day and enter the Sea of Marmora. They planned to leave Constantinople but the British had lost their confidence and now believed that to be effective they needed the army. However, the army did not really know what was expected of it. Kitchener had only appointed Chief of the Imperial General Staff General Sir Ian Hamilton to lead it on 12 March. He knew nothing about a Gallipoli campaign and the maps of Gallipoli produced in London were inadequate.

Hamilton left London the day after his appointment and reached the Dardanelles in time to see the naval attack on 18 March. With this battle unresolved, the onus was on him to achieve a result on the Gallipoli peninsula and he planned with what resources he had to attack on 25 April. The 29th Division would land at the tip of the peninsula at Cape Helles, while the ANZACs would land 13 miles away to the north-west. The French would land nearby on the Asian side.

The attack at Cape Helles was five-pronged and at one prong there was a massacre of the British troops. At Anzac Cove, there was a great loss of life but the ANZACs penetrated for a mile and a half and then by chance came up against Mustafa Kemal Bey, who had marched a reserve battalion to the action and was claiming the heights overlooking the cove. This in a nutshell summed up the campaign until Christmas. Claim the heights and you would control the battle.

No one knew how the Turks would fight as they were a motley army, poorly clothed, poorly fed and their pay was in arrears. However, they had a German military adviser in Lieutenant General Liman von Sanders and a minister of war in Ismail Enver Pasha who were ruthless and effective. They also had a superiority in manpower and in May decided to use it to drive the ANZACs off the peninsula. Mustafa Kemal led a full-frontal attack. His brilliance is undimmed but he was as wasteful of men's lives as any Allied general.

The attack failed, resulting in 4,000 dead Turks in no-man's land, plus the wounded, many of whom cried for help. In the heat of the Aegean, this would become a health hazard if they were left to rot and, despite mutual suspicion, a short armistice was arranged to bury them. Apart from prisoners, both sides knew little of the other and ignorance fuelled contempt and hatred but, once they met in the open and exchanged food and cigarettes, they created a mutual regard for each other, which was translated into a live-and-let-live arrangement in the front lines.

With stalemate, Gallipoli went quiet. Hamilton needed more soldiers, equipment and shells before he could try to break through to the high ground. There was a shell crisis in England, which had erupted in the press after the Battle of Neuve Chapelle when a journalist, Colonel Repington, highlighted the situation and it escalated. The Germans had used poison gas in this battle, which, like the battles in Gallipoli, had been indecisive. Although the Germans suffered similar casualties, the British were stung by their sacrifices, to which in time the sacrifices of Gallipoli added.

The war had only been going for ten months, people had thought it would soon be over but this was the first intimation that it would be drawn out. Hamilton was undoubtedly low on shells and this shortage reverberated in the press, not helped by Admiral Fisher resigning in May 1915. Fisher saw the difficulties in purely military terms and emphasised that this was a sideshow. The strategic objectives of wounding or knocking Turkey out of the war and helping Russia were secondary to defending the North Sea and winning the war in France. His resignation triggered a political realignment as Asquith realised that he needed a coalition to keep the country united. Bringing in the Conservatives meant that Churchill left the Admiralty and there was less of a driving force in the Dardanelles.

There was another development of great importance in May 1915. Although the surface fleet was of the second division, there were submarines and aircraft bringing modern warfare to the Middle East. The Germans sent Kapitanleutnant Otto Hersing in U-boat *U-21* via the Atlantic into the Mediterranean in April. The British were already at the Dardanelles with submarine *E. 14*, commanded by Lieutenant Commander Boyle. He wanted to reach the Sea of Marmora by passing through the Narrows on the surface but was harassed and forced to go under. It took him six hours to make his passage and he was unmolested for three weeks, during which he sank a liner with 6,000 Turkish troops, none of whom survived.

Boyle came out of the region in the middle of May and was replaced by Lieutenant Commander Nasmith in *E. 11*. He had a lethal effect, including a hit on a freighter berthed next to the arsenal in Constantinople, which caused chaos and panic in the city. Alerted to the danger, the Turks shelled the boat whenever it was near to land but had no luck, so Nasmith was able to make his way back to his own lines.

While he was away he was incommunicado, so no one knew of his success. Instead, they were worried that Hersing's U-boat had passed through the Straits of Gibraltar without being hit and the navy feared his torpedoes. The commander-in-chief, De Robeck, had transferred his flag to a sloop.

Although defended by destroyers, a torpedo hit and sunk the battleship *Triumph*, with a loss of seventy-one men. The navy, which had positioned itself just offshore to help the army, now dispersed but *Majestic* was ordered back to Cape Helles where it was torpedoed and sunk.

Hersing made his way to Constantinople, where he was feted. British fear of him remained but he eventually retired. Meanwhile, Germany sent many U-boats to patrol the Mediterranean, although they had little effect on the Gallipoli campaign. The Allied submarines in the Sea of Marmora had had a major effect, especially on the smaller craft. Turkey had lost one battleship, one destroyer, five gunboats, eleven transports, fourteen steamers and 148 sailing boats. This had a major impact on trade and the supply of soldiers on the peninsula. No longer would ships transport them, so they would have to rely on the roads. If this supply line could have been cut it might have made a difference to the campaign but intelligence and communication was poor and neither the military nor naval authorities were aware of the great damage done to the Turks by the submarines.

The Turks proved to be brilliant defensive soldiers who were aggressive and held the high ground. This was the Allied tragedy; they could never get to the high ground and dominate a part of the peninsula. For a time they attacked with naval guns but the Turks had their front line so close to the enemy that there was always the possibility of hitting one's own lines. When the Germans sank two British ships, the British retired. Supply was a problem for both sides as British submarines sank half the Turkish merchant fleet, while Allied supply ships were always susceptible to Turkish fire as they unloaded.

The supply of water was a particular problem for the Allies as there was little on the bits of parched peninsula they occupied. With the lack of water there often came disease and a large proportion of the casualties were disease-related. The Allies attacked to overcome these problems, above all to gain high ground, which would defend a port so that the supply problems could be overcome, but by August 1915 it was looking grim. The laudable ambition of having a direct link with Russia and bringing in the other Balkan nations was fading, leading to discussion about evacuation.

At the end of 1915, evacuation became a reality and Gallipoli became a triumph for Turkey, who had found a great leader in Mustafa Kemal. The Turkish army was now a great power in the land and it was not necessarily the sultan's army. Some 86,000 Turks had lost their lives compared with 70,000 Allies but it was a Turkish victory and one that probably prolonged the war.

The attempt to link with and help the Russians continued. Britain was using the Indian Empire to form an army, which had already entered Mesopotamia from Basra and would hopefully fight its way up the Tigris to capture Baghdad. From there it hoped to link with the Russians in Persia and Azerbaijan. The twin problems that plagued the Gallipoli venture existed there as well. The logistics of providing food and water and the problems of disease were proving insuperable. The troops from the Indian Empire were of average quality and not helped by being poorly supplied. Nevertheless, they outnumbered the Turks by two to one in Mesopotamia.

By the end of September 1915, the British had occupied the whole province of Basra up to Kut-al-Amara. General Charles Townsend, the commander, had orders to press on to Baghdad but the Turks stopped him at Ctesiphon in November. With supply lines attenuated and disease rampant, he fell back on Kut. Half his British officers were sick at Ctesiphon and had to be taken back to Kut, which was put under siege. A German general, Colmar von der Goltz, had taken control and the Turks had also formed grand strategic plans whereby Goltz would lead them through Persia and Afghanistan to India.

The Ottoman Empire's ambitions had left Europe and North Africa and were heading east. On a more practical level, the British made four attempts to relieve Kut but they all failed, with the flooded Tigris making life difficult. There were 23,000 casualties in attempting to relieve Kut, which was much more than the numbers they were trying to relieve. On 29 April 1916 Kut surrendered and 13,000 men went into captivity, the majority of whom would not return to their homeland.

The Second Armenian Massacre

At the outbreak of war, Russia had three corps in the Caucasus, which it could deploy to the Eastern Front. The Central Powers soon realised that it would benefit them if these corps could be kept in place. Turkey's racial ambitions extended into the Caucasus, where people with a Turkic identity were part of the Russian Empire and Turkey was keen to gain their loyalty. In late December 1914, Turkish attempts to defeat the Russians failed at the Battle of Sarikamish, where the former suffered approximately 75,000 casualties, mostly from supply difficulties or disease.

This was a great blow to the Turks, who in their eastern provinces were hundreds of miles away from their capital and they were worried about the loyalty of the inhabitants. There were at least 150,000 Armenians in the

Russian army and the Turks blamed the desertion of Ottoman Armenians for the loss at the Battle of Sarikamish. The Kurds and the Turks ganged up on them and Russian foreign minister, Sazonov, made an international protest in May 1915, stating that the inhabitants of a hundred villages had been killed. At the same time, Minister of the Interior Mehmed Talaat of Turkey decreed that Armenians living near the war zone would be deported to Mosul and Syria.

It is thought that one million Armenians lost their lives in the killings that started in 1915, which was about 50 per cent of the population. However, it may have been in excess of that as population statistics were very crude, especially in that area at that time. Along with the massacres of twenty years previously, this amounts to genocide, an accusation that today's Turks refute and Armenians endorse.

Genocide is the gratuitous killing of defenceless people because of an affiliation to race, religion or class and where the majority of the group is exterminated. Although it is an extreme manifestation of human behaviour, it occurs regularly in human affairs and among a variety of races and religions. The problem of genocide for the perpetrators is that killing of individuals is not difficult but mass killing is tough and exhausting. The Turks had not industrialised the business like the Germans would twenty-eight years later but their killing mirrored their capacity as soldiers, where there was a level of crude competency.

Gallipoli – June to December 1915

Anzac Cove was quiet during June and July 1915 but Cape Helles had five minor battles with the British or the French attacking individually or in tandem. There was one Turkish attack and, all in all, the gains could be measured in yards rather than miles. The effect was attritional on both sides, although Turkey suffered more than the Allies.

Lack of ammunition was hampering both sides, although neither was aware that the opponent was suffering. Both sides needed to replenish their armaments and their manpower, which was the reason for the desultory lull in fighting and no real attempt to resolve anything. The high command, however, decided that there would be an attempt to gain important high ground in August, with a third beachhead at Suvla Bay, where the Turkish defence amounted to only three battalions. Five new divisions were sent to Gallipoli to make a force of thirteen with 120,000 men, while the navy was reinforced with monitors replacing battleships and with landing barges designed by Fisher. Amphibious warfare was developing. Hamilton had to find a general to secure the beachhead at Suvla Bay and attack the heights, so he asked for Lieutenant General Julian Byng or Lieutenant General Henry Rawlinson, who were in France. His request was vetoed, although this was now the prime line of attack and shells were being diverted from France to Gallipoli. Instead, the powers appointed Lieutenant General Sir Frederick Stopford.

Mustafa Kemal suspected that there would be an offensive in August 1915 and a landing at Suvla Bay. Germany's Major Willmer had been sent there and had reorganised the defences, taking men away from the beaches and digging trenches in the foothills. This allowed Stopford to establish his beachhead with his neophyte soldiers from Britain. At Anzac Cove there was a tigerish struggle to capture the heights at Sari Bair, hoping that the troops from Suvla would cause the Turks to divert their troops there. Some 20,000 British soldiers were against 1,500 Turks and, although they captured two hills and were only a few miles from their major objective, the attack stalled and the complications of amphibious warfare were too much for the commanders.

As is usual in warfare, there was a chain of events, such as a shell killing General Hammersley's staff, inadequate maps, problems with water supply, lack of communication between the front line and the staff, and inexperience of soldiers and commanders. This led to failure but it was a close-run thing. Lieutenant General Liman rushed reserves to Anzac and Suvla. At Suvla, he sacked the commanding officer and put Mustafa Kemal in charge of a long line from the Anzac heights to Suvla. Kemal was unwell and sleep-deprived but it was a masterstroke as he organised the attacks that halted the British.

At Cape Helles, the Turks were prepared to retreat across the sea to Asia but Liman forbade it and they held on. The battle continued until the last week of August. Liman considered that the Irish at Suvla had a chance of taking the Turks' main ammunition dump, which would have outflanked their army. On 21 August the British nearly succeeded in taking two hills and were only halted by the last of the Turkish reserves.

There was now stalemate and exhaustion on both sides. No one knew what would happen next and there were those who advocated evacuation. Admiral of the Fleet John de Robeck was of this opinion but Admiral Rosslyn Wemyss and the influential Commodore Roger Keyes wanted to press on. The army was also split but understood that there would be no winter campaign so it meant a wait until spring before anything meaningful could happen.

Kitchener was vacillating. At first, he was for leaving the Dardanelles, then he was persuaded to produce a plan, in conjunction with the navy, for capital ships to brave the Narrows and reach Constantinople, where the inhabitants were fearful of the submarines still in the Sea of Marmora. The navy would also land troops at Bulair, where it would cut the supply route to the twenty divisions in the Hellespont. This was a fine idea but difficult to implement.

Kitchener visited the Dardanelles, inspected the bridgeheads and had a full discussion with all commanders. In October Hamilton was relieved of his command and replaced by an able, level-headed, professional general in Sir Charles Monro, who believed that the war would be won in France and was determined that evacuation should take place. Politicians would make the decision, influenced by the Northcliffe press in London, who were eager to end the campaign.

This was particularly true of Bonar Law, who was influential in cabinet as leader of the Tories. Less influential was Churchill, who said of Monro: 'He came, he saw, he capitulated,' and so it proved.[5] The evacuation was a brilliant military operation with 82,000 men taken from Suvla Bay and Anzac Cove in December. The Turks thought that the Allies would remain at Cape Helles but they were taken off in January. The casualties were negligible during these retreats.

In defeat, there is always blame. Justice is another thing and blame can be apportioned in only small quantities and with qualifications. This, for the Allies, was a complex operation of amphibious warfare of which there was no modern precedent. Hamilton was given command just five weeks before he had to establish bridgeheads and storm the heights in the Dardanelles, which was totally inadequate. The politicians and the Admiralty could be blamed for sending poor ships and minesweepers, with personnel who had insufficient training. The politicians could be blamed for inadequate supplies, especially shells. The War Office could be blamed for refusing to allocate the generals that Hamilton requested.

Gallipoli, like all battles at this time, was a gamble, where the sacrifice was no greater than at other battles during the war. Its objectives were imaginative in trying to knock Turkey out of the war and to open the trade route to Russia. This would probably not have happened even with the capture of Constantinople, as Germany would have intervened to prevent it unless the Russians had confronted them.

Russia can be blamed for Gallipoli for its inactivity and for stopping the Greeks from fighting. Russia badly needed the trade route and, if it had been established, it might have saved the tsar and his government. Those like Fisher and Monro who said that to win the war in France was all that mattered, were right but they had ignored Russia in their calculations. All in all, it is impossible to apportion blame and it is far easier to highlight inadequacies.

The French in 1915

France was in an attacking frame of mind as it wanted to be rid of the invaders who were still on its soil. However, when they attacked in 1915 there were substantial casualties, which greatly weakened the French army. At the end of it all there was little advantage. There was a static line of 475 miles, of which 160 miles running south of Verdun was manned by second-class or recuperating divisions on both sides. There was occasional hard fighting to gain the advantage of high ground but, overall, there was a feeling of live and let live.

In this region, no one could envisage a breakthrough that could affect the outcome of the war. The Verdun region itself was a salient, with all its advantages and disadvantages. Attacking from a salient it is possible to make ground and surround the enemy but, likewise, in defending a salient it may become pinched off and the forces in it surrounded. Verdun and Ypres were the two salients in the west where battle, once joined, hardly ceased and the salients remained in Allied hands all through the war.

Joffre believed that the war would be won on the plains of Picardy and Champagne, with the emphasis on the Somme region. This would be achieved by an artillery barrage, which would obliterate the defences of the trench system and allow the cavalry to move forward into the open spaces beyond. In part it could and did work, as in the Battle of Neuve Chapelle, but exploiting the break was difficult as the artillery had created such a mess that a clear pathway had to be established and the defenders learned how to defend in depth.

At this stage there was no element of surprise. The build-up for an attack was easily recognisable, with rail links specially built, arms dumps difficult to disguise and, nearing the date of the attack, the concentration of men was obvious. Thus, the defender had time to construct a suitable defence in depth and bring in reserves. On the chalk lands of Champagne, defence was easy and the French army – brave, resolute and full of elan – suffered huge casualties.

Apart from Second Ypres, Germany was happy to defend throughout 1915 on the Western Front. Its high command, however, was divided between westerners and easterners – the eternal German dilemma. General Erich von Falkenhayn considered that to win the war Germany had to defeat

France first, then go east. Hindenburg and Ludendorff were easterners and wanted the main effort there. This duo had an ally in Chancellor Bethmann-Hollweg, which in time would lead to the undermining of Von Falkenhayn. Germany had a two-front war and, if it concentrated on one front, could be vulnerable on the other.

The tactics throughout 1915 and even 1916 would not change to any great degree but the Germans would be innovative with the use of gas. They had used a lachrymatory gas against the Russians with little success but in April they planned to use cylinders of chlorine gas, which, when the wind was in the right direction, would float towards the enemy.

The Germans attacked at Ypres where the French and British lines joined. Intelligence had made the defenders aware of what was happening but no one knew what the outcome would be. The whole matter was very primitive and the Germans had only modest ambitions. They did not have reserves ready to pour through a breach and their aspirations, in truth, amounted to eliminating the Ypres salient.

Thus, when the attack was a success, with the gas causing horrible problems to eyes and lungs and often leading to death through drowning, the Germans, with their primitive respirators in which they had little confidence, burst through. However, instead of continuing when they had reached their objectives, they dug in, which was a missed opportunity, as the French and British were not always acting in concert. When the gas dispersed and normal warfare resumed, the Allied counter-attacks led to substantial casualties for little gain.

The Battle of Verdun, February to December 1916

The events of 1915 established that Germany had the dominant army in the east but in the west it was stalemate. If Germany was to win the war or gain an advantageous peace, it somehow needed to resolve the situation in the west, both on land and at sea. Time was never on the side of the Central Powers. The resources of the British, French, Italian and Russian empires were significantly greater than those of the German, Austro-Hungarian and Ottoman empires. Germany's strategy at this time was to knock out Russia and France, make an accommodation with Italy, then deal with Britain on its own.

Germany's method to beat France was one of attrition, an attempt to bleed it into submission. The Germans would attack on a small front, pull in the French to defend the area and wear them down. Even now it is not entirely clear whether the strategy was to create a breakthrough and with a pincer movement encapsulate a significant part of the French army or to make it cry for mercy with heavy casualties.

There was a degree of hope and opportunism in Von Falkenhayn's strategy but it soon became inescapable that the Verdun salient would be where the great land battle of the war would be fought. It started on 21 February and lasted until just before Christmas. Woods and verdant pastureland were reduced to a muddy, lunar landscape and hundreds of thousands of men in their prime were prematurely silenced.

Field Marshal Erich von Falkenhayn had caught the kaiser's attention after service in China and rapidly rose in rank and responsibility until he became minister of war in 1913, a surprising appointment. When Von Moltke was replaced as overlord on the Western Front, Von Falkenhayn succeeded him with the kaiser's backing.

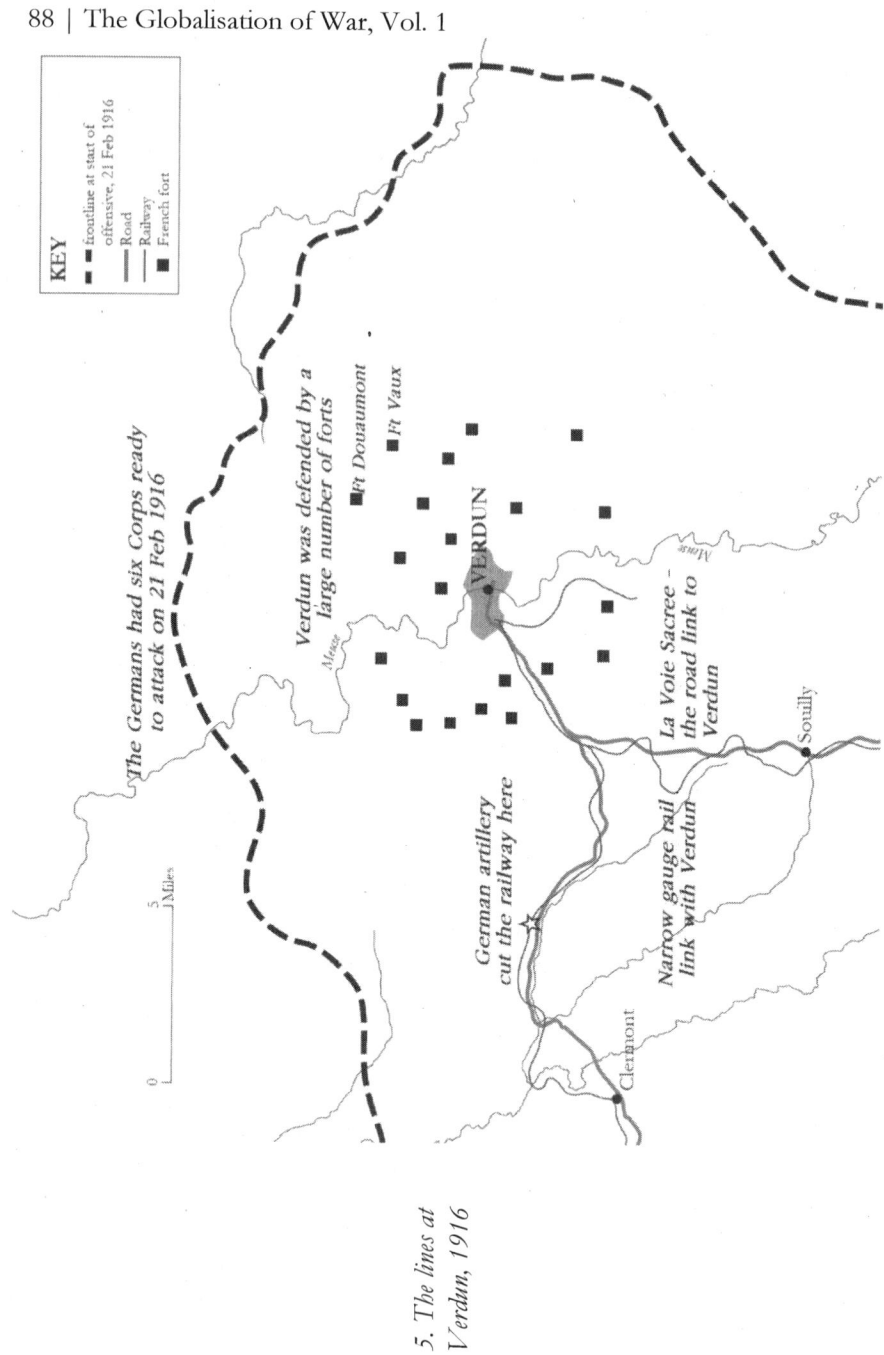

5. The lines at Verdun, 1916

Being on the defensive in the west was not going to win the war but Von Falkenhayn knew that Britain was his main enemy and had to be defeated. This was easier said than done even though Britain was not a great power in terms of its army and its presence on the Continent was subordinate to that of France. Von Falkenhayn's reasoning was to eliminate France, Russia and Italy, leaving Britain on its own, at which point he would advocate unrestricted submarine warfare. He did acknowledge that this could anger the United States but believed that Britain would have lost before the Americans could act.

His attempt to defeat the French was attritional and crude and resided in the brilliance of the German army. He ignored his ally, the Austro-Hungarians, infuriating Conrad, who was not told of his plans and had transferred five crack divisions to the Italian front. He also ignored the easterners led by Hindenburg and Ludendorff, who wanted to defeat the Russians and capture Ukraine, although this might cause Romania to defect to the Allies. It was all a very complicated puzzle.

Verdun was defended by a series of forts of which Fort Douaumont and Fort Vaux were the most significant. Observing the vulnerability of the forts in Belgium, Joffre had denuded his forts of guns and prepared most of his defences outside them. This part of the front had been quiet for some time and there were only three French divisions. In preparing for the battle, Von Falkenhayn had deployed ten divisions plus a huge quantity of artillery and shells, including thirteen Krupp 420s. The French observed this build-up but responded slowly. When the battle started, they were still under-strength and the artillery barrage blew them backwards. Within five days, the Germans had advanced up to 4 miles on an 8-mile-wide front, culminating in capturing Fort Douaumont, which succumbed to an infantry attack.

The French reaction was to fight for every inch of ground, which fitted in with Von Falkenhayn's strategy. Philippe Pétain was appointed to lead the fightback and organised his own artillery to give the Germans measure for measure and the logistical support indispensable to maintaining his army. A single road linked the 50 miles between Bar-le-Duc and Verdun, with 2,000 tons of supplies needed daily, so territorials had to improve and maintain this road. Also, 3,500 trucks were found to get the supplies to Verdun, the fate of which had captured the French imagination, so the struggle had been given a spiritual dimension, symbolised by the naming of the road as La Voie Sacrée.

After a week, the Germans were 4 miles from Verdun but were just being held. They decided to change their tactics in response to the effectiveness of the French artillery, which was protected by the heights on the west bank of the Meuse. Thus, the front was extended and successful German attacks inspired French counter-attacks. This heroic violence was symbolised by the village of Vaux, which swung from French to German and back again thirteen times, while the French retained control of the fort.

In April the Germans changed tactics again when they attacked along the long extended front of 20 miles, trying to gain the high ground. The casualties were horrendous. German territorial gains were not significant and with almost equal casualties they were not winning the battle of attrition. The French had defended gallantly and they cleverly rotated their troops, which made them better able to deal with the carnage. Forty-two French divisions had taken part in the battle against thirty German. The killing continued through May and June, with casualties doubling, until a final German effort on 11 July was parried and the main endeavour on the Western Front had moved to the Somme.

Crown Prince Wilhelm of Germany was the influential leader of the 5th Army and his initial enthusiasm buoyed Von Falkenhayn's bid for glory. He had General Schmidt von Knobelsdorf as his chief of staff making most of the decisions, which the kaiser approved of as he had a difficult relationship with his son.

Crown Prince Wilhelm may have been dissolute but he was no sycophant. On 21 April he came out against renewing the battle at Verdun, declaring that 'a decisive success at Verdun could only be assured at the price of heavy sacrifices, out of all proportion to the desired gains'.[6] His views were supported but not by Von Knobelsdorf, while Von Falkenhayn was ambivalent. The bid for glory was with Von Knobelsdorf, who put backbone into his commander, while the kaiser ignored his son. The crown prince was therefore in charge of an army fighting a battle in which he did not believe.

The Victor of Verdun

This sobriquet fell upon General Philippe Pétain. France was looking for a hero to mitigate the losses of Verdun and there was reasonable justification in nominating Pétain. Because the soldiers were rotated, a lot of Frenchmen fought at Verdun and a man who had been there was justly revered by his countrymen. The highest accolade fell upon Pétain, although he was only in charge for two months but played an important ancillary role thereafter. Within a few days of the battle starting, Joffre decided he needed Pétain's 2nd Army and put him in charge of the defence.

Pétain was a great lover and was with his chief mistress, subsequently his wife, so had to be tracked down and told to direct the battle. It took him some time to get to his HQ and, when he arrived, his staff were not there. The following day he was diagnosed with double pneumonia, so five days into the battle he was not fully operational. From his bed he was responsible for upgrading the road from Bar-le-Duc to Verdun, which was supervised by a civil engineer on his staff.

At the same time, Pétain initiated the system of rotation of units. The rapid widening and upgrading of the road eased the movement of troops, armaments and victuals. With the Germans attacking and getting to within 4 kilometres of Verdun, Pétain had to fight a very determined defensive battle, at which he was adept. As Clausewitz pointed out, defence has serious advantages over attack; and as Foch was to point out, Pétain was not as good an attacking general as a defensive one, and his defence at Verdun was outstanding.

There was much human sacrifice and Pétain was always requesting more troops. The forty-two divisions he used encompassed half the French army and Joffre was finding it difficult to help him, so wanted to replace him with Robert Nivelle, one of his corps commanders. Pétain did not get on with Joffre or Poincaré, the president, while Nivelle was a politician to his fingertips.

In the middle of April Pétain was promoted to the command of the Centre Army Group and Nivelle took over his job and HQ as commander of the 2nd Army. Consequently, Pétain became sandwiched between the two, with Nivelle wanting to attack at Verdun and Joffre hoping that the French and British attack on the Somme, due in six weeks, would relieve Verdun. When the Germans attacked on 1 June the situation seemed to become critical and Joffre gave in to Pétain's request by giving him four more divisions, taking them out of the Somme attack and putting the onus on to the British.

The attack on the Somme, plus the Brusilov Offensive, neutered the Germans but the French counter-attack did not come until the middle of October, directed by Nivelle and Mangin. By the middle of December it could be construed a success insofar as the territorial status quo ante was achieved at a horrible cost to both sides. For the time being, Nivelle was the winner as he was appointed as commander-in-chief of the French Army in succession to Joffre, leapfrogging Pétain. This upset Pétain but he had the benefit of press attention. They were interested in him and bolstered him, which did not diminish with Nivelle's success. According to public opinion, fostered by the press, Pétain was the victor of Verdun.

Chapter 6

The War on Land at Sea and in the Air

Charles de Gaulle

In 1914, Charles de Gaulle was a lieutenant in the 33rd Infantry Regiment of Arras and as a professional soldier was in battle within weeks of the declaration of war. His regiment was sent to the Ardennes region to defend the crucial area around the Meuse. He was leading his platoon in an attack on a bridge in Dinant when he was hit in the leg and fell, while a sergeant who had just been killed fell on top of him. His platoon was decimated but he was rescued and returned to Arras with a damaged fibula and sciatic nerve.

By October De Gaulle had recovered and re-joined his regiment in the Champagne area, soon becoming its adjutant and, in January, was awarded the Croix de Guerre. In February and March there was more fighting, with casualties increasing, including De Gaulle, when a shell splinter pierced his left hand. He paid it little attention and it became infected, paralysing his hand, swelling his arm and causing a fever. He was taken out of the trenches for two months, returning near the Aisne in June. This was a quiet sector where his regiment remained until the Battle of Verdun.

On 1 March 1916 the regiment was in a sector to the north of Douaumont and Captain de Gaulle was sent to reconnoitre the ground, find where the enemy was and make a link with both flanks. It was a landscape of blasted mud with no front line or linking trenches and no defences, so finding points of recognition made orientation difficult. The Germans had captured the fort at Douaumont and would use it as the base for the next attack unless the

French artillery could negate it.

The next day, the German attack came, starting with heavy artillery and followed by the infantry, which attacked in waves. One account claims that the French repulsed five attacks until the enemy made a breach and got to the rear of what remained of the regiment. De Gaulle led his men in trying to regain his lines but, in the confusion of hand-to-hand battle, he was bayoneted in the thigh and lost consciousness. When he came round, he was a prisoner.

The war had thirty months to run and De Gaulle was in captivity for most of that time. Being a man of spirit, he did not relish being under the German yoke and spent his time escaping, then ending up in prisons for difficult cases. His build and manner were not ideal for escaping and he did not blend easily into a crowd, so he was always recaptured. For a true soldier it was a time of bitter frustration.

Submarine Warfare and the Blockade

To win the war, both Britain and Germany realised that they had to dominate each other on the trade routes of the sea. Britain would do this by blockade with capital ships and Germany by submarine warfare, although there were manifold difficulties in carrying this out. Britain incurred the ire of neutrals by impounding ships that may have been sailing from one neutral country to another but whose goods might have been in transit to a nation at war. Likewise, the Germans had the dilemma of stopping ships to see whether they were truly neutral before sinking them. Often there were ships with mixed cargoes and passengers from neutral states and nations at war.

The blockade procedures had been discussed at a conference in London five years before the war. All ships going to or from a blockaded port could be subject to search, ships from a hostile nation could be seized and, if contraband were found on a neutral ship, this could also be taken. Contraband was defined as all materials useful to enemy armed forces.

Neutral nations had considerable rights and could trade with nations at war, even selling them munitions, but these could be confiscated. In the grey area of contraband – goods that could be of benefit to the belligerent, such as food – the ship could be impounded and the goods subject to the decision of a prize court. Such were the complications that Britain and the United States refused to ratify the Declaration of London, saying that it neutered naval supremacy. The other great trading nations of the world did ratify it.

On the whole, blockade came to mean the blockading of the enemy's ports, just as Nelson's navy blockaded the French ports in the time of

Napoleon and the Union blockaded the Confederate's ports during the American Civil War. The Americans wanted to trade with European nations, especially the neutrals, and did not like Britain interfering. Britain, however, was not going to blockade the enemy's ports as it did not control the Baltic and there was extensive mining by the Germans in the Heligoland Bight. Therefore, the British established the blockade deep into the North Sea. It was not considered that it would have an immediate effect on the fortunes of war but the longer the war lasted, the greater would be the effect.

In a sense, Britain was much more vulnerable than Germany to an interruption to its trade as it imported nearly 60 per cent of its food compared with 25 per cent for Germany; however, the latter had problems as it relied on fertilisers for its yield, which came from outside Europe. Other raw materials such as cotton came exclusively from the United States, as did 60 per cent of Germany's copper.

The blockade also decimated the German merchant marine, which was either locked in neutral ports or impounded, with less than 40 per cent remaining to trade in the Baltic. Germany could improvise but its need for immediate conquest and a short war was obvious. To begin with, imports from the United States diminished to a trickle but there was compensation in greatly increased trade with Scandinavia and the Netherlands. The British government, aware of this, closed the loopholes by the end of 1914. With this came inevitable American complaints.

The German Empire had only existed for forty-three years and its western and eastern parts were not fully integrated. The industrial west imported large amounts of food and raw materials via Rotterdam and Antwerp, which went down the Rhine into Germany, while the eastern part produced surplus crops and sent them into Bohemia or further east. It should have been a simple matter to transfer them to the west of Germany but the railways were being used for military purposes and were not geared to this change in trade.

At the beginning of the war, the surface fleets' actions occupied both sides' attempts to beat the blockade. The Germans made raids on Scarborough and Hartlepool, often pursued by the Royal Navy, which made Admiral Hipper think that fishing vessels, neutral or otherwise, on Dogger Bank had provided intelligence to the British. He determined to clear the area of trawlers and the light warships that were patrolling and protecting them. To do this he intended to use battle cruisers, which the High Seas Fleet would cover.

Kaiser Wilhelm had forbidden any large action that could be decisive but this was regarded as only a minor skirmish. The plan was to set out on the evening of 23 January 1915, survey Dogger Bank the next morning, attack any enemy ships thereabouts and return that evening. The only trouble was that there was no element of surprise as the British were reading the German codes and preparing to intercept the raiders.

For Germany, the Battle of Dogger Bank in January 1915 would turn out to be a disaster. Vice-Admiral Beatty intercepted Hipper's battle cruisers and the Royal Navy reasserted its authority over the North Sea. The British sank the German battle cruiser, *Blucher*, and there was a severe fire in the two after turrets of *Seydlitz*. Although Beatty's flagship, *Lion*, was repeatedly hit and was incapacitated, there were only two men killed and only fifteen British killed in the entire action compared to about 1,000 Germans. Although a British victory, there was much criticism of the navy's inability to destroy the remainder of the German force but there was quiet satisfaction at the result. The Germans, on the other hand, would learn from it and especially the torching of the magazines on *Seydlitz*. They would subsequently introduce a system of compartmentalising the transference of powder and ammunition, which would mitigate the effect of a direct hit.

This action temporarily ended any German pretensions to end the blockade by fleet action. The only alternative was to use submarines, a new means of warfare for Europeans, where the rules of engagement were yet to be established and accepted. There were two main possibilities: restricted submarine warfare would see the submarine surface, confront its antagonist, establish its credentials and, if hostile, it would allow all those on board to take to the boats, then sink the ship; unrestricted submarine warfare would ignore the niceties and just attack without warning. It did not matter whether the ship was hostile or neutral, or whether it carried contraband or passengers. All that mattered was that it was in a certain zone.

Because of the effect and the seeming inhumanity of the blockade on Germany, influential Germans, such as Chancellor Bethmann-Hollweg and the naval high command, were in favour of unrestricted submarine warfare. The kaiser, however, forbade it, although he did not rule out its future use. Within a few weeks, Bethmann-Hollweg had second thoughts and realised that neutrals would be appalled by unrestricted submarine warfare.

Thus, the dialogue continued among the Germans, with much confusion. In the end, they threatened unrestricted warfare to frighten the neutrals but in practice it was severely restricted, respecting neutrals and allowing hospital ships free passage. There were only twenty U-boats that could be used for this campaign and only seven or eight could be active at any one time. In the first month, they sank twenty-five merchant ships but over 4,000 ships entered and left British ports. The slaughter of merchant ships took time to develop.

The Americans and other neutrals protested but were not molested to any great extent. Bethmann-Hollweg was now becoming extremely sensitive to the neutrals' position. The British, on the other hand, saw German actions as an unrestricted blockade on their island and declared that there would be an unrestricted blockade on Germany. Consuls in neutral ports were exceptionally active. One German ploy was for food or raw materials to be designated for a neutral destination and loading would proceed. Then a German ship would moor alongside and the goods would pass over the neutral ship to the German one.

The great crisis came with the sinking of *Lusitania*. The Cunard Line owned the ship, the British government having subsidised its building in a time of peace so that it could be used as a merchant cruiser in time of war. However, *Lusitania* was still a passenger liner that could transport a considerable cargo. The ship had made four return journeys across the Atlantic since the U-boats had threatened merchant ships and, despite there having been a warning from the German Embassy in the United States, it had been ignored.

In the ship's cargo were artillery shells and rifle ammunition plus 10 tons of explosive powder. Near Kinsale in Ireland, a U-boat captain recognised the ship and classified it as a merchant cruiser used for carrying troops. As another ship, *Mauretania*, was 150 miles away embarking troops for the Dardanelles, this was plausible, so the U-boat fired a torpedo from 800 yards and struck *Lusitania*. There was an explosion, possibly the powder, and the ship immediately began to list, making the release of the lifeboats very difficult, so only six out of forty-eight were used. It took eighteen minutes for the ship to sink and 1,201 people lost their lives, including 94 children and 128 Americans.

The reaction in Germany was triumphant. There was a school holiday and a medal was struck. American reaction was full of fury and indignation. Two former US presidents, Roosevelt and Taft, demanded that the United States declare war but current president, Woodrow Wilson, was cautious. After all, the Americans were also indignant about the British blockade, even though that did not cost lives. Wilson continued his diplomatic offensive, to which Germany was sensitive and, by the beginning of June, formal rules of engagement had been established. This enraged Admiral von Tirpitz, the begetter of the modern German navy, who could not bear to see it emasculated with limited submarine warfare.

In August 1915, a White Star liner was sunk, with three Americans dead, so the kaiser announced that no passenger ships, enemy or otherwise, were to be attacked. However, another British liner was sunk in September, before Germany took its U-boats away from the Western Approaches.

The German U-boats were not a threat but the blockade remained. Almost 800 tons of Allied and neutral shipping had been sunk, of which nearly three-quarters was British. However, the amount of shipping in Allied control was greater at the end of 1915 than before the war because of the use of the Central Powers' merchant marine. Nevertheless, this was a one-off and the building of new merchant ships was down to 615,000 tons because the manpower was needed to fight the war in other ways. So, Britain would be vulnerable to an attritional attack.

The Germans continued to attack British shipping during 1916 and had not abandoned the submarine war, as with fifty-two operational U-boats at the end of February and another thirty-eight expected in the following five months, they were in a position to strike hard. In March and April they sank about 160,000 tons but there were still mistakes. At the end of March a cross-Channel ferry was mistaken for a troopship and four Americans lost their lives. As the orders went to back off, another passenger liner was sunk because the U-boat had not received the signal. This disaster stopped U-boat activity. Admiral von Pohl, dying of cancer, was replaced by Admiral Reinhard Scheer, who determined that the blockade should be resolved by a battle between the High Seas Fleet and the Royal Navy. Thus, the attempt to keep the United States out of the war led to the Battle of Jutland.

The Battle of Jutland, May to June 1916

6. The Battle of Jutland, 1916

Both the British and German surface fleets were kept in harbours where they were relatively safe from attack. This suited the British, who were happy with the blockade of Germany and strategically were intent on maintaining their superiority. For Germany it was very frustrating. Submarine warfare was subject to such limitations that the only solution was to confront the British fleet and overcome it. Then the mastery of the seas would be with Germany, patrolling the Western Approaches, the Channel and the North Sea, and Britain would be blockaded. With Admiral Scheer in command, Germany's navy had become more aggressive and he planned a conflict.

In May 1916 Germany made its attempt to confront the British fleet, which in most respects was stronger than the German fleet. The British had thirty-seven modern capital ships to twenty-nine German, Britain's superiority in guns was 272 of 12-inch or greater calibre to 176. In cruisers there were thirty-four against eleven and in destroyers eighty against sixty-three. The speed of the British ships was greater, mainly because they were lighter due to less thickness of armament, although this made them more vulnerable to shell fire.

These ships, on both sides, were magnificent creations, products of fine technology and in complexity the most finely tuned artefacts of aggressive warfare. The range and accuracy of their guns was immense but each fleet was subject to severe limitations. To engage the enemy there had to be a sighting and, in 1916, aircraft were only just being used for this purpose. In fact, the British put up an aircraft that located the German fleet but communications broke down and the intelligence was of no use.

This illustrated how erratic communications were and the use of the wireless was in some ways sophisticated, in other ways primitive. Often, ships communicated in battle by flags and lights. Wireless was subject to cyphers on both sides but the British had the use of the German cypher and signal books. Although the Germans modified them, British penetration continued and the Admiralty picked up the fact that the German High Seas Fleet was in the North Sea on 31 May and sent a fleet to intercept it.

Both fleets were blind and came across each other by chance. The battle had three components: the first was the initial contact by Admiral Beatty when his cruisers were sunk or mauled by superior German gunnery in the afternoon; the second phase was when the fleets coalesced in the firing line and, from 6pm until darkness fell, fought without significant advantage to either side; in the third phase, during the night, the British ships placed themselves between the German fleet and their ports and were willing to fight but the Germans wanted to return to port. In darkness, the German ships evaded the British, although they lost a battleship sunk by a destroyer.

On the morning of 1 June the Germans were nowhere to be found on the open seas, which acknowledged British suzerainty. The British Grand Fleet returned to base having lost six cruisers and eight destroyers to one battleship, five cruisers and five destroyers of the Germans. The Germans fared better in terms of manpower losses, as 6,097 British were killed compared with 2,545 Germans, while the Germans rescued 177 British prisoners from the sea.

The immediate significance of any sea battle is hard to discern. There are a series of incidents taking place 10 or more miles apart. Both sides observe each other but most of the time it is difficult to know the effect of a direct hit unless it is spectacular, such as a shell exploding in a powder magazine. This happened with five of the British cruisers and is the reason for the greater loss of British lives. A direct hit repeatedly led to the loss of a thousand lives. The Germans, on the other hand, had learned from the fate of *Seydlitz* at the Battle of Dogger Bank and compartmentalised their magazines. Thus, the greater loss of British lives was regrettable but not significant in the long term.

Admiral John Jellicoe was not a man to sensationalise a battle. On 1 June the world did not know that it had taken place. As Jellicoe retired, knowing that the German fleet had fled, he tried to piece together what had happened. The ships that had been sunk could be tallied, some sort of figure could be calculated for the casualties, the damage to the ships could be assessed, but what had happened to the enemy was more difficult to ascertain.

On the British side there had been spectacular explosions and quick sinkings, therefore the Germans were able to announce from Berlin that a victory had been obtained before Jellicoe had even informed the Admiralty of his opinion of the battle. Britain felt that it should respond to Berlin's claims and Balfour made an objective assessment of the facts as he knew them. The British press felt that information was being withheld and that Britain might no longer rule the waves.

The bare facts dented British prestige as the fleet had fought a battle and suffered greater losses than its adversary. But this was a superficial view of the contest. The British fleet could afford minor losses and those of the Battle of Jutland did not in any way upset the balance of power. Basically, it had been a cruiser battle and the great dreadnoughts of the two navies had survived, the only battleship to be sunk being obsolescent. Moreover, British gunnery had been very good, although the shells did not always explode.

Germany's shipbuilding was geared to keeping its ships afloat. Many of its warships had been badly damaged after being hit more than twenty times. After the battle, three of its dreadnoughts were in dry dock for several weeks compared with one of the British. Overall, the damage to the British fleet that remained was probably less than that suffered by the German fleet.

To retreat was not necessarily a defeat for Germany but, if it wanted to

The War on Land at Sea and in the Air | 101

break Britain by attrition, it had to come out and fight. However, the Germans were wary of fighting, although Admiral Scheer wanted to attack. On 9 August there was another foray into the North Sea, this time with airships to help. The object was to shell Sunderland but, despite the British sending their fleets into the North Sea, the Germans thought better of another confrontation and retired to base, where they stayed. The strategic victory went to Admiral Jellicoe and the Grand Fleet and the blockade inexorably weakened Germany.

The Brusilov Offensive, June to August 1916

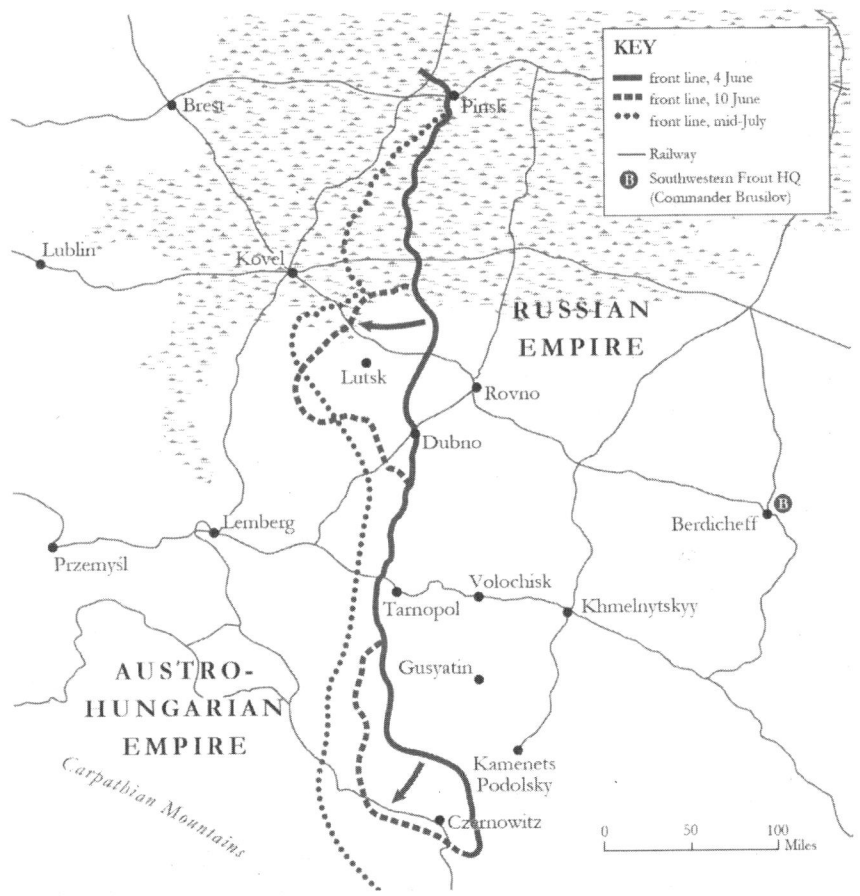

7. Front lines of the Brusilov Offensive, 1916

With the Germans occupied at Verdun, Russia considered decisive action in the east. It wanted to attack in the centre under General Alexei Evert, with help in the north from General Aleksey Kuropatkin, while General Aleksey Brusilov would have a defensive role in the south. As it happened, the Austrians had taken troops from where Brusilov opposed them to fight on the Italian front. Evert became more and more cautious about attacking on his front, while Brusilov had an attacking frame of mind. He had thought deeply about how to penetrate the enemy lines.

With a superiority of men and guns, which was not substantial, Brusilov decided to attack on a very wide front without a massive build-up in one place. He forbade a long and cacophonous artillery attack that announced where the attack would be and so give the defenders time to assemble reserves. Moreover, he assembled his troops in deeply dug positions and made them dig trenches forward of the front line to get near to the enemy.

These simple measures were brilliantly successful and the Russian 8th Army attacked on 4 June, penetrated the Austrian lines and captured large numbers of prisoners. Further south, the 11th Army was held but the 7th Army pushed the Austrians back. Even further south, the 9th Army captured territory in Bukovina. These were substantial gains over a wide front, as can be gauged from the 200,000 Austrian prisoners captured.

Evert, in the centre of the Russian army, became dilatory and pessimistic about his attack but the tsar was fearful of replacing him and decided that some of his troops should be deployed to help Brusilov achieve a greater breakthrough. The difficulty was in moving, as north-south communications were poor and, in the end, little came of it and Brusilov received little support from elsewhere.

In the south he reached the foothills of the Carpathian Mountains and tried to move on the great city of Lemberg; however, by August he was taking heavy casualties and the great offensive, one of the more successful of the war, petered out. He had suffered about a million casualties, a high price, but it was not in vain as far as his allies were concerned. Von Falkenhayn had sent seven divisions from the west to the east, which had a bearing on the Verdun and Somme battles.

The victories of the Brusilov Offensive had another outcome, which was the entry of Romania into the war. Both France and Russia had been working on Romania and had promised it Transylvania and a bit of Hungary after the war. Romania was going to rely heavily on Russia and, like many an opportunist entrant to war, declared at the time when its ally's effort was spent and all it wanted to do was consolidate. Romania's entry also decided the fate of Von Falkenhayn, who made way for Hindenburg and Ludendorff in the west but returned to active command against the Romanians.

The Battle of the Somme, July to November 1916

To relieve the French at Verdun, a great battle was planned in the region of the Somme river. Although it was initially to be fought by the British and French in equal numbers, the continuing attrition at Verdun meant that the French contribution to the Somme offensive was reduced, while certain French corps were removed from the front line in the north so that the British had a continuous line from the Ypres salient to the Somme. Prior to the battle, the Somme, rather like Verdun, had been a quiet region but the Germans had dug deep sophisticated defences in the chalkland, some of which went down 30 feet. Communications were good, as linking trenches were well protected and telephone lines were buried. There were thick coils of barbed wire in front of the trenches, so a pathway had to be found through this simple defence.

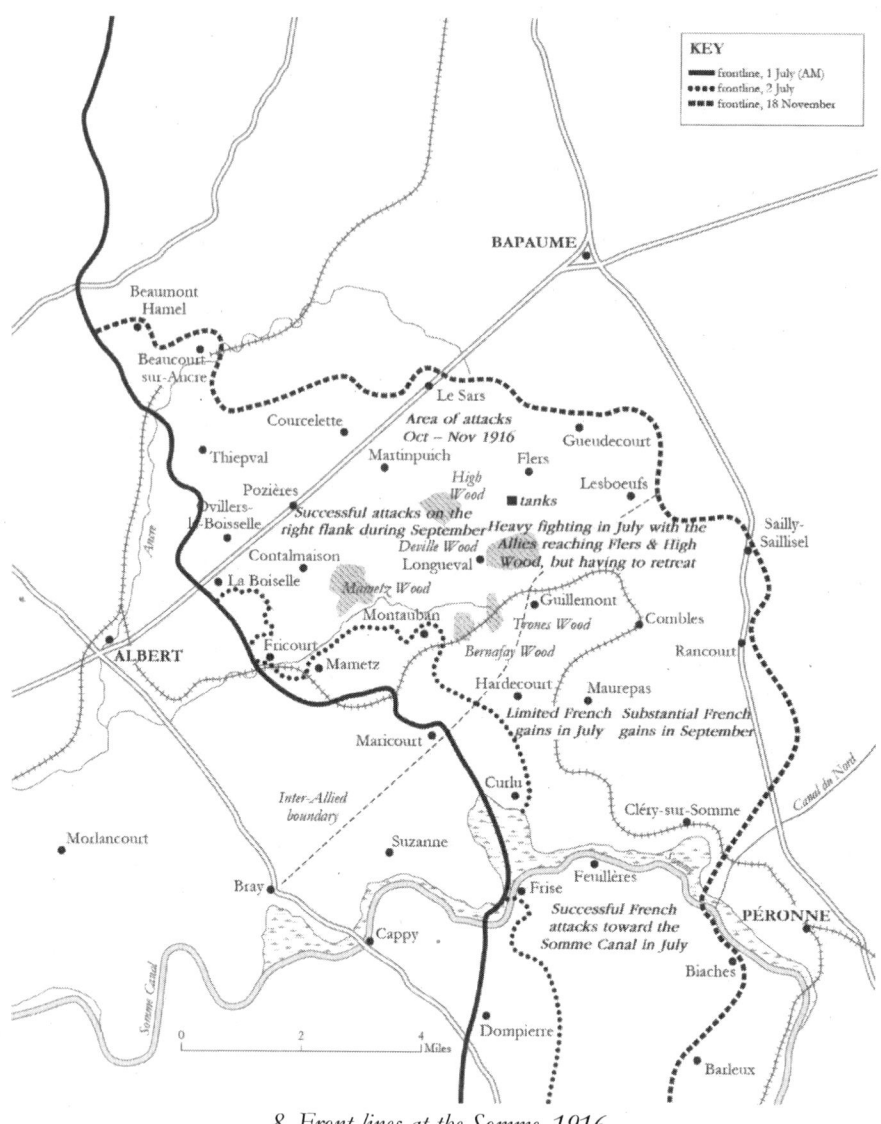

8. *Front lines at the Somme, 1916*

General Sir Douglas Haig provided the British with ample supplies but such a build-up, with railway spurs and arms dumps, signalled the attack and allowed the Germans to prepare in depth. Haig, like Von Falkenhayn, believed that artillery would blast a hole in the front, which would allow the infantry and cavalry to pass through. When the artillery started, it continued for the whole of the last week of June and was mind-numbing in its intensity, with a million shells landing in the German lines.

At dawn on 1 July nineteen British and three French divisions attacked. The British, on the whole, were neophytes, a patriotic, volunteer, citizen army that should advance in regular lines with their 60-pound packs and, as the sun rose, with glinting bayonets. The million shells had done immense damage but not to the deep defences, nor had they obliterated the barbed wire. The heavily laden, upright soldiers, without benefit of mist or smoke, were slain in their thousands and the cacophony of modern warfare could not obliterate the cries of the many more who were wounded. Only five of the attacking divisions reached the German positions. In round figures, of the 100,000 who had attacked, 19,000 were killed and 40,000 wounded or taken prisoner.

German losses were nothing like this in the initial attack but, when the Allies won ground, frenzied German counter-attacks led to slaughter on their side. By the end of July there were 160,000 German casualties compared with over 200,000 British and French. As at Verdun, the loss of life was horrendous but, as with the Brusilov Offensive, it was believed that a savage artillery onslaught would allow a breakthrough.

The British learned from what seemed crass ineptitude and changed tactics by attacking at night or in half-light, which was more effective. Then in August came the first major tank attack of the war between Albert and Bapaume. With the firepower and protection of this invention, the infantry advanced 2 miles until artillery fire halted the tanks, along with mechanical breakdown or rough ground. This was success but it was just as well that it was not a great success (all thirty-six tanks were disabled) as it meant that Germany's high command did not see great significance in this innovation.

The fighting continued in the autumn but petered out in the wet and cold of November, with the Allies only about 7 miles from their start line. The British had taken the brunt of the fighting but the French, using first-class troops, were more successful in that they had gained more territory. Casualties were now about equal on both sides, around 600,000. Thus, at Verdun and the Somme, it did not matter who attacked or defended, the casualties were about the same and the loss or gain of territory was not of any significance. Verdun and the Somme were the nadir of war on the Western Front, solemnly tragic, but all great wars are subject to attrition when both sides are evenly matched and where the protagonists lock antlers and fight to exhaustion.

The Early Air War

In 1914, aircraft were very primitive and their ability to make war was not great and the troops on the ground did not fear them. After all, it was only eleven years after the first flight had taken place and six years after the first aircraft had flown the Channel. In fact, it was still an adventure to cross the Channel by air. However, even a few years before the war, certain soldiers had realised the value of aircraft in a reconnaissance role and, in 1914, the French used them to report General von Kluck's move east of Paris, the Germans in discerning Russian dispositions at the Battle of Tannenberg and the British when Haig and General Smith-Dorrien's armies lost contact.

The aircraft industries in the main belligerent countries were still in their infancy but the French were the most developed, followed by the Germans, with the British a poor third. The aircraft were not offensive machines, although they tried to be. Most were two-seaters, with a pilot and an observer. Soon, a light machine gun stripped of its cooling apparatus was installed for the observer's use but the field of fire was limited because of the aircraft's structure. There were occasional dogfights but, once the front lines became static in the west, aircraft were predominantly used for artillery spotting. In time they were fitted with wirelesses, which could report the position of the artillery and could then report on the effectiveness of the resulting bombardment. The accuracy of this exercise was not good but it would evolve.

Aircraft were not the only way to observe artillery fire. There were balloons along the Western Front on both sides, which could be hauled up and down from the ground. After a time, aircraft were able to destroy these balloons but other aircraft would defend them and dogfights would ensue. The observers in the balloons had a perilous existence and were issued with parachutes, which they often used. The big technological breakthrough of the air war came from France. The idea was to synchronise the machine gun with the propeller action so that the bullets would pass through the propeller. Roland Garros, a French aviator, first did this, modifying his propeller by attaching steel blades to deflect bullets to counteract any malfunction in synchronisation. It was a brilliant idea, which worked, although he and his aircraft were captured.

The Germans seized on the idea and the Fokker firm developed it. From winter 1915 to spring 1916, the Fokkers dominated the sky but the Germans were timid in attacking over enemy territory and the Allies held back. Thus, losses in combat were not significant but there was a pay-off at Verdun. The

Germans had air superiority and the French did not know the degree of German troop concentrations, nor could they easily observe the battle from on high. By the time of the Somme, however, the new British aircraft established superiority over the battlefield through a brave attacking policy but at the cost of high casualties. This battle in the air had another twist in September when the Germans introduced the Albatros D.III, which was to prove superior to the Allied aircraft.

At sea, the German High Seas Fleet relied on Zeppelin balloons. As the fleet rarely ventured from its bases, it was thought that the Zeppelins could be used offensively to bomb England. In May 1915 they started to bomb London, during 1915 killing 127 people and injuring 352. To begin with they were immune from attack despite being easy to pick up by wireless interception, as it took time to develop artillery that could seriously damage them. Likewise, special explosive bullets had to be developed for aircraft. During 1916, the Zeppelins ranged all over Britain but the defence overcame its problems and started shooting them down. By the end of the year they were withdrawn and replaced by bombers.

In Britain, as elsewhere, the Flying Corps was a fledgling institution. It was not a service on its own but a part of the army or navy. As time went on, it became more a part of the army, which provided most of its personnel. In Britain, its leadership was centred on a tall, extrovert personality, Lieutenant Colonel Hugh Trenchard. Men, with few exceptions, revered him, despite a ruthless streak. He decided, in simple fashion, that the function of the Royal Flying Corps was to serve the army to the utmost, to seek air superiority at all times and under all conditions and to accept the casualties that would accrue from this policy. He carried out this strategy and the casualties endured by the corps were horrendous. Average life expectancy of pilots and observers could be measured in weeks rather than months.

By the end of 1915, ace pilots were beginning to gain publicity. The Germans had two in Captains Immelmann and Boelcke, who flew Fokkers and whom the British feared. Immelmann had such skill as a pilot that he devised the loop that bore his name. This consisted of a steep climb and a twist to one side at the height of the loop, which allowed the plane to fly downwards and reverse direction.

On 29 December 1915, six Fokkers confronted two B.E.2c's, one of which contained a young Sholto Douglas. His companion was shot down and took with him two Fokkers, while Douglas faced the remaining four. His observer managed to shoot down one Fokker but suddenly he witnessed an acrobatic loop prior to an attack. It was Immelmann, and one of his companions was Boelcke. Douglas let his plane fall out of the sky and levelled out as he hugged the ground. There was no scope for loops at ground level but Boelcke got so close that he would have destroyed Douglas's plane if he had not run out of ammunition. Douglas's observer had been passive because of the manoeuvres but recovered in time to give Immelmann a burst, which sent him on his way. By now, Douglas was over the British lines and was forced to land as his engine seized. The story made headline news in Britain and forged Douglas's reputation. Despite stories like this and even more as the war progressed, it was difficult to evaluate the role and effectiveness of the belligerent air forces. No one thought in terms of them winning battles. There was combat, of course, but rather like the sea, the air remained as it was once combat ceased.

On the Western Front, men saw static warfare and, when it became dynamic, the results were shown in terms of a few miles of territory won or lost and thousands of casualties incurred. But the air war was not static, in fact it was highly dynamic, an evolving amalgam of tactics and technology. By the end of 1916, no one could say that the air war was having a dominant effect but it would be a foolish man who could predict that it would not do so in the future.

Verdun, the Somme and the Brusilov Offensive

These were the three great battles of the First World War that determined its ultimate outcome. By the time the Battle of the Somme had started, there was stalemate at Verdun and the Germans became preoccupied with this front and the Brusilov part of the Russian front, where fighting had started in early June.

Von Knobelsdorf refused to acknowledge that his superior, Crown Prince Willem, was right and that any result at Verdun would involve sacrifice that was disproportionate. Von Falkenhayn, even at this date, was ambivalent and indecisive about the battle but Von Knobelsdorf persuaded him that an attack in July would have an impact. Sacrifices continued with no significant gain of territory and the Germans now realised that their antagonists had a numerical advantage as they were fighting France, Britain and Russia in unison. The attempt to knock out the French by attrition had failed, as German casualties were only about 10 per cent less than their opponents.

The crown prince beseeched his father to stop the battle but the kaiser would not listen and allowed the commander to overrule his chief of staff. To be fair, the breaking point of armies is very hard to discern and, in a battle of attrition of such intensity, it can happen at any time. However, Von Knobelsdorf's optimism was undermined by obstinacy. In August 1916 he was sent to Russia to command an army corps.

On 27 August Romania went to war on the side of the Allies. The timing was unexpected as it was thought that the Romanians would first want to collect the harvest. Bethmann-Hollweg was not a fan of Von Falkenhayn and persuaded the kaiser to send him to fight the Romanians. Hindenburg was recalled from the east, together with his lieutenant, Ludendorff, and when they viewed the battlefield at Verdun, they recoiled with horror at the sacrifice that had been made and they stopped all attacks.

Romania Enters the War

When Romania attacked, it did so against the Austro-Hungarians. If it had attacked with speed and panache, it could have caused a lot of trouble. The army, with twenty-three divisions, was in terms of manpower a formidable force but it lacked weaponry and leadership. It was not a straightforward decision to attack in Transylvania. The British had suggested that Romania attack the Bulgarians so that the army in Salonika could attack them from another front. As the Romanians advanced into Transylvania, the Bulgarians waited on their border, which was only 30 miles from the capital, Bucharest. Likewise, Turkey had forces looking with predatory eyes into Romania.

As the Russian front fell quiet, all eyes were on the Romanian front. Germany deployed forces of superior quality under Von Falkenhayn in Transylvania and General Eberhard von Mackensen south of the Danube near the Black Sea. Russia came to Romania's help but the German-led Central Powers were far too strong and swept through the country, entering Bucharest on 6 December and pushing the Romanian army into a tiny enclave in its own country. The advantage to the Central Powers was substantial as they garnered 2 million tons of grain and a million tons of oil. These were tangible fruits of conquest, which would help prolong the war.

Chapter 7

Talk of Peace

The Rhythm of War

The war had an inexorable rhythm of its own, a pace and inevitability that made peace difficult. If one takes as the trigger point the assassination of Grand Duke Ferdinand at Sarajevo, then action and reaction followed each other without a break. Austria's response to the Serbs caused the mobilisation of Russia, which led to Germany going west before the Russians were able to intervene.

To dominate the west of Continental Europe, Germany needed to control Belgium and dominate France. This threatened Britain and led to it going to war to maintain the balance of power in Europe and maintain its own dominance on the sea and its colonial empire. Thus, three great powers confronted two and the three great allied Triple Entente powers knew that if they did not split or weaken, they had the resources and the space to triumph over the two great Central Powers. The weakness of the Triple Entente was that it was either side of the Central Powers. Meanwhile, Germany had to fight on two fronts, while Russia could only trade with Britain and France with difficulty. The fight on two fronts led to a great victory for Russia in East Prussia and a stalemate in Belgium and France.

Turkey's provocation in the Black Sea soon hampered British and French trade with Russia. Germany had usurped Britain as guardians of the Turkish navy so came to Turkey's aid. Russia was Turkey's traditional enemy and had ambitions to control Constantinople, the Straits and parts of the Caucasus. Turkey therefore joined the Central Powers, which led to the British and French quests at the Dardanelles and in Kut to link up with the Russians to try to knock Turkey out of the war. The Russians were initially too strong for the Austro-Hungarians but Germany came to the rescue and pushed the Russians back. Italy felt that it could not tolerate Austro-Hungarian success and, being wooed and bribed by the Allies, entered the war.

During 1915, the Germans were happy to be in defensive positions in the west and inflict heavy casualties on the French, who attacked to remove the Germans from their soil. The German strategy was now to destroy France by attrition through removing the Verdun salient. The French response was not to yield any part of this salient. This great battle caused an Entente response in both east and west. Brusilov attacked in June 1916 on his part of the front because the Austro-Hungarians had weakened it by sending troops to the Italian front, where battles stopped and started.

The initial success of the Brusilov Offensive was followed by the British and French offensive on the Somme but all four of these attacks – Verdun, the Brusilov Offensive, the Italian front and the Somme – turned out to be stalemates. Only the defeat of Romania gave Germany hope but this was of little significance in the west. Romania apart, there was no advantage to any of the warring nations on the continent of Europe in attack or defence. The outcome was a bloody draw with millions of lives lost, which had a profound effect on all the warring nations. It troubled their consciences and sapped their vitality.

Germany needed to split the Allies and knock them out of the war one by one. It failed with France, although it had been badly weakened; it was superior to Russia but its territorial ambitions were limited; the Austro-Hungarians were at war with Italy but Germany did not help; while Britain was a formidable opponent on land but vulnerable if it could be blockaded.

The resources of the Triple Entente were so much greater that the logic of Germany's position demanded peace, which Chancellor Bethmann-Hollweg understood, but there was another viewpoint. Russia could be defeated, followed by Italy, then Britain could be expelled from the Continent and blockaded, which would leave France to collapse on its own. Germany did not, however, acknowledge the role of the United States in all this. The war had a momentum of its own and the warlords were in the ascendant.

Peace Feelers

The object of war is to gain an advantageous peace. The thought of peace amid the war occupied statesmen's minds all through the conflict. On the whole, these thoughts were not translated into action and the war aims of the belligerent nations fluctuated along with the fortunes of war. When they were up, they wanted more; when they were down, they were prepared to settle for less. However, at the end of 1916 there was one salient fact that dominated all: the Central Powers occupied much of the territory that they coveted and the Allies were not prepared to relinquish this territory. Likewise, the Central Powers were not willing to concede territory for which they had suffered greatly.

The British were fighting to keep Belgium intact as a sovereign state and to loosely control the attachments of the Ottoman Empire in the Middle East, together with the French. The French wanted the Germans out of France and Alsace-Lorraine and to regain key coalfields, which the Germans coveted. The Serbs wanted to reclaim their homeland. The Russians wanted to retain Poland in their empire, even if it gave Poland increased rights to rule itself, and they also wanted to reclaim Courland and Lithuania.

The Central Powers were in occupation in most of these places and psychologically wished to retain them. Another salient fact that made peace difficult was that, very early in the war, statesmen on all sides felt that the casualties suffered demanded some sort of territorial compensation to justify the suffering and the sacrifices. This was the feeling by the end of 1914 and it was greatly magnified by the end of 1916. Churchill, writing after the war, said that the only chance of peace was at Christmas 1914. After that the suffering and the sacrifices required a winner.

Germany's declared war aims were not analysed publicly for over forty years and then they were not conclusive, since no one knew what could be delivered. What Bethmann-Hollweg believed in September 1914 as the Germans wheeled in front of Paris for the knockout blow in the west differed to what he believed he could possibly get in November 1914. Even then, he realised that the Central Powers could never defeat the Allies if they fully mobilised their resources. Von Falkenhayn shared this view but Hindenburg and Ludendorff did not, while the kaiser hovered between the two poles. Nevertheless, up to the end of 1916, there was a consensus within the German camp on what they wanted but it was based on the miscomprehension of what the Allies were prepared to offer.

From the beginning, the Allies had a dialogue among themselves and were actively encouraging other nations to enter the war. In 1914, Russia instigated a pact that the Triple Entente countries would not make a separate peace with the Central Powers. Later, in the Treaty of London, Italy was persuaded to enter the war with the offer of territory, mainly at the expense of the Austro-Hungarians. Romania was seduced into war by being offered Transylvania, while Japan was offered islands in the Pacific and concessions in China in exchange for destroyer escorts.

The three main Allies had very different agendas. Britain was not going to allow Germany to control Belgium and its ports in the English Channel. It also wanted the surrender of the German fleet, including the U-boats. German colonial possessions would be relinquished and Britain wanted German East Africa.

Germany, on the other hand, was prepared to offer Belgium weak independence, with Germany controlling its railways, taking over Liège and Antwerp and, through its financial power, controlling Belgium's foreign policy and the Channel ports. The Belgian king sent an emissary to talk about these proposals but there was little chance of an agreement. In Africa, Germany coveted a great swathe of territory stretching from the west coast to the east in central Africa. Britain did not like this, as it saw competition from the German navy with coaling stations established in the Atlantic and Indian oceans. Likewise, Britain had ambitions in the Middle East so that it retained control of the Suez Canal and the Persian Gulf. For this reason, it wanted to control most of Mesopotamia and Palestine.

France was interested in the Middle East, especially Syria, where it had historical and economic interests, and the area around Mosul. François Georges-Picot and Sir Mark Sykes brokered this war aim for their respective countries, which became known as the Sykes–Picot Agreement. Like most war aims, it was modified with time. France, however, was more interested in its borders with Germany, where it wished to recover Alsace-Lorraine and wanted the Saar and Rhineland for economic and defence purposes.

At the end of 1916, financial reparations were not a major issue and to make Germany pay for the war was something that crystallised in minds over the next two years. Nevertheless, the French were worried by the Mitteleuropa customs union, which could create a powerful financial block, and in June 1916 the Allies agreed to discriminatory tariffs if the block were created.

The benefits to France of winning the war were not really commensurate with the sacrifices it had made and were certainly not commensurate with German war aims towards France. Germany now regarded itself as a world power and required France to acknowledge that dignity. The Hohenzollern dynasty had only unified Germany after it had defeated and humiliated France in 1871 and the kaiser was intent on sealing the dynasty's legitimacy in the eyes of the world by further diminishing France's economic power. Germany was intent on making France a dependent appendage but France was intent on breaking this dependency and controlling Germany's power through alliances.

This was relatively straightforward compared with the problem of Poland, where three empires vied with each other for a solution. There was a general opinion that the Polish people constituted a nation and that meant at least a limited but controlled sovereignty. All three empires wanted this controlled sovereignty within their own empire. Russia governed most of the Polish people but a proportion were part of the Austro-Hungarian Empire, while there were substantial Polish communities in Silesia and East Prussia. German conquest had reduced Russian control but they intended to regain it.

The dual monarchy thought of a triple monarchy during their period of martial success but the Brusilov Offensive and the rescue by the Germans put a stop to these ambitions. Bethmann-Hollweg did not want a great territorial expansion for Germany, mainly because of the racial problems that might ensue, but he was prepared to allow an Austrian solution. He changed his mind on reflection because he felt the Slavic influence would be too great in the dual monarchy. He therefore planned for an independent Poland linked to Germany by economic and military ties. This did not please the Austro-Hungarians, who wanted Poland included in their empire, or the Poles, who wanted a truly independent nation. The Germans thought the Poles would be sympathetic to them and, noting that there was much resentment of the Russians in the areas they conquered, they tried but failed to recruit the Poles to their army.

Bethmann-Hollweg's realisation that Germany would be unlikely to win the war if the Allied alliance held together, led him to try to split the Allies. His primary objective was Russia and, because of this, the Germans did not try to penetrate deep into Russia or to conquer it. Germany's objectives were limited. Russia, in turn, realised that being split from its allies would lead to defeat and was strong in its resolve to keep the Triple Alliance together.

Russia's territorial ambitions were mainly in the Caucasus and the Straits linking the Black Sea with the Mediterranean. It did not have an insoluble dispute with the Austro-Hungarians, although it was Serbia's protector, yet when the Austro-Hungarians put out peace feelers in the spring of 1915, Russia rejected them and in strong terms told Britain and France, who were interested, to ignore them. Russia feared Germany but was contemptuous of the Austro-Hungarians and Turkey and felt that they could be easily defeated.

Bethmann-Hollweg was a realist. When the kaiser appointed him chancellor before the war, his policy was to ease the financial strains of Germany's ambitions to become a world power. Spending on the German navy had escalated and he reined it back, wanting to abandon ambitions to rival the British navy. The German army became stronger but he strove to compete with the powers of the Triple Entente outside Europe rather than confront them on their own doorstep. The war changed this. He was a statesman of subtlety who, by the end of 1916, recognised the dilemma that Germany faced. He could not see how the war could be won and he wanted peace. With the overwhelming triumph in Romania, he felt that Germany could search for peace from a position of strength but in fact it strengthened the resolve of the Allies to win. Even the acknowledgement by all sides that the war was a horrible mistake and a return to the status quo ante would not have produced a result.

The changes taking place in all empires were seismic. Yet the horrible truth is that all nations involved suffered from the continuation of the war over the next twenty-three months. It benefited no nation and only compounded the tragedy. If Germany had given Belgium its independence, neutralised the problem of Alsace and Lorraine and allowed Poland its independence, the tragedy of war would have been mitigated and a German economic hegemony over most of central Europe would probably have ensued during the next thirty years. Mitteleuropa was Bethmann-Hollweg's great objective and this customs union would have greatly added to Germany's power and prestige.

The United States wanted to broker peace and President Wilson asked the main protagonists to declare their war aims. Germany did this in December 1916 but Britain and France ignored the offer. Britain, in particular, wanted to win and then sort out the mess. There were people such as Lord Lansdowne who suggested a compromise peace but with little support. The British had decided that Asquith should go. He was competent and measured but they required the passion of Lloyd George, who believed in victory and was by nature combative, although not particularly aggressive.

Germany was gung-ho for war and Bethmann-Hollweg got nowhere. The military wanted unrestricted submarine warfare, which Bethmann-Hollweg now abhorred, and there was a fight in the following year to get it. The fleeting chance for peace was gone, the combatants stirred themselves to make greater efforts and the war would grind on inexorably to the detriment of all, especially the great powers in the east.

Russia started the war, which triggered action by the Austro-Hungarians and Germany in the east. Germany was essentially defensive but made the mistake of going for conquest in the west. The regimes of all three imploded, together with the Ottoman Empire. In 1916, none of them believed that this would be the outcome, so they kept on fighting.

Keynes and World Finances

John Maynard Keynes was thirty-one at the outbreak of war. After a brilliant scholastic career at Eton and King's College, Cambridge, he had divided his time between economic posts in the civil service in London and being a don at his old college. He had been elected as an undergraduate to the Apostles, a group rejoicing in its own intellectual distinction and tending to reject customs of the day. It was a distinguished discussion group and in it Keynes evolved as an economist, a discipline with little standing in the university at that time.

On Sunday, 2 August 1914, before Britain had declared war, Keynes rushed from Cambridge to London to be at the financial centre of the world, which was in turmoil because the transfer of money had stopped and the banks and discount houses that loaned money short term to Russia and Germany could not get their funds. Stockbrokers who dealt abroad were going broke and the banks were panicking and demanding gold for paper money from the Bank of England.

Keynes prepared a paper for the chancellor of the exchequer, Lloyd George, which in the end succeeded in pouring oil on troubled waters. If London were to continue as the great European and world financial capital, it had to keep its nerve and, if it were to finance its allies through this war, it had to retain gold convertibility. To do this, it would be necessary to use gold between countries but to regulate and use paper internally. There would be losses but the Bank of England would guarantee those losses before 4 August, making new pledges so that trade would not come to a halt. To Keynes, the joint stock banks were weak and leaderless, while he praised the Treasury mandarins. However, he put the dagger into Lloyd George, claiming that he had not 'the faintest idea of money'.[7]

Keynes was the protégé of Edwin Montagu, a member of the cabinet, who recommended that he become a member of the Treasury for the war period. In February 1915 Lloyd George, Montagu and Lord Cunliffe (the Governor of the Bank of England), with Keynes as an adviser, went to Paris for a conference to agree to an Anglo–French loan to Russia and to arrange Russian and French gold transfers to the Bank of England. This was just the start of complex deals between allies that was centralised in London.

From this point on, Keynes would create the financial framework whereby Britain's allies would finance the war. In May 1915 Lloyd George became minister of munitions, Reginald McKenna replacing him as chancellor. Keynes worked with Lloyd George on his budget. As it was first thought that this would be a quick war, income tax was not initially raised, but the big increase in munitions was paid for out of a £350 million war loan. By the middle of 1915, the war was becoming expensive and income tax was raised to 17.5p in the pound in today's nomenclature. There was also an excess profits duty of 50 per cent, while luxury imports were taxed at 33.3 per cent. These last two taxes were repealed in 1924, reimposed by Churchill the following year, and were only abolished by Harold Macmillan in 1956.

This exceedingly costly war put Britain's finances in peril. By the middle of 1916, the Continental allies were in dire straits as Britain was paying for just about all of Russia and Italy's war costs, half of Belgium and Serbia's, and two-thirds of France's. They did this through borrowing from the United States, which had now become the great creditor nation, and Britain could only retrieve its situation when the conflict was over and it had won.

The war in Europe had now led to the United States becoming the world's great financial power and, for the rest of his life, Keynes would be dealing with this problem. At the end of November the US Federal Reserve Board told banks to restrict this lending to continue the war, which was a political decision as the United States wanted a negotiated peace. Keynes concurred with them but the immediate result was a run on Britain's gold reserves. The Treasury mandarins were prepared to let the reserves run down and were less than frank with the politicians about the situation as they feared they would abandon gold convertibility. Keynes was worried that, if this happened, Germany would know that Britain was in financial trouble.

In January 1917 US President Wilson was talking about peace without victory, which struck a chord with Keynes but with few others in high authority. It was a time of change, with Lloyd George having become prime minister in December and Bonar Law his chancellor. Keynes liked Bonar Law, as being a Canadian he was untrammelled with establishment contacts and loyalties and would look at problems with a fresh eye.

In February Keynes became head of a new department at the Treasury with wide powers, reporting directly to the chief Treasury mandarin and to Bonar Law. At the same time, Germany started its campaign of unrestricted submarine warfare. The war would continue and the financial bond between Britain and the United States would be strengthened.

Economics was a young and little understood science. The war was taking place at several levels and people were striving to understand it. Wars cost money and this one was costing big money. Where was this money coming from and how was it going to be repaid? Even a hundred years later this has not been answered satisfactorily.

Europe had dominated the world for a few centuries but it was squandering its wealth and prestige in a stalemated war. If only it had been over by Christmas 1914 but it was not. It was starting to be called the Great War and in its scope that was a justifiable title, but the war had just started and had a long way to run.

Chapter 8

The First World War 1917

The Rejection of Peace

The rejection of the possibility of peace was a great tragedy. With hindsight, the rise of nationalism would probably have broken up the Austro-Hungarian and Ottoman empires but the German and Russian Empires might have remained intact. Therein lay the tragedy, for the next two years of war would break these four empires and out of the chaos and disorder would come leaders peddling philosophies whose orthodoxy did not allow deviants.

The next two years of war were concerned with the breaking point of nations and their empires. All were near breaking point, even the British. In Britain there were strikes, while the people absorbed the fact that their citizen army had suffered terrible casualties on the Somme. During Easter 1916, the opportunistic Irish had also rebelled in Dublin. However, Britain had reserves and had not committed a large proportion of the nation to the trenches. That was to come but there was a careful monitoring of soldiers and civilians to see how much they could take.

France, which had suffered more, was in a worse state, with strikes triggering a rebellious mood in the army. The French had initially attacked with great elan and sacrifice, then borne the brunt of attrition and could not take much more. The triumph of the Russian Brusilov Offensive had been secured through terrifying sacrifice and the distortions of war were making life difficult throughout Russia. The war had gone on too long.

The Austro-Hungarians faced the same problems. The new emperor was personable and he had a French wife, which was a basis for détente, but the cracks in the empire from wealth destruction, nationalism and a far from competent army were visible for all to see. The Ottomans, fierce defenders of Turkey, were aware that their empire was not defensible except through German help.

In Germany, the soldiers were dreaming of victory as soldiers should, but they held the ultimate power and the German chancellor's musings, knowing that Germany could not win the war and could only negotiate a reasonable peace, were swept aside. The logic of the situation demanded peace but men could not advocate this because it was a sign of weakness and a failure of the will to triumph.

The Return to War

The Allies were making plans for spring offensives and scented victory. This was illusory but they knew that the Central Powers had been gravely weakened and they had superiority in manpower, which gave them confidence. Russia, more in hope than reality, wanted to attack in the spring, so an Anglo–French attack was planned on the Western Front, while the Italians would continue their attacks on the Isonzo.

Germany, on the other hand, acknowledged the weakness of its Austro-Hungarian ally but saw the possibility of the collapse of Russia, Italy, France and even Britain. However, if Germany were to achieve victory or an advantageously negotiated peace, the war would have to be resolved within the next eighteen months. Thus, desperation crept into German strategy, realising that Britain would only be crushed through unrestricted submarine warfare.

The strains of war among the great powers were first manifest in Russia. Without knowing it, the tsar and the ruling class started operating in a political vacuum. A system of local government, or soviets, formed in Russian cities, towns and villages and the army supplanted the established system of ruling. Often, without a great revolutionary intent, these soviets became the real source of power as they strove to remedy injustices and stop needless suffering.

At the end of February 1917 there was a strike in Petrograd, which the army supported. This dominating soviet received support from the others and suddenly the power of the tsar had been usurped. He abdicated on 2 March and designated Grand Duke Michael as his successor but he declined and the Duma rejected the tsarevich. The monarchy fell, there was no continuity and the system of government had broken down. Provincial governors lost their powers, while district councils were subject to the Petrograd soviet's veto, who were essentially socialists but with a wide spectrum of belief. Prince Lvov led the provisional government but its powers were weak until the emergence of Alexander Kerensky in May.

The essential dilemma was the conduct of the war. No one wanted Germany to rule Russia, therefore Russia had to be defended. In May Kerensky became minister of war with Brusilov as his chief of staff. The Russians had seemingly rediscovered their enthusiasm for war and in June planned an attack.

The Entry of the United States into the War

For Germany, Britain was becoming the great enemy as its manpower in northern France started to increase. The French were running out of steam and Nivelle had replaced Joffre in December 1916. Joffre believed that the French were good for only one more major battle as they would have trouble replacing casualties despite using colonial contingents.

Nevertheless, the Allies were optimistic on the Western Front as their manpower was more than 50 per cent higher than Germany's and they felt they could make it tell. The Germans, in desperation, were destroying Allied and neutral shipping through submarine attacks and attempting to throttle Britain but, in so doing, they were harming the great neutral, the United States. American public opinion did not automatically support Britain but these acts made the them question German intentions.

It was on the diplomatic front that Germany cracked. In the United States, the German ambassador, Count von Bernstorff, was a paragon of his service and a fine German. Coming from a diplomatic family, he spoke many languages and was particularly comfortable in the English-speaking world. He was intelligent, cultivated and both men and women enjoyed his company. Sometimes he had strong opinions, not always the case with ambassadors, and he made no secret that the United States must be kept neutral and that it would be a tragedy for Germany if the United States joined the Allies. Being the senior German government representative in the Americas, he was responsible for all German diplomatic endeavours. To do this, he had to communicate with Berlin, requiring the transmission of coded messages.

One of the first things the British did on the outbreak of war was to send a cable ship to the Dutch coast and cut the cables that linked Germany to North America. This did not stop the Germans communicating as they could use wireless and there was a cable between West Africa and Brazil, which the

British could not cut as the United States predominantly owned it. Nevertheless, cable traffic was getting through by other methods and, although British intelligence had the requisite German codes, they did not know how diplomatic mail was being transmitted.

Captain Reginald Hall of Room 40 at the Admiralty, who was in charge of intelligence, took a long time to solve this problem, although he did it in a simple way. A Swedish diplomat in Mexico was observed receiving what was deduced as far too much diplomatic mail. Room 40 investigated and found that German mail was intermingled with the Swedish. Thus, the Germans sent their coded mail from Berlin to Sweden and the Swedes sent it from Sweden to Mexico, where the Germans then transmitted it to Washington.

Germany had ambitions in the Americas and was forever meddling, which started before the Great War was declared. In April 1914 Germany was sending arms to President Huerta of Mexico, which caused an uncharacteristic armed riposte from US President Wilson, who tried to stop the German ship from docking and unloading. There was an armed clash, with ninety United States casualties and over two hundred Mexican. The ship was turned back but went to another port and offloaded arms with another ship. To the Germans this was a great diplomatic coup.

Mexico continued to be unsettled, with German influence continuing. In March 1916 President Carranza had a rival in Pancho Villa, the Mexican revolutionary general, who caused unrest in the border region of the United States. Wilson sent in a punitive expedition under General Pershing but Villa escaped. Wilson, in the position of either getting Villa or getting out, decided in January 1917 on the latter.

The Germans thought that the Mexicans could preoccupy the United States, which in turn would stop the Americans worrying too much about unrestricted submarine warfare. Germany also tried to involve Japan, only superficially linked with the Allies and open to a deal in a new world order. By this time, Arthur Zimmermann, Germany's foreign secretary, was directing the diplomatic effort and, in a series of telegrams to Bernstorff, he targeted President Carranza of Mexico. The intermediary was Heinrich von Eckhardt, the German envoy in Mexico, and the message to him read:

> We intend to begin unrestricted submarine warfare on the first of February. We shall endeavour in spite of this to keep the United States neutral. In the event of this not succeeding, we make Mexico a proposal of alliance on the following basis: make war together, generous financial support, and an understanding on our part that

Mexico is to reconquer the lost territory in Texas, new Mexico, and Arizona. The settlement in detail is left to you.

You will inform the President of the above most secretly as soon as the outbreak of war with the United States is certain and add the suggestion that he should, on his own initiative, invite Japan to immediate adherence and at the same time mediate between Japan and ourselves.

Please call the President's attention to the fact that the unrestricted employment of our submarines now offers the prospect of compelling England to make peace within a few months. Acknowledge receipt.

The telegram was sent in three ways: State Department cable, wireless and via the Swedish route. Room 40 intercepted all three but it was the convention that countries did not read each other's so-called friendly traffic. This interception of intelligence was of enormous benefit to the British as they could not only monitor the Germans but also get a feeling for American intentions.

Bernstorff was trying to use Wilson as a peace mediator so that Germany could get out of the war and retain its position in the world. Wilson wanted this role so, in his address to the senate on 22 January, he spoke of peace without victory, which did not strike a chord in battling Europe, where each side was fighting a war they wanted to win and were purblind to the consequences.

The dangers in the telegram were obvious to the Allies. If Japan joined Germany, Russia could sue for a separate peace. This would be very dangerous as Germany needed to be kept preoccupied in Eastern Europe. The telegram also offered the opportunity to bring the United States into the war but it would require subtlety from the Europeans. It was decided that the telegram should first be divulged to William Page, the anglophile American ambassador in London. Page was a longstanding friend of Wilson but the friendship was now fragile as Wilson pursued peace, while Page, like former President Theodore Roosevelt, pleaded for an American declaration of war.

The British knew, as did Page, that the telegram had little validity on its own. It could be a hoax or a plant and the Germans, Mexicans and Japanese were likely to repudiate it – it would be stupid for any of them to acknowledge it. More to the point, the Americans had to be convinced, so it was decided that they could look at the telegrams that had passed through their system, with the British providing the code books to translate them. Thus, the Americans had the means to learn that the telegram was true and not a bit of

Allied chicanery.

True to form, there were vehement denials from the Mexicans, the Japanese and influential Germans. Many influential Americans did not believe the contents of the telegram and its source could not be revealed. Horrific as it was, dumbfounding Americans by its hostility to their country, they could not act on this one bit of evidence, which was of doubtful provenance.

Then came the diplomatic gaffe of the war. Zimmermann acknowledged that the telegram was true. He probably confirmed his authorship because, with unrestricted submarine warfare, he could not see how the United States could stay out of the war. He thought that the Allies in Europe would soon be defeated and the United States would not be a factor. It was a dreadful miscalculation and, on 6 April, the United States declared war on Germany.

The Submarine War

April 1917 was the high point for Germany in the submarine war. The British defence was by minelaying, especially in the narrow channels the Germans used to get into the North Sea. British destroyers laid the mines and German minesweepers defused them. The submarines got through but there was a small price to pay, which over time was attritional.

In April, however, the submarine was king and destroyed 516,000 tons of British shipping, along with another 336,000 tons belonging to the Allies or neutrals. Britain only had food for six weeks and, if this continued, the war could be lost. Politicians and junior naval officers had for some time suggested that a convoy system should be started. Naval high command had rejected this because it considered that Britain could not afford to allow ships to escort convoys because the home-based fleet would not be able to defend the British Isles.

The entry of the United States into the war helped solve this problem by providing extra ships and by May a convoy system was tentatively introduced, with brilliant success. This was developed and extended for the rest of the year.

Battle and Mutiny

Joffre's successor in France, Nivelle, persuaded Britain that a successful Anglo–French attack at the two sides of the neck of the Somme salient was the requirement for victory. However, Britain favoured of an attack in the Ypres area and wanted a breakthrough to the Belgian ports from which the

U-boats sailed.

Britain acquiesced to Nivelle's plan after several conferences and, behind these bald, bare facts is a considerable story. Lloyd George had become the prime minister in order to wage war with more panache and success than Asquith. He demanded success from his generals and told them he did not mind where it happened – the capture of Jerusalem or Damascus would do – but success was what he wanted so that he could trumpet it to the nation and the world. Nivelle also wanted success and proclaimed that he could finish the war with one mighty offensive. He spoke good English and persuaded Lloyd George to support his strategy and battle. Lloyd George did this but went further and intrigued with Nivelle against Robertson and Haig. He wished to cut his commanders down to size and subordinate them to the French but did this without his fellow politicians' support.

At the Calais conference at the end of February Nivelle put forward his proposals and was very upset when Robertson and Haig were affronted. Even Lloyd George was taken aback when he found he had little support among his cabinet. Nevertheless, it was agreed as a temporary measure that Haig would be subordinated to Nivelle for the duration of the attack.

The Germans had little difficulty in picking up the thrust of the next offensive and had built advantageous defences. They then retired to the Hindenburg Line about 10 miles to their rear and left a desolate lunarscape for the Allies to traverse. However, the axis of the main French attack on the Chemin des Dames had not witnessed a retreat, as the Germans occupied the high ground and had a good defensive position. None of Nivelle's three subordinate generals were happy with the plans and Paul Painlevé, minister of war, was not convinced, although Nivelle's optimism propelled them all forward.

Haig's attack was to the north of the Hindenburg Line near Arras. This battle would be fought without much benefit from the air. The weather was overcast and the Royal Flying Corps was taking a beating from the Germans. On 9 April 1917 General Edmund Allenby's 3rd Army started the battle by using gas shells, which were effective in disrupting and destroying the enemy's artillery. The defenders manning the guns had to wear gas masks and fully cover themselves, while the horses, indispensable as pack animals, could not be protected.

Allenby tried to introduce the element of surprise by attacking after a sharp burst of artillery fire but was overruled and the artillery barrage continued for five days. When the attack went in there was a sophisticated creeping barrage, the wire was cut, the gas shells were lethal and the line moved forward by three to 5 miles. The four divisions of the Canadian Corps fought brilliantly and captured the high ground of Vimy Ridge, which overlooked and dominated the plain below.

The main French thrust at the other side of the salient's neck started a week later at the Chemin des Dames, about 80 miles away. The Germans on the high ground could easily watch the French, who telegraphed their intentions, so the Germans avoided the artillery barrage by moving back and forming strong points. The French gained ground when they attacked but, as they came to the new defences, they were slaughtered and 29,000 were killed. It was a terrible disaster that bit into morale. Nivelle had not done that badly but his optimistic predictions, coupled with his statement that the French were only capable of the one offensive, meant his time was up. Lloyd George was also damaged.

At this time, the French and British economies were under pressure and there were many strikes. People could not see imminent victory and were not prepared to make sacrifices without leadership. Inflation was increasing, with its concomitant unfairness and, with war industries making large profits, the discontent in the workforce was mirrored on the French side by mutiny in the trenches. This involved, in some form or other, about half the army and was not necessarily a refusal to fight but varied from a reluctance to a refusal to attack. Most soldiers remained in the trenches, although their lack of leave was a real grievance.

The upshot was that Pétain replaced Nivelle and managed to stop the discontent by putting most of the French army on standby for a year and attending to grievances. Nevertheless, the ringleaders were pursued ruthlessly, and there were 3,427 court martials at which 554 soldiers received the death penalty and forty-nine were executed. The French were not entirely negative, as there were limited and successful attacks at Verdun in August 1917 and on the Aisne, but the they had temporarily shot their bolt.

The Collapse of Capitalism in Russia

The crisis in Russia went from bad to worse. The Russian economy was dynamic and the war made it more so but fuelled it artificially. Governments live by taxes and, because of this, their primary function is to provide sound money. Since the war had begun, inflation had increased four times from August 1914 to the beginning of 1917; however, this was not the product of a stagnant economy but of a dynamic industrial one, which was sucking men from the countryside into the cities by offering them higher wages than they could earn on the land or from cottage industries.

Up until 1914, Russia was a land of cottage industries and the war led inexorably to their decline as products were industrialised and men moved to the cities and into the army. Banks proliferated, money was lent in profusion as Russia came off the gold standard and a distorted economy linked to war was forged. The distortions could have been mitigated if the government had some sort of control of taxation and its imposition, to dampen down the distortions and lessen the increases in prices but there was not a suitable mechanism. Income tax was of negligible importance and only introduced in 1916 and the bureaucratic ability to introduce it on a wide scale was not readily available.

Those linked to the war economy made substantial profits and those in the dynamic part of the economy did very well. There were, however, those on fixed salaries, working for the government, who suffered from the effects of inflation, especially as by the end of 1917 it was ten times the pre-war level. This especially pertained to the railways, which had increased the workforce by 500,000 to 1,200,000 since the beginning of the war. There was also an increase of 10 per cent in locomotives and rolling stock so that there was no under-provision. The railway workers had a great esprit de corps and pride in their profession, which had enabled the government to stop them striking during the troubles that the Russo–Japanese War caused and allowed troops to be moved to put down insurrection. This time inflation had blown away their pride and they went on strike like everybody else.

There was also the problem of food, which was plentiful in Russia. Its production was not a problem and its price was within the reach of the great majority. The shortages were in the towns. In 1917, in both Petrograd and Moscow, there was a lack of grain, exacerbated by their inflated populations. This could, in some respects, be put down to a failure of distribution. The railways, the main means of distribution, did fail occasionally through strikes and had also become less efficient through not being able to adapt to the changing patterns of distribution. Although manpower had increased on the railway, its quality was reduced. This meant that there were inefficiencies in timetabling and getting trains to the right places, while there was less maintenance and repair of rolling stock.

The army had to be fed, bringing in new patterns of distribution but this was no different from the problems of the other combative nations. Although there was no more exporting, supplying the army used up a third of the rolling stock and used it inefficiently. The farmers producing the grain also affected the amount going to the cities. The price of grain was such that it made little sense to the supplier to sell it until the price improved. This meant that what was needed was used locally, both for household and animal consumption. There had been a distinct movement to a greater animal economy and for middlemen and producers hoarding grain. When the price mechanism for primary produce breaks down, there is chaos and there would be turmoil and famine for years to come.

The army was still patriotic and the provisional government, under the inspiration of Kerensky, wanted to fight. However, the Russians, like the French, had little stomach for an attacking policy. They hoped not to yield Mother Russia to the imperialist ambitions of Germany and all parties of the left – Socialist, Menshevik and Bolshevik – held to this opinion.

The break came when the Germans returned Vladimir Lenin to Russia in a sealed train in July 1917. To begin with, he had to assert his authority among the Bolsheviks and, when he had done so, he persuaded them to break ranks and advocated stopping the war with Germany. Lenin revelled in the anarchy of increasing inflation and put his finger on the crucial areas that would allow him to rule and control the country, which would be through the provision of food and oil. He did not have to worry about taxation as such, as all profits and surpluses would automatically accrue to him wherever his writ ran. Thus began a deep, deep tragedy for the Russian people.

Similar Problems in Germany

There were modifications to the same problem in Germany. The railway system was more compact and efficient but the effect of taking men and horses from the land was the same. The British blockade stopped fertiliser coming from Chile, fertiliser that had increased the production of cereals by over 50 per cent in the twenty-five years before the war. Germany was self-sufficient in food, in the sense that it could provide an adequate diet for its people and its distribution was adequate. However, the yields were down, farms were run less efficiently, there was an inadequate harvest in 1916, while food controls were poor in their psychology. With lack of food and the food distribution being controlled, there are always black markets.

In war, the army is fed first and old men, women and children come next. When price controls are placed on a commodity, the profit motive invariably decrees the amount of production and it does not matter whether the farmer is Russian, German, French or British. In Germany, when price controls were placed on the price of milk at the point of production, less milk was produced, while the production of butter and cheese, which had no controls, went up.

Thus, distortions were created in the market and the black market vied with the price control market as to which was the real one. It has been calculated that a third of the German army's food requirements were purchased on the black market in 1918.

The Third Battle of Ypres

At Messines, a ridge overlooking the Ypres salient, an imaginative attack had been planned for some months. Miners on both sides were busy digging underground and the British penetrated under the German lines. It was a cat and mouse affair, with the sounds of the digging being picked up as both sides came close to each other. The British had 8,000 yards of tunnel and had placed twenty mines in position, which could blow up the German front line. On 7 June General Hubert Plumer gave the order to blow the ridge and the front line exploded in the air, making its capture straightforward. It was a limited but important action, starting the Third Battle of Ypres, where Haig wanted to break the Germans.

Lloyd George was in favour of the attack, provided the French attacked too, but when he realised that they would be passive, he turned against it. The British cabinet, including Churchill, supported him and thought it better to harbour their resources and wait for the Americans, with the Russians semi-paralysed and the Germans redeploying their manpower.

Haig still believed that Germany was weakening, which his intelligence appreciation supported, although in retrospect they had not sufficiently discounted the weakness of Russia. The argument was finely balanced but the Admiralty supported Haig, wanting the Germans out of the Belgian ports. This tipped the balance and Haig continued the attack on 31 July.

This hiatus after the success of Messines allowed the Germans to stiffen their defences. General Hubert Gough, in command of the 5th Army, with Plumer protecting his left flank and two French divisions on his right, provided the Allies' cutting edge. The axis of the attack was important and Gough attacked along a line to the ports, tending to ignore the axis of the plateau of Gheluvelt and Roulers, the key railway centre of the region, which was 12 miles from Ypres.

Mid-summer was prime fighting time but the initial bombardment had smashed the drainage system in the area and unseasonal and continuous heavy rain resulted in swampy conditions. This hampered both sides because the Allies attacked and the Germans counter-attacked, the rains nullifying any attempts at modern warfare. Haig used tanks but was ill-supplied and only achieved tactical success with them.

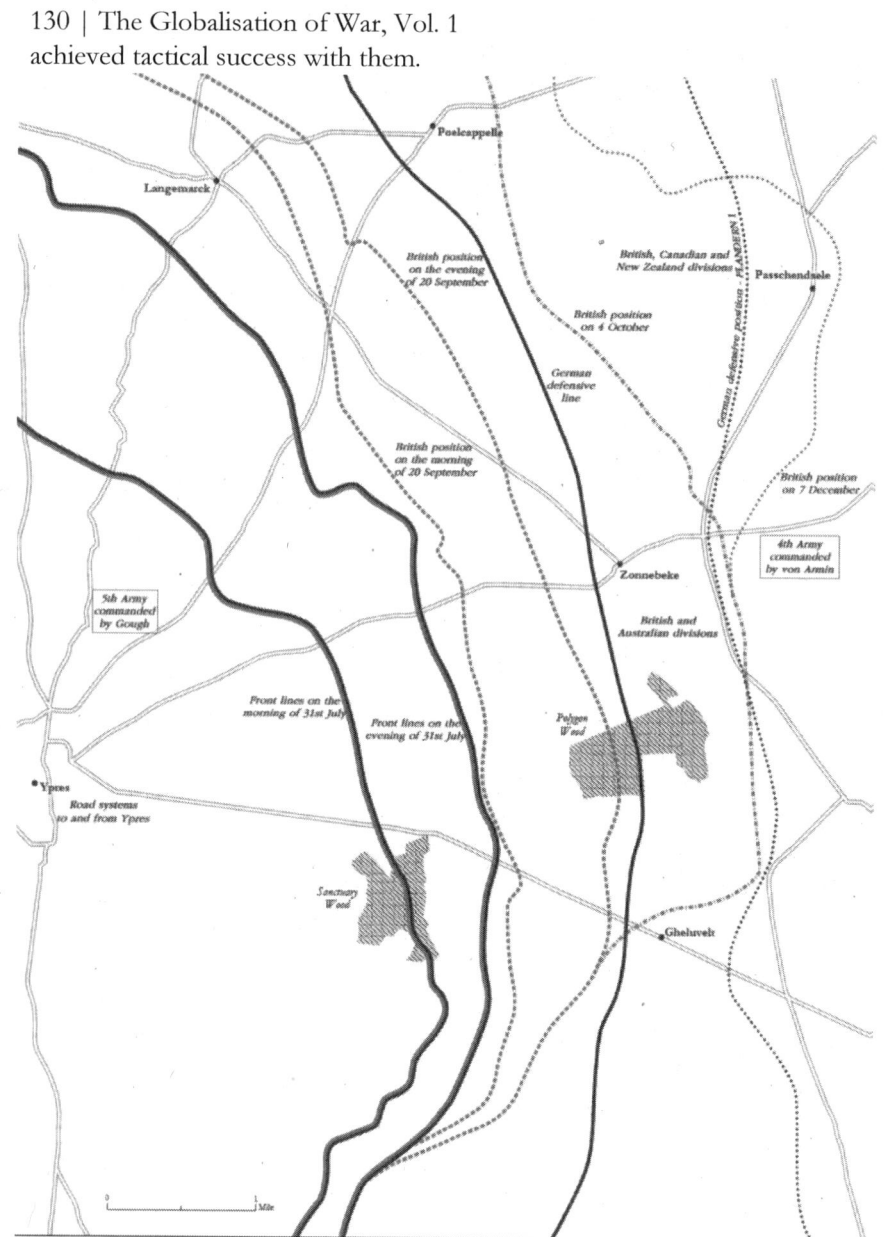

9. Relative positions at the Third Battle of Ypres, 1917

The weather also made the task of identifying artillery targets very difficult for the aircraft. At Messines, aircraft had found 200 previously unidentified targets. In the early part of the Ypres battle this was impossible and the infantry broke through and found a large amount of artillery intact. There were also concrete pillboxes, which had to be eradicated. In some sectors the advance was rapid but had to be held back because the line could not tolerate a small salient awaiting a counter-attack.

The key position was the Gheluvelt Plateau (Gough's critics say that he did not realise its crucial importance, although Haig did) and the Germans fought hard to keep this high ground. It was there that the majority of tanks were used, which suggests that it was not thought unimportant; however, the attack was unsuccessful.

It was at Ypres that the real fighting occurred at this stage of the war, although there were Allied attacks elsewhere. The Russians were not active, which allowed some reinforcements to come to the Western Front. Pétain, who was keen to help, attacked at Verdun, capturing 10,000 prisoners. Likewise, the Italians made their eleventh attack on the Isonzo.

All this helped and there was no doubt that the Germans were suffering at Ypres. At the end of August Ludendorff acknowledged the strain and that the weight of Allied artillery was weakening morale. Haig, on the other hand, was dissatisfied with the results and went back to Plumer, a fine general, very thorough in his approach and one who fought with well-defined, set-piece objectives. Once he had gained one aim, he would go for another and, in this way, he would break down the enemy.

There was great success during late September and early October. The rains had relented, the ground had dried and in some places was dusty. Three battles were fought at the Menin Road Ridge, Polygon Wood and Broodseinde, spearheaded by the Australians. Aircraft were pinpointing targets and the artillery was so effective that Ludendorff was becoming convinced that it was better to attack than defend. For the first time for many years in this sector, the Allies were seeing green fields in the distance. The Australian commander, General Sir John Monash, was optimistic and reckoned that it only needed a few similar attacks to the ones that had taken place for the Germans to crack. Ludendorff acknowledged that 4 October was a black day for the German army and they only came through it after enormous losses.

Then the rains came again and the rest of October was filled with the dismal battles of Poelcappelle and Passchendaele. In the end, Passchendaele was captured on 6 November and the Third Battle of Ypres ended six days later. The Allies' casualties tell a sorry tale: from 31 July to 3 October, 138,787; from 4 October to 12 November, 106,110. The hopes and prospects of the middle part of the battle were not fulfilled. But what of the Germans? To this day, their casualties are a guess. Few say they are less than the Allies, most say they are about the same, while others say they suffered more. There was still stalemate but it was becoming increasingly difficult for Germany to win.

Montgomery

As a regular officer, Bernard Montgomery was in the war from the beginning. At twenty-seven he was a subaltern in the Warwickshires, meeting the British army retreating from Mons and becoming involved in the tumult. They were redirected to the Ypres area where, in October 1914, Montgomery took part in the First Battle of Ypres. In two consecutive days he displayed powers of leadership that led to him receiving the DSO but being badly wounded. He led his men into action with only a sword but, in the heat of battle, he jettisoned it. When confronted with a German about to take aim, he threw himself at him feet first, taking him prisoner in the melee. This, he claimed, showed the importance of surprise in warfare. The action petered out and the front lines restabilised themselves but the attack continued on a wide front the next day, the first formal British attack of the war.

Montgomery wanted to see how his lines looked from the enemy's point of view and went on reconnaissance. A sniper hit him through the right lung and he fell. One of his soldiers went to his rescue and applied a field dressing but was shot through the head, slumping over him and probably saving his life as the sniper hit both of them again. Understanding the plight of his fellow soldier, Montgomery shouted an order that no one should try to rescue him in daylight; however, he was rescued several hours later. Montgomery was in hospital in England for two months but, as he described it: 'I recovered quickly, being very fit.'[8] He had suffered minor damage to a kneecap but a lung was badly damaged and would limit his breathing under duress for the rest of his life. He returned to duty as an acting major in a training brigade.

By 1916 he was back at the front with this brigade but it was quiet, especially as they were pulled out before the action at Neuve Chapelle, which was a feint to try to get the Germans to ignore the Somme area. The brigade was also spared the opening Somme attack but joined the battle later in July, suffering terrible casualties. Montgomery was in constant danger and appeared on the wounded list in Britain but it was only a graze to the palm of his hand, which he reported in case it became septic.

In August he was with a general and two others when a shell burst 4 feet away. He and the general were blown flat on their faces in opposite directions, while the shrapnel of the disintegrating bomb shot into the air. Although shaken and covered in dust, the four of them survived without injury.

The heavy fighting ended when the brigade was sent to the quiet Arras area in September. In January 1917 Montgomery started a new life as a staff officer in the 33rd Division. By the middle of 1917 he was involved in training at the corps level and a 60-page manual issued for the autumn offensive in the Third Battle of Ypres bore his imprint. It was in his own inimitable style, which banished complexities and enunciated objectives with clarity. It was General Plumer's corps and his principles were modern. There was the creeping barrage, the method by which units would bypass forward units to sustain the attack; the use of wireless intelligence from the air; the methods of dealing with counter-attacks; the provision of supplies, etc. Plumer made three successful autumn attacks but they faded into the relative failure of Passchendaele.

The next six months, including the German spring offensive, were quiet for Montgomery but in July 1918 he became a temporary lieutenant colonel and chief staff officer of the 47th (London) Division. At the age of thirty it was obvious that with luck he was destined for high rank in the British army. The division was full of neophytes but they had the right man to train them. They saw battle to the north of Amiens in August and September, performing creditably but not with the elan and experience of the Australians and Canadians.

On leaving the line, Montgomery made them reflect on their performance. He taught them the necessity of communicating among themselves and with the artillery, of achieving tactical surprise, of taking the initiative and of methods of knocking out enemy strong points. Better trained, they returned to the line at the beginning of October but the Germans were in retreat and hardly fighting. Having supply problems, the British did not chase hard.

The division reached Lille and, on 28 October, there was a triumphal march-past, recorded in a photograph. Sitting down is Winston Churchill, a pleased minister of munitions, and standing in the foreground is a trim Lieutenant Colonel Montgomery.

Chapter 9

The Central Powers Advance

The Gothas Attack

When a Zeppelin turned into a fireball after being attacked over England, they were perceived as a failure and replaced by bombers. These twin-engined Gothas had a speed of 80mph and carried a payload of 1,000lbs. They found that London was easier to attack than Paris, although Paris was nearer, and as a more compact city was susceptible to bomb damage. As the Gothas had to cross the lines, it was easier to alert Paris and defend the city. With London, special squadrons had to be taken out of the line and used specifically for its defence. There was also an increasingly sophisticated means of defence, with advanced warning posts, warning sirens, balloons and anti-aircraft guns. In addition, with night raids they employed searchlights.

The Gothas initially came by day but their visibility helped the defence, so they then only came by night. The first Gotha raid was in May 1917 but London was foggy and the raiders dropped their bombs on Folkestone, killing ninety-five people. A subsequent raid on London hit Liverpool Street station, killing 162. However, most raids did not kill as many but they put fear into the hearts of Londoners and up to 300,000 people went into the underground stations each evening. The Gothas made 397 sorties over Britain for the loss of twenty-four aircraft in combat and thirty-seven in accidents. As the loss of life through the Zeppelins and Gothas was under 1,500 and the damage done was not significant, the Germans stopped the raids in May 1918.

The British did not take kindly to these attacks and responded, causing little damage or loss of life but losing 140 bombers and causing 746 deaths in Germany. The significance was that it represented a further evolution of the air war, which was becoming increasingly dynamic and extending its scope. Britain was planning ahead and could have used a four-engined bomber in 1919, the Handley-Page V/1500, which could have reached Berlin.

This was not the only outcome, as the British government asked General Jan Smuts to chair a committee to report on the future role of the Royal Flying Corps. This was because it needed to make strategic decisions that went far beyond the front line and there was a need to prioritise services between the British Army and Royal Navy. At the time, both Haig and Trenchard opposed a separate service, not with particular fervour but in purely functional terms. For Haig, in the front line, it was necessary for airmen to pursue his objectives, to which Trenchard agreed. He was happy to be subordinate and pursue the strategic objectives of the army. At this particular time they were right but Smuts was far-sighted and recommended that the Royal Air Force should be a service in its own right and it came into being on 1 April 1918.

Mussolini

Benito Mussolini was born in the Romagna in 1883. The region was not particularly fertile or rich, had a tradition of violence and was a natural breeding ground for socialism. Mussolini wholeheartedly embraced socialism in his youth. Giuseppe Garibaldi and Karl Marx were his heroes but the creator of the Italian nation and the creator of internationalism had incompatibilities, which Mussolini would, one day, have difficulty in reconciling.

At the outbreak of war, he was an effective orator for the socialist cause and a talented journalist on the newspaper, *Avanti*. During September 1914 he spoke at a rally defending Italy's neutrality and published an article in *Avanti* developing the theme and the goals of international socialism in response to his friends' pleas for Italy to enter the war. The debate continued in *Avanti* and, by the middle of October, Mussolini was changing his opinions. He was a member of the National Executive of the Italian Socialist party and an *Avanti* article that advocated a rejection of absolute neutrality, which would be replaced by an active and working neutrality, disturbed them. They debated it at length without coming to a conclusion, so Mussolini moved a resolution that the party reaffirm its opposition in principle but affirm that there should be flexible rather than absolute neutrality. Out of fourteen members, he was the only one for the motion. Unwilling to give up the fight, he asked for a party congress to debate the problem but this was not forthcoming.

Mussolini broke ranks and on 15 November published the first edition of his new newspaper, *Il Popolo d'Italia*. A few days later the Socialist party expelled him. His enemies asked where he had obtained the money to launch his newspaper. The Germans said the French government was financing it. They were right, although the Belgian government was also helping. Of course, the French and Belgians denied it.

The paper was staunchly republican, supported the Allies and wanted Italy to enter the war. The republican in Mussolini wanted to see the defeat of the aristocratic Central Powers. The Italian government of the time was also moving towards intervention and was striving for the best deal between the two power blocs. Austria, on Germany's advice, offered to cede the Trentino but, in the Treaty of London (April 1915), Britain and France offered the Trentino, Trieste, Fiume and its hinterland, Rhodes and the Dodecanese Islands, and Jubaland in British East Africa if Italy declared war with the Allies. This treaty would have immense repercussions.

With Italy entering the war at the end of May 1915, Mussolini was ecstatic and visualised a united Italy advancing to Vienna. As a man of action, he wanted to be part of this adventure and joined the army. By September he was in the front line at Udine and soon became a corporal. He kept a diary, which was published in his newspaper, and in 1916 he saw action and received a shrapnel wound.

In February 1917 his unit was looking after a gun that had become hot. The officer was warned but insisted that one more shell should be fired, whereupon the gun exploded, causing fatalities. Mussolini was badly wounded, which led to his army discharge. By June 1917 he was back in Milan at *Il Popolo d'Italia*. It was not difficult to modestly play the role of war hero, although modesty was not one of his most striking qualities. His catchphrase was 'Delenda Austria' (Austria must be destroyed) and he was full of offensive spirit. The socialist who was now the great nationalist was, however, blind to his nation's weaknesses.

Churchill

It was not until July 1917 that Churchill re-joined the cabinet as minister of munitions, which Lloyd George had previously occupied. Churchill streamlined the ministry and liaised with the French and Americans, spending much time at the front. He set up a factory in France to modify and repair heavy guns and acquired over 400 aeroplanes for the Americans. He also set up an Anglo–American tank factory in Bordeaux to produce, in July 1918, 1,500 tanks per month, which he believed would bring victory. His target for aero engines was 4,000 per month.

Even though the Germans broke through in 1918, they were not in a position to win the war. Allied production of tanks, aeroplanes, artillery pieces, shells and ammunition was overwhelming. Churchill had rehabilitated himself in his new role, even though he had only been in office for a short time. His success was recognised and he was able to enjoy power on the path to victory.

The Battle of Caporetto

Since Italy had entered the war, it had made a series of attacks on the Isonzo, gaining territory and wearing down the Austro-Hungarians by attrition. There had been eleven battles on the Isonzo, and the Austro-Hungarians reckoned that they were no longer strong enough to repel another, so they called for Germany's help. They sent seven elite divisions, including the Alpenkorps, a Bavarian mountain division, in which Erwin Rommel served. The Central Powers now had thirty-five divisions on this front against Italy's thirty-four. Their attack on 24 October, as the Third Battle of Ypres was coming to an end, reversed Italy's dominance in the region and, by the capture of a few strategic points and speedy penetration, they created chaos in the Italian ranks.

This initiated a general retreat, which Hemingway's *Farewell to Arms* brilliantly describes. The Italians wanted to make a stand at the Tagliamento river but were forced back to the Piave river. They had retreated 80 miles and surrendered with alacrity, as there were 275,000 prisoners, although only 10,000 killed. The Italian commander, General Cadorna, was ruthless with his army but unable to stop a chaotic retreat, so was replaced by General Diaz, who was a Pétain-like figure and more sympathetic to the plight of his countrymen.

The attack by the Central Powers had run out of steam but it was a decisive defeat for Italy, although it was not out of the war. The Allies now realised that they had to coordinate their efforts to a far greater extent, so decided to form the Supreme War Council consisting of Britain, France, Italy and the United States. There was now a front line running from the North Sea to the Adriatic and it had to be coordinated. The formation of this war council might seem straightforward but it was not, as Lloyd George wanted it not only as a strategic unit to unify war aims but as a means of blunting the strategic power of Robertson and Haig. Therefore, he appointed Sir Henry Wilson, while the other nations appointed their chiefs of staff.

Georges Clemenceau had only just become France's prime minister – against the odds, as he was seventy-six and disliked by President Poincaré. Clemenceau believed in fighting and hated defeatists. There was a strand of French thinking that wanted a negotiated end to the war, which Joseph Caillaux represented. Clemenceau defeated him for the premiership and then had him arrested for treason. The phrase 'total war' was coined to describe Clemenceau's approach.

The French army would once again start thinking about the offensive. Here was a radical of the left and an atheist getting most of his support from the right, determined to expel the Boche from France. Lloyd George found a kind of mirror image of himself and lobbied Clemenceau not to appoint the chiefs of staff as members of the Supreme War Council. Clemenceau, in exasperation, appeased Lloyd George and appointed Foch's subordinate, General Maxime Weygand to the post, which was not exactly what Lloyd George wanted. Wilson was the only council member without a direct responsibility for the war.

The Air War Develops

During the first three months of 1917, the Germans were in the ascendant on the Western Front through their superior aircraft. This did not stop Trenchard from attacking but he was losing machines and aircrew at great rates and a pilot's life expectancy had come down to seventeen days. This did not escape comment of both the Flying Corps and parliament but Trenchard retained the loyalty of his superiors and his aircrew. He needed new and better planes. The navy flew the Sopwith Triplane, which could hold its own against the German Albatros, but there were few of them and they were in the north. By the summer, the S.E.5 had been produced and, a little later, the acrobatic Sopwith Camel. These two aircraft, plus the French SPAD planes, had sufficient quality to attack the Germans with confidence. The Albatros was still being developed and refined but it was an exceptional aircraft, so no new German plane was being developed because of this supremacy.

During the battles of Ypres and Cambrai, the British continued to concentrate on dominating air space and reconnoitring both for artillery and the movement of armies. Foul weather at Ypres badly hampered this but the Germans introduced new tactics at Cambrai. They formed Schlachtstaffein (Schlastas), or battle wings, to strafe the British and regain lost ground. This was a major reason why Cambrai was so disappointing to the British after the successes gained by the tanks.

The Central Powers Attack | 139

By March 1918 the air war was predominantly in the British sector. Germany had 1,680 aircraft situated there, while there were only 367 opposite the French sector. Trenchard's aggressive tactics and the quality of his pilots and their machines caused this imbalance. The Germans were only concerned with holding the French and concentrated their aces in the north.

Germany's breakthrough at the end of March involved the use of rolling artillery, poison gas shells and elite stormtroopers but the Schlastas strafing of the British greatly helped. The British 5th Army was in full flight, so communication with aerial spotters stopped and the Royal Flying Corps' function was to protect the air space and to bomb and strafe. Its retreat, however, was better organised than the German advance, as they destroyed their abandoned airfields and fell back to airfields in the rear.

Brigadier Brooke-Popham was the organiser, who had also been responsible for the retreat from Mons. As the front line retreated about 40 miles, this reduced the number of sorties the Germans could carry out. The British became adept at bombing and strafing German concentrations and bottlenecks, especially around bridges, and this, together with the German problem of moving their artillery, was the major contribution to the offensive petering out. By now the war in the air had a personality of its own.

On the ground there were few individual heroes; it was the collective action of the regiment, battalion or division that was praised, although there were outstanding acts of bravery rewarded by decorations and fame. In the air, however, there were heroes and personalities who were attacking and scoring victories on a daily basis. Germany and France were keen on promoting these aces and put them in elite formations. Britain was more reticent and did not form elite groups.

The first great French ace was Captain Georges Guynemer. He survived Verdun, by June 1917 had forty-five victories and was made an officer of the Legion of Honour. He then took his elite unit, Les Cicognes, to Messines and Ypres but in September he was killed – the fate of most of the aces. Britain caught up later with the razzmatazz and produced many aces, most of whom received the Victoria Cross. For some, such as Captain Albert Ball, flying was a drug, an excitement that gave that glorious feeling of rhythm, freedom and the illusion of being in control of one's destiny. Ball's talent was enormous. Within a short time he had won the MC, three DSOs and the VC. He was given two planes: one for squadron work and the other so that he could fly as a lone ranger. He was killed over the German lines in 1917.

Billy Bishop, a Canadian, was someone else who could not be kept out of the sky. At twenty-seven he was thought too old to be a top-flight pilot but would spend seven hours in the air each day, never seeming to tire. He would gain seventy-two victories. Then there was the ex-mechanic, Jimmy McCudden, who was measured, calculating and always assessing the odds. He had a friend, Mike Mannock, who many thought was the greatest ace of all. After his death, his kills were reassessed and he was given one more than Major Billy Bishop, which may or may not be justified, but his contemporaries were adamant about his brilliance and bravery. After the war, they prevailed upon Churchill, then minister of air, to give him a posthumous VC.

Germany clustered its aces together in Richthofen's Circus and many think that Manfred von Richthofen was the greatest ace of the war. From an early age he had hunted and shot so it was natural to him to kill his prey. His elite group roamed the sky in Jasta 4s. By May 1917 he had fifty victories and was sent home as a hero to inspire the young. He authored a book, as did many of the British aces, then returned to battle. On 6 July 1917, he was wounded by a bullet that struck his head. He tried to come back the following month but he needed time. He was at hand when the Germans struck in March 1918 but, on 21 April, he was shot by either another aircraft or from the ground. His aircraft landed safely behind the Australian lines but he was dead. The man was a legend with eighty victories and was buried with full military honours. In the air war there was mutual respect – heroes and chivalry.

As the tide turned in the summer of 1918, the Allies gained overwhelming superiority in the air. The blockade was hurting Germany, not least in the production and maintenance of aircraft. There was not enough of such simple things as dope and linen, or major items such as lubricants and fuel. This was something new, as was the air wing as an offensive weapon, which had been gradually developed and was now becoming powerful, although difficult to quantify. Airmen flew over troops and released their bombs or allowed their guns to blaze but rarely were able to witness the mayhem they had caused. The troops on the ground, likewise, would dust themselves down and leave the casualties behind. Thus, the effect of air action was rarely assessed on its own but it was now undoubtedly a powerful force.

Erwin Rommel

The one characteristic that all great fighting soldiers possess is an intuitive feel for the battlefield. Amid the movement and cacophony of war, amid its perilous silences, they always have a contempt for but an awareness of danger and an intuitive ability to weigh up a situation. Of all soldiers, Rommel had this in spades.

He first saw action as a twenty-two-year-old lieutenant on 22 August 1914 as the Germans were advancing to the Marne. In the village of Bleid, he was in the lead, found fifteen to twenty French soldiers on the road and opened fire. His platoon followed up and overwhelmed the surprised French. On 24 September, near Varesmas, he was wounded in the thigh during an incident where he was awarded the Iron Cross, 2nd Class. Recovering quickly, he was in action by the end of January 1915, where he led his platoon through barbed wire, captured four blockhouses and repulsed a battalion counter-attack before retiring. This earned him the Iron Cross, 1st Class.

A leg wound led to a period of inactivity but, by April 1915, Rommel was transferred to a new mountain unit in Austria, experimenting in a form of combat that emphasised mobility. He returned to the front in the Vosges mountains, where there was little fighting. The year of 1916 was quiet for him and he had time to get married. At the beginning of 1917, his battalion had joined the Alpenkorps in Romania and he led an attack on the village of Gagesti, capturing 400 prisoners. In August, although wounded in an arm, he led four companies in the capture of the heavily defended Monnet Costa.

Rommel's battalion now became part of the German 14th Army on the Italian front and, in October 1917, took part in the Battle of Caporetto. His battalion had six companies and he set off with two of them to infiltrate an Italian flank position. Capturing an Italian battery, he left one company there and pushed on with the other. The company he had left was counter-attacked, so he immediately turned round and sandwiched his antagonists, capturing 1,000 prisoners. He then called up the other four companies and they proceeded for 2 miles, intersecting a main road used as a supply route and capturing over 2,000 crack troops. Proceeding, he captured a garrison of over 1,500 troops, then attacked the high ground of Monte Matagar from the rear.

Rommel had been attacking for fifty hours in enemy territory and had captured 150 officers, 9,000 troops and 81 guns. After recovering from these exertions, he and six men capped it by swimming the Piave river, while his companies gave fire from dispersed positions, magnifying their strength. Rommel and six companions walked into the village of Longarone, demanding and receiving the garrison's surrender.

For such feats, the Pour Le Mérite was mere adornment but it was the end of his battlefield experience. From now on he was part of the staff and he passed seamlessly into the tiny German army of the peace. He was a true professional, fully honed in war.

The First Battle of Cambrai

British observers from other sectors were pained at what they thought was the unintelligent use of force at Ypres. The area around Cambrai was deemed suitable for a tank attack and, as Passchendaele came to an end in November, the tank corps assembled 381 tanks under General Julian Byng, commander of the Canadian Corps. They attacked on 20 November. The initial plan envisaged a smash and grab raid to expose and maul the German lines, followed by retirement. This was then thought to be inadequate and it evolved into a plan for a general breakthrough.

Unlike the previous attacks on the Western Front, which were preceded by several days of artillery barrage, this one had been carefully planned to dupe the enemy by means of minor attacks and feints in other parts of the line, together with the assembly of dummy and real tanks in these areas. When the Cambrai attack went in without artillery warning and fortunately covered in mist, the Germans were only half ready. Their trench defences were formidable and it was difficult for the tanks to cross them, as they were wide and deep.

The tanks went into battle in sections of three, with fascines of birch attached to their front. They dropped the fascines into the trench, so forming a bridge, to be followed by the next tank bridging the next trench and so on. Thus, a way was formed that allowed the infantry to follow through. The attack was brilliantly successful, in one day covering 5 miles, and there were only minor defences before open country. But the tanks, infantry and cavalry had to pause before they could exploit the potential hole and, by this time, the Germans had plugged it.

The Central Powers Attack | 143

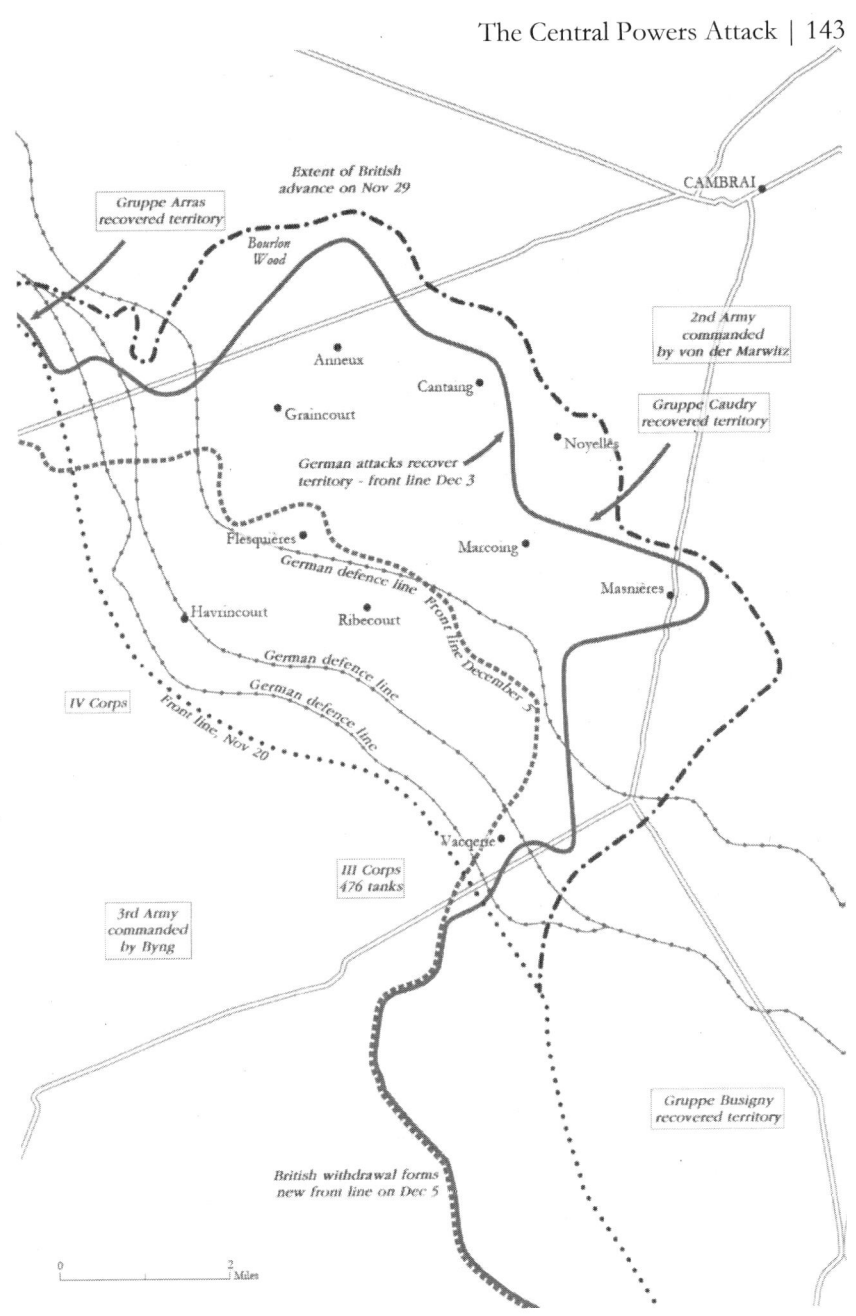

10. Relative positions at the First Battle of Cambrai, 1917

On 21 November the bells were rung in London to celebrate a great victory. There was prescience in this but it was premature; this was not to be a great victory but was the harbinger of one that would change the face of war. This time the Germans fought back with tactics they felt were superior and would see them through to victory. The tanks disconcerted them but they did not see it as the great breakthrough, the means by which fluidity would return to warfare and paradoxically would lead to a lesser loss of life.

The Germans retorted by using gas and smoke shells, the former successfully hampering the lines of communication, the latter providing cover for infiltration, while their air force successfully attacked troops on the ground. The tank was not yet flexible enough, the means by which it was serviced and kept in action had not yet reached an acceptable level of competence and, once it had broken through, it was vulnerable. The brilliance of Cambrai was annulled and by 7 December a new line was formed, with the Allies gaining territory in the north and the Germans in the south. Cambrai was another stalemate battle.

The Russian Revolution and the Treaty of Brest-Litovsk

In a way, Germany triggered the October revolution in Petrograd by attacking in September and threatening the city. The provisional government wanted to leave and move to Moscow but the Bolsheviks appealed to the patriotism of the people and formed a defence committee to defend the city. On the night of 24 October the Red Guards used their power to take control of the city and the provisional government was no more. Lenin's new programme was fundamental and concerned with the ownership of land, the provision of bread and an appeal for peace. He offered Germany a three-month armistice.

The soldiers' belief that they could possibly own their land made them vote with their feet and wander home. Those who did not go east often became prisoners and there were about four million of them in German hands, an enormous number. Germany was suspicious of Lenin's offer of an armistice and only gradually realised that he was being serious. On 2 December an armistice was agreed for a month and peace talks started the next day.

All the Central Powers were represented, including Turkey, while the Bolsheviks included a representative from Ukraine at this meeting at Brest-Litovsk. Germany wanted Poland and other territories to the east. The talks dragged on and Germany upped its demands and was not conciliatory. The Bolsheviks were split, with the revolutionary left wanting to continue the war, while Lenin wanted to give Germany what it wanted. The Bolsheviks were aflame with romantic revolutionary thoughts that the proletariat would revolt and nation after nation would join their cause.

The armistice was extended and, in the second phase of talks, Leon Trotsky led the Bolshevik delegation. Here was someone who would, in time, prove himself pugnacious in the extreme but, with the Germans holding all the cards, he turned the whole thing upside down on 10 February by declaring that Russia was no longer in a state of war and that a decree was being issued for the total demobilisation of its troops. Trotsky believed that he was revolutionising the revolutionary movement in other nations and all soldiers would eventually ignore their weapons and demand peace.

The Germans, thereupon, walked 150 miles into Russia and took territory, which was sobering to the Russians. Some Bolsheviks thought that the regime would fail if they did not fight back but Lenin was for peace and the acceptance of Germany's terms. Peace with Germany was the overriding objective and Russia achieved this in humiliating fashion when the treaty was signed in March, as Germany took Poland and parts of Russia that were three times the size of Germany itself.

Hermann Göring

Göring was born into the ruling class. His father was the governor of a German colony, German West Africa, now Namibia. At the outbreak of war, aged twenty-one, Göring saw action from the beginning as a platoon commander, then as a battalion adjutant. After five weeks, having been awarded the Iron Cross, 2nd Class, he developed arthritis and was sent out of the front line. While recovering he became friendly with Bruno Loerzer, who was learning to fly, which stimulated Göring's interest in this new form of warfare. He became Loerzer's observer and together they were at Verdun in the greatest of battles.

With photographic, radio and Morse signalling skills, Göring covered the battlefield, relaying the vital intelligence of airship hangars, ammunition dumps, the outline of enemy trenches and the digging of new ones, and the effectiveness of artillery barrages. This gave him access to the high command. Crown Prince Wilhelm, the commander of the 5th Army, decorated both pilot and observer in March with the Iron Cross, 1st Class.

Göring now learned to fly and to be in control of his own destiny. His first kill was in November 1915. For the next year he fought with distinction in various localities until his luck ran out when attacking a bomber and he was hit by fighters. A bullet lodged in his buttocks and he crash-landed in a cemetery without further injury. Three months later he joined his friend Loerzer's squadron and, after another three months, he was promoted to the command of his own squadron on the Ypres sector. The battles at Arras were still smouldering and Ypres was about to start again; it was a crucial sector.

Göring was hugely ambitious and craved the ultimate decoration, the Pour Le Mérite, but as yet he was not in the top echelon of aces. Manfred von Richthofen had sixty-one kills, Göring and Loerzer fifteen each, while Ernst Udet, a future administrator of the Luftwaffe was on fourteen. Consumed with ambition to be a great ace, Göring was often thwarted by illness. When Richthofen's Circus was expanded into a large wing he was not in action and missed promotion. Richthofen was killed on 21 April but Göring, with eighteen kills, had not done enough to become his successor, although he was awarded the Pour Le Mérite in June. It was the death of Richthofen's successor that secured the baton of command that allowed Göring to lead Germany's greatest aces. By now, kills were not so easy as armour plating had been introduced to Allied aircraft but he finished with twenty-two to his name and his morale high.

There is no doubt that Germany was losing in the air as well as on the ground but it was a fantasy life of adventure, suffusing the body in adrenaline. Göring was not all that downcast by defeat and was intrigued and stimulated by the future potential of the aircraft in warfare. He had fought a brave, chivalrous war and was to be rewarded for it. At war's end he took his planes to Darmstadt and sent his men away with the words, 'Our time will come again.'[9] When he arrived in post-war Munich, his luck was in as the armistice terms were enforced by a British officer who had been shot down and who Göring had subsequently treated with great chivalry. As was customary, until his luck ran out a quarter of a century later, Göring's charm and talent obliterated the scoundrel in him and he was handed a lifeline to future fame.

Palestine – The Capture of Jerusalem

The Turkish Empire still territorially dominated the Middle East but it was under threat and if Germany disintegrated then it would also go. Even with Russia quiescent, the defeat of the Turks could weaken the Central Powers and allow an attack through what Churchill called the soft underbelly of Europe.

After the attack at Arras, Allenby was sent to Cairo to command the Allied forces against the Turks. He was a general of substance and intelligence who gave added vitality to his command. He believed in being close to his troops and took his HQ from Cairo to near the front line. He also believed that surprise was worth a lot in a battle, so he built up a portfolio of false plans, which he allowed the Turks to capture, and he supplied them with drugged cigarettes, which they rashly smoked.

On 20 October Allenby bombarded Gaza to draw the defences in that direction, captured Beersheba on 31October, inducing Falkenhayn to counter-attack, and on 1 November made his overwhelming attack on the weakened Turkish centre. The flight of the Turks foiled Falkenhayn's counter-attack and there was a general retreat. By 14 November the Turks were in two groups. The Allies pressed on and captured Jaffa, while the right wing went inland, captured the passes to Jerusalem and, on 9 December, captured Jerusalem itself.

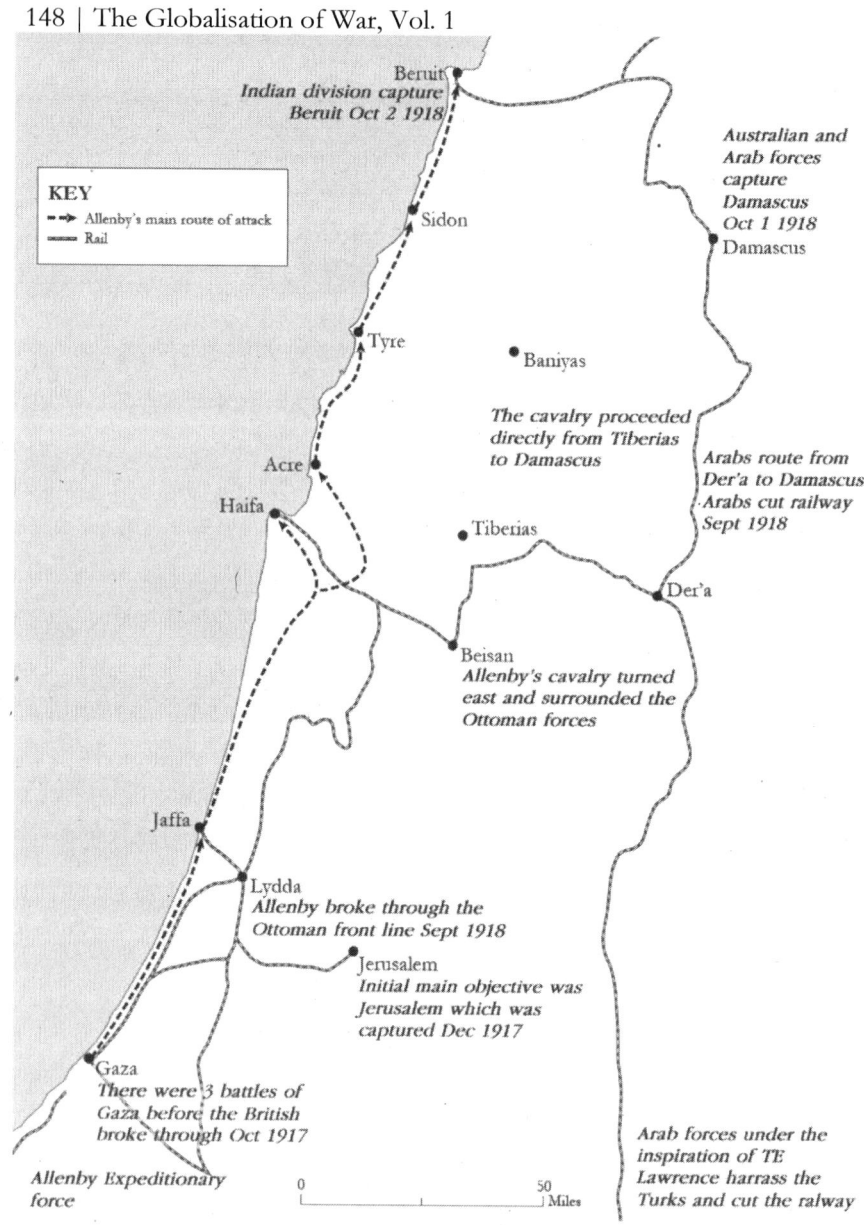

11. *The route to the capture of Jerusalem, 1918*

East Africa, Von Lettow-Vorbeck and Smuts

The German colony of Tanganyika was isolated by British control of the seas. British East Africa went to war with the colony and the British Empire found itself taking on a resourceful general in Paul Emil von Lettow-Vorbeck. He only had 5,000 troops, 250 of whom were German, and they involved 130,000 British Empire troops, nearly all of whom were native to the region. The expense was considerable for the British, as were the losses through disease, but there was one major plus in that South Africa was involved as a united nation, thirteen years after the Boer War.

An enemy of Britain at that time, Jan Smuts led the Empire troops against the Germans but only after Von Lettow-Vorbeck had formed a formidable force on the Kenya–Tanganyika border, which threatened the crucial railway line from Mombasa to Lake Victoria via Nairobi. Smuts arrived in Nairobi in February 1916 and was not particularly welcome, as an enemy guerrilla general from the Boer War, and someone who was regarded as a bit of an amateur. However, he soon removed the German forces from the border region and went on to take the fertile region around Moshi, forcing the enemy south of the railway running from Lake Tanganyika to Dar-es-Salaam. Communications such as roads were very primitive, as were cars and trucks, so the logistics of the whole operation became very difficult. Disease, especially malaria, decimated the armies and it was decided to use native levies, who were more resistant.

Von Lettow-Vorbeck was a nuisance and, although Smuts's successor, Van Deventer, pursued him further south, he remained undefeated to the end. His success was not dissimilar to Smuts's success in the Boer War. Much fuss was made of him in Berlin amid the wreckage of defeat but he achieved little apart from keeping British forces in the field. In some ways, having South Africa fighting as a united nation was a greater plus to Britain than an abject surrender by Germany.

Smuts was relieved of his command so that he could attend the Imperial Conference of Dominion Prime Ministers as the South African representative. With stalemate on the Western Front, the success in East Africa was magnified and he was lauded by politicians and the press. Even Churchill described Smuts as 'a new and altogether extraordinary man from the outer marches of the Empire'.[10] Smuts was far too modest and grounded to let this go to his head and, when he went to stay with King George V at Windsor, he wrote to his wife about his desire to be in his beloved South Africa and how upset he was that Luis Botha was ailing.

Smuts was very influential in the last years of the war. At the Imperial Conference, the British, under Milner's influence, wanted to form a centralised parliament with an executive that would run the empire. Smuts opposed this, knowing it would cut no ice in South Africa. His proposal was that the individual nations would be autonomous within an imperial commonwealth and would control their own affairs.

This was accepted but Smuts's greater achievement was in his dealings with the Royal Air Force. As London and the south-east were raided from the air and there was general anxiety, Lloyd George asked Smuts to prepare defensive plans. Lloyd George subsequently described Smuts as the Father of the Royal Air Force. He was undoubtedly a truly successful soldier-politician of the First World War.

German Success

Now Russia was out of the war, the Allies' great numerical strength was nullified until the Americans arrived. This was Germany's great chance and its divisions in the east moved west for what they hoped was the denouement. The Allied forces had a national loyalty that sometimes hampered harmonious command, even though soldiers and politicians were constantly conferring on equalising the burden and using resources for the common good.

During 1917, the British, with fifty-eight divisions, were holding 100 miles of the line, while the French, with ninety-nine divisions, were holding 325 miles. These bare figures suggest the French were badly burdened but the British were on the offensive, had their backs closer to the sea and were opposed by a greater density of German divisions. Nevertheless, it was agreed that in 1918 the British lines should be extended to 125 miles, which was still proportionately less than the French. However, this posed difficulties because the casualties suffered during Passchendaele had not been fully replaced.

Lloyd George stopped sending reinforcements into this attritional battle and had not made up the leeway. He was greatly affected by the British death and suffering endured during the battle and it would cloud his thinking for the rest of his life. To understand Lloyd George one has to understand the effect of the Third Battle of Ypres on his thinking. It had an immediate effect, as he limited the movement of troops from Britain to France, which stretched British manpower in the trenches.

In the middle of 1917 the ratio of divisions was 3:2 (178 Allied to 129 German) but in March 1918 the Germans had about 200 divisions and a 10 per cent advantage. With numerical advantage, they could use all their skill as soldiers to split the British and French and roll the British back to the sea and their homeland, which would enable the Germans to break through the French defence and capture Paris, which not be easy, though, as the French had recovered. Haig was scathing about French capabilities and their willingness to attack but Pétain had led a renaissance by conducting a defensive strategy, saving lives and bringing new young soldiers into the war.

152 | The Globalisation of War, Vol. 1

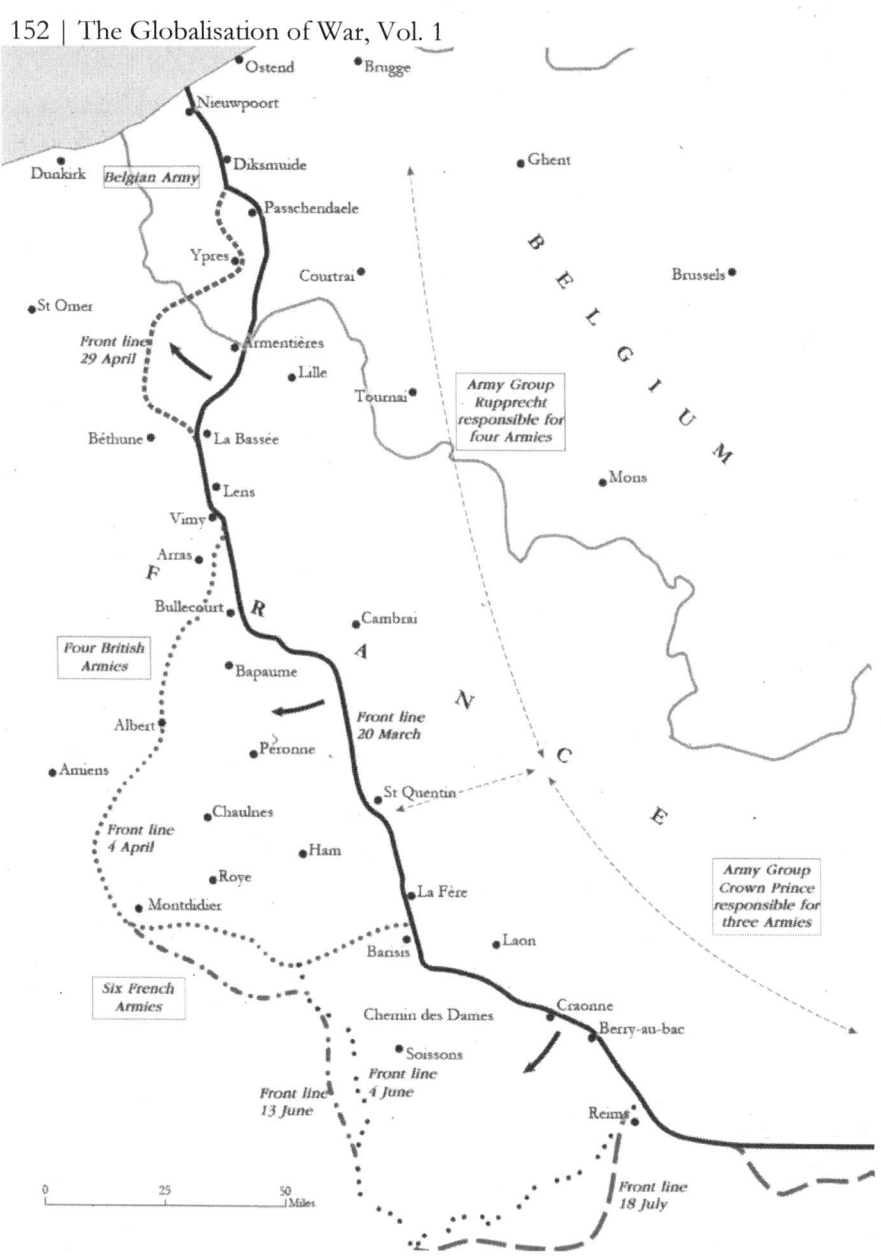

12. *The advancing German front lines, 1918*

On 31 January the Supreme War Council met at Versailles and Foch accused the British of not providing enough troops. Haig backed him up, telling Lloyd George that his soldiers were tired and there were insufficient numbers. Men needed to be called to the colours and trained. Lloyd George created a diversion by suggesting that there were enough men in France and that surplus resources should be sent to the Middle East. This infuriated Premier Clemenceau, who vigorously addressed Prime Minister Lloyd George in French, which he did not understand. Concerning military matters, Foch argued that to stop a major German attack, which was expected, it was necessary to mount a counteroffensive, as at the Somme when Verdun was relieved. Both Pétain and Haig said that this was impossible due to lack of resources, although there was a large American army waiting to earn its spurs.

Germany's plan was to attack the British sector between Arras and Saint Quentin using gas and smoke shells in a short artillery barrage to use the advantage of surprise, which stormtroopers would exploit. Success came along the southern part of this 43-mile front, while the Germans were held around Arras. This was not what Ludendorff wanted, as his plan was to roll the British up in the north using Arras as a hinge, while a breakthrough in the south would enable him to guard his flank and stop the deployment of reserves. Thus, he persisted in trying to get a result at Arras, while to the south his army was moving unopposed to Amiens.

The gap that had been opened was huge, with Gough's 5th Army streaming back in retreat and Pétain nobly sending French reserves to plug the gap. Even without the tank, the Germans had brought mobility back into the war by advancing up to 40 miles and capturing 80,000 prisoners and 1,000 guns. The only trouble was that they did not have the means to move the heavy artillery forward. Meanwhile, this was increasingly becoming an air war but the Luftwaffe was too far behind the front line to be effective. Pétain had successfully held up part of the German offensive by ordering the French air force to strafe the assembly of troops.

At long last but out of fear, the Allies appointed a supremo, Marshal Foch, to try to coordinate their activities. Foch had to leapfrog the unhappy Pétain but could then theoretically direct the French armies. Pershing, the American commander, and Haig wanted to keep the integrity of their armies and have the right of appeal to their governments if they were not happy with Foch's decisions, which was agreed. Morale was raised, even if there was little immediate scope for coordination that would make a difference. Although there had been arguments, Pétain and Haig had successfully redeployed reserves but with Foch in command, the decision could be quicker.

The Germans were now being held in front of Amiens and were regrouping. All was not well, however, with the Fatherland. Hunger and famine was the lot of many and people were dying. This was reflected in the sparse supplies for the German army, which was amazed by the great cornucopia of food, drink, clothing and equipment found behind the British lines. They realised that they were winning at that moment but the disparity in resources disturbed them and the temptation to indulge was too great for many of them. There was another factor that held the Germans. The Allies had air superiority, which was not control but a generalised dominance that allowed them to attack attenuated lines of communication and troop concentrations. It also provided the intelligence of where the Germans were likely to attack. While the German stormtroopers were brilliant, the artillery could not act with the same speed to provide them with accurate gas and smoke shell fire to continue the breakthrough.

On 9 April 1918 Ludendorff attacked, again in the Lys sector. The attack was not a major effort but such was the collapse that Ludendorff attempted to expand it and was only stopped by fresh French divisions after a 10-mile incursion near to the railway junction of Hazebrouck. The French had saved the British, who had been hard hit with 300,000 casualties, but the Germans had now run out of steam and had to pause to regroup.

Breakthrough to the Marne

The next major attack did not take place until the end of May 1917. Germany's dilemma of how to deliver the knockout blow to the Allies was still unresolved but, in Ludendorff's mind, it would be through success in Flanders. However, there was always the thought that Paris could be captured and the threat to the city could cause a disequilibrium in the Allied front. Therefore, Ludendorff assembled a strong force of fifteen attacking divisions, with twenty-five in reserve, plus 6,000 guns on the Chemin des Dames, 70 miles from Paris.

The guns produced one of the most powerful artillery bombardments of the war and, as the front had been quiet and was manned predominantly by recuperating divisions, three French and three British from Gough's army, the Germans had little problem in breaking through. The ease with which they did surprised them, as they crossed the Aisne, capturing Soissons, then the Vesle, until by the evening of 30 May they had reached the Marne, only 56 miles from Paris.

The next day the Allied left wing retreated further, so the Germans were occupying a large stretch of one bank but they had been unable to capture Rheims. The Germans were held on the Marne with the help of two large American divisions at Château-Thierry. As they were coming to the front and French troops retreated, it was suggested to a US Marine captain that he should also retreat, to which he retorted, 'Retreat? Hell, we just got here.'[11] It was another triumph for the Germans but they could not sustain it any longer. Their resources were stretched, then influenza struck.

Adolf Hitler

For a man who was twenty-five and had no job or qualifications, the onset of war was a godsend. Hitler welcomed it with enthusiasm and Hoffman, who would become his court photographer, pictured him among the crowd in Munich. As an Austrian, Hitler petitioned King Ludwig to be accepted into a Bavarian regiment, which he granted. On 29 October 1914, Hitler was under fire on the Menin Road near Ypres, where there was chaos and casualties. According to Hitler there were only 611 fit men at the end of it from a regiment of 3,600.

Within the next ten days, Hitler's role was determined when he was promoted to corporal, a rank he would hold for the rest of the war, and he was assigned to the regimental staff as a despatch runner. This was a responsibility that involved taking orders from regimental HQ to battalion and company commanders, who were usually about 3 kilometres away. As he spent most of his time at regimental HQ, it was less dangerous than being in the trenches but was extremely perilous in times of battle, so two runners were sent in case one was killed. Of the eight runners on 15 November, three were killed and one wounded. On 2 December Hitler's worth was recognised when he was awarded the Iron Cross, 2nd Class, one of sixty in his regiment to be decorated.

Hitler was called Adi and known as the artist. His comrades accepted him as a lonely and solitary figure with puritanical inclinations. He was friendly enough with his comrades but was not part of the rough, rude soldiery, cursing, moaning and looking forward to hedonistic relief away from the trenches. Early in the war he had found a terrier, which was thought to have come from the enemy lines. It became his friend and companion and he was deeply upset when it disappeared later in the war.

Hitler's fanaticism and love of Germany became apparent to his comrades. He loathed the fraternisation at Christmas and his comrades soon learned how easily they could bait him with defeatist talk. For a year and half his regiment opposed the British on a mile-and-a-quarter strip near Fromelles. In October 1916 they moved to the Somme, where Hitler was wounded in the left thigh. He recuperated near Berlin and found that the enthusiasm for the war was muted. He returned to his regiment in March 1917, near Vimy, but then went to the Ypres area for the big battle there. He was soon out of the front and had a two-month break, spending the last part of the war in the Rheims area.

In July 1918, Hitler was in the Second Battle of the Marne. On a Jewish officer's nomination, he received the Iron Cross, 1st Class on 4 August, a remarkable achievement for a corporal and part of a bribe to deliver a message during a particularly heavy attack. He then went on a telecommunications course, followed by leave, so was spared the German army's defeats. Returning to his regiment at the end of September, he found that they were very much on the defensive. On the night of 13 October in the Ypres area, when leaving his dugout, he was gassed along with his comrades. Being unable to see, he joined a gaggle of men holding on to each other and was led to safety, ending the war in hospital at Stettin. His intense patriotism called the armistice the greatest villainy of the century, a classic case of pot calling the kettle black. He would find uses for lethal gases but his suffering could well have been why soldiers would not use them in combat during the next big war.

Influenza Epidemic

It was in April 1918 that another factor came into play that would be debilitating for everyone. It is now thought to have originated in the United States but, as is the way with viruses, no one was sure then and no one is sure now. It was a pandemic in its infancy, not yet a real killing pandemic, but a horrible one all the same. It was called, unfairly, Spanish influenza because the Spaniards, being neutral, reported what was happening, while most of the world covered it up.

The three-day variety started to affect troops in France and nearby countries during April 1917. The sick person would have the usual symptoms of flu – a high temperature, splitting headache and aching bones and muscles. In most cases it would be resolved after three days by a great perspiration but it was mightily infectious and affected the prowess of every army. The Germans called it Flanders fever and Ludendorff complained that it was affecting his battle plans and troop morale.

There were three weeks in May when the British fleet had over 10,000 men sick and was not truly operational. In June the British 29th Division had to postpone an attack because of the flu. In July, when Ludendorff wanted to attack and finish the war, he found his numbers were diminished because of sickness. Then, in high summer, it mysteriously disappeared for a couple of months. When it returned it had mutated into a killer.

Ludendorff Attacks Again

The control of the railway system was fundamental to the supply of men, food, armaments and ammunition to the front throughout the war. Although the Germans had reached the Marne, the front was such that it was only supplied by the Laon–Soissons line, which was vulnerable to Allied air and artillery attack. Ludendorff decided he needed Rheims as an alternative railway centre and also wanted the French reserves in Flanders to be redeployed to the Rheims area, as his decisive blow was to be in Flanders.

He attacked with forty-nine divisions either side of Rheims and attempted to surround the city by pinching it off. Good intelligence meant the French were aware of his plans, so they got their artillery barrage in first, then retreated beyond the range of the German artillery, ceding territory but occupying a strong defensive position. This was Pétain's inspiration and was brilliantly successful. The Germans were held, suffered debilitating casualties and the French counter-attacked on the German right flank. This was Foch's inspiration. He and Pétain disagreed on how to organise the defence. Pétain wanted a weak first line of defence and a second line that was out of range of artillery. Foch demanded a strong first line and, if that were breached, he would advocate a counteroffensive.

In this case, Foch had assembled a corps under General Charles Mangin, a ruthless operator, and with the use of tanks knocked the Germans backwards. Pétain's defensive tactics, brilliant as they were, had been superseded. The salient that the Germans had formed was now difficult to defend and they were forced to withdraw. Although the French could not break through, they had halted the German offensive and the French reserves had not been drawn away from Flanders. This was a setback to Ludendorff's hopes but he was still planning his masterstroke in Flanders.

Chapter 10

The Allies Strike Back

Franco–British Advances

Britain and France were planning a joint operation where their armies met near the old Somme battlefields. Air superiority was such that Germany's intelligence was weak, so surprise, that vital element in war, was a possibility. For surprise it was necessary that no soldier in the front line knew through information or intimation that an attack was imminent. For this, heavy guns were brought up at night, crack troops were not deployed in the area until the last minute and tanks were camouflaged and concealed. This was a war where the artillery dominated, the British used air superiority to pinpoint where the German heavy guns were placed and by accurate fire were able to knock them out.

At 4:20 a.m. on 8 August, without an early artillery barrage, the attack went in with artillery, infantry and tanks acting in concert and achieving surprise. Although the Germans had some suspicions of this attack, they had rejected this evidence. The British had assembled 360 tanks plus 96 whippets and over 2,000 guns, whose main function was not to pulverise the trenches but to knock out the enemy artillery. The crack troops were Canadians and Australians and the attack was on a 14-mile front held by only six German divisions. The attackers did not need smoke, as a ground mist assisted them, so they achieved the first day's objective of 6 to 8 miles, except on the flank where there were fewer tanks. The next day there were small gains but, subsequently, the attack became bogged down in the old Somme battlefields, while the Germans rushed in reserves who held the line.

Although it was not an overwhelming territorial gain, 8 August became

The Allies Strike Back | 159

known as a black day for the German army. This was the day that hope was extinguished, the day when Ludendorff realised that his offensive power had gone. It was the day when the Allies' superior power became manifest and the awful sacrifices could be justified.

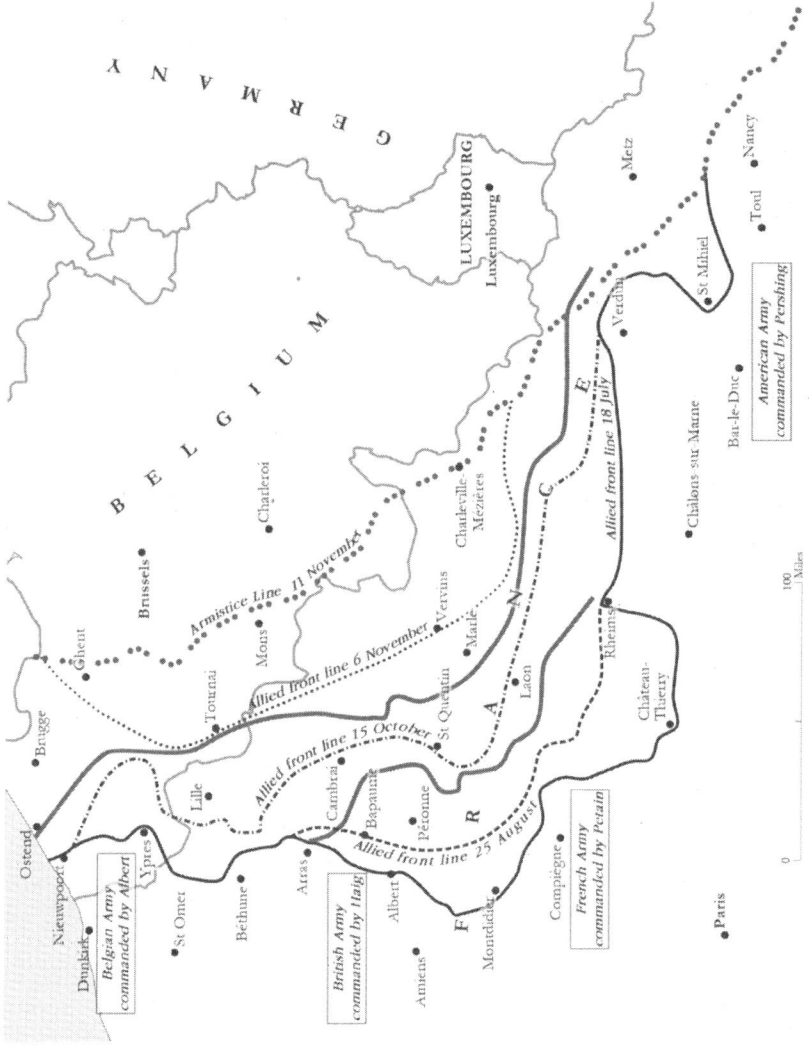

13. The Allied front line advance, 1918

Wars between great powers are won by attrition and technical prowess. Although Haig can be condemned for conducting attritional war at the unsuitable venue of Ypres, it helped break Germany's war machine. The Germans had tried to win the First World War by attrition at Verdun and now were finally broken by it. The day of 8 August was when they realised that they could take no more and Ludendorff's mind turned from the offensive to the defensive. He mentally prepared a retreat, which he hoped would be so costly to the Allies that they would make peace.

While this victory was predominantly British, the subsequent advance was a Franco–British effort, which stopped and started as German reserves poured into the area. There were ten British divisions and eight French, but the British provided most of the tanks. By 8 September the Germans had retreated 30 miles along a broad front.

Here was modern warfare as the twentieth century would come to know it, with aeroplanes bombing and strafing the enemy and providing intelligence. The infantry attacked with the protection of tanks, while the artillery and logistical support had become sufficiently mobile to enable armies to move forward without running out of steam. It was still elementary compared to what would come but it was mobile war superior to the enemy's stormtrooper version. Allied air superiority partially blinded the Germans and, in addition, they could not counterpunch effectively against the tank. There was now a buoyancy on the Allied side. They were confident, even though they were taking casualties, but they were enjoying the smell of victory.

A Great American Victory

The heavy fighting in the west took place in key areas such as Flanders, the Somme, the Marne and Verdun. The Verdun area was crucial right to the end of the war and the Germans had a salient at Saint-Mihiel, which interrupted the Allied railway communications with Verdun. Foch was keen to knock out this salient and the Americans were eager for action on a large scale as a predominantly American force. Although they had been in important actions, notably near the Marne, they had carefully husbanded their resources and did not want to commit themselves to a major offensive before they were ready. Coming late to the war and from across the Atlantic, they had a major logistical problem in being self-sufficient. They lacked heavy artillery, planes and tanks, relying on the Britain and France for these. What they did have was the offensive spirit and they were formidable against a tired but resilient German army.

The Allied offensive against the Saint-Mihiel salient was well telegraphed and the Germans yielded ground and retreated a few hours before the attack. However, the retreat was not altogether successful as the Allied bombardment caught them in the open. The Americans moved with zest and elan, especially on their right wing, and reached their targets on the first two days. The only problem was that Foch had set limited objectives, while Pershing was aflame with the thought of victory through the capture of Metz and the Americans pushing the Germans back along a line from Saint-Mihiel to the Swiss border.

It is a matter of conjecture whether Pershing could have captured Metz and thus disrupted the German lateral rail communications. It is probable that they could have got beyond the Michel line, an extension of the Hindenburg Line, which would have been a substantial achievement. However, they would have inevitably had the problems of mobility and logistics, which an untried army needs to learn by experience in battle. Nevertheless, it was a significant victory, which eased the supply pressure on Verdun. Germany recognised the United States as a formidable force and was deeply worried by the Americans' freshness and potential.

Douglas MacArthur

It seems as though Douglas MacArthur was always a general. From 1918 when he attained that rank at the age of thirty-eight, until 1951 when his commander-in-chief summoned him back from Korea, he was a general who led men in battle and has claims to be the most remarkable fighting general of the twentieth century. He was a soldier whom the gods adored and spared the merest brush with anything lethal. He was the bravest of the brave and, as a general, he liked to be in the thick of the fighting. He offered his life but came through unscathed.

MacArthur saw action in July 1918 with the 42nd Division attached to a

French corps in the French 4th Army. The Germans were attacking southeast of Rheims and the Allies retreated to nullify the German artillery, counter-attacking with their own artillery as the Germans assembled. The German attack was beaten off, with the 42nd suffering 1,600 casualties. The fighting general now galvanised his men into action, demanding they move forward when all they wanted to do was sleep. Although the 42nd had its companies reduced to platoons and casualties rose to 6,500, it advanced 7 miles.

The next action was at Saint-Mihiel on 12 September. There were 1,500 aeroplanes, predominantly French, commanded by Colonel Billy Mitchell, while Colonel George Patton commanded a brigade of thirty Renault tanks. Patton was out in the open with MacArthur when an artillery barrage passed over them. A shell landed nearby, they were splattered with dirt and Patton flinched, to be reassured by MacArthur, who said, 'Don't worry Colonel, you never hear the one that gets you.'[12] Patton always regarded him as the bravest of the brave. As a fighting soldier he was not satisfied with a mere 7-mile advance and saw the possibilities that the capture of Metz afforded, so appealed to Pershing to let him continue; however, Pershing refused.

The American effort was in the Meuse–Argonne area. On 26 September they went into action but there was great congestion. When the 42nd Division joined the fray on 11 October they were met with gas. MacArthur was not someone who cared for gas masks so inhaled doses on consecutive days, causing him to be ill. On 13 October he was back in action, vowing to capture the Côte de Châtillon or incur 5,000 casualties with his name at the top if he failed. He planned to take the heights by a stealthy bayonet attack but the officers, bewildered by his contempt of death and indifference to casualties, persuaded him to accept a rolling artillery barrage and a conventional daylight attack.

The attack went in the next day and, when there was trouble, MacArthur led a brigade forward with terrible casualties. By evening they held a precarious position on the hillside. Châtillon had nests of machine guns protected by concrete pillboxes. Five assaults went in on 15 October but were not successful. That night, MacArthur led a reconnaissance party to find weaknesses in the German defences. Crawling from shell hole to shell hole, they came under artillery fire and, when it had passed, he went round each man to reassure him that he would lead him back to his own lines but found that they were all dead. He attributed his survival to the guiding hand of the Almighty. The horror of it was humbling but to be spared gave him a feeling of divine exultation.

However, they had found the weakness in the German defences and MacArthur led a brigade that held down the Germans while the weak flank was overcome and the enemy was attacked from the rear. It was a great and significant victory, opening the way to Sedan. General George Marshall, Pershing's chief of operations, gave the order that there were no boundaries in the race for Sedan but France claimed the right to enter first. On 11 November 1918, MacArthur was on a hill overlooking the city as the French occupied it. The war was over, the bravest of the brave had survived with seven silver stars and a recommendation for the DSC and the Medal of Honour. He was one of the true fighting generals of the war.

The Balkan Front

For Germany, the large number of Allied troops in Salonika and Macedonia was a bonus. They did nothing and they suffered from disease. The French and British were there, the Serbs had come via Albania and Corfu after their awful retreat, and Greece had at last joined the Allies. It had been neutral for a long time, King Constantine and Prime Minister Venizelos having a difference of opinion on which side to support. The queen was the kaiser's sister, while Venizelos supported the Allies. He felt that this was in Greece's interests, as Thessalonica would then become part of Greece. In 1917, the difference was resolved when the British blockaded Greece, the French landed at Athens and the King abdicated.

During 1917 and early 1918, Bulgaria was not discontented with its lot as it controlled Serbia, while Romania had fallen to Germany. Bulgaria was hoping for something from the fall of Russia, possibly the Dobrudja region with its granary, but it was not to be. Bulgaria, like its neighbours, lacked food but the rest of the starving Central Powers were unable to help. The front remained quiescent until September 1918, when German divisions started to leave the Balkans to bolster the Western Front. Throughout the war, all the fronts had interacted on each other but now they were about to crash, one after the other.

A Franco–Serb force attacked on 15 September, gaining up to 20 miles of territory on a 25-mile front. The Bulgarians now retreated further and the bombing of the Kosturino Pass caused a panic flight and the splitting of the Bulgarian army into two parts. The war had become mobile and the French cavalry had ridden into Serbia, reaching the major rail junction of Skopje on 29 September. This was the day that the armistice was signed with Bulgaria, which had collapsed with remarkable speed.

The French commander, Franchet d'Espèrey virtually had control of the Balkans and, in his euphoria, he felt that with 200,000 men and commanding the railway system from Skopje he could march across Hungary and Austria, pass through Bohemia and attack the Germans at Dresden. It was indicative of the collapse of the Central Powers on this front but d'Espèrey was ordered to Romania and to contact the Russians in the south. The Serbs marched on Belgrade and d'Espèrey cut the Central Power's communications with the Ottoman Empire and Ukraine. This was a monumental blow to Germany.

The Ottoman Empire Disintegrates

The collapse of the Ottoman Empire was equally devastating. Turkey's ambitions were centred on the Caucasus and it was trying to unite people on racial lines. In other parts of the empire, Britain was winning without much opposition because it had command of the air, which provided intelligence on the whereabouts of Turkey's forces. Once the front lines had been breached, the cavalry could make deep incursions.

In the Balkans, British troops were able to advance through the Dardanelles and on to Constantinople. Allenby conducted a brilliant campaign through Palestine, which the Arabs aided under the guidance of Colonel T.E. Lawrence, moving in parallel to the east. Damascus was captured on 1 October and given to Faisal for the Arabs, although in the Sykes–Picot Agreement it was earmarked for France.

In Mesopotamia, the humiliation of the British on the Tigris in the past as they moved to the north and captured Mosul on 4 November, another city promised to France. It was Britain that was dominating the Middle East and it was Britain alone who accepted Turkey's surrender at Lemnos on 29 October.

Influenza as Killer

In September 1918, the influenza pandemic reappeared and became a killer. American youth had responded to the call to arms and there were thousands in camps such as Camp Devens near Boston, which at one time had 50,000 men but was decimated through September as men died at the rate of a hundred a day.

The ordinary symptoms of flu were superseded by a mortal pneumonia, where the sufferer coughed and gasped for breath as their lungs flooded, culminating in cyanosis and death by suffocation. American soldiers were arriving in France at the rate of 100,000 a month but diseases culled their numbers much more than war. The 88th Division arrived in France on 17 September and saw action in the last 16 days of the war. Deaths from flu were 444, while casualties, including wounded and captured, were ninety.

The flu was ubiquitous. Ludendorff, seeking some comfort for the awful German position, received intelligence that the French army was suffering badly from the flu but was told that the German army was in as bad a way. Pershing called for a new large-base hospital and thirty-one evacuation hospitals to deal with the problem, which was just as bad back in the United States, with the draft suspended, camps put into quarantine and training modified for the remainder.

Death had been the constant companion of the soldiers of the warring nations for four years. Now there was exhaustion, hunger and disease to add to the misery. The ending of the war, with its concomitant relief, was the great event of 1918. However, its euphoria for the victors and depression for the losers masked the influenza pandemic, which was the great killer of the time. The figures for the flu pandemic range from upwards of twenty million deaths. No one knows the true figure and no one will but it far exceeds the deaths in the Great War, which are reckoned at about fifteen million, and it affected the same age group.

Another ten million deaths occurred from civil war, mainly in Eastern Europe from 1918 to 1923, but even if these figures are added together to make a loss from war and civil strife of twenty-five million over a ten-year period, the influenza pandemic almost certainly exceeded it. Yet there is no memorial to those who died from it and it barely rates a mention in memoirs and books on the Great War. The population explosion is one of the most salient facts of the twentieth century and it is sobering to think that upwards of fifty million could die in their prime over a ten-year period, purely a blip in this population explosion.

The pandemic was strange in that it affected certain age groups. It was at its most virulent among young adults. It is well known that viral diseases affect children less than teenagers, who are in turn less affected than young adults. It is usual that the elderly would be affected because of their frailty; they were susceptible but between the ages of forty and seventy there was a certain immunity. It is thought that this was because flu viruses are related and the epidemic of 1890 had given a certain immunity to the awful virulence of 1918.

No army could publish the fact that its soldiers were dying in large numbers through disease, as it would give comfort to the enemy and cause confusion at home. In consequence, the whole matter was brushed aside with the ending of war and the advent of peace. People were bemused by it; its incidence was localised, distinguished people over forty did not die of it, although King Alfonso of Spain and King George of England recovered from it. It was a quick, prosaic termination of life, unaccompanied by artillery bombardment, the rattle of machine guns and the cries of the wounded.

The deaths of twenty to fifty million people hardly figures in the history books and the question has to be asked: what is its significance? Spread around the world, picking off the susceptible, the effect of the influenza virus was insidious and surreptitious, killing actual or potential mothers and fathers in their prime. Some tried to make political capital out of it, such as Mahatma Gandhi, who accused the British of introducing it into India, but it was a worldwide pandemic of obscure origin.

Its significance may be that the loss of fifteen million men in war was of no great moment to the species, nor the loss of another ten million in the Russian civil war or the loss of many more to the flu. The species could dispense with these men and women and hardly notice the loss. What was significant was that men were losing their lives in war for a belief in something more important than themselves and it was the living who had to be reconciled to death in war because man creates war. Those dying of disease were subject to the hand of God.

The Central Powers Collapse

Nothing was going right for Germany and its allies. Although there was peace with Russia, the Balkans and the Ottoman Empire had collapsed. Only on the Italian front did the Austro-Hungarians prove a threat. Just as Germany had been able to release men to the Western Front when Russia stopped fighting, so the Austro-Hungarians increased their strength on the Italian front and attacked on 24 June. They made very little headway, leading to the replacement of General Franz Conrad, the long-serving chief of staff. British and French divisions had bolstered the Italians and this stalemate produced war weariness and, for the Austrians, the realisation that they could not produce a result.

This, in addition to the suffering endured, filtered through the whole Austro-Hungarian Empire, so at the beginning of October, Emperor Charles sent President Wilson confirmation that he wanted an armistice. He hoped for a federation of nationalities but, on 6 October, the Croats, Serbs and Slovenes formed a provisional government of Yugoslavia. An independent Poland was formed the next day, then one day later Czechoslovakia came into being. On

1 November, Hungary reaffirmed that it was an independent kingdom. This left only the Ruthenes and Romanians to pronounce on their destiny.

During this disintegration, the Allies attacked on the Italian front on 24 October and a week later were in Austrian territory. The Austrians were demoralised and beaten and initiated a ceasefire on 3 November, which Italy accepted the next day.

Franklin Roosevelt

Roosevelt was born with a silver spoon in his mouth and his talent was commensurate with the privilege he enjoyed. He cut his teeth in New York politics and was elected to the state senate in his late twenties. Soon after, at the start of Woodrow Wilson's administration, Secretary of the navy, Josephus Daniels, selected him to be his assistant. President Theodore Roosevelt, a relative, formerly held this post. It was 1912, Franklin was thirty-one and on a learning curve, especially in national politics, but he liked his post, regarding himself as a sailor, and his amateur experience of sailing boats would colour his judgement through two world wars.

When war broke out in Europe, he wanted to go to England to see how his counterparts were organising themselves. He made soundings but Winston Churchill was preoccupied and politely refused his request. For the duration of the war their paths hardly crossed, although Roosevelt kept his post to the end. Daniels, his boss, was cautious about being involved in the war but Roosevelt was Anglophile. He felt the Central Powers were wrong in starting the war, although Russia could certainly be blamed, and he wanted the thrill of action in a just war and to put his manhood to the test in combat.

Although a major pretext for the United States going to war was Germany's links with Mexico and its offer of the border states of the United States if it won the war, the greater issue was unrestricted submarine warfare. This was a running sore between the United States and Germany and, when the two states declared war, Roosevelt was in a position of influence.

The British and French had successfully blocked the English Channel with mines and the Americans asked why something similar could not be done in the north, thus blocking German submarine activity in the Atlantic. Roosevelt was the great protagonist of mining but there were problems. Admiral Fisher said of mining, 'Mine in haste and sweep at leisure,' while Balfour pointed out that Norwegian neutral waters could not be mined.[13]

However, Roosevelt correctly retorted that belligerents could not use the territorial waters of neutrals and, if they did, they could be stopped if the neutral country did not act. Theoretically this was true but it was not as straightforward as this. Roosevelt, however, persisted over the next few months, initiating the production of a new firing device, persuading Daniels and Wilson of the good sense of his strategy and getting Britain to accept his policy. All in all it was no mean political achievement.

In October 1917, the mine barrier was Allied policy but, because of problems with mine production, it was not started until March 1918. It was a big undertaking involving thirteen sorties of two days each. The Americans laid 56,000 mines in the central 130 miles, while the British laid 15,000 on the two wings. The mines were laid at three depths at hundred-yard intervals and it was reckoned to hold up a submarine for one to three hours.

It was undoubtedly one of the technical wonders of the war and, at a cost of $80 million, was a monument to American financial muscle. It had two gaps, one 3-mile gap to the east of the Orkneys for British ships and another 3-mile gap in Norwegian territorial waters. As Britain knew of the German use of the latter, there was a demand for Norwegian interference but the world of diplomacy moves slowly and the war ended before the demand could be met.

The barrage could also be breached if the submarines went deep but this put pressure on the captains and their navigation. It cost the Germans little in losses, with only three confirmed with another three probable, which was minimal compared with the losses from convoy escorts. With only six U-boat losses at the very most, the barrage could not be said to be cost-effective but there was no doubt it was a major psychological barrier. The Germans hated the mines, which faced them going out and coming in, and it undoubtedly lowered their offensive efficiency because it took time to circumvent. Roosevelt claimed that it helped win the war, which it undoubtedly did, but it is difficult to quantify its significance.

Roosevelt came to England in July 1918 and was treated royally, being the first American of his rank to visit since the United States had entered the war. Balfour persuaded him to intervene with Italy so that its navy would go into action under the British. He rejoiced that the marines had gone into action and repelled the Germans at Château-Thierry, which he subsequently visited, and was also received by Clemenceau.

Roosevelt went everywhere, from Verdun to submarine bases in the Bay of Biscay, to the Firth of Forth to see the Grand Fleet and then on to his North Sea mine barrage. He went to Rome and used his persuasive powers on the indolent Italian navy, which did not want action, forging an agreed unified command. He reported this back to Daniels, who was unimpressed

The Allies Strike Back | 169

and reprimanded him for overreaching himself. This deflated him.

Having seen the war at first hand, Roosevelt became eager for action, so he returned to the United States and entered the navy. First, however, he caught the dreaded flu, being susceptible to bugs all through his life, despite being a man of fine physique. Luckily for the world he recovered but the war was drawing to a close and his hopes of active service had been thwarted. He had experienced a lot and seen war in all its complexity.

The End

The Allied strategy in the west was to break through the Hindenburg Line and, if possible, end the war in 1918, although there was no great optimism that this would happen. The two main thrusts, planned for 26 and 27 September, were for the Americans and the French to attack towards Mézières, while the British attacked on the Saint Quentin–Cambrai line. The Franco–American attack had more than a 3:1 superiority in numbers, while Germany had perhaps a numerical superiority in the north.

As it happened, the British with two American divisions had broken through in the north by 5 October but could not follow through decisively. Although the Germans had been pushed back, they held on and their appeal on 3 October to President Wilson for an armistice seemed premature. But at home Germany was crumbling and there were now over two million Americans in Europe eager for action.

On 23 October Wilson asked for unconditional surrender, although Germany did not interpret it that way. On 26 October Ludendorff resigned and, with the Austro-Hungarian Empire disintegrating, Germany hardly had an ally. Everything on Germany's side was now breaking up, its navy refused to fight and its rebellion was not put down. Revolution was in the air and, once the kaiser had abdicated and like the tsar brought down his own throne, the socialists took over. Peace came on 11 November 1918.

Germany had one bargaining tool, its army in the west. It had retreated in good order and was still a formidable force that the Allied commanders respected but it had been beaten by modern warfare, methods it would hijack for the next conflict. It had been beaten industrially by the production of tanks, aeroplanes and other munitions, and it had been beaten because the Allies were not hungry and the Germans were. The blockade had taken a terrible toll and, as a nation, Germany just did not have enough food.

It is said that 250,000 Germans died of hunger in 1917, then in 1918 it was worse. The blockade was not removed until Germany signed the peace treaty in 1919. By the end of the blockade, it was thought that 900,000 of those most vulnerable had died of hunger and malnutrition. As this was the objective of the submarine war against Britain, few wept about it there, nor did they weep about it in France, which, unlike Germany, was physically scarred by the war.

The blockade and its effect was a terrible event for Germany, arguably worse than the bombing in the next conflict. The Germans had also been beaten in the field by the products of industrialisation: the concentration of tanks to form a *schwerpunkt*; the control of the air to strafe and bomb the enemy and to supply intelligence; the selective use of artillery to knock out the enemy's artillery and to hinder movement; the use of camouflage, disguise and other stratagems to fool the enemy and produce surprise.

These were the Allied keys to victory, best exemplified in the British army, which briefly had become the most potent and effective in the world, a title it would never have in the next big war. Through muddle and ineptitude, which was the lot of all armies in the Great War, it had found the key to modern warfare and it would be unjust if its commander, Douglas Haig, who had undoubtedly made mistakes was not given his due deserts.

Haig, Lloyd George, Foch, Pétain and Clemenceau

The awful casualties suffered in this war profoundly affected all participant nations. Patriotism can never override grief – it can only modify it. In coming to terms with grief there is always the blame factor and in history this can continue for centuries. A seemingly incompetent politician or general can easily be targeted, justly or unjustly.

The First World War was a series of events that impinged on each other. Nothing was isolated and, although Germany led the Central Powers, the Fatherland was part of an alliance that had to stick together as a coherent whole. The same was true of the Allies. Nor were the fronts isolated; each affected the other. The Eastern and Western Fronts were interacting with each other and the defeat of Russia was a terrible blow to the Allies. The Italian front, which was at one time a straight fight between the Italians and the Austro-Hungarians, eventually sucked in the France, Britain and Germany. Likewise, the war against Turkey involved all the major combatants. Of those nations that fought throughout the war, Britain, although profoundly affected, suffered the least. Nevertheless, the blame factor was still potent, although not coruscating. The politicians were on the whole well treated, although Churchill, arguably the most creative politician of the war, was the fall guy of the Dardanelles.

There were plenty of generals who were judged not to have the talent for war command at the highest level and their careers were sidelined at the cutting edge. Hamilton, who commanded the army at the Dardanelles, was one of those. At the time he was the only realistic challenger to Haig as commander-in-chief of the British army on the Western Front but his reputation did not recover from the Dardanelles debacle, which was rather unfair as he was not involved in its planning and was only appointed a few weeks before the attack.

Most of the faults levelled at Haig are justified; it is how they are weighted that must be considered. The debacle of the first day of the Somme was awful but the German defence was brilliant in digging deep into the chalkland, thus being able to survive the murderous artillery barrage. The idea that the British could walk into the first line of trenches with their heavy packs was presumptuous but the lesson was learned immediately. The attack had to continue to lighten the French burden at Verdun, so tactics were changed to increase effectiveness and lower casualties. And at the Somme the first tanks were used in warfare.

Haig and his commanders were learning and modifying. Likewise, Haig the cavalryman has been criticised for his support of the cavalry arm, which was hardly a factor on the Western Front in four years of war but it was certainly a factor in Palestine and on the Eastern Front. If warfare had been more mobile in the west it could have been a factor. Haig's critics have justly questioned his intelligence appreciations. At the beginning of the war he was over-optimistic; during the latter part of the war his intelligence information was said to be faulty, leading to optimistic predictions at Third Ypres. Nevertheless, many of his prognostications during the war were perspicacious.

Haig should be compared with his peers on either side. The German professional soldier in high command was usually of high calibre but they did not see the potential of the tank, which was placed under their noses in 1916, much to Churchill's consternation. Haig, on the other hand, saw its potential and was unwavering in its support and development.

It was the same with the aeroplane. From the first tentative reconnaissance role in directing artillery fire and locating troop concentrations in 1914 to the bombing and strafing to gain air superiority in 1918, Haig was supportive. He had very cordial relations with Trenchard and, although initially they both opposed it, in the end they supported the formation of the Royal Air Force as a separate entity in 1918, which had immense implications for the future.

The British army and air force worked in harmony and with effectiveness during the war, which is to Haig's credit. He has been criticised for his use of artillery, and this war was primarily an artillery war, but he learned throughout the conflict and became more subtle in its use, with the prime aim being the eradication of the enemy's artillery and garnering the intelligence that enabled his gunners to do this.

Haig believed in victory and was unwavering in its pursuit as a model professional soldier. His relationship with the French was ambivalent. He had no high opinion of the French army and was contemptuous of its rebellion in 1917. His opinion was summed up by a diary entry of 22 August 1916, when the French were tired by the attrition of Verdun and had sent less than top-quality divisions to help the British on the Somme: 'A return compiled by my Intelligence Branch shows that whereas a German Division is worn out in four and a half days opposite the British, opposite the French they last much longer, sometimes three weeks.'[14]

He continued to be disparaging of French martial prowess to the end, only partially justified. He respected Foch and, although he had no wish to be subordinate to him, accepted this role with good grace and worked well with him. However, he regarded Pétain as defeatist. Pétain was a genuine French national hero, the victor of Verdun who had come to the rescue of the British during the retreat in the spring of 1918 and had won a partial victory over the Germans at the Chemin des Dames in the summer, but Haig perceived his weakness. Pétain did not have the bulldog virtues that could pursue victory when facing the prospect of defeat, which was revealed by his pessimism when the Germans broke through in 1918.

Lloyd George was not a fan of Haig but never had the courage to replace him. Lloyd George understood that the casualties endured were breaking nations, so he tried to control the bloodletting and to stop the winning of the war through attrition. He knew that the Allies had the whip hand, especially with American help, and reckoned that they should wait until they could use overwhelming force. Churchill supported him in this but time and tide wait for no man and the war had a natural momentum of its own. If the British had not fought with such tenacity at Ypres and Cambrai, both of which were hardly successful battles in territorial terms, then Italy might have been forced out of the war. Certainly, the killing on the Italian front would have increased.

Peace was in the hands of the politicians and the permutations of peace were manifold. On the Allied side, in September 1917, Britain was the lynchpin with its navy, helped by the Americans, strangling the Germans through blockade, while Germany's attempt to blockade Britain had been countered. On land the crucial battles were being fought in Flanders. There was a feeling that peace could come at any time but how was the big conundrum. It was thought that Russia might sue for peace, which it soon did; Italy might capitulate, which it could have done without Allied help; and France might also seek peace, which it had done in the 1870s and would do 23 years later. It was also felt that there was a case for Britain getting out of Flanders and letting the navy bring Germany to its knees.

That September a German peace offer did come to the Allies, offering a return to the 1914 boundaries in the west and the Balkans, provided that Germany could do what it liked in the east. This was discussed in high secrecy but was rejected, as Germany would dominate Europe as it had never done before. Haig was privy to this and, in March 1918, he thought Germany's offer was reasonable but it had also redoubled his determination to try to get a result at Ypres.

Haig's relationship with Lloyd George was difficult. Haig bottled his emotions and paraded a stiff upper lip, while Lloyd George was mercurial and emotional. His genius was revealed by the spoken word, which gave him mastery of his contemporaries. In a group of people he was a positive stimulus who could enhance the contribution of individuals and creatively bring everything to a conclusion.

Lloyd George undoubtedly exists in the pantheon of great British prime ministers. He was a successful chancellor of the exchequer, an energetic and creative minister of munitions and he won the war as prime minister. He was creatively chaotic as an administrator but the civil servants could sort the chaos. Yet there was something lacking in Lloyd George, which Haig revealed. He labelled two of his most important contemporaries as defeatist and, in the end, he was to be proved right. During the Second World War, Pétain was the arch defeatist and Lloyd George was labelled Britain's Pétain.

The blame that is still attached to Haig for the bloodbath of the Great War is because of a British misconception that this war was a greater bloodbath than the Second World War. In general terms, the number of dead in the 1939–45 war greatly exceeded the dead in the 1914–18 war in the rough ratio of 3:1. For the British, however, the rough ratio is 2:3. Thus, the British perception is that the longer second war was much more economical and sensible in the number of lives lost. Apart from Turkey, which was neutral in the second conflict, and France, which was traumatically beaten within a few weeks, this did not pertain to any other nation of importance. To this day, Haig is the maladroit commander who spilt the blood of his nation in an incompetent way. In the context of the First World War this was nonsense. Verdun was by far the worst bloodbath and the French, Germans, Russians,

Austro-Hungarians and Turks had far greater casualties per head of population.

The German breakthrough in March 1918 was through the British line, which they had attenuated and not properly manned. It was a compliment to the merit of the German army but the British had few tanks, they could not move their artillery quickly enough and they lost air superiority. By August and the start of the Hundred Days on 8 August, Haig, although under Foch's overall command, pushed his way forward in a way that the Germans would imitate in 1940. There were many progenitors of modern warfare but Haig was the first chief progenitor. Because of this he lays claim to be the ablest and most successful army commander of the war.

Foch must not be ignored, because he too was successful. He was highly intelligent and his writing had influenced Haig before the war. Haig conducted staff rides, which were field exercises without troops but with the issuing of orders, and during these exercises he would quote from Foch. It is surprising that Foch did not rise to supreme command more quickly as he was a successful commander in the early part of the war but became unstuck as the commander of an army group on the Somme when Joffre was sacked.

Pétain became the great figure in the French army and, in May 1917, Foch became his chief of staff. In the spring of 1918 he leapfrogged Pétain to become the Allies' commander-in-chief. He did not stand on ceremony, was down to earth in his dealings with all men and he knitted the alliance together without fuss. Rawlinson, who had worked with him on the Somme, thought he had learned and developed since that time and enjoyed being subordinated to him. At the political level, Lloyd George had confidence in Foch, the diplomatic general par excellence, but he also had a powerful strategic sense that enabled men of high standing to hide or jettison petty jealousies or partial views for the common cause. Sometimes he had difficulty in communicating with people and had an important alter ego in Weygand, his chief of staff, who could interpret his various gestures and taciturnity. Foch's weakness was the weakness of the French army, which by 1918 had only partially recovered its strength. Despite his success as Allied leader, he was intensely French and knew little of the rest of the world. His hopes and fears centred on the Rhine, which he regarded as the river of life and death. He believed in absolute victory over Germany and the concessions that were to come in the peace treaty made him apoplectic.

The revival of France as a potent military force owed much to Clemenceau as well as Foch. France underused Clemenceau's talents before 1917 but he then became the man of the moment and rejuvenated the country.

Clemenceau wanted victory and would pursue it resolutely. Apart from putting Caillaux in prison, anti-war protestors were arrested and tried and traitors executed. Although he was seventy-six, Clemenceau was full of energy and in Foch and Pétain he had two great commanders with different gifts. They repulsed the Germans at the Chemin des Dames, which triggered the British successes in the Hundred Days and the supporting actions of the Americans, who were about to become a dominant force.

The actions on the Western Front led to Germany forsaking the Balkans and the predominantly French forces caused Bulgaria to surrender, thus enhancing the reputation of General Franchet d'Espèrey. The soft underbelly of Europe had been exposed and Germany knew that whatever happened on the Western Front, the Austro-Hungarian Empire had become vulnerable. At the political level, Lloyd George and Clemenceau respected each other but Clemenceau did not have the rift with his generals that afflicted Lloyd George, who was constantly intriguing against both Robertson and Haig.

It had started with Lloyd George's backing of Nivelle, which had misfired, and continued with the formation of the Supreme War Council, where the heads of government and the military liaised. It had an advisory, predominantly strategic function and was rife with political rivalries and expediencies. Likewise, Lloyd George used General Henry Wilson to offset the influence of Robertson and Haig, who were the effective commanders of the British army. This enabled the Council to make a major strategic decision to the liking of Lloyd George in that the Allies would act defensively in France and Italy during 1918 but attack in the Middle East. The only condition was that no troops were to be diverted from France and Italy. Neither the French nor the British commanders agreed with this, although Clemenceau was not against it as long as the manpower condition was met.

Now that Germany was threatening to have a majority of front line troops in the west as Russians crumbled, manpower was becoming a crucial factor. France wished to release older soldiers and to reduce its line. Clemenceau reckoned that this would hinder Britain's ambitions in the Middle East as it would need extra manpower to fill its line. Lloyd George, on the other hand, was keen on the extension of the line, as it would keep Haig on the defensive through lack of manpower.

Haig and Pétain came to an agreement that the British would extend their line by 25 miles to just south of the Oise, with the proviso that if the British 5th Army was attacked in the south, the French would come to the rescue with six divisions and the British would reciprocate if the French were attacked. Having extended the line with British troops, Haig found that his command was too attenuated and statistics were bandied to and fro as proof. In fact, the total number of troops had increased over the previous year but the number of combat troops had declined by 4 per cent. This led to an investigation as to whether an investment in tanks and other life-saving technology would mitigate the manpower crisis. This was plausible but difficult to quantify. The waging of war had become very complex.

Another major recommendation from the Supreme War Council was the Allied General Reserve. The governments concerned agreed that Foch should control a reserve of thirty divisions to cover the Western, Italian and Macedonian fronts. Haig and Pétain opposed this, as expected, but the upshot was that Haig became estranged from Robertson, whom he thought was not giving enough support to the Western Front. In Haig's opinion, this was the decisive front. Lloyd George was not with him on this and took the opportunity to get rid of Robertson and replace him with Henry Wilson. Haig threatened to resign rather than have his troops siphoned off into a general reserve, and Pétain supported him. Foch was furious but Clemenceau would not intervene and the idea of the general reserve collapsed. In the end Haig was vindicated. Although all the other fronts collapsed before the Western Front, this was because the Germans could no longer support these fronts.

So the Great War seemingly came to an end but it proved not to be the war to end all wars. Its end excited the imagination of the defeated, the members of a warrior tribe of great ability whose honour had been sullied and who were determined to retrieve that honour. They would not acknowledge that the war was of their own making, certainly not in the east where they had a good case. Many Germans thought they had not been beaten but stabbed in the back by irresolution in the Fatherland. This was far from the truth and led inexorably to another conflagration.

In Flanders Fields

In Flanders fields the poppies blow
Between the crosses, row on row
That marks our place; and in the sky

The larks, still bravely singing, fly
Scarce heard amid the guns below.
We are the Dead, short days ago,
We lived, felt dawn, saw sunset glow,
Loved and were loved, and now we lie
In Flanders fields.

Take up your quarrel with the foe:
To you from failing hands we throw
The torch; be yours to hold it high
If you break faith with us who die
We shall not sleep though poppies grow
In Flanders fields.

John McCrae

Chapter 11

The Peace Conference

Introduction

Soon, very soon, too soon, the victors convened the peace conference in Paris. Of all the meetings of politicians and statesmen in the twentieth century, this would be the greatest, most comprehensive, most profound in its consequences, and its reverberations are still felt.

President Woodrow Wilson was the inspiration behind the conference and the core of his belief resided in the nation state and its formation through ethnic, religious, cultural and historical ties. The creation of nation states from the breakdown of empires, known as self-determination, was simple in some cases but exceedingly complex in others. In a sense, it was a strange kind of idealism to be initiated by someone from the United States, for that empire was not very interested in the ethnic, religious, cultural or historical ties of its inhabitants and would not tolerate self-determination for any separatist group. However, in Wilson's idealism these nations would come together in a forum to resolve disputes and thus enable the nations to live in harmony. These were the two great pillars of the new world order: self-determination and a league of nations.

The war had badly destabilised Europe. In the west there were victors and neutral countries, in the centre there were the defeated Germany and Austro-Hungarian Empire, while further east the Russian Empire, although allied to the victors in the west, had been defeated, made a disadvantageous peace treaty and was in the throes of civil war. Turkey was also part of a defeated empire, and its peripheral parts were in thrall to the ideas of self-determination. Even the British Empire was not immune, as the Irish continued to negotiate for an independent state that would soon come into being, while India, the jewel in the crown, was also stirring.

It was Woodrow Wilson's Fourteen Points that helped to guide Germany to an armistice and in which he had expressed his idealism. Many of the points were straightforward and not contentious: the demand that Germany leave Belgium and France; the return of Alsace and Lorraine to reward France; Italy to gain some Austrian territory in the Adriatic; the Treaty of Brest-Litovsk between Russia and Germany was void and Russia regained much of its lost territory. There were few quibbles about the formation of nation states in the Austro-Hungarian and Ottoman empires, although the precise borders were difficult. The creation of Poland as a sovereign state between Germany and Russia did not have natural borders. There were other points with which most nations agreed, such as open diplomacy, free trade and freedom of navigation in peace and war. Crowning it all was the formation of a league of nations.

Germany felt that it could live with this, although it was plain that it had been defeated. Nevertheless, the end of the Great War was described as an armistice and, because of this, Germany felt it had certain rights in negotiations, which would not have been so if the war had ended in unconditional surrender. It was not long before Germany discovered that the armistice was a euphemism for unconditional surrender, but not only that. Because of the Austro-Hungarian Empire's collapse into its component parts, the burden of paying for the war would fall upon Germany. Turkey was in a similar position to Austria but Germany, the great powerhouse of central Europe, was reasonably intact and was thought to have the ability to pay for the war.

This was how France and, to a lesser extent, Britain saw it. For France, the war had been costly and it needed compensation, quite apart from the necessity of breaking Germany's power. The war in the west had been fought predominantly on French territory. France had lost 20 per cent of its fertile land, while 90 per cent of its iron mines and 65 per cent of its steel production had been made useless.

The scar that had disfigured France was ugly and raw and, whenever the enemy delegates came to Paris, the French drove the train at a snail's pace through the ravaged areas. France was a debtor nation and even more in debt because it was a creditor to the Bolsheviks. Even Britain, which was a creditor nation, became a debtor because of communism, which refused to pay back what it owed. Only the United States was a true creditor nation. To alleviate their position, the debtor nations needed Germany to pay for the war.

Prime Minister Georges Clemenceau of France had been a young man at the end of the Franco–Prussian War. He had witnessed the loss of Alsace-

Lorraine and the financial reparation of the equivalent of £200 million to pay for the war, leading to the dwindling of France's power over the next forty-eight years. His aim at the peace conference was to reverse this and stop German imperialism on the European mainland. Britain, likewise, wanted to prevent German imperialism overseas by emasculating Germany's merchant marine, taking away its colonies and accepting the ships of its navy. Britain also wanted financial settlement but France was, with justification, more strident in its demand for financial compensation. Then there were other nations, such as Belgium, that had claims.

The peace conference came at a bad psychological moment. Lloyd George had already had an election and the inevitable anger against Germany had spilled over into vengeance. He had not wanted Germany humiliated but, always the politician, he had to acknowledge overwhelming public opinion, which wanted its pound of flesh. He was pushed firmly into the Clemenceau camp.

Structure of the Council

In the early part of 1919, an enormous number of representatives assembled in Paris from nations small and large and from those as yet unformed. They thought they might be able to influence the titans who controlled the peace conference. At first, there was a Council of Ten, which contained the leaders and foreign secretaries of the five great victorious powers: the United States, Britain, France, Italy and Japan. Britain represented its empire in all its diversity. Australia and New Zealand had interests in the Pacific, and South Africa in its region of Africa. India, although part of the empire, had representatives of its own, while T.E. Lawrence accompanied the Arab representatives in their quest for self-determination.

Although Japan had played little part in the war, its navy had helped Britain, who mediated Japan's position at the top table through a common treaty. However, Japan's diplomacy was very low key unless its interests were at stake. As time went on, the Council of Ten was unwieldy, so in March a Council of Four was formed, excluding Japan and all foreign secretaries. These foreign secretaries formed a second tier, which was how important decisions were henceforth taken.

Poland

Poland had not existed as a nation since 1795 but the Poles had no doubts they existed as an ethnic group and as such formed a natural nation. There were many points of contention, the most obvious being that the ethnic Poles were scattered, a big Polish nation would have many non-Poles and a small Polish nation would exclude many Poles.

Of course, there could be a compromise but the ethnic Poles had been divided between three great powers: Russia, Germany and the Austro-Hungarians. Three million Poles lived in Germany and had become increasingly German, others lived poorly in Galicia under the Austro-Hungarians and many emigrated to the United States because of their poverty. The majority of Poles, however, had lived under Russian rule. A Polish nation would be a miscellany but what they wanted was an economically viable nation of ethnic Poles that would, if possible, have coal, iron ore, steel mills and control of a port.

They had found a leader in Josef Pilsudski, who was born in Vilnius (then Russian, now in Lithuania) and had fought against the Allies in the war. This was characteristic of this part of Europe, where loyalties were mixed. There were large Jewish populations but in towns with many ethnic Poles they felt Polish as well as Jewish. The Poles were predominantly Catholic but there was a big Protestant enclave in East Prussia with strong German loyalties. Likewise, some Lithuanians felt Polish but most were strong Lithuanian nationalists.

There were endless potential problems in creating a nation. Rivers, lakes and railways were, if possible, kept in one country, but there was no port that could be construed as Polish, although they wanted Danzig. It was at the mouth of the Vistula but was 90 per cent German, although surrounded by Poles in its hinterland. Before the 1790s it had been a free city under Polish rule. This was not the only problem. Silesia covered an area of 4,200 square miles, with coal and iron mines, productive steel mills and other mineral deposits. It was 65 per cent Polish speaking but was the product of German industry and capital, producing 25 per cent of Germany's coal, 81 per cent of its zinc and 34 per cent of its lead. Germany would be in great economic trouble if it lost Upper Silesia and the Saar.

The problems of Poland fully tested the leaders at the peace conference. Lloyd George was sympathetic to Poland, understood its problems but was its biggest critic. Clemenceau wanted to give Danzig to the Poles and was keen on its role as a buffer state, while Wilson was obviously worried by the breaching of the principle of self-determination. It would take time for the peace conference to decide over Poland if it were to make a just decision. Wilson tried to resolve the problem in Silesia through a plebiscite, which only resulted in ambivalence as the result varied in different areas. The resolution of the problem was given to four minor powers, who returned 70 per cent of the area to Germany but gave the majority of the industries and mines to Poland.

Because of the fighting in Russia and the doubtful legitimacy of any government, Poland's eastern and north-eastern borders became a nightmare. The Baltic states were in chaos as they tried to become independent, with Russia trying to retain control, while a German army was still active. The victor's writ was not working here and the victors took the view that they should not intervene in Russian affairs. Nevertheless, they did produce a border called the Curzon Line but this did not satisfy the Poles, who found many of their ethnic brothers on the wrong side of the border. The Poles were combative and fighting the Bolsheviks. The peace conference called for a truce as the Poles captured swathes of Belarus territory.

This did not provide a solution, as the fighting continued, mainly in Ukraine, whose people were treated as part of Russia and were ignored by the peace conference. The Bolsheviks rallied as the Polish effort became attenuated; by August 1920 they had pushed the Poles back to Warsaw. This, in turn, unified the Poles, with Pilsudski organising successful attacks on the Bolshevik supply lines, causing the Russians to retreat. The following month Lenin asked for peace. In the Treaty of Riga the Poles received a border well to the east of what the peacemakers at Versailles would have given them. There were four million Ukrainians, two million Jews and one million Byelorussians in this area.

There were inevitable problems in the former Austrian province of Galicia. Czechoslovakia claimed the Duchy of Teschen, while many other towns were Polish but their hinterland was not. For example, Lvov's hinterland was one-third Polish, with 14 per cent Jews, who might or might not consider themselves Polish. The majority were Catholic Ukrainians, who had strong links with their Orthodox Ukrainian brethren and, through history, with the Hapsburgs.

The problems with Poland were intractable. Lloyd George wanted a settlement that Russia and Germany would both accept as just and he did not have high hopes that Poland would survive as a nation. Danzig was made a free port with a customs union with Poland. In 1920 the Bolsheviks gave Vilna (Vilnius) to Lithuania but the Poles took over the city. Two years later a plebiscite was held and there was a large majority for the Poles. Lithuania then seized the port of Memel, which was 92 per cent German, and so it went on. Poland was surrounded by enemies who had a vested interest in territory. This involved Lithuania (Vilna), Russia (ceded territory that it had ruled), Germany (Danzig and Silesia) and Czechoslovakia (Teschen). This new nation was a powder keg.

Czechoslovakia

The story of Czechoslovakia also had its complexities, its roots being deep in the history of Europe. The Czechs and Slovaks had links through language and race but their history had differences. Bohemia had grown grand and imperial until the seventeenth century when the Hapsburgs took control, while the Slovaks had been under Hungarian control for centuries and remained so in the Austro-Hungarian Empire. The Czechs became largely Protestant at the Reformation, while the Slovaks remained Catholic. The racial bond was the strongest link and the new nation was looking for Russian protection as fellow Slavs.

In 1917, Thomas Masaryk went to Petrograd and persuaded the provisional government to release the Czech prisoners of war and use them to fight the Austrians. The Czech Legion was 50,000 strong, so the Bolsheviks, after taking power, wanted to get rid of them, suggesting they fought on the Western Front. They would get there via Vladivostok, then by boat to France. In the chaos that was Russia, they clashed with the Hungarians, who were supporting the Bolsheviks, which led to the Czechs opposing the Bolsheviks. The war in the west was coming to an end and there was little reason for the Czechs to go there, even if it was via the east, but in the most bizarre of circumstances they found themselves in control of most of the Trans-Siberian Railway and the gold reserves of tsarist Russia.

Like the Poles, the Czechoslovaks wanted a coherent and defensible border and lobbied hard at the peace conference for portions of Poland, Hungary, Austria and Germany. A mere footnote of interest were two requests: they asked for a substantial settlement of Czechs near Dresden to be incorporated into the new nation and a tongue of land that would enable Czechoslovak Slavs to be linked with the Yugoslavs. Both suggestions provided an insight into the minds of nation formers but did not influence the peacemakers.

The new nation was a nightmare as far as self-determination on a racial basis was concerned, as there were three million Germans in this state. The dangers and seeming injustice of this was recognised but Czechoslovakia used Switzerland as its model and pointed out that the Sudeten Germans had never been a part of Germany in their long history and to add the crescent they occupied to Austria would produce the oddest-shaped nation in history. When Hungary turned communist, Czechoslovakia tried to add to its territory but the Hungarians soon rejected communism, although Czechoslovakia did manage to annex Bratislava, a predominantly German town on the Danube.

Austria

Austria was now a state of twelve million souls stripped of empire but with a grand capital in Vienna. Small and vulnerable, its thoughts turned to links with Germany. This was known as Anschluss and appealed to socialists, as the link would be with socialist Germany. The peacemakers in France were against this as it would add to German power and territory.

It worried Wilson that Austria would not be subject to self-determination but, as the conference ensued, the demand for Anschluss waned. Clemenceau and Lloyd George wanted some provision that would prevent Germany linking with Austria, so Lloyd George found a political compromise. It was agreed that a merger could take place if the League of Nations agreed. As it had to be unanimous, this gave certain nations, such as Britain and France, a veto. Like everywhere else in Europe, ethnic anomalies abounded and Austria lost control of German-speaking communities in Slovenia, Hungary and Czechoslovakia.

Hungary

Hungary's border with Romania was exceptionally contentious and the peacemakers did not know what to do about it. France and Italy favoured Romania, while the Anglo-Saxons supported Hungary. Although defeated, Romania had been on the side of the Allies, so demanded favours, especially as Hungary had a communist regime, which led Romania occupying Budapest. While the peacemakers tried to unravel this imbroglio, Hungary had representatives at the peace conference who eloquently presented their case but with little success. In June 1920, with Hungary a defeated nation, its representatives were forced to sign an agreement that ceded Transylvania to Romania. Flags in Hungary flew at half mast, creating bitterness that has never been assuaged, because even with the vicissitudes of the next German war and Russian overlordship, the boundaries remain the same.

Italy Decamps

There was a spring break at the peace conference but by April 1919 everything was coming to a head and was ripe for resolution. Horse trading and stormy meetings were resolving the terms to be dictated to Germany, with France having to compromise with the Anglo-Saxons but getting, in essence, what it wanted. The strain was beginning to tell but Clemenceau got as good a deal as could be expected for France.

It was Italy that cracked. Although one of the big four, it was not in a strong position, being a debtor nation of $700 million, which was manageable for a strong economy but Italy was weak industrially and suffering from bad inflation. In addition, it had fought a patchy war on land and a weak one at sea, although it was a victor and Britain and France had inveigled it into the war with promises that had treaty status – the Treaty of London. The United States refused to acknowledge this as it was not a party to it, which caused a monumental problem.

Italy had new territorial ambitions in Africa (Abyssinia and parts of Somalia and Kenya), parts of Turkey and its adjacent islands, and parts of the Adriatic coast and hinterland. On this Adriatic coast was Fiume, which Hungary used as its port on the Adriatic. Its ethnic make-up was a few Hungarians, a larger group of middle-class Italians and a Croat working class. In Fiume itself, the Italians were in a majority but, if its close environs were included, the Croats were the majority.

Wilson's self-determination would not allow Fiume to go to Italy. He had already made over a part of the Tyrol, where the Germans were in a majority, but which was contiguous to Italy. Italian Prime Minister Orlando, who got on well with Wilson, was driven on by patriotic fervour from home, then a flamboyant leader appeared who, with flowery rhetoric, whipped the Italians into a frenzy. D'Annunzio was brave, a war hero and adored by the Italians, including Mussolini, who observed and learned from him.

The others in the Council of Four recognised the Italian connection with Fiume but felt it should be a free port like Danzig but Orlando would not accept this. He demanded that the Treaty of London should be acknowledged and Fiume should become Italian. To appease Italy it was offered islands on the Dalmatian coast, with the ports remaining free, but Yugoslavia intervened and said it would fight for Fiume. The whole matter became so inflamed that Italy said that it would not sign the peace treaty without Fiume.

There was a crisis among the Allies. If Italy walked out, Japan might follow. The interpretations of self-determination were burning a hole in the peace treaty. Wilson agonised over the problem of Danzig and the Tyrol, where he knew there were anomalies. Orlando went back to Italy to get a vote of confidence and received the plaudits of his people, who sneered at Allied treachery. It did not change matters; the three most powerful leaders were obdurate and Italy left the conference.

Japan

Japan had taken part in the war and was keen to collect German possessions and concessions in China and the Pacific. Island groups such as the Marshalls, the Carolinas and the Marianas were conceded to Japan but the United States and Australia were watching developments carefully. Japan was justifiably one of the big five nations, certainly with its powerful armed forces and positive economy making it a greater power than Italy and not inferior to France; however, it played little part in the peace proceedings except when its interests were at stake. Its representation at the conference was led by Prince Saionji, a cultivated and experienced statesman, educated for ten years in France, who rarely appeared but operated behind the scenes. In consequence, Japan made little fuss when the Council of Ten was whittled down to four. It was still included at the next tier of decision-making.

Japan had not backed the Allies out of any ideological fervour but out of pragmatic self-interest. Apart from the Pacific Islands, it saw an opportunity to capture German concessions on the Shantung peninsula of China. Germany had developed the area, including the port of Tsingtao, with a great deal of money and sensitivity to Chinese nationalism and willingly allowed the port to be subject to Chinese customs. Early in the war Japan had taken over the German concessions but did it in a way that incurred China's wrath. This was followed by diplomatic ineptitude through making twenty-one demands that would have made China a Japanese protectorate, so despite their political weakness, the Chinese rejected them. Japan back-pedalled and concentrated on the Shantung concession, demanding it remained Japanese ad infinitum.

At the peace conference, the Shantung concession cut across Wilson's ideas of self-determination but the Japanese knew this and were subtle in their approach. Their major objective was to get a clause of racial equality written into the covenant of the League of Nations. Japan was acknowledged as a world power but without the same rights as others in being able to move around the world. The Japanese were not allowed into the British dominions and they had limited rights in California, such as the right to buy or lease land or to take their wives to live with them. Acknowledging the problem, the

Japanese said they would limit emigration but no rights were conceded.

The United States, Canada and Australia continued to oppose the racial equality clause but, overall, the leaders at the conference were unhappy at the implications. Australian Prime Minister Billy Hughes hated the Japanese for their manners and seeming obsequiousness, while the Japanese found him rather rough-hewn. It was a case of mutual cultural incomprehension. The Japanese pressed for the clause but Wilson, even if he wanted to, knew the west coast politicians would have none of it and he needed their help to get the founding of the League of Nations through Congress. The Japanese decided to concede on this point but they wanted a quid pro quo in the acknowledgement of their right to the Shantung peninsula.

China

China had also taken part in the war on the Allied side, sending 100,000 men to France to dig and maintain trenches, thus releasing soldiers to fight. Many Chinese died on the front line, so when peace came there was rejoicing in China. Wilson's Fourteen Points, with their emphasis on self-determination, struck a chord with China's intelligentsia, who looked forward to their nation being freed from foreign influence. The trouble was that this vast country did not have strong unified leadership and Japan covetously eyed the vacuum.

The weak Chinese leadership had signed a defence treaty with Japan before the war had ended, including an exchange of notes regularising Japan's position on the Shantung peninsula. The peace conference discussed this early on but made no decision, which did not look good for China. The subject came up again in late April when the Italian crisis over Fiume was raging and the principle of self-determination was paramount. The Chinese representatives seized upon this and, after the Japanese had presented their case, put forward China's, leading to deadlock. Italy had already left the conference, so if Japan left, as it threatened to do because of the racial equality clause, the peace proposals would not have much backing.

Wilson appealed to Japanese altruism, telling them it would be for the good of Asia if Japan left Shantung, but this appeal fell on stony ground. The Chinese pitched in and said that if this sort of thing continued, they might link up with Japan, have Asia for the Asians and take away all European concessions. Britain, which had always supported Japan and owed it a debt for its naval help during the war, feared its increasing power but was still supportive.

It was the Japanese who suggested to Balfour that a deal could be done. If

Japan's claim to Shantung was recognised, the racial equality clause could be left out in the founding of the League of Nations. To Wilson, the founding of the League was of supreme importance. Without Italy and Japan it would be a weak institution. Thus, he compromised. When the news broke, all the idealism that had been engendered in China was squandered and the students demonstrated in Peking.

There was another effect, as China was holding a national peace conference in Shanghai to reconcile north and south China. The meeting broke up in anger as the south demanded the rejection of the arguments made on Shantung and demanded its return to China. Such feeling may have been an excuse to break up the meeting but the failure of reconciliation further weakened the country. It was very apparent that Japan had ambitions in China.

The Ottoman Empire

The Ottoman Empire, a truly great empire in world history, straddled Europe, Asia and Africa. It had been in retreat in Europe before the war and was defeated in the Middle East during it. However, its people had great hopes in Wilson's idealism. Britain set rigorous armistice terms with the Ottoman Empire, which caused a rift with Turkey that would become increasingly serious. On the other hand, Sultan Mehmet VI, whose rule was weak, wished to accept the terms. However, many nationalists opposed him and created a power base from which Kemal Atatürk, the remarkably successful army commander, emerged. He was a complex character who rejected Islam, hated its fanaticism and found in the army the stepping stone to power. It was he who would determine the future of Turkey but the rest of the defunct empire was up for grabs.

Turkey may have held hopes in American idealism but the United States had never declared war against the Ottomans and had little interest in the future of the region. France had historical interests but it was predominantly the British Empire that had broken the Ottomans and it was not prepared for France to become an equal power in the region.

New nations were going to be formed from the provinces or districts of the Ottoman Empire where nations had never existed and they evolved from the United States' dislike of colonial government. The League of Nations gave mandates whereby it would have trusteeship of a new embryo nation, although there was a strong case for creating independent nations.

British interest revolved around guarding the Suez Canal and recognising the importance of oil in the modern economy. At this time, it was thought that Mesopotamia had the world's largest oil reserves. France also recognised the area's importance and lobbied hard for influence but Clemenceau was prepared to bargain away parity in the Middle East for Britain's support for reparations and annexations in Europe.

There were other factors in the equation. Russia had always coveted Constantinople, the straits and the Turkish provinces bordering the Caucasus. Britain and France had been in negotiation in 1916 (Sykes and Picot) about the breaking up of the Ottoman Empire and had agreed with Russia that it would have what it wanted. However, when the Bolsheviks signed the Treaty of Brest-Litovsk and made peace with the Central Powers, this was invalidated.

The Bolsheviks still registered their interest, however. The Russian and Ottoman Empires, like most empires, had areas of historical dispute where they were contiguous. Then there were the Ottomans' relations with Greece. The Ottomans had ruled Greece for several centuries but, having been defeated, the Greeks felt it was time to reunite its people with their communities in Asia Minor. As it happened, Greece had produced an able advocate in Venizelos, who charmed the delegates at the peace conference and caused Lloyd George to descend into hollow hyperbole by describing him as the greatest Greek statesman since Pericles. Britain was keen for Greek power to increase in the Mediterranean as a counterweight to other powers such as Italy. Italy and Greece had conflicting interests in Asia Minor and the Dodecanese, while Albania was a nightmare to resolve.

In the Council of Four, Britain and France were pro-Greece, the US neutral, while Italy was understandably against. There was considerable negotiating of the territories, with Italy getting most of Albania, which it was soon to lose as Wilson put his foot down when Italy proved difficult over the peace treaty. Likewise, Italy's influence waned in Asia Minor, although it retained Rhodes.

Venizelos's undoubted ability was a mixed blessing to Greece. Charm and persuasive oratory had to be backed by power and Greece had very little of this. Gains in Albania and Thrace were plausible but a large tract of Asia Minor that was inhabited by Greek communities was too much and had terrible consequences for the Greeks. Symbolic of this was the tale of Smyrna. This was a great port with important railway links to the interior. The building of the railway had attracted Greeks in the nineteenth century and it was thought that more Greeks lived in Smyrna's population of 250,000 than in Athens. Although they had a large percentage of the population in the town, the Greeks also wanted its hinterland, where they were in a distinct minority. The Turks and Italians did not like Greeks on the Turkish mainland and the Turks were not averse to killing a Greek or two to remind them.

In May 1919 the peace conference made a decision that became of great import. It was one that it took quickly, as the Italians were returning on the following day and were to be provided with a fait accompli. Lloyd George, Wilson and Clemenceau had fallen for Venizelos's romantic vision and had encouraged him to send Greek troops to occupy Smyrna, while the British and French would occupy forts that guarded the harbour. Everyone knew what was happening when the plan was put into action. The Turks banged drums during the night, while a Greek Orthodox bishop blessed the troops as they arrived. Greek flags appeared all over the place and, amid Greek rejoicing and Turkish fury, one rifle shot incited another. By the end of the day the death toll was 300 to 400 Turks and 100 Greeks. The Turks on the mainland became fearful, strengthening Atatürk's position.

Although Turkey had been defeated in the war, the Allies did not have much hold on the nation. If necessary, they could probably control Constantinople and keep the sultan as a figurehead. Recognising this, Atatürk retreated to the interior to create a powerful nationalistic force that would fight for Turkish rights. He was a great realist who believed that if the Turks behaved passively they would be finished. He was effectively an outlaw in his own country and was soon forced to resign his commission but he had become the leader of the resistance, dedicated to the integrity of the Turkish homeland and prepared to fight for it.

No one at the peace conference had much clue about Turkey, or little inclination, despite Smyrna, to play power politics with it. Italy's ambitions had been rebuffed and it was now out of the equation. However, the British had to act circumspectly. With millions of Muslims under its suzerainty in India, Britain needed to respect the sultan's position as he was also caliph, so was responsible for the holy shrines of the Muslim world.

Most of Europe was indifferent to Smyrna's fate but certain people viewed the Greek capture of the port as a disgrace. One of them was Curzon, who had great personal knowledge of the region and was acting as Britain's foreign secretary. He was sensitive to Turkish nationalism and of the opinion that the occupation of Smyrna was the greatest mistake made in Paris. He became foreign secretary in October 1919 and was at loggerheads with Lloyd George on this point. However, at this stage he did not have the influence or prestige to put pressure on Lloyd George. But events were moving his way.

Italy, with a change of government, was not interested in Asia Minor, while

Clemenceau became less interested in the Greeks after realising that 60 per cent of the Ottoman debt was owed to France. Atatürk's power was now growing and he had created an alternative capital in Ankara. In March 1920 the Allies took over Constantinople and arrested nationalists. Atatürk responded by creating a parliament in Ankara and arresting as many Allied officers as he could.

Curzon was prepared to recognise a new Turkey under Atatürk but Lloyd George was not. In April there was a conference in San Remo with the Turks but without Atatürk. Turkey was to have Constantinople but the straits would be under international control. France and Italy were to have areas in Anatolia, and Greece would gain Smyrna and Thrace. Armenia would be independent and Kurdistan would be an autonomous authority within Turkey.

By 1920, Bolshevik Russia was the power to the north of Turkey. The White Russians were in disarray and the Turkish nationalists and Bolsheviks agreed to stop Armenia's independence. The Allies did not have the will or the power on the ground to intervene. The Turkish people were scathing about the San Remo Treaty, which helped to unite the people under Atatürk. The Greeks were still acting belligerently in Smyrna and in other parts of Turkey but Venizelos was worried and craved Greek success.

A plan was hatched and in June 1920 Lloyd George approved the capture of territory in Anatolia and Thrace by Greek forces. The Turks retreated and the Greeks moved 250 miles inland. At the same time, the sultan's government signed the Treaty of Sevres, a capitulation that caused the Turkish people to close their shops and fill the mosques in mourning. Atatürk bided his time and negotiated with Russia on Armenia, as the Russians took control of that nation. It paid off, as Russia gave back two provinces to Turkey in March 1921.

In November 1920, Venizelos was defeated in an election. Although the army was purged, the aggressive policy towards Turkey continued, which Lloyd George encouraged. The Greeks pressed on to Ankara but with attenuated lines of communication they were hopelessly overstretched and Atatürk pressed them back to the Aegean. The denouement came in August 1922 when he rode triumphantly into Smyrna. The Turks systematically burned the city and a million Greeks fled from Asia Minor.

The Allies still controlled the straits but the French fled. Although Britain called on its empire for support, little was forthcoming. Lloyd George wanted to go to war but Atatürk wanted to mediate, so did not provoke him further. A peace conference was called, the plan being for the sultan and Atatürk to represent the Turks, but Atatürk claimed to be the legitimate ruler based on popular support and forthwith abolished the sultanate. In negotiations, he got what he wanted, as the victors of the Great War did not have any power in the region. It was a remarkable success for the new Turkish nation.

The Arabian Part of the Ottoman Empire

The policy of self-determination posed all sorts of questions in the break-up of the Ottoman Empire. Most of the empire could not be construed as nations but were administrative units, although Egypt had a certain coherence. There were, however, big cities in this area that were, as such, an index of civilisation and economic sophistication. The area known as Mesopotamia highlighted the problem. In the north was Mosul, mainly Kurdish, a race also numerous in Turkey and Persia; in the middle was Baghdad, whose natural links were with Persia; and in the south was Basra, whose trading links were with India. This area had never been a nation and the concept was new.

Syria, with its capital of Damascus, bordered part of this area. It had claims to be a nation through its extensive hinterland but had no borders and would have trouble in defining them. Syria claimed the cities of Mosul and Beirut in any new nation. Palestine was another area with an undefined northern and eastern border but it was the Holy Land to the Christians, the Promised Land to the Jews, while Jerusalem was a shrine to Muslims, Christians and Jews. The deserts of Arabia, the Empty Quarter, were ignored at this time, but the holy shrines of Mecca and Medina were of great importance to the Muslims.

The treaties and arrangements made under the pressure of war were almost always found to be disastrous when viewed dispassionately after war had ceased. The Sykes–Picot, Anglo–French agreement of 1916 divided the area into a French part (Lebanon and parts of Syria), a British part (Baghdad and Basra), Palestine under international administration and an area that included Syria, Jordan and Mosul and its environs under Arab control. France in the north and Britain in the south would be protecting powers. Today's Saudi Arabia was ignored.

By the time of the peace conference, this pleased neither Britain nor France. Britain wanted to be the dominant power because of oil and its trading link via the Suez Canal to India. France also wanted oil and to develop its historic links with Greater Syria, including Mosul and Palestine, which could be traced back to the Crusades. Italy had no influence in the Middle East but the United States felt, as the new world power, that it should exert influence. Although it was not interested in any involvement, the United States did not want a colonial system imposed.

The British had been looking for Arab leaders of substance who could create new nations, not necessarily independent but with the ability to create a cohesive whole. During the war, Hussein, a Hashemite of ancient lineage, seemed able to fill this role. He had a son, Feisal, who fought with Lawrence of Arabia. Lawrence wanted Feisal to have the throne of Syria and, in the capture of Damascus, proclaimed that Feisal's forces had won a great victory, which did not please the down-to-earth Australians, who had done most of the work. Lawrence, in Arab headgear, and Feisal turned up at the peace conference to plead their case and stirred the enmity of the French.

Then there was Palestine and another wartime declaration. It was a story of two men who were able to marshal forces in the cause of Zionism. Chaim Weizmann was a Zionist zealot who despised Jews who were happy to be assimilated into other nations or thought that they could have a national home in any other place than Palestine. He came from Russia but his home was now in England, where he was reading biochemistry at the University of Manchester. His enthusiasm for Zionism caught the imagination of Balfour, who had a reputation for not being a man of enthusiasm. By the time of Balfour's declaration, they had known each other for eleven years.

Prime minister from 1902 to 1905, Balfour was greatly influential in any administration but famous for seeing both sides of a question and for being able to succinctly present them. This is shown by his remarks on the Jews. On the one hand, he described them as the most gifted race that mankind had seen since the Greeks of the fifth century; on the other hand, he also said that all Bolshevism and similar disturbances were directly traceable to the Jews of the world. Balfour was a detached figure who never married and was not a person to be emotionally engaged. Churchill said that if you did not want anything done, Balfour was the man for the task, while Lloyd George, when asked of Balfour's place in history, said it would be just like the scent on a pocket handkerchief. However, the Balfour declaration would be the precursor to the state of Israel, thus creating one of the most intractable problems of its kind.

Further south, Egypt had stirred and was demanding that the peace conference receive its nationalists. For a long time there had been a strong diplomatic and defensive presence in Egypt to protect the Suez Canal but, up until the Turkish declaration of war, it was technically part of the sultan's domains. The British immediately made it a protectorate and used it as a base for the Gallipoli campaign, which some influential Egyptians did not like.

When war ended, nationalist leaders appeared excited by prospects of self-determination, supported by thousands of signatures. Britain took a strong line, arrested the leaders and sent them to Malta. Allenby was sent to Egypt to sort out the problem and was conciliatory, so much so that the nationalist leaders were released and Egypt was given self-government in 1922, apart from control of foreign policy and the Suez Canal.

The resolution of Turkey's Arabian provinces was not easy. France had the support of the Christian communities, which were predominantly in the Beirut area and determined to have this area that Syria coveted. Lawrence's promotion of Feisal as king of Syria had some British support but official British feeling was that he would have to accept French overlordship. Feisal was representing his father, with his power base in the Hejaz. Wilson asked him whether Greater Arabia wanted one mandate or several, a question he dodged by stating that the Arabs wanted unity and independence.

Clemenceau did not budge from his relative indifference about France's fate in the Middle East, despite prodding from his officials, whom he did not try to disappoint. Lloyd George was perplexed but resolute about British interests and was pro Feisal. It was Wilson, however, who brokered the solution. His hatred of all agreements made during the war scuppered Sykes–Picot and he proposed that Britain should control the Mesopotamia of Mosul, Baghdad and Basra, diverse as it was. Wilson had formed a Commission of Inquiry, with the support of France and Britain, over the borders of Syria. Its conclusions were that the people of the region wanted Palestine and Lebanon incorporated into the state of Syria and they wanted to be independent.

Feisal was proclaimed king of Greater Syria in March 1920, which did not suit the French. Meanwhile, his brother Abdullah was proclaimed king of Mesopotamia. In the same year, Mesopotamia revolted and Britain, even with the confrontational Churchill as colonial secretary, felt that it might not have the power to keep it. In the end, air power quelled the rebellion and, in March 1921, Churchill sought a solution.

Feisal was not acceptable to the French, so he was offered Mesopotamia. Abdullah was compensated with the throne of Transjordan. Their father, Hussein, had a fragile hold on the deserts of southern Arabia. He would retain power until 1924, when Ibn Saud defeated him, and the kingdom of Saudi Arabia was formed. The French, meantime, had helped the Lebanese Christians to form a state, which was expanded to include many Muslims. They also had a mandate over Syria and were given a share in the oil from Mosul. The peacemakers had little inkling that the Middle East would be among the most fragile of all their decisions.

The Signing of the Peace Treaty

It only took four months for the fundamental treaty to be put together and another month for it to be ready for formal signature. In those four months, nations had been formed and other nations that had created themselves were about to receive formal legitimacy. Territory the world over had been redistributed. The process had been speedy and the big three were pleased with their work, although realising that there were many imperfections. However, Wilson, Lloyd George and Clemenceau, each in his own way, had respect and regard for each other and felt that they had done the world a service.

Wilson was an idealist who took pride in imposing his theology of creating a world assembly for all people to be represented via self-determination as credible nations. Lloyd George was the pragmatic politician who had a world vision and looked to the balance of power to achieve his aims. Clemenceau was the practical realist who wanted German power truncated so there would be no resurgence. Between them they felt they had compromised to form a just peace. When the terms were published, the compromises, which were made with such difficulty and idealism, were blown away with cries of pain. On the one hand, a great figure like Marshal Foch exploded, saying that the German border should be on the Rhine, otherwise the next time they would break through to the Channel ports and attack Britain. He was heard but not heeded.

On the other hand, Germany was in despair. Although it had intimations of the outcome, it still had hopes that the treaty would be based on the Fourteen Points and it would lose little territory. Germany hoped it would not lose its colonies and merchant fleet, that Austria could link with Germany if it so wished, that it would not be treated as a pariah nation and could join the League of Nations. The Germans were given the terms on 7 May and their hopes were dashed. Their leader, Brockdorff-Rantzau, made a speech, in shocked but not humble terms, which alienated most of the delegates.

The martial Germans did not concur with the opinion that Germany was a defeated nation and guilty of starting the war. More pertinent, they felt that Germany alone was being made to pay for the war, ignoring the rest of the alliance. Moreover, the alliance of which Germany was only a part was not guilty of initiating the war in the east and Germany had mitigated its guilt in the west by usurping the ruling class and becoming a republic.

The Germans were not alone in worrying about the terms. Future US President Herbert Hoover, who was a relief administrator, met the South

African, Smuts, and Keynes, representing the British Treasury, and they agreed that certain parts of the treaty spelled trouble. Bullitt, from the American delegation, who had been sent to Russia on a diplomatic mission, led a group who considered that American idealism had been exchanged for European revenge on Germany.

This highlighted the great problem of the treaty. It was massively complex and had involved much negotiation. Smuts, who felt the terms were harsh, had lobbied and succeeded in getting the financial reparations raised to include pensions, which many agreed was the straw that broke the camel's back. Meanwhile, when asked if he was prepared to give South West Africa back to Germany, Smuts was non-committal. Everyone had their own agenda and was under pressure from their own constituency.

The Germans tried to counter-attack and put forward proposals based on the Fourteen Points, which the French received with indignation and reiterated the view that the treaty was not sufficiently severe. The British, however, were having second thoughts, especially Lloyd George, who thought a weak and dispirited Germany might turn communist and be a destabilising influence in central Europe. He did not think, however, in terms of restoring the German colonies or the merchant marine, which were mainly in Britain's pocket.

Lloyd George, the politician par excellence who had never wanted a harsh result, was prepared to compromise. The big three came together and he suggested that the people of Upper Silesia should determine their future by plebiscite, that the French occupation of the Rhineland be shortened and reparations should be lessened. After much ill-tempered debate, the plebiscite was agreed but there was only cosmetic agreement on the other two points. It made little difference, as the Germans felt deeply humiliated, as if the nation had a gaping flesh wound that would not come together. Brockdorff-Rantzau and his delegation, egged on by public opinion, took the view that they would not sign. Britain prepared to renew the naval blockade and Foch prepared forty-two divisions to occupy Germany.

The German navy, at anchor at Scapa Flow, reflected Germany's desperation. Two days before the treaty was to be signed, it acted cohesively and sank most of its fleet under the eyes of its captors. As 400,000 tons of shipping sank to the bottom of the sea with ensigns flying, the Germans felt that they had retrieved their honour. It certainly made the Admiralty look stupid but it hardened Allied attitudes and there would be no extension of the deadline.

On 22 June Germany agreed to sign but did not accept the war guilt clause or the clause requiring the surrender and trial of those starting the war. To Germany, this meant unconditional surrender, which its army did not want to accept but, at the last moment, it buckled and agreed to sign. Brockdorff-Rantzau and his delegation resigned and Ebert was left to form a government to represent Germany.

The formal signing was on 28 June but there were notable absentees. Foch, the victorious marshal on the Western Front, was enraged by it all and did not attend, saying that Clemenceau had lost the peace. The Chinese, likewise, did not attend or sign because of the disputed Shantung peninsula. The signing acknowledged that this was the structure on which the world would be governed but it was still only skeletal. There were still endless problems, some of which could be resolved quickly and others that remain to this day.

The heads of government departed from Versailles, dealing with the outstanding questions from their capitals or in special conferences. Lloyd George attended thirty-three such conferences until he lost power in 1922, partly because of his incompetence in Turkey. One important decision was not resolved until 1921 in London, when the reparations bill was fixed at 132 billion marks (£6.6 billion, $33 billion). It was not as onerous as it seemed as some assets lost in the transference of territory were credited to Germany and payments would only be made when its economy was doing well.

This was the rub. Germany had lost 13 per cent of its territory and 10 per cent of its population. Its capacity for steel production had been decimated, so the engine of the economy was inadequate and spluttering. It had been cut down to being a European power by the loss of its colonies, its navy and merchant marine. It had lost control of its railways and waterways. With the best will in the world it knew it could not generate surplus wealth in the near future.

Yet, in a sense, Germany could not complain. As the Treaty of Brest-Litovsk showed, if it had been the victor, it would have added large swathes of territory to its empire in the east. If victorious in the west it would have substantial territory, together with many colonies of the defeated powers. Moreover, in forming its empire in 1871, France had provided Germany with a substantial indemnity, which some say was not much different in value from what the French were demanding as victors in this war. The trouble was that Germany refused to acknowledge that it had lost and there were consequences. At no time was there humility or a plea for mercy.

The Great Inflation

There were many great men at the peace conference. One man, John Maynard Keynes, a true genius, made an international reputation with his book, *The Economic Consequences of the Peace*, in which he recommended that reparations should not exceed £2 billion and this should include £500 million for some assets that the Allies would take, such as merchant ships, submarine cables and state assets in ceded territory. He also recommended that Germany's coal and steel production should compensate France in a sensible way and that the Saar and Upper Silesia should revert back to Germany. Finally, a loan should be set up that had to be repaid, in order to kickstart trade, but inter-allied debt should be cancelled.

It is a short work that is tautly written and filled with insight. Take this seemingly innocuous description of 1919 Germany described in economic terms:

> The note circulation of Germany is about ten times what it was before the war. The value of the mark in terms of gold is about one-eighth of its former value. As world prices in terms of gold are more than double what they were, it follows that mark prices inside Germany ought to be sixteen to twenty times their prewar level to be in adjustment and proper conformity with prices outside Germany. But this is not the case. In spite of a very great rise in German prices, they probably do not yet average much more than five times their former level, so far as staple commodities are concerned; and it is impossible that they should rise further except with a simultaneous and not less violent adjustment of the level of money wages. The existing maladjustment hinders in two ways (apart from other obstacles) that revival of the import trade which is the essential preliminary of the economic reconstruction of the country. In the first place, imported commodities are beyond the purchasing power of the great mass of the population and the flood of imports which might have been expected to succeed the raising of the blockade was not in fact commercially possible. In the second place, it is a hazardous enterprise for a merchant or manufacturer to purchase with a foreign credit material for which, when he has imported or manufactured it, he will receive mark currency of a quite uncertain and possibly unrealisable value. This latter obstacle to the revival of trade is one which easily escapes notice and deserves a little attention. It is impossible at the present time to say what the mark will be worth in

terms of foreign currency three or six months or a year hence, and the exchange market can quote no reliable figure. It may be the case, therefore, that a German merchant, careful of his future credit and reputation, who is actually offered a short-period in terms of sterling or dollars, may be reluctant or doubtful whether to accept it. He will owe sterling or dollars, but he will sell his product for marks, and his power, when the time comes, to turn these marks into the currency in which he has to repay his debt is entirely problematic. Business loses its genuine character and becomes no better than a speculation in the exchanges, the fluctuations in which entirely obliterate the normal profits of commerce.

There are therefore three separate obstacles to the revival of trade: a maladjustment between internal prices and international prices, a lack of individual credit abroad wherewith to buy the raw materials needed to secure the working capital and to restart the circle of exchange, and a disordered currency system which renders credit operations hazardous or impossible quite apart from the ordinary risks of commerce.[15]

The inability to reconcile these differences in the four years that followed led to the printing presses disgorging money. The price of commodities triggered wage rises, which forced another rise in prices, and so on, until wheelbarrows of paper money were required to purchase the simplest needs. The currency became worthless, those with physical assets had the means to hold out, those with paper savings could be ruined. The 1923 inflation was blamed above all on reparations, which was just a minor part of it, and with this blame the justice of the Treaty of Versailles was brought into question. Keynes's diagnosis was sound and he would be further vindicated as time went on.

The League of Nations

The year of the big inflation in Germany was also the year of Wilson's death but his power had long since waned. Narrow interests had shattered his hopes of the United States participating in the League of Nations. In September 1919 he went on a tour of his nation to persuade the people that it was right to ratify the Treaty of Versailles and form the League of Nations. The opposition was varied, coming from isolationists, idealists not comprehending the compromises that had to be made, varying party deviants, plus Irish Americans obsessed with Ireland and the failure to wring independence from Britain.

Wilson was vulnerable on the specifics; however, his greatness does not lie there but in his application of his two great principles. By the end of September he had collapsed, then suffered a stroke, which affected one side. He was never the same again and the fight went from him. He was defeated in the senate on the question of the League of Nations and the United States never joined this institution, a setback from which the League never recovered.

Decisions at the peace conference created the modern world. Russia, the power that opted out, rigidly controlled but unconventional in its violence and ideological fervour, ploughed its own furrow. In the future, wretched Germany would seek revenge, while two of the big five, Italy and Japan would seek empires of their own and were already signalling their disaffection. The pattern of the next twenty-five years was already established. The creative good that the peace conference had established would eventually triumph but the selfish narrow evil that it engendered would lead to short-term disaster.

Chapter 12

The Russian Revolution

Russia 1918–19

At the armistice, Germany had to restore large areas to Russia or whoever was in control of its government. Russia, the key to the eastern parts of Europe with Germany out of the equation, was absent from the conference, which made it difficult to achieve an acceptable solution for the region. Russia's borders were contiguous with Finland, the Baltic states, Poland, Romania, Turkey and Persia, and there were contentious issues with all these states.

No one liked Bolshevism, which controlled the two main cities of Russia, but it was Churchill who summed it up at this stage of its development in prophetic terms that trumpeted his greatness: 'The essence of Bolshevism as opposed to many other forms of visionary political thought is that it can only be propagated and maintained by violence. Of all tyrannies in history, the Bolshevik tyranny is the worst, the most destructive, the most degrading.'[16]

Lloyd George, who saw the weakness of Bolshevism, did not think their power and influence would last long and thought that Churchill's rhetoric was a class thing, ducal blood reacting against the murder of Russia's dukes, while Balfour thought Churchill was exaggerating. Public opinion felt that Churchill was erratic and unreliable. The Dardanelles operation had not been wiped off the slate.

The Bolsheviks made no secret of the fact that they ignored democracy, pursued their ends by terror and repudiated all foreign debts. But many in the world saw this as a product of revolution and, in time, the Bolsheviks would settle down and become reasonable in the Western bourgeois sense. Lloyd

George wanted to do business with the Bolsheviks but Clemenceau hated them – he knew the extreme left from the end of the Franco–Prussian War. Wilson wanted to play for time and let them evolve a sense of responsibility. The Bolsheviks' triumph, which was not clear at this stage, would not be unexpected. The White Russians in Paris cut little ice, while the world watched their attempts to topple the Bolsheviks with little optimism.

The Bolsheviks controlled the productive part of Russia and could not be ignored, while the peace conference needed their approval on many matters. They were not invited to Paris, but it was agreed to hold a meeting on an island in the Sea of Marmara. No one knew how they would react to diplomatic niceties but they responded in a way that would not change for forty years. They used the diplomatic tactics of taking extreme, intransigent positions, of blowing hot or cold, and of being contemptuous of the capitalist world, the ideas of self-determination and the League of Nations. Then, to get attention, they would become conciliatory and give hope that they would repay some of their debts and might modify their ambitions for world revolution. This was too much for the White Russians, who demonstrated in Paris, while Churchill dashed to see Lloyd George to get a consistent policy for British and other Allied troops who were fighting in Russia.

As the war in the east ended and the Germans retreated from Russian territory, so the civil war in that country gained momentum. The defeated Germans were still in areas of ethnic German influence, while the victorious Allies were in peripheral places such as Archangel and Vladivostok. The Bolsheviks controlled the big towns and the most populous areas. All counter-revolutionary activity was from the periphery – from the east along the Trans-Siberian Railway, from the south with its links to the outside world via the Black Sea, and from the Baltic states in the north-west. There were major armies in the east and the south that tried to coalesce and capture Moscow. The army in the north-west was small and its objective was Petrograd, which they would observe with the naked eye but would not capture.

The civil war casualties would be far greater than those on the Western Front during the Great War, widely regarded as an awful bloodbath. Some have postulated a figure of ten million killed in the civil war but that is a statistic of which there is no categoric proof. There is little doubt that there was a dreadful slaughter, of which battlefield deaths did not form an overwhelming part. The influenza epidemic is hardly mentioned in histories but it must have killed tens of thousands, as did typhus. The terror also gratuitously killed thousands of many different nationalities and different ethnic groups within the Russian Empire, with the Jews being especially targeted.

With the ending of the Great War, the Allies were in confusion with their old ally Russia, which had walked away from the conflict and had ignored the agreement that no one nation would make a separate peace. What the Allies wanted was a stable Russia that could deal with the problems of that part of the world. They tried unsuccessfully to intervene in an even-handed way. With war over, there were plenty of munitions available but real aid was only available from the United States, whose support was crucial for the Whites.

Prince Lvov, the leader of the provisional government after the abdication of the tsar, was the political leader of the Whites and he went to the United States to see President Wilson to ask for support. Wilson gave him fifteen minutes of his time, admired his beard but was non-committal about any support or giving them a part in the peace conference. Lvov then went to the peace conference, where the Allies took a neutral stance towards Russia but gave the Whites enough arms to fight the Reds. In the first half of 1919, they received 15,000 machine guns, 700 field guns, eight million rounds of ammunition, plus clothing and equipment for 500,000 men. This was equivalent to the annual Bolshevik production.

Kolchak, an admiral who had contained the revolution in the fleet and had taken control of the ground forces, could now advance along the railway into Siberia. He had 100,000 men and advanced 200 miles towards Ufa and Orenburg. Advances of such magnitude led to supply problems. They may have had arms and equipment but food was a different problem and it was difficult to pay for. There were the tsarist gold reserves, which could stabilise the currency, but they did not use these, which led to great paper inflation. The men on the railway, who were their supply lifeline, also needed paying and, when this was not forthcoming in any sensible way, they helped themselves to the goods carried on the railway, while the disaffected along the line helped themselves to much of the rest. Kolchak's army was also top heavy in the officer class, while local officials swelled the numbers that had to be looked after along the line of communications.

Just as with the Bolshevik army, deserters fled in their thousands, but the long thin line of the Trans-Siberian Railway was very vulnerable compared with the Reds' internal lines of communication. In Siberia, there were few great landlords, so the land question was of lesser import, but once Kolchak reached Russia proper, he found it difficult to recruit the peasantry to fight. In the southern Volga region, where he wished to link up with Denikin, land reform had been extensive and the peasants had become happier with their lot. There were also peasant revolts all over Russia, including Siberia, and these peasants were often deserters who had taken their equipment with them, which the Allies had supplied.

To maintain discipline, Kolchak was drawn into the terror business – terror against deserters, terror to get the peasants to join up and fight, terror to get food and terror to protect his lines of communication. Both sides were acting in the same way but the Bolsheviks had the advantage of the support of the urban proletariat and those who had benefited from land reform, plus the fact that they were new in power and the old regime was discredited. From the end of April through to August 1919, the Reds, reinforced by conscripts, forced Kolchak's forces back to Omsk and by now his original 100,000 soldiers had shrunk to 15,000.

The Reds and Terror

The Red Army was not very disciplined during 1918 but it had certain advantages, among which were an outstanding leader in Trotsky and the control of key munitions factories such as Tula, just 100 miles from Moscow. At its conception, the Red Army elected its leaders but, as time went on, Trotsky recruited from the tsarist officer corps, which amounted to 22,000 by the end of 1918. This was sensible, as the middle-class specialists, such as doctors, vets and engineers, could not be trained overnight. And anyway, the tsarist officer class included many from humble backgrounds. However, the egalitarians of the revolution were horrified. They hated differentials in pay and uniform and having to show respect by saluting, which Trotsky reintroduced.

In the summer of 1918, communist Russia was under martial law, a state that would endure. The Red Army strength was roughly one million in 1918, three million in 1919, rising to five million in 1920, but its enemies surrounded it. There were Germans in Ukraine, British in the north around Archangel, Czechs on the Volga, Japanese and their allies in the Far East, while the Whites were predominantly in the south. The Russian Empire was up for grabs. The Red Army's ambition was to be big in numbers but an army needs supplies, equipment and training. When soldiers have no role, they desert, and desertion was rife. A quality army would have been better than a quantity army, which was badly shod, clothed and fed, and went home to bring in the harvest. When people congregate closely, disease is apt to follow and in 1920 a million soldiers caught typhus. With the fronts moving with some fluidity in the open spaces of Russia, hospitals were few, as were doctors. It is thought that more people died from diseases than from fighting in the civil war.

Discipline, on the whole, is hierarchical in character, which cut against the grain of the communist ethos. With desertion rife (up to one million in 1918) they created a new class of commissars, who acted outside the law and fined and confiscated grain and livestock, if their mood was mild, or destroyed villages and shot their leaders if they thought fit. This was how the terror came about but it would become more sophisticated and ruthless with the formation of the Cheka, the Bolshevik secret police.

As the paper economy broke down, so the barter system grew and, for the cities to thrive, a barter system was too clumsy. Cities exist on an advanced division of labour, which precludes an efficient barter system. It worked in the simpler conditions of rural villages, which exchanged city-made goods for food. The Moscow population halved between 1918 and 1920 even though it was the seat of government. Petrograd was even worse hit, with its population diminishing to a quarter of what it was in 1918. With this loss, city services disintegrated, rubbish accumulated in the streets, pipes burst, disease was rampant, death was ubiquitous and the dead lay unburied.

The breakdown between the cities and the countryside was critical and, as in 1916, it was not the lack of food but the means of getting it to the cities that was the problem. Railcars full of food arrived empty in Moscow or Petrograd. There was indiscipline in the railway system, with its processes still geared to war and its rolling stock badly maintained. The factory workers, whose wages were reckoned to be worth about a fiftieth of 1913 values, spent three-quarters of their wages on food. To get this, the city dwellers would take time off and go to the villages with tools, penknives, primus stoves, kerosene and cigarette lighters. They were known as bagmen, with thousands passing through the Orel station every day.

Once the big landowners were removed and their lands reallocated, village communities felt remarkably egalitarian. Of course, there were talented farmers, competent farmers and less competent ones. The more talented ones would have a few more cattle or a few more acres and might be recognised in the community as the best qualified to lead it. Thus, if a distinction had to be made, there was a kulak or yeoman class but it was not very distinctive over most of Russia.

However, in 1918 the Bolsheviks needed a scapegoat for the failure to get food to the cities, so Lenin blamed the kulaks as the enemies of the Soviet government and as bloodsuckers who grew rich on the hunger of the people. To deal with this, a lumpenproletariat brigade, which in time grew to 76,000, terrorised the peasantry and requisitioned all that they considered surplus. The battle raged, with the peasantry concealing their grain, which was predominantly food for the winter and seed for the next harvest. But Lenin was determined to drive a wedge between what he called the rural proletariat and the rural bourgeoisie, which was a rift in the social order that the peasantry did not really recognise.

Here were the seeds of terror. In the early days of the revolution there was ruthlessness but the terror was benign. Kamenev even tried to abolish the death penalty in 1917 and the Second Soviet Congress passed a resolution along these lines, which prompted Lenin to fly into a rage and ask how one could make a revolution without firing squads. The Cheka, the secret police, was formed in 1917 and grew through 1918 into an organisation that would apply widespread terror. It started slowly, compared with its later reputation, by killing less than a thousand in the first eight months. But two events, apart from the ebb, flow and peril of the civil war, would signal that arbitrary terror was in the ascendant and was causing fear everywhere.

The first started in August 1917 when Kerensky sent the tsar and his family to the remote Siberian town of Tobolsk as he feared for their safety. They were a problem, as denuded of power they retained a potent symbolism. Trotsky wanted a public trial to expose their failure, which could be broadcast by wireless all over Russia. Their guards, therefore, were instructed to keep them alive but the influential Ekaterinburg Bolsheviks wanted them dead. In the chaos of Russia, they considered that they had the authority to get rid of them.

Tobolsk was 150 miles from Ekaterinburg and the Bolsheviks got the family transferred to the latter. The Czech Legion surrounded Ekaterinburg and managed to capture the city on 25 July 1918; however, before that, on 17 July, the tsar and his family were murdered. This was attributed during the untruthful days of communism as being due to the actions of the local Bolsheviks but Moscow, and probably Lenin, ordained it.

That was the terror that unleashed the floodgates but the second incident, the attempted assassination of Lenin, propelled it onwards. On 30 August Lenin was told that the head of the Petrograd Cheka had been assassinated. It was a Friday and Lenin often addressed the workers on this day, so he went to a factory in south Moscow, where a woman came out of the crowd and fired three bullets at him. He was hit in the shoulder and neck and there was blood in his lungs. His life was in danger but within a month he had recovered enough to go on convalescence. With his recovery from seemingly near death, the cult of Lenin started – the beloved leader who had been in mortal peril. The terror was ratcheted.

Russia – Denikin in the South

The war in Russia continued in early 1919. Kolchak was successfully moving forward, while Denikin, who commanded the Whites in the south, was based at Rostov. He had two options: capture Tsaritsyn, the future Stalingrad, and link up with Kolchak on the Volga; or repel the Reds who were invading the northern Don region and the Donbass. The latter was a major coal-producing area, which the Reds coveted. Apart from coal, they wanted control of the land, which was in the hands of Cossacks who, with their swashbuckling independence, were easily classified as kulaks and enemies of the people.

The Reds were ruthless with the Cossacks, executing 12,000 of them. As Denikin had to protect them, he had to confront the Reds and put on hold any plans to link up with Kolchak. The Reds wilted under Denikin's thrust as the Whites had Cossacks in the vanguard, superior supplies and even aircraft supplied by the Allies. The Whites advanced from the Donbass into southeastern Ukraine and pushed aside the Reds and Ukrainian partisans under Makhno. They captured Kharkov on 13 June, then Ekaterinoslav on 22 June. The Red supply line had broken down and, when there was mass desertion, peasant uprisings and terror were used to restore order. The problem for the Reds was shown by Makhno's partisans. Makhno believed in a pure form of communism, a rule based on the local soviets but stateless. There was a strain of anarchy in him, which the centralisers in Moscow would crush, but he linked up with the Red Army and was supplied by it.

The partisans were no match for the Whites. When Trotsky tried to bring them into line he had some shot to encourage the others. Makhno's 15,000 followers melted into the forest and became enemies of the Reds. This was the perpetual problem for the Russians and Ukrainians. The Little Russians of Ukraine wanted to be Ukrainians and not puppets of Greater Russia.

Denikin had a rival, Baron Peter Wrangel, who with his Caucasian army had captured Tsaritsyn in June and was trying to consolidate in the region. Denikin was in no position to link up with Kolchak as he once hoped but he felt he had a strategy to win Russia. Moscow was the objective as it was the great rail junction and the attack would be along the railway lines. The Caucasian army would be one pincer and would advance along the Volga, then via Nizhniy Novgorod. The Don army would go via Voronezh, while Mai-Maevsky's army, further to the west, would go via Kursk, Orel and Tula.

The Whites had a formidable cavalry arm, much superior to the Reds, and it would range far and wide, ostensibly in control of the territory but with no secure lines of communication. In the early days of the offensive there was much success as the Whites dominated Ukraine, capturing Kiev and Odessa in August. In September Kursk and Voronezh fell, and in October, Orel. The Whites were 250 miles from Moscow and General Yudenich was threatening Petrograd in the north.

The Germans had formed the North Western army, which tried to take Petrograd from the Reds and had retreated into Estonia as the Reds advanced after the German defeat in 1918. In May 1919 it had 16,000 men, mostly prisoners of war that had been released, plus a few Red deserters. Yudenich, its commander, had little political instinct and as he marched into Russia was indifferent about appealing to the locals and recruiting them.

This lack of popular support, plus the connection with the Germans, caused the Allies to give him little support. If Yudenich had courted the Finns, this would not have mattered, as Finland was only 20 miles away from Petrograd and, if the Whites had guaranteed Finnish independence, which was almost a matter of fact, their lines of communication would have been simplified and they would have received help with supplies. The Finnish army was formidable, having 100,000 men and, although they would not act together, they would provide a threat to the Reds. But Yudenich was in thrall to Peter the Great and the creation of a Greater Russia, so ignored the Finns. The same happened in Estonia, where he refused to do a deal but continued to recruit. The Reds, however, offered Estonia a peace accord in exchange for neutrality.

Yudenich took a roundabout route with his army, which had grown to 18,000 men who would be opposed by 25,000 Reds. On 20 October 1919 he was overlooking Petrograd from the heights. Lenin was prepared to leave the city but Trotsky provided the backbone for the Reds and arrived to organise the resistance. With ruthlessness and terror, Trotsky galvanised the population.

The railway link to Moscow was still open and men came from afar to fight for the Reds. Within days they had 100,000, even though their equipment was rudimentary. Yudenich had the advantage of Allied tanks but he had no reserves, nor did he have the acceptance of the rural population along the lines of communication, which meant he could not hold his position. Within a few weeks his army was back in Estonia. Trotsky wanted to pursue but this was not necessary, as the peace treaty had been signed with Estonia.

With the capture of Orel and with Yudenich overlooking Petrograd, the Whites had been at their most threatening. In the east, Kolchak's power was ebbing. His forces remained at Omsk until November, reinforcing themselves but not actively preparing to advance. This obvious lack of momentum, so important in a situation where loyalties were fluctuating, led to a fall in support, with even the loyal Cossacks leaving.

The Reds were outnumbering the Whites by two to one and attacking Orel, capturing the city and 30,000 men plus their equipment. Kolchak and his remaining followers fled to Irkutsk, 1,500 miles to the east, in six trains, the biggest of which had twenty-nine cars and carried the tsarist gold reserves. Kolchak hoped to get Allied protection but his power was dwindling. He resigned his post and the Czechs probably betrayed him in return for their safe passage to Vladivostok. The Bolsheviks had gained a great victory and, after interrogation, Kolchak was executed on 6 February 1920.

1920 – The Blunting of Polish Ambitions

The relations between Poland and the Soviet Union were complex. Poland had once had dominion over territory from the Baltic to the Black Sea, where there were Poles, Russians, Ukrainians, Jews and other ethnic communities. Polish ambitions in 1920 did not extend as far as this but did extend into Ukraine. Pilsudski, the Polish leader, had a pact with Petliura's Ukrainian nationalists whereby they would instal Petliura in power in Kiev, with western Ukraine to come under Polish sovereignty. This triggered a profound effect on Russia.

Brusilov, the most successful Russian commander of the war, was an aristocrat who had remained in that part of Russia controlled by the Reds. At the time of the Polish capture of Kiev, he lived in Moscow. He was a Russian who regarded Ukraine as Little Russia, part of the Orthodox firmament, where he and his ancestors owned an estate and had fought to defend it against the Poles. In the Great War he had defended Ukraine against Austrian predation and his instincts were strongly against Polish incursion. For the past two years he had lived humbly on the breadline, suffering severe humiliation. His son had joined the Reds as a cavalry commander, hoping that the Cheka would save his father's life, but the Whites captured him at Orel in September 1919 and it is likely that he was executed.

Brusilov was ambivalent towards the Reds, regarding their atheism as temporary but calculating that they would win the civil war because overall they had the support of the people, while the Whites needed Allied support. He was first and foremost a Russian patriot but in May 1920 he joined the Reds. He was sixty-six and could not bear to see the Reds and Whites fighting each other while the Poles threatened a part of Russia. Trotsky saw the advantage of Brusilov joining the cause and promoted him as the figurehead of patriotic Russia fighting the invader. This struck a chord, much to the Bolsheviks' amazement. Some 14,000 former officers joined the Red Army, 100,000 deserters returned, and there were many patriotic demonstrations. The Whites were mortified by Brusilov's actions when thousands of tsarist officers formerly under his command were in Cheka-run jails. Brusilov got amnesties for some of them but, as Trotsky pointed out, the Cheka were a law unto themselves.

The Bolsheviks crossed the Curzon Line, which demarcated the agreed Polish–Russian border at Versailles, and pressed on to Warsaw. There they felt that the great ideological force of communism would induce the working class to join them and they could put a Polish communist regime in place. However, all that happened was that they engendered Polish nationalism and they were beaten back. In October 1920, with the fronts stabilised, the Russians and Poles accepted the borders as agreed in the Treaty of Versailles and signed the Treaty of Riga in 1921.

Joseph Stalin

The rise of the Bolsheviks, a small communist sect, was remarkable and not easy to foresee. When there is a power vacuum and no recognised constitutional method of filling it, the fight for power can be raw and elemental, with two factors coming into play: first, the talent of the old power structure needs to be temporarily harnessed to the cause; second, all opposition to the cause needs to be ruthlessly obliterated.

Above this sordid realpolitik, there must stand a figurehead who can appeal to the minds of men and manipulate the forces that have been unleashed. Lenin turned out to be this leader. In April 1917 he returned from exile to Russia in a sealed train, financed by Germany, as it wanted chaos to settle on Russia so that German influence and power could stretch eastwards. There was chaos but Germany's influence was circumscribed by its defeat in the west.

Under Lenin, two acolytes emerged who were chalk and cheese. Trotsky had been the leading light of another communist sect, the Mensheviks, which had merged with the Bolsheviks after the revolution, but the wounds caused by the abuse of nit-picking ideology remained. Lenin recognised Trotsky as a great military leader who had recruited talent from all ranks and classes in the tsarist army, creating an army of formidable competence.

Stalin was a Bolshevik of undeviating loyalty to Lenin. In 1917 he was nearing forty and had been a politically astute revolutionary for some years, having been sent to Siberia for his subversive actions. He was a successful political journalist and became a supreme party functionary with an instinct for manoeuvre and promotion. Lenin recognised his qualities, especially those of ruthlessness and loyalty. Stalin became the Bolsheviks' hatchet man and, in his loathing of dissent, his hands dripped with the blood of dissenters and would never be cleansed.

Stalin's loyalty to Lenin and hostility to Trotsky drove him on. Trotsky had created a force without which the communists would have been buried but gratitude did not come easily to Stalin. His practical role was now an economic one – he had to feed the people and in 1918 there was great hunger in Petrograd and Moscow. Decrees had gone out that the kulaks, the medium-sized farmers who produced surpluses, should release their grain stores but they refused to release them without payment. The whole system of production and distribution broke down and was replaced by speculators cornering food markets and selling at key points.

In the south, around Tsaritsyn, a former tsarist general who reported to Trotsky commanded the troops. Stalin complained about this to Lenin and, as troops arrived in the city from the Don region, he found a comrade in their commander, Voroshilov. There was pandemonium, as the Germans were in the area and the Cossacks were asserting themselves wherever they could. The railways were repaired, with much ruthless exploitation, and by July wagon loads of grain were sent to Moscow.

Oil was the other essential commodity but, at Baku, where large amounts were produced, the soviet had collapsed and all its leaders were shot apart from the young Anastas Mikoyan. Through Stalin, he became the link man with the capitalist producers, who as a matter of expediency were paid in gold. Thus, Stalin oversaw the passage of grain and oil to the big cities, although in a muddling and inefficient way.

Stalin continued to undermine and belittle Trotsky and demanded full authority from Lenin. With Voroshilov's help he increased his military power and went into battle, starting an offensive, which was ineffective. Lenin, seeing his plight, gave him control of the district, which he celebrated by inviting Trotsky's military advisers to a boat in the middle of the Volga, where he murdered them.

The fight continued in September but went against the Bolsheviks, with Trotsky telling Stalin that Voroshilov was capable of commanding a regiment but not an army. Lenin recognised the truth of this and Stalin beat a retreat. Voroshilov was sent to Ukraine, while Stalin was sent to Perm in the Urals to put backbone into a disintegrating Red Army. He did this by the use of terror, which inculcated discipline.

The key year for Stalin and the communists was 1919. Lenin was ambivalent towards his subordinate's ruthless bloodletting but recognised his great talent as an organiser, allied to his loyalty. With Sverdlov's death, Lenin needed someone to implement his orders and to neutralise Trotsky's growing power, so he appointed Stalin to the politburo and numerous commissions.

The threat from the Whites was great, as Yudenich, Denikin and Kolchak menaced the Reds in the two main cities of Petrograd and Moscow. Stalin was sent to Petrograd and created the fear that was his hallmark. Anyone who might be a potential ally of the Whites was murdered, electricity was cut off, mutinies in two forts were put down, as were similar mutinies in the Baltic fleet. Yudenich, who only had a corps under his command, was held, then retreated, but in October he returned with a bigger army. This time Trotsky opposed him and managed to just survive, being as ruthless in action as Stalin. In future Soviet histories, the two battles would be merged into one and there would be no credit for Trotsky.

At the time of the second attack on Petrograd, Stalin was in the south trying to deal with Denikin, who had captured Kursk, then Orel, and was advancing on Moscow. However, the further the Whites advanced the less the peasants supported them. Although Stalin and his henchmen were inordinately cruel, their actions were ostensibly in the name of the people, while the Whites were equally cruel and rapacious, on the surface offering less in return.

Stalin was not directly involved in resisting the Polish advance to Kiev in 1920 or in pushing them back to Warsaw but he believed in the spirit, the glory and the inexorable march of the revolution. Because of this he was sure that the Polish people would receive them as saviours; however, this did not happen.

Stalin was in the south as commissar for the southern army group in which Budenny's First Cavalry Army was the key component. Trotsky wanted this army to be transferred to him for the main attack on Warsaw but Stalin refused. He wanted to take Lvov, then with his imagination aflame he would move to Warsaw, to be followed by a move through Austria and on to Germany, where the revolution needed support. It was not to be, as the Red Army was unable to subdue the Poles and retreated back to the homeland.

In 1921 Stalin suffered from septic appendicitis. He had an operation with partial anaesthesia when it was found that his gut needed resecting. It took him time to recover but he knew this was the time to be close to Lenin in

Moscow and to organise the nuts and bolts of the party. In 1922 Lenin rewarded Stalin by appointing him general secretary of the Communist party. The power base was now secure.

Pogroms

The Jews in Russia had for centuries occupied the Pale of Settlement but, with the disruptions caused by industrialisation and war, had migrated all over Russia. They were influential everywhere, certainly among the Bolshevik intelligentsia but also among the Whites. As the hatred of the civil war welled up, the Jews tended to be regarded as wealthy, unaligned aliens with the potential to increase the coffers of any needy group. The Whites accused most Jews of supporting the Reds. If they captured a town, they treated the Jewish quarter as the spoils of war and allowed their men to rob and kill. The Cossacks were past masters of this and included women and children in their bloodlust.

The Reds were just as bad if they suspected the Jews of any sympathy for the Whites. They were also merciless towards the Ukrainian peasantry, whether they be followers of Makhno or Petliura. To this one can add the Poles, who carried out pogroms as they marched through Ukraine. Jewish deaths in the civil war were substantial, probably exceeding 100,000. Dwarfed as this is by the genocide to follow, it indicates that what the Germans later did was not abnormal but a continuation of an abjectly brutal and merciless phenomenon.

The End for the Whites

Ukraine was a place of fluctuating fortunes and great complexity because it was not like the rest of Russia. The great difference was the strength of the peasantry in a fertile land whose prime loyalty was to the independent village rather than to the city or the nation. Within these villages was an egalitarian spirit but with greater wealth and tradition of private and inherited property than in the rest of Russia. The Bolshevik means of undermining the coherence of the village by pitting the poor against the more prosperous was not popular and the rift between the villages and the big cities was considerable.

In 1918 and 1919, there were spells when the nationalists controlled large parts of Ukraine but each time the Bolsheviks counter-attacked. In 1919 it was probably through Stalin's orders, acting without Lenin's approval, that a fierce Bolshevik regime was formed, backed up by terror. Russians installed themselves in all the most important posts and the peasants had reasons for their revolts. Lenin was furious and demanded that there should be sensitivity towards the Ukrainians, respect for their language and culture and a recognition of the bond that the peasants had with their villages.

Kiev at this time consisted of less than one-third Ukrainians and the commercial thrust of the city was in Russian hands. The urban proletariat of the towns was broadly sympathetic to the Bolsheviks but Lenin realised that he needed support from socialist sympathisers in the villages. The Borotbists had been formed as a party that tried to fuse socialism with a rural cultural nationalism reflecting Ukrainian aspirations. It had the biggest following in the villages and when it linked with the Bolsheviks in March 1920 it was a triumph for Lenin, who had courted it at the Party Congress at the end of 1919. The Borotbist strain, not in tune with Moscow control, proved influential in Ukrainian politics for a decade and helped the Reds to break the Whites.

Brusilov was right, the Whites could not win as long as they depended on foreign aid and did not have the loyalty of the people. With the Poles in Ukraine, the people identified with the Bolsheviks. Brusilov hated the White leader, Baron Peter Wrangel, for fighting the Reds when the Poles were at their throats. The Allies also acknowledged that they could not indefinitely help to sustain a Russian civil war and Britain stopped its aid at the end of 1919. The Whites were now only a power in the south, with their base in the Crimea, while the Reds were unable to concentrate on the Whites until they had reached agreement with the Poles.

Wrangel led his White forces into the fertile Tauride and tried to go north. He, like everyone else, tried to force obedience through terror but he was more politically aware than Denikin and had produced new land laws to appeal to the peasantry. However, they were complicated and had much less appeal than the Reds' simple confiscation and redistribution methods.

The Reds were given the benefit of the doubt as a new regime, even though the state had not always liberated the peasants but had kept vast tracts of land in state ownership. By the end of 1920 there were 16,000 collective farms controlling ten million acres farmed by a million men. They were often run by opportunists with little skill on the land. With the Whites unable to gain the sympathy of the people and the Poles quiescent, 135,000 Reds were able to confront 35,000 Whites in October 1920. They pushed them back into the Crimea, where the Whites took defensive positions and prepared to evacuate. By the middle of November, 126 ships had taken 150,000 refugees to Constantinople.

The Whites had behaved despicably but the Reds were no better. They shamelessly used Brusilov, who was offered the command of an army staffed by White officers. This army would be given an amnesty in Brusilov's name. Leaflets were dropped by planes and hundreds of officers accepted the amnesty. However, within days the offer of command of this army was rescinded. Later, Brusilov would learn that all the officers who had accepted the amnesty had been shot.

Doctor Zhivago – Boris Pasternak

Doctor Zhivago was first published in 1957, not in the Soviet Union but in Italy. It is primarily a love story, a sublime one, where love is all but extinguished by the civil war of 1918–22. It is marvellously evocative of pre-war Russia, of Russia at war with Germany and the Austro-Hungarians, and of Russia at war with itself. This is the bulk of the book.

The love story depicts the universal experience of love, marriage, procreation and duty clashing with the romance, guilt and hope of a new love. Tonya, Zhivago's wife, summarises it in her farewell letter. She has not seen her husband for a few years and does not know whether he is alive or dead. Her letter is full of pain and love and there is a rebuke for his lack of love for her. She claims that even if she were indifferent to him, his heart would have hidden it from him because not to love is almost like murder. Lara, Zhivago's mistress, is a friend of the family and helped in Tonya's confinement. In her letter, knowing of their love, Tonya is generous to Lara, up to a point:

> I must honestly admit that she is a good person, but I don't want to be a hypocrite – she is exactly the opposite of myself. I was born to make life simple and to look for sensible solutions, she to complicate it and confuse the way.[17]

The anguish continues as the letter ends when she asks Zhivago whether he realises that they will never see each other again. She and the family are going into exile and she instinctively knows that Zhivago would prefer to suffer rather than leave Russia.

Zhivago and Lara are the heroes of the book. They fall deeply in love, which causes feelings of guilt in Zhivago, who resolves to tell Tonya of his love but also of his decision to abandon Lara. Riding back home, three Red irregulars stop him and take him into the forest to act as a doctor to the men fighting the Whites. For over two years, despite attempts to escape, he becomes part of the forest brotherhood and is totally cut off from his family and Lara. Tonya has his child and the family returns to Moscow. Zhivago is released, chastened by his experiences and uncertain of his future, but he arrives back in Yuryatin, a small town on the Trans-Siberian Railway, finds Lara and their love is rekindled.

With the civil war ended, there is a triumphant imposition of the Red political system. This is the new world when the only free day is one that has a seven in its date. For nine days man labours and on the tenth he can rest. Zhivago works hard as a doctor but is indifferent to the political orthodoxy of the murderous new regime and stands out like a sore thumb. These are perilous times, and in times of peril the astute and worldly Komarovsky, who had seduced Lara when she was a schoolgirl, tries to help with his brutal common sense. This makes Zhivago bristle, although Komarovsky is intent on saving them both. Kolchak and the Whites are beaten but there is still a chance to get away and to escape to a new life. Komarovsky implores them to go but Zhivago refuses and Lara will not dream of leaving him even though they know that Komarovsky is probably right.

Lara also has responsibility for her daughter by her husband Strelnikov, and Zhivago tricks her and her daughter into leaving. It is death to him and it is also death to Strelnikov, who although being a successful revolutionary and arch puritan, has fallen foul of the regime and been undermined. Zhivago and Strelnikov meet at Varykino after Lara has departed and talk of their respective loves and how to survive in the new Russia.

For Zhivago, Moscow is the magnet. Exhausted, destitute and in rags, he reaches the holy city of the Russians. The fire and spirit have departed from him, but he has another decade of life. His heart is weak and, as a doctor, he understands his predicament. He has a brother who is thriving in the regime and has become a major general. He protects and looks after Zhivago, who marries again and has two children.

One day in Moscow, Zhivago takes a tram, which is proceeding intermittently because of a lack of power, when he glimpses a middle-aged lady who happens to have been born in Russia but is now a Swiss national and wants to regain her Russian citizenship. Her mannerisms stir him and he tries to open the tram window, which was nailed up. Such are his exertions that he has a fatal heart attack. Lara, the love of his life, passes by unknowing.

Zhivago's coffin stands in what was Strelnikov's old home. Lara, visiting old haunts, attends the funeral. She has found Zhivago again and helps to sort his papers. She talks with his brother, then, in one immortal paragraph, there is comment on the regime that won the civil war but is unworthy of the peace:

One day Lara went out and did not come back. She must have been arrested in the street, as so often happened in those days, and she died or vanished somewhere forgotten as a nameless number on a list which was later mislaid, in one of the innumerable mixed or women's concentration camps in the north.[18]

The hero and heroine are dead but Pasternak was a survivor. He was primarily a poet and, in the Russia of the time, an important and influential one. Stalin and the communist regime had a finger in every pie and were intent on imposing a common orthodoxy on everyone and everything. Even an autocrat needs a court jester, although autocrats tend to dispense with them quickly. In Stalin's case, the poet Demyan Bedny was given rooms in the Kremlin and would amuse Stalin with his antics and earthy jokes. Before Stalin threw him out, Bedny had reported to another poet, Osip Mandelstam, that Stalin left greasy marks on the books that he borrowed. Mandelstam made use of this in a sixteen-line poem, where he referred to Stalin as a Kremlin crag dweller, a peasant slayer with fingers as oily as maggots. Yagoda, the murderous head of the NKVD, memorised this poem and related it to Stalin. For most people that would have meant death but Stalin the merciful gave the order: preserve but isolate. Thus Mandelstam was exiled for three years and Pasternak was one of the first to plead for him.

It led to a telephone call between Pasternak and Stalin, which was full of the dictator's hypocrisy. Stalin called the arrest disgraceful and reassured Pasternak that everything would be all right, praising Pasternak for supporting his friend. Pasternak, emboldened, asked for a meeting with the great dictator. When Stalin asked what the meeting was about, Pasternak replied that it was about life and death. The dumbfounded Stalin put down the phone.

Pasternak only just survived in the following years. As the relations of the regime with Gorky testified, writers had an ambivalent but special role. They were censored and told what to write but they also had licence because of their otherworldliness. It was this that saved Pasternak until he was awarded the Nobel Prize, when Stalin's successors took deep offence and hounded him to his death. The Nobel Prize for Literature is only sometimes awarded to a man of genius and rarely with such alacrity. Pasternak had lived in Moscow most of his life.

The epilogue of *Doctor Zhivago* is not altogether convincing but for an artist of his temperament it had to end on a note of hope. The civil war had destroyed a generation and out of it came little good. Moscow was the holy city, the city that distils from its citizens, across the generations, a creative spirit. Out of the suffering of the wars and the awful years that followed came *Doctor Zhivago*, a true representative of the times. Truth was a rare commodity in Russia, where it was usually skewered to a weak political philosophy. For thirty years, the truth about those times had been obscured but in this book Pasternak provided the resurrection of the Russian spirit and, at last, had talked to the dead Stalin about life and death.

Chapter 13

Boom, Depression and the League of Nations

The Treaty of Rapallo

The Treaty of Versailles had been implemented but it was not long before it was modified and the history of the 1920s and 1930s would revolve around its implementation, modification and repudiation. For Germany, reparations were the major difficulty but the inability to pay was often blamed on the loss of such territory as Silesia and Danzig and the loss of colonies. The burden of payment was truly on Germany, while the Austro-Hungarian Empire, which was just as much to blame for the start of the war but by the end had disintegrated, hardly shared the burden. This could be construed as unfair but did not resonate with the victors. The Ottoman Empire also disintegrated but many of its successor states were controlled by the victors.

Lloyd George tried to ease reparations in 1922, calling a conference at Genoa. Russia and Germany, the wounded tigers of the war denied the salve of victory, suspected they would be played off against each other, so had a pre-meeting at Rapallo and made their own treaty. The Russians were suspicious that Germany would be persuaded by the West to isolate Russia, while the Germans feared that the Russians would be used to demand reparations.

They united in their resistance to this perceived diplomacy and, in so doing, undermined the Treaty of Versailles, as Germany would use Russia as a base to rebuild its armed forces. The United States did not attend and France would not allow any modification of reparations repayment, so in the end

Germany and Russia were the only beneficiaries in what became known as the Treaty of Rapallo.

Albert Einstein

Beginning with papers that he produced in 1905, the world of physics made a dramatic leap with Einstein's theory of relativity, which supplanted Newtonian physics as the bedrock of the science. Only a few people understood what he was saying and many of his peers rejected the theory, just like those of Charles Darwin with his theory of evolution.

Einstein had very little status, being an employee of the Swiss Patent Office and not even a professor. In the world of science, Swiss universities were not very prestigious but he received no offers and thought of teaching in a local school. In the end, he did not do this but word circulated that he was not a very good teacher and this was probably true as he was not didactic and needed dialogue for inspiration.

At Zürich university, Alfred Kleiner, the Professor of Physics, was promoting Einstein. He recognised his worth and the genius in the theory of relativity and had arranged Einstein's doctorate. However, the faculty was concerned about Einstein as an Israelite and whether he exhibited overt and damning Semitic qualities. Having passed this test, they offered him a junior professorship in March 1909, which he refused because the pay was below what he was already getting. This caused the university to relent and offer him more.

Einstein was now on the academic ladder and his fame was gradually spreading, which resulted in the University of Prague offering him a full professorship after only six months at Zürich. This was not straightforward, as the faculty at Prague was very keen to accept him but the city being part of the Austro-Hungarian Empire had to get the approval of Emperor Franz Joseph and his ministers. Max Planck endorsed the recommendation, the most celebrated political scientist of his time, but it was overruled and an alternative candidate approved.

Gustav Jaumann, to his eternal credit, refused to take the job when he heard he was second choice and had not won on merit. However, there was another impediment: it was necessary for a professor in the empire to have a religion, otherwise they were barred. Einstein had written on his application form that he had no religion but he was persuaded to change this and to apply to become a citizen of the empire. In 1911 he was appointed to the post, with a salary twice that of his post in Zürich.

Prague did not work out for Einstein, however. His wife did not like the city, was showing signs of depression and they found the whole place rather stuffy. He had not cut his ties with Zürich, so when the university was upgraded and was looking for a professor of theoretical physics, Einstein was the obvious candidate. He returned to Zürich in 1912 but this was not the end of his wanderings. The next year, Max Planck and Walther Nernst, a chemist, came to Zürich with an offer. There was a vacancy in the Prussian Academy of Sciences and they offered him the directorship of a new physics institute plus a professorship at the University of Berlin.

Einstein was struggling intellectually in trying to link his theory of relativity with that of gravity and would be obsessed with this problem when the war started and would not solve it for a few years. The war was a hated interlude. By nature a pacifist and an internationalist, Einstein could see no sense in this nationalism run riot. He was a wanderer, who by his middle thirties had been a citizen of Switzerland, Germany and the Austro-Hungarian Empire, giving loyalty to all in his way; however, he was a citizen of the world committed to revealing its secrets.

Fritz Haber, who with Walther Nernst and Max Planck, had persuaded Einstein to come to Berlin, was a scientific giant whose synthesis of ammonia was a great boon to the armaments industry during the Great War. He was instrumental in making chlorine and supervised the first gas attack in April 1915, which killed 5,000. Nernst and Planck also supported the war, the former making a tear gas, which was abandoned.

By the end of the war, Einstein had resolved the link between the theory of relativity and gravity to his theoretical satisfaction. This would lead to a new cosmology and the discovery of the formation of black holes, which he was busy explaining to his peers. Meanwhile, as he was going through a divorce there were financial problems. To relieve them Einstein was hoping for an emolument, which a Nobel Prize would bring.

By 1919 Einstein had worldwide fame as the result of English scientists' observation of an eclipse in the south Atlantic, which he had predicted. The observation showed that gravity was capable of bending the path of a light wave from a star. When this became known and accepted, there was an outpouring of euphoria, with the *London Times* proclaiming: 'Revolution in Science'. Einstein became the recipient of universal adulation. However, there was still no Nobel Prize. Max Planck had been awarded a prize in 1919 and had been active in recommending Einstein, a process that had started with his peers in 1910. The problem was that relativity was a theory that had no practical proof, even with the eclipse observation, which the Swedes viewed with scepticism.

In 1921 Einstein had fourteen Nobel nominations, many of them effusive as to his ability as a world-class scientist; however, no prize was awarded that year. In 1922 a Swedish physicist, Carl Oseen, joined the Nobel committee and suggested that the theory of relativity should be temporarily ignored and Einstein should be given the prize for the discovery of the law of the photoelectric effect. By this time Einstein had arranged to go to Japan and would not be available for the presentation, even if he won the award.

In the end, he was awarded a retrospective Nobel Prize for 1921, while Niels Bohr won the prize in 1922. The Nobel committee hedged its bets by stating that it would not consider the value of Einstein's relativity and gravitational theories until they had been confirmed. He would never receive another Nobel Prize. Einstein's life was rich in variety and deep in worry at this time. He was a Zionist and, together with Chaim Weizmann, toured the United States in 1921, although he lectured on physics, while Weizmann recruited for the Zionist cause. Einstein was always very wary of becoming too involved in any political cause but tried to convert his friend Walther Rathenau to Zionism.

Rathenau, a proud Jew, believed that he was, above all, a fully assimilated German and his religion did not conflict with this fact. In 1922 he was foreign minister, his family owned the electrical firm AEG and he believed that anti-Semitism could be modified if Jews were prepared to take positions in public life. Chaim Weizmann strongly dissented from this line of thought and told him so. The humiliation of Germany through losing the war and being subject to the strictures of Versailles was such that the blame factor kicked in and, although there was hatred of Britain and France, the Jews and the communists were the biggest targets.

Such hatred found an outlet in Rathenau's murder in June 1922. This was the man who had negotiated the Treaty of Rapallo with Russia and there was an outpouring of sympathy for this distinguished politician. Conversely, Hitler applauded the assassination and accused Rathenau of being part of a Jewish communist conspiracy. This anti-Semitism appalled Einstein, who thought of leaving Berlin and taking a job as an engineer in Kiel. Nothing came of it but he now knew he was a citizen of the world and to live in the United States was a tempting prospect.

The World Economy in the 1920s

The United States was the powerhouse of the world economy and the only interruption in that country to the post-war boom came in 1921, when there was a short, sharp recession, with an increase in unemployment and a fall in prices. From then on it was growth and prosperity throughout the 1920s, with industrial production rising in 1925 to 48 per cent above its 1913 level.

In Europe it was different. Britain had difficulty in making good the disruption of the war and the wealth it had lost. In 1925 industrial production was 14 per cent lower than the level in 1913. In Germany there was galloping inflation, with prices doubling in 1919, trebling in 1920, standing still in 1921 and rising fifteen times in 1922. The currency was out of control and no sensible person would invest. France had no sympathy and, to enforce reparations, occupied the Ruhr in 1923.

Germany was gripped by hyperinflation, with the mark being meaninglessly traded in billions to the dollar compared to 4.2 marks to the dollar in 1913. France was not immune to this and found that its foray to enforce reparations was of little use, which started a run on the franc, combined with increased inflation. Germany had to stabilise its currency, which it managed after much suffering. With mild inflation but much unemployment, Germany managed well enough over the next six years; however, of all the nations it was most aware of the evils of inflation. Likewise, France realised that it could not continue to weaken Germany and expect it to pay reparations.

Germany by now had produced a leader of quality in Gustav Stresemann, who became chancellor in 1923. After the debacle in the Ruhr, France was forced to negotiate. Stresemann was genuine in his policy of adhering to the Treaty of Versailles and equally genuine in his wish to modify it. In other words, he believed in the rule of law, goodwill and the mutual obligation of treaties. However, he also believed in the injustice of the Treaty, in peace and in Germany's ability to play a creative part in world affairs.

Stresemann was a great man and a true German nationalist but his nationalism was not blind. He could acknowledge the nationalism of other leaders with their perceived rights and virtues. His abilities, combined with Aristide Briand, the French foreign minister, and Prime Minister Ramsay Macdonald, led to the Treaty of Locarno in December 1925, the lynchpin of peace until Hitler overturned it.

The Treaty of Locarno

The essence of this treaty was that France, Britain, Germany and Italy acknowledged certain realities. Germany acknowledged the sovereignty of

France in Alsace and Lorraine and that the Rhineland would remain demilitarised. In return it was accepted that foreign powers would not occupy the Ruhr. In the east, Germany would pursue a policy of arbitration with Poland and Czechoslovakia over the frontiers, with the rider that they would have to be revised.

France, for its part, kept its alliances with Poland and Czechoslovakia and could go to their aid if they were threatened. Although Russia and the United States were not parties to the Treaty of Locarno, the importance of their power remained. Both were looking inwards and grappling with the problems of their great territories, although the United States was the financial engine of the world, whose money was lubricating the industrial regeneration of Europe and the Soviet Union. At the same time, Germany was being brought back into the family by the decision to admit it to the League of Nations.

There was a problem, however, in that public opinion in France and Germany saw the treaty in different ways. The French, on the whole, did not like the concessions made and saw the treaty as the end of the process, while the Germans felt that what they were offered was inadequate and there was more room for bargaining. They wanted to rearm and defend themselves, to be rid of the excessive burden of reparations, for occupation forces in the Rhineland to go and the return of lost territory in the east.

There was movement in some of these areas before the advent of Hitler: in 1927 the Control Commission on German rearmament left, reparations were negotiated downwards in 1929 and, in 1930, the occupation forces left the Rhineland. With the Russians, the Germans had pursued limited rearmament and there was no doubt about which nation was dominating central Europe and whose power was burgeoning.

Churchill and Keynes

In the 1925–29 Conservative government in Britain, Prime Minister Baldwin appointed Churchill to the post of chancellor of the exchequer. It was one to which he was ill-fitted and where he made one of the greatest mistakes of his career by putting Britain back on the gold standard. Many people wanted to return to the old pre-war certainties, including the pegging of the currency to gold, which would stabilise the exchange rate at the expense of price fluctuation. Rising prices, as long as the rises were not too large, could be absorbed; falling prices, with the concomitant fall in wages, were less easily absorbed psychologically.

This is as true today as it was then – governments are terrified of deflation.

Keynes recognised and warned about this phenomenon. He called the gold standard a barbarous relic and pointed out that a regulated non-metallic standard had slipped in unnoticed and a paper money supply could be managed. Before Britain returned to the gold standard the economy was sluggish, with high unemployment of over 10 per cent. Afterwards, it was not helped by the limited liquidity that gold provided.

Keynes was arguably the foremost practitioner of economics between the wars. Just as the gold standard was to go, so economics as a science began to burgeon. Economics relies greatly on historical statistics to present its case and as the quality of statistics improved so did the science, becoming recognised as a discipline on its own. The great classical economists, such as Adam Smith, were recognised as such in retrospect. He held the chair of moral philosophy at Glasgow in the eighteenth century and lectured on several subjects. His curiosity steered him to investigate the science of society, which led him to write *An Inquiry into the Nature and Causes of the Wealth of Nations*, which became the seminal book of classical economics.

Economic inquiry grew throughout the nineteenth century and became more professional, until in the 1920s it was regarded as a science in its own right, becoming more and more mathematical in the process. The only trouble was that, unlike the physical, chemical and biological laws of nature, economics was often subject to unpredictable political and financial whims, thus earning the tag of the dismal science. This did not mean it was useless, as economies did often follow certain economic patterns. The trouble was that it was often undermined by the use of data, which by its very nature tends to be inaccurate, and by society in general, which does not always act rationally and in its own self-interest.

Economics and politics went hand in hand and the great shock of the depression made economists and politicians think. There is little doubt that one of the major causes of the depression was over-optimism and too much lending by the banks. This is a perennial problem of capitalism, which leads to business cycles. When the wild investment spree stopped, the banks had to rein in their lending.

In the United States, numerous banks went broke and were not saved when some could have been. The Bank of England had suffered from a spate of bank failures in the 1860s and had established itself as a banker of last resort; however, in the United States there was no sophisticated banker to take on this role. The Federal Reserve did not regard itself as a bank that could provide the liquidity for other banks to survive, so a failure of one bank could lead to a domino effect. The United States was the banker of last resort on the world stage, as every major nation was a debtor nation to it. If there was a slump, even a short one, the debtor nations would not repay their debts. This is what happened to every nation apart from Finland, whose constancy became a future diplomatic plus with the United States.

There were many economists moving towards a solution, including Keynes. In 1930 he produced *A Treatise on Money* in two volumes: *The Pure Theory of Money* and *The Applied Theory of Money*. He was moving towards a general theory but was not there yet, although the ambition was, and he was comprehensively linking together the strands of economic thought. He may not always have been right but he was producing the benchmark and articulating the thoughts that would overcome the depression. In retrospect, the political and the economic solution went hand in hand. Hoover and Roosevelt both stumbled on aspects of the solution just as Keynes incorporated strands of the solution into *The General Theory of Employment, Interest & Money*, published in 1935.

In essence, confidence had to be restored and, with Roosevelt, this started to happen. Put simply, an ordinary investor had to have the confidence that if they put money into a bank, they would not lose it. With unemployment in the region of 25 to 35 per cent in the capitalist world, those out of work needed the opportunity to work again. It was common sense and the government had to manage part of it through public works. If a person is employed in building a road, part of the money they earn is used in consumption of goods, which in turn increases the need to employ people to produce these goods, while the part they save can be used in investment, and so the cycle goes on.

Hitler, too, understood this. Over the next five years Germany's economy would be the most successful in overcoming unemployment. Hitler was a brilliant builder of roads but a major part of his public works programme, which pulled the rate of unemployment down to 2 per cent, was in the production of armaments.

The World Crisis

At the same time as Hitler was writing and publishing *Mein Kampf*, Churchill was writing and publishing *The World Crisis*, which was subsequently published as *The Great War* in an illustrated and popular edition. This is a brilliant book, not in the sense that it is a balanced and dispassionate assessment, as he was too close to events for that, but in the sense that he was able to distil the drama and tragedy of the years between Agadir and Locarno.

Being first lord of the admiralty at the beginning of the war, Churchill describes in detail how the fleet was prepared and protected from a pre-emptive strike, how Germany was defeated on the high seas and how the rest of its ships were holed up in ports around the world and the blockade created. His immense knowledge of naval matters leads to substantial coverage of the German submarine counter-attack and the attempted blockade of Britain.

Even more skewed is Churchill's treatment of the intervention at Antwerp, in which he participated. He gives this greater coverage than the crucial Battle of the Marne and later gives the Dardanelles intervention significant coverage, while treating the crucial events of 1916, such as Verdun, the Somme and the Brusilov offensive with due seriousness but with a lack of Churchillian brio. If one accepts this lack of balance, then *The World Crisis* is a work of genius. In one sense, because it is different, it makes one weigh up the difference between the conflicts on land and sea.

When one thinks of the Great War, one tends to think of the great land battles in Europe and the Middle East, with maybe the Battle of Jutland coming into the picture. However, with Churchill, the Battle of Jutland, which lasted a couple of days with about 10,000 casualties, is much more fully analysed than the Battle of Verdun, which lasted almost a year with hundreds of thousands of casualties. Yet in the scheme of things, the blockade of Germany and the counter-blockade of Britain were as momentous as the great land battles.

However, a Frenchman, a German, a Russian or an Austro-Hungarian would not write a history in this way. It is Anglocentric but it was in Britain that the fulcrum of world affairs were situated, just as in 1939 they were situated in Russia, to move back to Britain and then on to the United States by the end of the Second World War. Germany in 1914 was a great worldwide trading nation but this was immediately truncated once it went to war. This was a great British victory but was hardly acknowledged. The consequences haunted Germany and were the reason that it needed quick victories and peace in two world wars. There was no chance of long-term autarchy even within the curtilage of Germany's territorial ambitions. The blockade was the long-term war winner, and the blockade was effected by throttling Germany on the high seas.

The *World Crisis* acknowledges this but is very sketchy on how the blockade affected Germany. Most histories on the subject reflect this, as the effect was real but mainly anecdotal. Death by starvation takes time and is not overly dramatic. Some commentators have tried to quantify the number who died and have suggested a figure well in excess of the circa 600,000 who died by bombing in the Second World War. One of the more disturbing facts was that the killing by starvation went on well after the war had ended, as the blockade continued for some months to encourage Germany to ratify the peace treaty. And, of course, there was the interaction of the influenza epidemic, of which Churchill did comment on its inhumanity.

One of the great virtues of the book is its dignity, generosity of spirit and magnanimity. Churchill was a warrior who understood warriors and is imbued with the knightly virtues of the caste. One of the great acts of his life was to go to the front in his forties and once again share the experiences of a soldier. Although in a quiet part of the line, his bravery was never in question but he did not seem to greatly enjoy the random odds of life and death, especially when he was without air cover. He also fretted over being shackled by the minor command of a colonel. However, it alerted him to the awful sacrifice and the general's dilemma. Wars can only be won by fighting and defeating the enemy – a truism but fundamental to understanding the general's dilemma. The generals knew that sacrifices had to be made to achieve the breakthrough that could lead to a definitive end. From time to time there were false dawns. Attacking with gas was one that was tried to end the war. Attacking on a wide front without great preliminary bombardments allowed Brusilov to break through and gain hundreds of square miles of territory, But again it was a false dawn and the great sacrifice would only lead to revolution.

Towards the end of 1917, Churchill sided with Lloyd George in deploring the sacrifice made at Third Ypres (Passchendaele) but it was not entirely straightforward, with Russia collapsing, the Germans bringing troops from the east, the French quiescent and the Italians retreating. The surprising fact is that he does not blame Haig for the sacrifices made but is scathing about Chief of the Imperial General Staff, General Sir William Robertson.

All the time Churchill is looking for a solution and describes well the genesis and production of the tank. In some respects it was his baby and he was worried by its initial use at the Somme because it was revealed to the Germans, its misuse at Passchendaele in unsuitable conditions, but he rejoiced in its relative triumph at Cambrai. His descriptions of air power are less good, acknowledging its influence but having difficulty in describing it in concrete terms. By the end of the Great War, Britain had the biggest air force in the world, the only one with its own independent command, and it was very potent.

The greatest tour de force of the book is the Dardanelles campaign. It is a brilliant apologia for a failure but one, in Churchill's opinion, caused through lack of resources and the commanders' lack of verve and imagination. It was a sideshow but you would not think so from this book. In Churchill's view it was the greatest tragedy of the war.

If only the British and French had pushed on and been given adequate resources, the war would have been different. In 1915 Germany was still powerful, had suffered little attrition and had internal lines of communication, while Britain and France had only sea-borne lines of communication. The Turkish armies could have collapsed and the link with Russia made but there would have been a mighty German riposte. Perhaps it was here that the great battles of 1916 should have been fought but the odds were that the same kind of attritional warfare would have developed with the concomitant logistical problems and the same shedding of blood as elsewhere.

In 1915 it was too soon for a result in such a contest. Yet, once again, the greatest tragedy of the war could be said to be Russia's political, moral and psychological collapse and its consequences. The inability of Western Europe to remain in easy trading contact with Russia was an immense blow.

Churchill clearly saw the artifice of the Great War. The term 'battle' was changing its meaning. Before the war a battle was a cathartic event of short duration, usually with a decisive result. In this war a battle tended to be something of long duration, which gradually attained the dignity of the title and was not often decisive. The beginning and end were often hazy and there was an attritional component in all of them.

What Churchill recognised was the great triumph of the British Empire and its triumph as a world power against the continental empires of Germany, Austro-Hungary and Turkey. France was indispensable on the Western Front, but Italy and the United States were bit players. If France had collapsed, the British Empire would have had to rely on the United States, as would happen in the next war. Britain was propping up France and Italy economically, while the United States, propping up Britain in a financial sense, had come late to the war and had long lines of communication. The war ended just as the United States was making its mark. The British Empire defeated Turkey on its own and overcame the submarine menace with help from the United States, while its merchant fleet of 20,000 ships was trading unmolested on the seaways of the world when peace was declared.

The British were not dominant on the Balkan and Italian fronts but were influential. It was here that the crash came as the Germans needed help on the Western Front, where a modern conflict was being fought for the first time. Churchill witnessed a great deal of this, often at crucial moments. For instance, on 9 and 10 August 1918, the two days following the black day for the German army when Ludendorff knew the war was lost, Churchill was at the front witnessing the victorious army's attack. As minister of munitions, he spent a good deal of his time in France on official business.

What did not perturb Churchill much was the cost. He was marvellously insouciant and aristocratic in his attitude to money, both as a minister and as an individual. The surplus wealth of a great nation had been lost in war and wealth is the bedrock of power. The book gives little recognition to this, nor to the fact that the power of the United States had greatly increased and that of the British Empire had diminished.

With the peace, Churchill became minister of war and, as such, responsible for British actions in Russia. He was keen for action but the British people were tired of war as were most of his colleagues. They sympathised with his position and recognised that it would be preferable to have a certain continuity and evolution rather than revolution in Russian politics but Churchill saw the evil in Bolshevism. His description of the Russian civil war is masterful for the times. He was one of the few people who knew what was happening.

Likewise, his description of the peace conference is full of perspicacity. He rounds on Wilson for being idealistic in his solutions for Europe's woes, while failing to sell to his Republican opponents the concept of the League of Nations. On the other hand, he is fair to Wilson and is not an opponent of the League. Churchill's strictures are specific and he acknowledges Wilson's genius, coupled as it was with political failings.

The book's last chapter is entitled 'The End of the World Crisis', where Churchill firmly accuses Germany of aggression, even in the east. Germany willed the Battle of Tannenberg, lauded it as the nation's greatest victory and vigorously pursued the territorial dominion that came to it at the Treaty of Brest-Litovsk. He continues with much historical reflection on modern warfare and how it had developed. Sometimes he saw the future:

> Next time the competition may be to kill the women and children, and the civil population generally, and victory will give itself in sorry nuptials to the diligent hero who organizes it on the largest scale.

Later he refers to the Germans and what would have happened if they had not surrendered:

> The campaign of the year 1919 would have witnessed an immense accession to the power of destruction. Had the Germans retained their morale to make good their retreat to the Rhine, they would have been

assaulted in the summer of 1919 with forces and by methods incomparably more prodigious than any yet employed. Thousands of aeroplanes would have shattered their cities. Scores of thousands of cannon would have blasted their front. Arrangements were being made to carry simultaneously a quarter of a million men, together with all their requirements, continuously forward across country in mechanical vehicles moving ten or fifteen miles each day. Poison gases of incredible malignity, against which only a secret mask (which the Germans could not obtain in time) was proof, would have stifled all resistance and paralysed all life on the hostile front subjected to attack. No doubt the Germans, too, had their plans. But the hour of wrath had passed. The signal of relief was given, and the horrors of 1919 remained buried in the archives of the great antagonists.[19]

Churchill describes the ending of the world crisis through the creation of the twin pillars of the Treaty of Washington in 1921 and the Treaty of Locarno in 1925. The lesser known Treaty of Washington between the United States, Britain and Japan was essentially naval in character and looked to peace in the Pacific through arms limitations and a balance of power. The Treaty of Locarno between France, Germany and Britain, supported by Italy and the lesser European powers, provided for the stability of Europe. Treaties need goodwill to make them work and, when Churchill's book was published towards the end of the 1920s, there was optimism; however, the Great Depression and the foolish opportunism of the 1930s would wash this away.

Church and State

Out of the Great War came the communists' attempted extermination of religious belief. The Russians and Ukrainians were predominantly Orthodox, which was the state religion. The communists broke this link and the Orthodox Church was persecuted, together with the Catholic minority. The papacy tried to continue providing priests but the persecution was such that believers had to practise their faith underground and the papacy acknowledged that its influence was negligible.

Pope Pius XI was a substantial figure who clearly saw what was happening but had no clear vision of what to do about it. He left the direction of the Roman bureaucracy in the late 1920s and the 1930s to Eugenio Pacelli, a young man of many talents. For several years he was papal nuncio to Germany and negotiated the Reich Concordat, which had a notable effect on

German politics. Pacelli was tall, lean and ascetic, beautifully mannered, with an authoritative charm. He was a talented linguist, a skilled diplomatist, not a man of passion or enthusiasm but one who engendered enthusiasm worldwide as he seemed to embody the aristocratic glory of the Roman Catholic Church. To Stalin, Hitler and Mussolini, the populist heroes of the time, he was of little moment.

The war and revolution of 1914–22 had done damage to the Christian religions. There had been great poverty in Europe before the war but the economic and moral breakdown of the conflict had damaged the social fabric. The tenets of socialism held great appeal and all European states had to make their own accommodation with it. Only in the New World were there states unsullied by socialism and thus evolving in a more natural way.

A form of national socialism evolved in Central and Western Europe that made use of the historical past of the state and the glory and identity that accrued from it rather than rejecting the past as was the way of the communists. Because of this the communists were anathema to the papacy but they could try to form some sort of relationship with the National Socialists. For the papacy, this was the most important form of diplomacy during the inter-war period.

In 1929 the Holy See and the Italian fascists signed the Lateran Treaty. Although Eugenio Pacelli had little to do with this, his brother Francesco was party to its negotiations and drafting. The Italian state and the Holy See had been in a state of tension ever since Italy's unification in 1870. The pope was still the ostensible leader of a substantial territory but, with the Lateran Treaty, he abdicated power over all his former dominions except for the Vatican's 108 acres, a few churches in Rome and Castel Gandolfo, the pope's summer home.

The Italian state did pay a sum of money and acknowledge Roman Catholicism as the country's only religion and gave validity to all marriages performed in church. In politics, however, the papacy was neutered. The Catholic Partito Popolare was forced to disband and its leader was exiled. The Church was allowed to propagate the faith but was discouraged from political action, which was transferred into support for Mussolini, with the agreement of Pius XI.

The terms of the Lateran Treaty appealed to Hitler. Germany had a Catholic centre party with a fairly constant support of 15 per cent of the electorate and, because it was a centre party, it often played a crucial role in the formation of coalitions. Two successive chancellors, Bruning and Von Papen, were staunch Catholics and they tried to hold the centre in power and the extremists at bay. It was a forlorn hope, with the depression fuelling extremism and the extremists allowed to use intimidation, often of a violent nature, to gain their aims.

Nevertheless, Catholic opposition at the ballot box could have shackled Hitler or created a more viable opposition. But this did not happen, as Pacelli negotiated a concordat with the German fascists in the same way as had been done in Italy. To Pacelli, the advantages of a concordat were that they guaranteed Catholics' religious rights and retained their influence in education in exchange for a clergy that distanced itself from politics and the disbandment of the Catholic political party. To Hitler, the educational concessions were of little importance and they could easily be overturned as long as he had emasculated the clergy and persuaded Catholics to vote for the Nazi party.

In certain areas of Germany at this time there was a very strong, parish-based, social organisation that linked Catholics together. Its links were in the workplace as well as in the Church, so were quasi-political. The young were loyal to it and, as such, it was a rival to the Nazi Youth movement. This was not to the Nazis' liking and they created fights. In June 1933, 25,000 young Catholics met in Munich. The Nazis tried to ban the march but, in the end, allowed it to proceed as long as banners remained unfurled. The Catholics marched in orange shirts but were beaten up by brownshirt thugs, which caused the open-air mass of the following day to be cancelled. This was not an isolated incident and was before the concordat was signed.

The other characteristic of the concordat was that it ignored the strong views of the bishops and the clergy. It was an agreement between two authoritarian administrations, one in Berlin, the other in Rome. Pacelli was friendly with Ludwig Kaas, a priest and a politician who had led the Centre party since 1928. The strength of Kaas's loyalty was more to the priesthood and the Holy See than to his country and he was prepared to go along with the disbandment of his party without receiving any political favours in return.

As the concordat was being negotiated over the first six months of 1933, it was obvious to the members of the Centre party and the clergy that they were being thrown to the wolves and Heinrich Bruning replaced Kaas. As a former chancellor he had great experience of politics, understood what was happening and alerted German Catholics to the danger but was defeated. Pacelli and the Holy See imposed their vision and discipline on the German clergy and concurred with the distinction between the religious and political functions of the priest. Hitler spent much time and energy on the small print of this distinction as he hated the political priests and wanted to neutralise or eradicate them.

The concordat was signed in July and ratified in September 1933. Bruning continued to oppose it but had to be circumspect in Hitler's Germany, which was a land of gangsterism. Bruning, disillusioned, in ill health and hounded, went into exile in 1934 and did not return to Germany until after the war. He left before the mobs struck in earnest on 30 June 1934 when, in the Night of the Long Knives, Hitler's associates, whom he wished to discard, were murdered, as were four influential Catholics who had opposed him.

The papacy was now on course for taking a more apolitical view of the world. Its concern was for the Church to be active in saving and ministering to people's souls. If humankind could live in the spirit of Christ, it would influence their political actions, but the papacy was not concerned with being overtly political. When Italy decided to invade Abyssinia in 1934, there was no Vatican condemnation, although it was rumoured that Pius XI was against it. The papacy was politically emasculated in Europe yet its influence across the world was huge. Pacelli, the heir apparent, was sent to North and South America, received with enthusiasm and accepted as papabile and the likely next pope.

Western Europe and the League of Nations

The alliance of Britain, France and Italy, supported by the League of Nations, was the basis of security in Europe. Hitler's rise made Germany and Italy ideological partners but there were areas of potential conflict as the Italians regarded Austria and Hungary as their sphere of influence, together with Albania, parts of Yugoslavia and Greece. Nothing had changed from what Italy had put forward at Versailles as one of the victors.

If anyone thought that they had been denied the spoils of victory, it was the Italians. They also had ambitions of historical origin in Abyssinia. In 1896 the Italians had been beaten at the battle of Adowa and Mussolini wanted revenge. At one time, Italy had been Abyssinia's protector and in 1925 had promoted it as a member of the League of Nations, as it feared that Britain might have an interest.

In 1934 Mussolini calculated that Abyssinia was easy to conquer and a natural part of the Italian Empire. As both countries were members of the League of Nations, it put the League in a délicate position, as it was obvious who was the aggressor. Britain and France were ambivalent to Italy's ambitions. France, represented by Premier Laval, wanted to maintain a solid front against Germany, while Britain, worried by this threat to the League's authority, also wanted Mussolini on its side.

Eden, then a junior foreign minister, put forward a compromise whereby Abyssinia would be given access to the sea via British Somaliland, while a part of Abyssinia recently conquered by that nation would be given to Italy. Senior Italian diplomats wanted to accept this but it did not fit in with Mussolini's ideas of glory. Although Britain's plan was rejected, it did not feel the situation was out of hand as it reckoned that Italy would have difficulty in conquering Abyssinia in a short time and, if the Italian army were caught in the highlands in the winter, it might seek a solution. The Royal Navy also made an assessment and calculated that, even with the addition of the Home Fleet, it would have difficulty in beating the Italians in the enclosed waters of the Mediterranean, although it had the bases of Alexandria, Malta and Gibraltar.

By the middle of 1935, in this potpourri of diplomacy and threatened action, the emphasis changed under Prime Minister Baldwin and his foreign secretary, Samuel Hoare. At Geneva in September 1935, Hoare called for collective security. The Italians attacked in October 1935 and sanctions were applied. Even Hitler's Germany applied them, while the neutral United States said it would apply them to both sides. France, sensitive to the break-up of the alliance with Italy, applied sanctions but would not interfere with Italy's oil supplies, which was one area of vulnerability. Here there was an enormous paradox because the future appeasers were trying to bring Mussolini to heel, while Churchill sat on the fence and Vansittart supported the Italians.

There were also the problems of legitimacy and power. The League of Nations was a new institution struggling for its legitimacy, unsupported by the United States, the departed Japan and the ambivalent Soviet Union, while the remaining nations tried to give it purpose, which would only come from the collective will of the nations that made up its numbers. The only real world power among its members was Britain, which had been powerless to act against Japan over Manchuria and was unwilling to act with force against Italy. Thus, the League's authority was undermined. Britain and France put together the compromise that had been proposed earlier of access to the sea for the Abyssinians and a slice of territory for Italy.

The French revealed this plan, the Hoare–Laval Plan, which caused an uproar among idealistic British supporters of the League, leading to Baldwin repudiating Hoare and replacing him with Eden. At the same time, Flandin replaced Laval. A new plan was formulated but the British expectation that the Italian army would not be able to conquer quickly was found to be unfounded. In May 1936 Emperor Haile Selassie left his country and Mussolini annexed it to his empire.

This was a disaster. The alliance of Britain, France and Italy was broken and Italy would move by degrees but inexorably into the German camp, while the moral force of the League was disintegrating. Italy would leave the League in the following year, so the three powers of Germany, Italy and Japan, who had aggressive intentions, were outside its influence. Although out of the League, Germany was playing a cautious game and waiting for the split between France and Italy.

Sanctions continued against Italy, which allowed the French to maintain good relations with Britain, although the French were annoyed that Britain had treated Germany well in naval matters. When Italy departed from the League of Nations, all pretence that the League was a forum of influence had gone. What Woodrow Wilson had hoped would become the lynchpin of international security had been treated with contempt and found wanting. A collective stance against aggressors would not happen, which was hugely to the benefit of the aggressor.

Chapter 14

Changing Times in Germany

All Quiet on the Western Front

Erich Maria Remarque's *All Quiet on the Western Front* was published in Germany in 1929. Its great virtue was that it recorded war as it was. Although Ernst Jünger had produced his initial version of *Storm of Steel* in 1920, very little had been published in the ten years after the war that dealt with the reality of the conflict. There was escapism and many were trying to absorb the overall effect, asking themselves the question of what it was all about.

Remarque's book is about the ordinary German soldier and his friends, how they all leave school and go straight into the army, the most professional and efficient in the world. It may have been the best army in the world in many respects but it behaved in a universal way, with any degree of individualism subordinated to the orders of a non-commissioned officer who inculcated the fact that he was in charge and demanded total obedience. When their individual wills have been subjugated and they have been bullied into obedient soldiers, they are sent to the front.

There are wonderful descriptions of battle as the platoon survives an artillery barrage, followed by an enemy attack, which is repulsed. Then there is a counter-attack using hand grenades and machine guns, which leads to stalemate. However, their work is not over, as the trench system is partially destroyed and in need of reinstatement. Later, tanks and gas play their part. It is all described with great beauty, with death all around and the cries of wounded men and animals adding to the horror.

Of course, a soldier does not just fight. The soldiers' life revolves around comfort, food, drink and tobacco, and thoughts of sex that the brothel can assuage. When out of the front line the resourcefulness of the group, which has become tightly knit through surviving danger, can meet the soldiers' desires. There is a feeling of being lost when the group is broken up.

There are harrowing but beautiful descriptions of the pain of being home on leave and the attempt to return to the pleasures of normality. Even more harrowing is the description of being sent to guard a Russian POW camp. By this time, the Germans were not getting much to eat and the poor Russians were getting even less. The prisoners were in an advanced state of lassitude and Paul, the hero of the book, is torn by humanitarian feelings of compassion for his foe and a feeling of helplessness.

The book does not have a happy ending. It reveals that Germany's resources towards the end of the war were running out. The Germans hardly had a tank, they were outnumbered in the air, the Americans had arrived and were eager for battle and even the army could not be fully supplied with food. The Fatherland's soldiers were in a parlous condition. In the end, not one of the platoon survives.

It is a cathartic and beautiful novel that was made into a film in 1930. Remarque was twice nominated for the Nobel Peace Prize but did not win it; however, the film was acknowledged and received the Academy Award for best picture.

Ernst Jünger – *Storm of Steel*

This book was published in 1920. It is remarkable in that Jünger participated in most of the actions on the Western Front and was wounded frequently but with nothing that incapacitated him for long. He was tough, lucky and had that natural instinct for war that could detect the sound of a shell, a mortar ball, a rifle shot or machine-gun fire. To protect himself he moulded into the terrain of trenches and craters in no-man's land. Shell craters were his best friend and shells his worst enemy. What is revealing is the use of hand grenades in trench warfare. The tortuous nature of trenches, to mitigate the effect of shells, and the links of trenches to the second and third lines made the use of grenades the easiest way of moving along them.

Jünger provides an unsentimental view of an officer's life, with its need for optimism in the leading of men. Death was a constant companion and he acknowledges the death of colleagues but quickly puts it to one side. Unlike *All Quiet on the Western Front*, Jünger only records what happened on the battlefield. There is no record of home leave, what was happening in Germany or being seconded to look after Russian prisoners, which makes

Remarque's book so interesting. His brother does figure but only on the battlefield and, at the end of it all, one salutes a great soldier, although one knows little about him except in that capacity. Nevertheless, this is an excellent description of what it was really like to fight on the Western Front from the German perspective.

Jünger participated in most of the great battles, especially towards the end of the war. He was at Passchendaele in October 1917 and gives the impression that as a soldier he could not grasp the situation as the rain poured down, drowning out easy communication and blighting action. He records that there were dead soldiers everywhere and there was a feeling of helplessness.

The subsequent Battle of Cambrai was quite different. The tanks broke through and the British won territory but in the German counter-attack the British lost territory elsewhere and Jünger's company was involved in this gain, capturing hundreds of prisoners.

The tank had entered Jünger's consciousness but it does not figure as a great weapon of war. Several burned-out tanks appeared on his flank and were examined. The means to combat them were discussed but they were not feared as they looked cumbersome and vulnerable to shell fire. In fact, Jünger describes them as helpless beetles. Their threat in no way stopped the great storm trooper attack of March 1918 where Jünger triumphantly led his men through the British lines and caused a great retreat.

He reveals the parlous state of the German army as it comes upon dugouts left with plentiful food and he describes how the soldiers devoured cartons of raw eggs. An army marches on its stomach but the German army had little to march on until it came upon the cornucopia of conquest. Before the attack stalled, Jünger suffered a bad concussion and lost much blood but continued fighting until taken to a casualty station. He took great pride in this temporary victory, which he describes as the great battle, but also reveals his fear, as it was obvious that Allied resources were much greater than those of Germany.

Jünger returned to the Western Front in June 1918 but at the rear, although within range of shell fire. His company reached the front line as a result of the flu, which he briefly describes:

> Following a week on the front line, we were again moved back to the resistance line, since the battalion which was to relieve us was almost wiped out by Spanish influenza. Several men a day reported sick in our company as well. In the division next to ours, the epidemic raged to such an extent that an enemy airman dropped leaflets promising that the British would come and relieve them, if the units weren't

withdrawn. But we learned that the sickness was also spreading amongst the enemy; even though we, with our poor rations, were more prone to it. Young men in particular sometimes died overnight.[20]

This was June, when the virus was not particularly virulent and not the killer that it would become later in the year. It is Jünger's sole reference to the flu that would decimate armies. Like the tank, he badly underestimated its effect but all through the book records the aeroplane's increasing influence, which started by directing artillery fire and ended by bombing and strafing. It was these three factors that gave the Allies superiority and determined the end of the war. By this time Jünger was in Hanover, his beloved home town, having been shot through the chest at the end of July before the great Allied advances of August. He thought he was dying. The shot had pinned him to the ground but there were men who worshipped him, one of whom was killed while carrying him from the battlefield. Another carried him to the casualty station. The bullet had gone straight through a lung. He recovered quickly at Hanover, took part in the next war and died aged 102. The book was written by a professional soldier of great talent, recording the play in the game of war.

Hitler, as could be expected, abhorred *All Quiet on the Western Front* and it became a forbidden book but the Nazis exalted *Storm of Steel*.

The Rise of Hitler

It would take twelve years of plotting, planning and action for Hitler to become chancellor of Germany. It was a measured march of moving forward and retreating according to circumstances but essentially it was the emergence of someone who possessed political brilliance and who came to dominate his party. Even at its peak the party only had the support of just over a third of the German electorate but, once it had the levers of power, it would usurp the system.

The party had political flair for publicising itself. It had its own newspaper, the *Völkischer Beobacter*, it had a quasi-military arm, the SA (*Sturmabteilung*), which could use bully boy tactics, have fights with the communists and parade and march to proclaim its power and unity. As its leader, the party had a great orator in Adolf Hitler. In essence, it was a nationalist party, more socialist than capitalist, geared to appeal to the mass of the German people, who were Aryans, linked to an undertow of racial hatred.

With national disaster it thrived. During the great inflation of 1923, it overreached itself and staged the beer hall putsch in Munich, which in retrospect looked like a comedy of errors involving, among others, Ludendorff. This was an attempt to take over the state by force and there were deaths for which Hitler could be held responsible. Arrested and tried, Hitler used the court for propaganda purposes. A sympathetic judge exonerated Ludendorff and gave Hitler a five-year sentence, which was a mere rap over the knuckles for the crime committed. He was sent to Landsberg prison where he was treated with deference, had many comforts, received so many visitors that he had to limit them, read voluminously and wrote *Mein Kampf*, which would become a financial best-seller in ten years' time.

To Hitler, this was his university and it gave him time to think and talk, for like many great politicians he talked as he thought, modifying and fine-tuning his opinions as he went along. In so doing, he was endlessly repetitious, which was a burden for his acolytes. His time in prison was not wasted. He knew he was a man of destiny but he had learned enough to know that to win power he had to both dominate his movement and pursue a constitutional path. Being in prison lessened his authority and he watched the military arm of the movement increase its power, knowing it had to be curbed.

Mein Kampf

This is an unusual book written by a man humiliated by defeat and lusting for the power to enact revenge. Just as the inexorable rise to power of the Bolsheviks in Russia makes a sane man blink with disbelief, so does the rise of Hitler and the fascists. Both grabbed power slowly and by degrees and, when they had it in their grasp, they would not relinquish it. Both were ruthless in their exploitation of power.

With the Bolsheviks it was the ruthless domination of the Moscow–Petrograd axis, the implantation of the communist creed through the soviets, a certain provision of land for the dispossessed and the control of such staple requirements as food and oil. With the Germans it would be more subtle, although that word is not too apt for the fascists. Nevertheless, they would go through the democratic route until such time as they could discard it. They made a great appeal to the minds of men through both the spoken and written word, they created mass displays of harmony and they provided work. The two creeds overlapped but historical and personal reasons made them different. Both Hitler and Stalin absorbed history in a selective manner and used it for their own ends. They were men of power, not dispassionate scholars.

Hitler's talents became apparent through oratory. He had an instinct, a highly developed sense of how his words were influencing people. He needed his audience, which he would dominate with his fluency of exposition. When this audience showed a flicker of interest in what he was saying, he would amplify and develop the theme. It was this particular gift that gave him the tools to carry him to fame and fortune.

With Hitler in prison, the orator was silenced, so he decided to put his thoughts down on paper. This meant that his words were rooted and could be analysed. The appeal to the emotions could still be made but they could also be dissected. Hitler despised the written word and wrote in scathing terms of the power of the pen. It was a second-best way of expressing himself and was very revealing. On balance, he hated much more than he loved, thus the appeal of his movement was in wide-ranging hates and narrow, exclusive loves.

What moved and inspired him? Above all, there was his idea of a Germany restored to a greatness far exceeding any nation in the world and receiving due homage for this position. He believed in a homogenous Germany, an Aryan Germany, where race mattered and there was exclusiveness. Hitler was an urban animal and had a love-hate relationship with cities. Munich, he adored, Vienna he abhorred. For an urban soul who in later life would love mountain retreats with wide vistas, he was wedded to the soil. Here, Hitler believed, man could find his roots and a nation its stability.

With Germany's population growing, Hitler wanted more land for his people, which would be at the expense of some other nation or race with their own territorial rights. *Lebensraum* for the *Volk* was his cry. This notion of *Volk* was the link of blood, of racial binding. Blood was what determined race and he proclaimed a biological might that comes through this bonding at the expense of lesser mortals. The strong established themselves and the weak had to adapt.

His list of hates is much longer. His hatred of Vienna extended to the whole Austro-Hungarian Empire, with its multi-racial group of nations. Being a native of this empire was not to his liking. He mocked its structure, ignored its magnificent history and welcomed its demise. He felt that Germany had made a grave mistake in having it as an ally in the war. The Jewish population of Vienna was roughly 10 per cent. The sophisticated bourgeois cosmopolitan, of whom the Jew was a prime representative and who develops hand in hand with any civilisation, was anathema to him. The Jews dominated the financial and legal professions, the twin pillars of a functioning civilised state, and he hated this dominance, which he believed was worldwide.

Hitler's economic views were autarchic, nationalist ones, predominantly but not exclusively socialist. In this he was wiser than his communist opponents. But the Jew was a pariah in his German state and he declared this baldly, repeatedly, and the turgid repetition made it obscene. The Jew was also the scapegoat, the begetter of all the sins, weaknesses and failures of Germany. He also repeated this bombastically and obscenely. So far, he was only attacking the Jews with the written word, which hurt no one and only added to the rabid anti-Semitic literature of central Europe, of which there was a ripe collection. He had not, unlike the Russians, Poles, Ukrainians and others, been guilty of the pogroms of the early 1920s when over 100,000 Jews were gratuitously murdered. He was just building up a head of steam but his intent was clear.

This is the extraordinary fact about the book. Nothing is fudged. Hitler plainly sets out his aims for the rest of his life. France must be humiliated in war because it had humiliated Germany. Italy and Britain would have to be wooed because their interests did not directly conflict with those of Germany. European Russia was the objective, one that had virtually been gained at the Treaty of Brest-Litovsk and then taken away from Germany with defeat in the west. His hatred of the Slav was almost on a par with that of the Jew but the latter was more easily bullied. He wanted to eradicate the Jews but only make the Slavs helots. Hitler did not conceal his contempt for the Slavs in Russia, who were committed to Marxism or its variants. He saw this as a Jewish creed, which was bound to fail, and the Russians, by embracing it, had made themselves vulnerable to a resurgent German nation. His views of the world were shouted from on high and from now on could be read as a book. It was remarkable that so few took notice.

Mein Kampf is in two parts: the first published in July 1925, the second in December 1926. The former sold 23,000 copies by 1929, the latter was less popular and sold 13,000. Eventually the two parts were amalgamated into a and by the end of 1933 had sold one and a half million copies. With Hitler as chancellor, the book was ubiquitous and was presented to school leavers and to brides and grooms on marriage. As such it had quasi-biblical status and eight to nine million copies were published during Hitler's life.

Mein Kampf is an oratorical work as it was dictated to his amanuensis, Rudolph Hess, who modified some of the rants and inconsistencies of the text. There were also other advisers, who failed to make the whole much more coherent. Max Amman, a war comrade who published the book, chose the title, which was succinct as opposed to Hitler's long-winded suggestion: *Four and a Half Years of Struggle Against Lies, Stupidity and Cowardice.*

Amman was very disappointed in the text because here was a remarkable story of a corporal in the German army rising to great prominence as a politician. It could have been a romantic, rags to riches story, with hope engendered through abnegation to a great ideal, but all he got was a text debased with hate and vitriol. Here were exhibited the raw, gaping, bloody wounds of Germany's defeat.

Hitler's Rise to Power

With Hitler still in prison, his supporters were badgering the German judiciary to demand his release and he was paroled after little more than a year. Imprisonment had an effect on Hitler, who changed his tactics by stopping the negative racial abuse of the Jews, which had always been part of his oratory, and making the party fight for parliamentary seats on the way to power. He spoke of the German people's need for *lebensraum*, or living space, and the need for unity.

Towards the end of the 1920s this became his great theme and was an attack on the Weimar system and the factionalism of democracy. His National Socialist party would transcend class and bring prosperity to all the people. Although it was making little breakthrough in an electoral sense, people were taking notice of the publicity that the militant brownshirts of the SA and Hitler's oratory were engendering and the propaganda Joseph Goebbels was organising in the press and elsewhere. The Nazis were becoming a political force in Germany because the communists could not trump their patriotism and the democratic parties could not come together to override their factionalism.

It was the depression that created the fertile ground for the Nazis. Before this they had won only 2.6 per cent of the vote in 1928 and a paltry twelve seats in the Reichstag. With the misery of unemployment and with no obvious solutions, people were prepared to listen. When Hitler spoke, he struck a chord. In September 1930, six and a half million Germans voted for Hitler, which was 18.3 per cent of the electorate, and he was the leader of the second-largest party in the Reichstag with 107 seats. The Nazi leaders were amazed – they had momentum, outright power could be theirs, it would only need a few more elections.

President Hindenburg was not blind to the Nazis' faults and he faced the dilemma that they created; however, his great dislike was the Reichstag's left-wing leadership. With Stresemann now dead, Gustav Bruning was the chancellor and was embroiled in the problems of the depression, which could only be solved by palliatives with the aid of time, patience and the wise use of liquidity. Hindenburg, who was old and aware of time and mortality, wanted a right-wing chancellor.

German politics were a matter of coalitions and, to hold on to power, some supporters encouraged Bruning to take the Nazis into government. Hitler talked to Bruning, determined to take the constitutional route to power but his method was to enter a coalition as chancellor and thus have control. Here Hitler lost contact with some of his own supporters. One faction wanted him to grab power by force, while another wanted him to take power, even in a subordinate role, by entering coalitions. By taking on these two factions, Hitler managed to gain power and have total control of his party.

The quirkiness of Hitler's personality was revealed to few. Many referred to his magnetic personality, his ability to fix his unblinking gaze on a person and mesmerise them. Many testified as to how when they came into Hitler's presence they were of one opinion and when they left they were enthusiastic followers of his view. His was a male world where his personality dominated but he did not ignore women. He treated them with gallantry and as subservient but he needed them in his idiosyncratic way.

In 1931 Hitler was living with his niece, Geli Raubal, who was his constant escort and was in love with him. She suffered the pain of mildly reciprocated love and a total subservience to his will. This led to her wishing to escape from his stranglehold, which he denied. One day, while Hitler was away, she found his gun and killed herself. Hitler was grief-stricken and in despair, which he only overcame with a massive effort of will. Two years later Eva Braun would behave in the same way but she botched her attempt at suicide and learned to exist within Hitler's dictated parameters of love.

The office of president was coming up for re-election and the other party leaders tried to achieve agreement among themselves to allow Hindenburg to remain in office. Hitler would not allow this, so Hindenburg had to stand for re-election, where Hitler and others opposed him. In the first round Hindenburg was just under the necessary 50 per cent for election, with Hitler on 30 per cent and the Communist party's, Thalmann, on 13 per cent. In the rerun the figures were 53 per cent, 37 per cent and 10 per cent. Hindenburg was ailing physically and Hitler was on a roll. He had campaigned brilliantly using an aeroplane to cover the country and speaking to about two million people at twenty large venues. The state elections soon followed and the Nazi vote held firm, with 36.3 per cent voting for them in Prussia, which was by far the most important state in the country.

After Hindenburg's re-election, Chancellor Bruning persuaded him to dissolve the Nazis' paramilitary organisations, based on evidence that the SA would probably take power if Hitler were victorious. Although Hitler denied this would happen, it was pointed out that there was a possibility that he could not control the SA. The communist paramilitaries had been left out of the ban and the Reichswehr, led by General von Schleicher, opposed this. Schleicher believed that Hitler could be tamed and act constitutionally, while Hindenburg, sensing that the mood of the country was moving to the right, ditched Bruning and put Franz von Papen in his place.

Von Papen was a Catholic and a conservative but hardly a match for the iron will of Hitler. In the middle of June 1932, the ban on the SA was lifted, which led to general mayhem, usually between the Nazis and the communists, with over a hundred deaths. Von Papen called an election to the Reichstag and, on the last day of July, the Nazis became the largest party in the state with 37.4 per cent of the vote and 230 seats. In fact, the Nazis were mildly disappointed, as they thought they would move forward from the presidential elections.

Now it was a matter of tactics. Hindenburg refused to offer Hitler the chancellorship, while Hitler refused to take his party into power without it. Hitler's tactics caused a rift in the party, although it was kept hidden until the emergence of Gregor Strasser as the advocate of taking power without the chancellorship. Hitler had to be careful but he knew that no government without him, the leader of a mass movement, would have much legitimacy. If he did not join the government, there would almost certainly be new elections. He believed in his powers of persuasion and this is what happened. The electorate, however, was exhausted and many were fed up with Hitler but he was in his element, doing what he did best, making speeches. He made fifty of them in less than four weeks but the rhetoric did not do its magic. The Nazis went down to 33.1 per cent of the vote and 196 seats, while the Communist party vote rose to 16.9 per cent.

It was Von Schleicher who emerged as the potential chancellor who would bring the Nazis into power and try to control them. Gregor Strasser supported this move and was in many eyes the number two in the Nazi movement. Outside the Nazis, Strasser's stance against Hitler's obduracy was well supported but Hitler outflanked and then ostracised him. There could only be one leader of the movement.

There was a crisis in Germany but, as elsewhere in the world, it was an economic resolution crisis, the final sweat of a weakened body before it recovered. Unemployment in Germany was dire, which the official statistics did not reveal, and it was estimated that about half the population was either unemployed or partially employed. Although there were soup kitchens and special shelters in other countries, they abounded in Germany.

The three major party leaders – the ex-chancellor Von Papen, the present one Von Schleicher, and Hitler – were in continuous negotiation with Hindenburg, who was resisting Hitler's advance, while Papen and Schleicher were prepared to make an accommodation. There were, however, other influences, such as the business leaders and the results of elections. A small state, Lippe-Detmold, voted on 15 January and the Nazi vote increased to 39.5 per cent from 34.5 per cent. By the end of the month, amid increasing high tension, Von Papen agreed that Hitler be chancellor and he would be his deputy, at the same time holding the important post of Reich Commissar for Prussia, a post that Hitler wanted for the Nazis. Hindenburg was out on a limb and had to compromise, which he did by having Von Neurath as foreign minister, Von Blomberg at defence and Von Krosigk as finance minister. None of these were Nazis but Göring became minister of the interior, which gave him control of the police.

Von Papen took the view that Hitler would be tamed by this arrangement but Hitler had his own package, as he had insisted on new elections and an act that would allow him to enact enabling decrees without depending on the president or the Reichstag. This was a danger signal and Hitler's hunger for power had exhausted everyone. It was a relief when he was at last sworn in on 30 January 1933. Germany was on the road to regeneration and damnation.

Chapter 15

Other Rising World Powers

The Rise of Stalin

After about five years of power, Lenin's health began to fail. He was only in his early fifties but a series of strokes sapped his energy and at times befuddled his judgement. His potential successors hovered around but he would give no indication of a favourite. There were four main contenders.

Stalin had great influence and power via control of the party, which through its functionaries controlled the country. Many thought that he lacked star quality, which his rival Trotsky undoubtedly had in abundance. The other two candidates, Kamenev and Zinoviev, a powerful duo, often acted in tandem. Kamenev had chaired the Moscow Soviet and had been close to Lenin as a deputy commissar, while Zinoviev controlled Petrograd and was president of Comintern. In the background was the influential Bukharin, who was the intellectual interpreter of Leninism.

In 1923 at the 12th Party Congress, when Lenin was still alive, Trotsky made a brilliant speech on industry and his supporters spread the word that he was Lenin's choice as his successor. This bid for power through acclamation had the effect of bringing his rivals together. Stalin loathed Trotsky, who had always been an enemy, but Kamenev, Zinoviev and Bukharin now sided with Stalin, who had an iron grip on the party, which would control and stage-manage Lenin's death. All news of Lenin's health was released by the party, which meant that there was a news blackout. Even Trotsky had difficulty in knowing what was happening.

Sometimes the control of the party lapsed, as Lenin recovered and became active, but he soon relapsed. He lasted until January 1924, by which time Stalin had prepared him for the part he would play. He would be embalmed and deified, his face preserved for the worship of future generations. The body was brought to Moscow, kept in the Hall of Columns and people filed past in their thousands, while Stalin kept vigil. His rival, Trotsky, had been advised by his doctors to take a cure well away from Moscow. He remained convinced to his dying day that Lenin had been poisoned.

With the leader dead, the thrust for power became more overt. At the 13th Party Congress, a letter from Lenin was read out, which was critical of Stalin. Stalin thought he should indulge in some humility and offered to resign the post of general secretary but his rivals prevailed on him to remain as they did not want a rival in the role. Confirmed in his post by Trotsky, Kamenev, Zinoviev and Bukharin, he strove to expand his power and influence by increasing membership of the party and he used Lenin's name to do it.

The juggling for power continued as Trotsky, adopting the mantle of Lenin, quoted his words; however, these were the pure words of the Revolution. For some they were outdated as Lenin had contradicted himself, for tactical purposes, in the New Economic Policy, which Kamenev and Zinoviev supported. Thinking this was an excellent opportunity to expel Trotsky from the party, they found that Stalin opposed them. This was purely tactical, as Stalin preferred to undermine Trotsky's power base and had him removed as chairman of the Revolutionary Military Council. With this act, the creator of the Red Army was no longer at its head.

Trotsky was incensed, made an impassioned speech from the Throne Room of the Kremlin and departed. He had one last chance by appealing to the army and ordering it to act. His rivals waited with apprehension but Trotsky refused to move. He did not want to be accused of Bonapartism and to act contrary to the party dogma that all activity outside the party was counter-revolutionary. This lack of ruthlessness cost Trotsky dearly, while the duo of Kamenev and Zinoviev thought they were the winners with the appointment of their man, Frunze, as Trotsky's successor, although he did not last long. He suffered from stomach ulcers and died while being operated on. It may or may not have been murder but his successor was Voroshilov, Stalin's man.

Stalin needed an ally to break his rivals and found one in Bukharin, described as a rightist who believed in Lenin's New Economic Policy. This gave breathing space and encouragement to the kulak, the urban capitalist and bourgeois intellectual. Kamenev and Zinoviev went for Bukharin's jugular, saying he was betraying the revolution. At the 14th Party Congress, Stalin used the members to create uproar and confusion, winning a vote of 559 to

65 for himself and Bukharin against Zinoviev and Kamenev. Everything was contorted and confused in a bid for power. Kamenev was removed from the chairmanship, Zinoviev lost control of Leningrad but was still in the politburo, as was Trotsky, whose oratory was stilled, defeated by the cynicism of it all.

The man on the move was now Vyacheslav Molotov. All opposition was being neutered. The army was purged of Trotsky supporters, while men of influence who were not Stalinists were sent abroad as ambassadors. At the 15th Party Congress, Trotsky and Zinoviev were still around but Trotsky had to use the underground press to further his ideas and if either of them dared to address the politburo they were shouted down.

On 7 November 1926 there were two public demonstrations. Stalin let them happen, noting who demonstrated and who was for or against. He determined to liquidate them all, as those who demonstrated against Stalin were ideologically right but wrong in protesting against him, while the others were right in supporting him but ideologically wrong. A week later, Trotsky and Zinoviev were expelled from the party, then a little later Bukharin told Trotsky that he would be banished. He was offered two days grace but, when he planned a demonstration, he was abruptly removed.

Stalin now firmly held the apparatus of power and in 1927 started to put pressure on the kulaks and began the process of collectivisation. This was one of the most evil political processes of the century and was a complete volte-face, which he wanted Bukharin to explain to the people; however, Bukharin was horrified. Stalin needed class warfare to fertilise the revolution and to bring terror, which would enable the Bolsheviks to remain in power. This was Churchill's thesis and Stalin upheld it. Bukharin thought he could start a fight with Stalin over this and sought allies everywhere, even among the murderers in the secret service.

Trotsky ended his banishment with exile in January 1929 and, as such, became a focus for dissenters from Stalin's regime. Stalin found this very useful as he knew who Trotsky's enemies were and, when they were also his enemies, he leaked titbits to Trotsky, who would publish them, thus giving Stalin a pretext for their removal or liquidation.

Terror was widespread and in 1927 was celebrated when the party lauded the secret police, the GPU. It was seen as the punitive sword of the revolution, while Bukharin praised it fulsomely as having accomplished the greatest miracle of all time by changing the nature of Russians. In its corrupt nastiness it was indeed one of the world leaders of the century. At this time it was preparing for the show trials by acting against the innocent intelligentsia such as engineers or scientists. In 1928, fifty-three engineers were brought to trial, primed, bullied and conditioned to confess their failings, even though they had been told they had done nothing wrong. The GPU explained that it was necessary to show the Russian people that the communists were winning the fight against the capitalists. Under duress, all confessed and five were executed.

Bukharin's opposition to Stalin continued. He likened him to Genghis Khan in his relationship with the kulaks and the peasantry and was intent on building sufficient opposition to get the policy reversed. Stalin watched him, gave him enough rope to hang himself, then attacked. It was not long before Bukharin folded, asked Stalin's forgiveness and pleaded for reconciliation. Stalin had him removed from the politburo. For Bukharin it was the beginning of the end.

By the end of 1929 the proclamation had gone out that the kulaks would be liquidated as a land-owning class and the peasantry remaining on the land would own nothing as it would be owned collectively. Getting rid of people who had been prosperous and had owned a stake in the land was no easy matter. A certain number, especially those who had the bravery to resist, were killed; another group were deported and dumped hundreds of miles away in unfertile areas; a third group, less likely to make trouble, were banished to areas outside the collective farms. Molotov was Stalin's agent in this class liquidation, where thousands of families were transported in cattle trucks, many perishing en route. When they were released in a desolate wilderness, the authorities who received them could rarely cope. It was a forerunner of the Jewish experience under Hitler and about equal in its effects.

With the kulaks gone and collectivisation of the land, there was a mighty famine. This was to some extent self-induced as it was Stalin's policy to export grain, as he needed the capital to build new factories. All through the famine, the poor peasant on the farm was subject to terror. The stealing of even a few grains could lead to execution. The peasants in the villages reacted by migrating to the towns, which led to the introduction of passports and further control of all movement within Russia. There are no real statistics on the effect of the famine but it is estimated that between five and eight million people died. Word leaked to the outside world of this carnage but it did not cause an enormous stir; after all, there was plenty of hunger and depression elsewhere.

In Russia, everything had now to be subordinated to the Communist party and its interpretation of the world. Churches were closed, some demolished; priests were not allowed to minister; musicians, writers, artists and scientists were subject to the dogma of Stalinism; and tame artists such as Maxim Gorky were put in charge of this intellectual utopia.

There was now only one living God, Stalin, from whom all belief and aspiration came, and it was verified by the dead God, Lenin. Their words were one – infallible and holy writ. For the people of the Soviet Union it was tragic and in large swathes of life the creative impulse was stilled or damped down, whereas it had flourished in the previous hundred years. By 1933 Stalin, the supreme autocrat, had done his worst but there was more to come.

Franklin Delano Roosevelt

Although Roosevelt had many enemies, which did not greatly diminish as he became older and more successful, he had even more allies. His charm, modesty, political competence, an ability not to gratuitously create enemies, together with an east coast aristocratic background, allowed him to climb the ladder. He was not enthusiastic when it was mooted that he would be invited to be a vice-presidential candidate in 1920. No one knew who would be nominated or whether Wilson would continue but the president was sick and incapacitated and public opinion had turned isolationist and rejected the League of Nations. The presidential nomination fell to James Cox, who favoured the League, and he chose Roosevelt as his vice-presidential candidate. The Democrats were out of temper with the times, while Cox carried the stigma of being divorced.

Roosevelt campaigned with fervour and passion, supporting the League of Nations, but this led to trouble, which he would not forget. He was asked why Britain and its colonies would have six votes to the United States' one, which he defended by saying that the United States was linked to the central American states such as Cuba and Haiti, which would vote with the United States. He then started to talk big and said he had something to do with the running of a couple of small republics and that he wrote Haiti's constitution himself. The press picked this up and attacked him, whereupon he claimed he had been misquoted. It was a gaffe that all politicians make from time to time but it was a lesson well learned.

Harding beat Cox by 404 to 127 votes in the electoral college but Roosevelt was young and the stigma of losing so easily was not attached to him. Meanwhile, he had received a fine training in national politics and could now return to his law business. His contacts were a bonus to the law firm but he was not a natural lawyer, as the detail did not engage his enthusiasm like politics. He had a genius for welding together people in the political process, matching the tiller to the wind in the sails and getting the boat to port.

Enemies, however, were lying in wait and did their best to discredit Roosevelt with the Newport scandal in 1921. This was an investigation into what had been happening at the naval base when Daniels and Roosevelt had been in charge. There had been widespread homosexuality and drug use, so Roosevelt had sent in naval personnel to discover what was going on and allowed them to proceed by entrapment. When a senate committee headed by Republicans put this into print and took the high moral tone, it did not look good. The *New York Times* headline was 'Lay Navy Scandal to F.D. Roosevelt – Details Are Unprintable'.

Roosevelt felt maligned and was indignant. Someone had once took a high moral stance about the traditions of the British navy, whereupon Churchill pointed out that the traditions were rum, sodomy and the lash. In applying the lash Roosevelt had got himself into trouble and it damaged his self-esteem. He regarded himself as an honourable man but the Newport scandal tarnished him.

The following month, August 1921, Roosevelt went on holiday. He was a fit, handsome, energetic, thirty-nine-year-old father who enjoyed being with his children on vacation. Out of the blue he was stricken by the poliomyelitis virus, although it took some time to diagnose. He was paralysed from the trunk down, which in time would only get partially better and he would never regain the use of his legs. With his natural optimism, he thought his condition temporary and it took him many months to come to terms with life as it was. It was only with the use of braces and support that he would be able to stand vertically. As for politics, he was very limited in what he could do and the future did not look bright. Would he ever be able to mount a local campaign, much less a national one? His future was dubious, yet over the next few years he clawed his way back with a courage that brought admiration.

In 1924 he attended the Democratic convention as part of the New York delegation. Al Smith was seeking the nomination, whom Roosevelt had helped persuade to become governor of New York in 1922. It fell to Roosevelt to make the nominating speech as it was felt that the Protestant patrician's support would complement the appeal of the Irish Catholic from the Bowery. This speech, which someone wrote for him and he did not much like, was a huge success. He was back in national politics. He was lucky, too, that he was not a vice-presidential candidate, as Calvin Coolidge comfortably beat Smith. However, Smith was the big noise in New York, dominated its politics and had Roosevelt's tacit support.

Four years passed, Smith sought the Democratic nomination again, won it and decided to relinquish his New York base as governor. In his bid for president, he recognised that he needed all those upstate votes, which Roosevelt could deliver, and he and other Democrats wanted Roosevelt to stand for governor. Roosevelt was in Warm Springs trying to regain his health, thinking that with vigorous exercise in a warm climate he would be able to walk again, so he declined the nomination. No one suitable could be found to stand, so they continued to twist Roosevelt's arm, but the best they could get out of him was a certain ambivalence.

The Democrats went ahead and selected him. His caution was rewarded, as the Republicans were favourites and it looked as though he was doing Al Smith a favour. In the presidential elections, Smith turned out to be no match for Herbert Hoover, who won in a landslide. It looked ominous for Roosevelt in New York but enough people who voted for Hoover the Republican as president were prepared to vote for the Democrat Roosevelt. He won by 0.5 per cent. It was at this point that his friends knew that here was somebody who was papabile and, unlike Al Smith, might be able to engage Americans away from the east coast.

Smith still felt that he was the true power in New York and tried to persuade Roosevelt to keep on his people. Roosevelt moved slowly but, over time, he moulded his own team. The depression was hurting and Roosevelt, like everyone else, did not know what to do, as something of this severity was a new experience. He was lucky in one sense that the people looked to the Republican federal government for a solution, so he could make suggestions as a Democrat without any responsibilities. Yet he could act on a practical plane in New York by offering the bare necessities of life to the down and out. In another respect he was imaginative in recommending the shortening of the working week, because if people worked shorter hours, surely more could be employed to take up the slack.

Being in the banking centre of the world, Roosevelt watched banks fall like ninepins. One was grandly called the Bank of the United States, although it was mainly used by garment workers. In the mayhem it went bust, taking with it the savings of thousands of innocent workers, although Roosevelt had tried hard to get the backing to save it through contacts in the banking world. He knew the banking system was crucial to recovery and had appointed Joseph Brodrick to supervise the system in the state and to initiate legislation to improve its regulation. Even this had not helped the Bank of the United States. When Brodrick incurred the populace's fury for allegedly not acting quickly enough, Roosevelt had the courage to defend him.

Roosevelt was no economist. He considered possible solutions, such as the dole, which he rejected, and employment insurance to be paid for by the employers, employees and the state. In fact, by the time he was elected president he had the wrong solution in advocating balanced budgets, no deficits and the reining-in of spending, while Hoover had the opposite and correct solution. Hoover, however, appeared hard-nosed and ruthless to the people in contradistinction to his help and compassion to the people of Europe after the war, while Roosevelt was genuinely concerned, slightly baffled, although still optimistic and seeking solutions.

With biennial elections for governor of New York, Roosevelt stood again at the end of 1930 and won with a substantial majority. His brand of politics, creating a broadband coalition of people of goodwill, made him a formidable vote-getter. The presidency was beckoning but there was no word of it except behind closed doors. His emollient and devoted friend, Jim Farley, was plotting and planning by putting Roosevelt's name in front of the great of Democratic politics across the nation, seeking their opinions on a range of issues and then card-indexing them.

The three great issues facing the American people were prohibition, isolation and the depression. Prohibition was a ridiculous issue for a great people but indicative of their puritan origins. Roosevelt finessed it, wanting to make it a state responsibility rather than a federal one. On isolation he was seemingly out on a limb as he had been a League of Nations man in 1920 and he realised that for political purposes he would have to renounce this, which would bring him enemies. On the depression he edged forward as a man seeking a solution but optimistic as to the outcome.

He made no song or dance as he moved on to the national stage with the primaries and then the national Democratic convention in Chicago. The Democrats were not the natural party of power, their only outstanding President in most people's lifetime being Woodrow Wilson, and the Republicans had been in power for twelve years. At the Democratic convention it was necessary for the winning candidate to carry two-thirds of the votes, which led to deadlocked conventions and a consequent lack of authority in the candidate. On the first ballot Roosevelt received 666.5 votes, while there were 203.25 for Al Smith and 90.25 for John Garner of Texas. As long as Roosevelt held momentum he would be elected. A ballot could take a few hours and in the next he edged forward by only eleven votes, then in the next by 4.75. There was now exhaustion and time for reflection and wheeler-dealing but Roosevelt could not be denied.

The tough part was over. The depression had induced a change in American politics just as it had done everywhere else. It was the great event between the two world wars but by 1933 had passed its peak. In 1932 events looked as grim as they could possibly be but now the healing process could begin. Roosevelt, like Hitler, was a beneficiary and was on his way. He was quintessentially American, someone who embraced the political temper and rhythm that Walt Whitman expressed in *Leaves of Grass*:

> Who are you indeed who would talk or sing to America?
> Have you studied out the land, its idioms and men?
> Have you learn'd the physiology, phrenology, politics, geography, pride, freedom, friendship of the land? Its substratums and objects?
> Have you consider'd the organic compact of the first day of the first year of Independence, sign'd by the Commissioners, ratified by the States, and read by Washington at the head of the army?
> Have you possess'd yourself of the Federal Constitution?
> Do you see who have left all feudal processes and poems behind them, and assumed the poems and processes of Democracy?[21]

Despite reverses with the Supreme Court, Roosevelt's answer to these questions is a grand and magnificent affirmation, a series of Joycean yesses.

Chiang Kai-Shek and the Kuomintang

In the 1920s China was struggling to survive as a coherent whole. The Japanese knew this and were waiting to exploit it and be recognised as overlords of the East. China's strength was in its great territory, enormous population and the intelligence of its people; its curse was that this enormous population was so difficult to manage consistently. The Kuomintang had been recognised as the successor to the Manchus. From its power base at Canton in the south, its influence radiated over the whole of China, winning the allegiance of most of the warlords who had sprung up with the demise of the Manchus. Its legitimacy, however, was not fully accepted. The curse of overpopulation divided the people into landed and landless. In the latter category were the under-employed and unemployed. Eighty per cent of the population was economically linked to the land and those who could not make a living drifted towards the army, which was inflated in number.

The landed class was linked to the Kuomintang but the regime's power base came from the army. The old-fashioned mandarin class and the new members of the civil service were trying to grapple with the modern world and to mould it to Chinese custom but the Kuomintang was having trouble forming a cohesive ruling class, so its authority tended to be local and did not give the traditional political coherence to China. The military world dominated the civilian world and gave China what political ethos it possessed but the army was not well organised. Distinguished military figures from Germany were hired to make it a formidable force but any success was partial. It was a mercenary rabble, low in discipline and weapons but high in manpower.

The Kuomintang had a rival in the communists, who had been inspired by the Bolshevik revolution and wooed the proletariat of the cities and the rural dispossessed. The Kuomintang had leaders who were ideologically sympathetic to the communists and looked upon them as a potential ally. If the revolutionary aspect of Marxism could have been rejected, there could have been some substance in this, but communist intransigence and revolutionary dogma soon led the Kuomintang to realise that compromise was impossible.

In 1927 the Kuomintang extended its power to Shanghai and with this success decided to break the loose alliance it had with the communists. This was a blow to the communists, who unsuccessfully attempted to form a power base with the workers in the cities, so they wooed the rural landless. This group often allied itself to bandit leaders. Such a power base was formed in the Kiangsi area, becoming known as the Kiangsi Soviet. With the Kuomintang's power secure in Shanghai and the communists trying to create power bases, Chiang Kai-Shek rose to prominence and became the Kuomintang's acknowledged leader. He promised the people that he would unite China and, because the communists would not come to some sort of arrangement, there was civil war.

During the 1920s Japan was muted in its ambitions and any potential threat to China was in the north. Nevertheless, Chiang chose to gamble that there would not be a debilitating civil war that would make China vulnerable to the Japanese. He had to break the communists, who surprisingly were not a power among the industrial proletariat in the cities but had support in the countryside from the landless. The communists were naturally against the landed gentry and for the redistribution of land, which went to families whose sons were in the Red Army. This land reform brought support but the problem for the communists was to establish a power base and control it.

From 1930–34 there was fighting on a large scale in the Kiangsi area, the main communist power base, with the nationalist forces initiating five encirclement campaigns before they were successful. The communists had little money and few arms, relying mainly on the rifle, the machine gun and guerrilla tactics. Their soldiers merged into the general population and only attacked when their opponents were vulnerable. The nationalists overcame this by creating a system of interlocking blockhouses and, when the communists tried to emulate them, they used their superior artillery to knock out the communist blockhouses. Within seven years, Chiang had triumphed over the Red Army and sent it on its long march. He had triumphed but the Red Army was not defeated.

The Japanese Army

Chiang may have triumphed over the communists and had the chance to unite China but to the north there was another potential foe with a formidable army. Japan's army was well trained in the art of war and well armed compared to the Chinese. It was not trained in the art of diplomacy and in its higher echelons tended not to be subordinate to the civilian power. It was a peasant army and its lower orders were brutalised into unthinking obedience and conditioned to give their life in battle for the emperor. One of the consequences of this was that they brutalised their foes when they gained the upper hand. The officer class came predominantly from peasant stock, although there were middle-class army families. The peasant soldiers left school at fourteen, were trained and the most successful creamed off to form an officers' cadre. At a later date there would be a further selection for the higher echelons of the army. This narrow, tough and competitive selection produced able but rigidly trained soldiers whose discipline and self-sacrifice was magnificent in battle but often broke in contact with the civilian and political power, which had very different values, whether it be at home or abroad.

The Japanese army became notorious for assassinations and three prime ministers would go this way in the next twenty years, yet the army achieved little from these murders. The perpetrators were treated sometimes as criminals but more often as men who had patriotic motives but were misguided. Some were executed but many plotters and activists returned to their commands. The civil power tried to appease this Japanese form of banditry; it was a fatal flaw in the system.

The army, in its high command, could barely control the call to action when it was triggered. The frenzy, the willingness to make the supreme sacrifice, blunted good sense. At the apogee of this system was the emperor, the mysterious symbol revered as a god who provided the inspiration and solace for the supreme sacrifice. The reality was that Hirohito was a mild-mannered figurehead who theoretically had absolute power but was a constitutional monarch in action, whose family embraced a wide spectrum of opinion. The politicians, of whom there were many from the armed forces, paid lip service to the emperor's views, only heeding them when it suited. The court class around the emperor was, on the whole, much less aggressive than the governments of the day and always advised caution regarding Japan's imperial ambitions.

Manchuria 1931

The Manchurian Incident of 1931 illustrates well the Japanese army's role in formulating the country's policy. Manchuria, from which the Manchus came to topple the Ming Dynasty in 1664, was regarded as part of China, although outside the Great Wall. After 1911 the powerful warlord Chang Tao-Lin operated under Japan's protection. As the Japanese controlled the railway, had forces along its length and controlled most of the trade, it was a symbiotic relationship with Chang. He also had a foothold in north China but the Kuomintang was forcing him to retire. Japan's foreign ministry thought this an opportune moment to emasculate him, but Prime Minister Tanaka overruled this, feeling that Chang was of benefit to Japan. An assurance was given to the Kuomintang that Chang would not in future interfere in north China.

This was in 1928 and, as the policy was being implemented, Chang was assassinated on a train journey. Who was responsible was baffling to all concerned, as it transpired that it was not the responsibility of anyone in high authority but of a clique of Japanese army officers whose highest rank was colonel. Their objective was to impose Japanese rule over Manchuria. The secret police found the culprits and the emperor requested that they be severely punished, as did the government. The army's general staff did not want the facts revealed because it would harm the army's prestige, so the right wing in Tanaka's party put pressure on the emperor, pointing out that the culprits had acted with patriotic motives. In confusion, Tanaka resigned and the culprits lived to fight another day.

Chang's son, Chang Hsueh-Liang, succeeded him. He was a thirty-year-old with ability and character. A former opium addict who had cured himself, he saw his role as predominantly diplomatic, siding with the Kuomintang and acknowledging that he was a Chinese subject but at the same time appeasing the Japanese, who had killed his father. This balancing of power, which he did well, increased his influence and was acceptable in political circles in

Tokyo, where the Shidehara Policy had been formulated. This policy tried to synthesise an acceptable way to accommodate Japanese, Chinese and the Western powers on the Asian mainland. The only trouble was that the Kwantung army in Manchuria regarded it as vague nonsense. As far as it was concerned, Manchuria should be conquered and annexed to the Japanese Empire.

The civil power did what it could, after all it ruled Japan and the army was subordinate to it. However, events dictated politics and the Kwantung army called the shots, while those in power in Tokyo reacted to them. In September 1931, the army unsuccessfully attempted to derail the Changzhou to Mukden express but used the inadequate explosion to blame the Chinese for sabotage and occupied Mukden. The plotters, convening that night, gave themselves authority through General Shigeru Honjo to occupy south and central Manchuria.

The West was in the grip of the depression and not entirely aware of the enormity of this act, while Japan's government assured the foreign powers that this was only a temporary expedient to restore order. Tokyo, however, could not control the Kwantung army, which had now hijacked Manchuria. This particular operation was referred to as the Manchurian Incident. There were endless repercussions. An incident it may have been but it was an excuse for war. China's forces outnumbered those of Japan by a ratio of 30:1 but quality was more important than quantity and the Japanese swept them aside without much difficulty.

The population of Manchuria was thirty-four and a half million, of which 3 per cent were Manchus and 90 per cent Chinese. There were just under a quarter of a million Japanese in Manchuria, a region of 380,000 square miles, to which can be added Jehol (60,000 square miles). It was mountainous, with the concomitant river gorges and fertile areas producing 60 per cent of the world's soybeans. It was also rich in mineral deposits of iron and aluminium ores, magnesite and molybdenum, which, allied to hydroelectric power, provided all the elements of a steel industry. The climate was extreme, with frozen rivers and numbing cold in winter, humid heat and monsoon weather in high summer. It was not very amenable to the Japanese offshore islanders.

The Kwantung army had become a law unto itself. In retrospect it is a mystery how it was allowed to act in this insubordinate way. To nip this in the bud would have required an example to be made of the officers concerned but the politicians were fearful of public opinion and of strands of opinion within their own support, so did nothing and paid the price.

Prime Minister Wakatsuki Reijiro, directed the war minister, Jiro Minami, to cease operations in Manchuria and had cabinet backing. Minami showed Wakatsuki lines on the map beyond which the forces would not go. Day by day the Kwantung army passed them, with an assurance that this would be the final step, while Wakatsuki watched the people rejoicing in the exploits of this army. It was an impossible position, so he and his cabinet resigned at the end of 1931. His successor accepted the fait accompli and the Japanese were de facto masters of most of Manchuria and Jehol.

However, Japan did not want to run the state directly, only to control it. Thus, a new entity was formed called Manchukuo, the land of the Manchus. Pu-Yi, who as an infant was the last Manchu emperor in 1911, twenty years later became the figurehead of the new state. This position was sealed by a gift of a sword and a mirror, two of the three objects that the Japanese throne regarded as sacred.

The Japanese had thought about their role as imperialists and colonialists and, on the surface, respected Chinese pride; however, in practice they showed scant respect for others. They were exceptionally efficient in developing the region, and the wealth they created would allow them to try to dominate Asia and the Western Pacific, but they were not good at appealing to the minds of their fellow Asians.

The army's triumph in Manchuria, which caused the fall of a government, had given it great prestige. It was a great political force, which was very dangerous. The navy looked at the army's swaggering confidence and was displeased. It was a different kind of institution to the army as its officer class did not come predominantly from the peasantry but from university graduates and middle-class families. Its ethos was forged in the puritanical struggle for survival on the sea and the technological challenges of a warship. The navy was attached to Japan and, as such, not involved in the politics of occupation. There is no doubt, however, that it was a formidable force in the Western Pacific and feared by both the British and American navies. Although the Anglo–Japanese Alliance was no more, there was a certain sympathy between the two navies, which the United States did not like. Likewise, the Japanese were aware that the Anglo-Saxons could collude at any time, having more in common than in division.

The Geneva Naval Conference of 1927 saw Japan and Britain in agreement in that they did not want naval expansion but the burgeoning power of the United States wanted growth to achieve parity with Britain. This caused much ill-will as one fleet's new build makes the equivalent in the other fleet obsolete, although the tonnage may be the same. In fact, what these arms limitation exercises revealed was that there were too many factors involved for any true agreement on parity. In addition, the whole thing could be made to look pointless by two nations linking together, such as Britain and France, which the Americans wrongly suspected in 1928. The Americans were also worried by Japan's developments of heavy cruisers and submarines, which they thought was giving the Japanese an advantage, so in 1930 a new arms limitation conference was held in London.

The Americans and British had patched up their differences. US Secretary of State Henry Stimson kept the Japanese, not particularly expansionist, in their place, a little unfairly it is thought. The negotiations were extremely complex and the end result was not a comfort to anyone. It certainly created a faction in Japan's navy that wanted to reject the deal but there were three major naval personalities, each of whom would become prime minister of Japan at some time, who accepted the deal. The only way for it to be rejected was for the army to side with the faction that wished to reject it. The army would not do this, which was just as well. It was preferable for the navy to be a countervailing force rather than the army and navy dominating the state.

Japan's navy did not get involved in the Manchurian Incident but China's government was appalled at the takeover and appealed to international opinion via the League of Nations. The League had been effective in minor disputes in Europe, so China was hoping it could restrain a more formidable power such as Japan. The worldwide depression made the Americans and British think before putting pressure on Japan. Only the Royal Navy at that time could have applied sanctions, which would have meant patrolling between Japan and the mainland. But this was an impossible task as the Japanese navy bases nearby could well have intervened and the Royal Navy would have been no match for them.

The League of Nations commissioned an enquiry, headed by Lord Lytton, which was sympathetic to Japan but pointed out that whoever controlled Manchuria had great influence on north China and, with these political and strategic advantages, endangered China's peace. The Lytton Report stated that Japan was guilty as an aggressor but China was partly to blame.

Such objectivity failed to placate the Japanese, so in March 1933 Japan resigned from the League of Nations. Having been an influential and constructive member of the League, its departure was damaging. The major power in the East had departed, the United States was isolationist, the Soviet Union treated the League with contempt, so the great hopes of Woodrow Wilson were dashed and there was worse to come.

Mussolini

During the twentieth century, Jewish influence in politics increased and the political Jew was a potent figure in many countries. In Britain there were cabinet ministers, in Russia there were influential figures in the Communist party, such as Trotsky, Zinoviev and Kamenev, while there was Bela Kun in Hungary and Rosa Luxemburg in Germany. Churchill had remarked on this and categorised the Jews into three: the national Jew who was a patriotic member of the country in which he or she lived, the Zionist Jew whose loyalty was to a national home in Palestine, and the international Jew who was part of a conspiracy to overthrow civilisation as it was known for some unknown utopia.

Mussolini was also perturbed by this and referred to the Bolshevik revolutions in Russia and Hungary as Jewish vengeance against Christianity, which Jewish financiers backed. This anti-Jewish stance did not last long. Friends dissuaded him from this line of attack on the Bolsheviks, who were becoming influential in Italy. He also found that the Jews were helping to finance the fascists and were only a tiny proportion of the population (0.1 per cent). The Bolsheviks and their international utopia were the enemy and by October 1920 Mussolini had written an article condemning anti-Semitism in Hungary where, after the predominantly Jewish administration of Bela Kun, the Jews had been denied the right to vote, to go to high school or to practise the professions.

In Italy, the left had split into Socialist and Communist parties, with the communists well supported in big cities such as Milan and Bologna. For a time it looked as though there could be a revolution but the fascists led the fightback, confronting force with force. They gained many middle-class supporters, although they were against established institutions such as the papacy, parliament and the king. For instance, in Ferrara, the left had triumphed, the red flag flew from the town hall, the day of rest had been changed from Sunday to Monday and from nothing a Fascist party was formed, mainly from old soldiers.

Sporadic fighting started to occur all over Italy, including the countryside, especially where collectives had been formed. The fascists had two main advantages: first, their appeal to the veterans of the trenches; second, the police's tacit support. Giacomo Matteotti's speech in February 1921 highlighted this partiality, asking why the police did nothing in Emilia to stop the violence.

With chaos and threat of civil war, an election was called in April. There was violence and intimidation on both sides, Mussolini campaigned with fervour in northern Italy, which led to the fascists winning thirty-eight seats after having been previously unrepresented. However, they were still outnumbered on the left, where the socialist parties had 122 seats. Mussolini decided that his party should occupy the right of the chamber, a not altogether appropriate position for a national socialist party with revolutionary tendencies.

The violence did not abate after the election. Mussolini's acolytes were now moving fast. When they tried to occupy Ravenna, they were resisted and nine fascists were killed. In revenge, all the HQs of the left were burned in the provinces of Romagna and Forli, while the Italian army looked on dispassionately at the anarchy. The socialist's response was a general strike in support of law and order and the authority of the state. The fascist's reaction was to take over the running of cities, especially the transport, which caused the strike to be called off.

In the Chamber of Deputies, the moderates who held power were confronted by the rage of the immoderates. The fascists were now becoming a national party but Mussolini had to speak with forked tongue to achieve it. At a party rally in Naples in October, he spoke in favour of the monarchy in an area where it had great support. At the same time he said the fascists wished to serve the state in government and wanted five ministries. If they were not given, they would march on Rome.

Mussolini returned to Milan, where a warrant was issued for his arrest; however, the prefect refused to act. Prime Minister Luigi Facta asked the king for rule by martial law, to which the monarch initially agreed but then changed his mind. The fascists were now marching on Rome and were not resisted. The king took advice from former premiers and the consensus was that the army, if instructed, would probably resist the fascists but it was better not to put it to the test.

The king was in line with the majority of public opinion. This, however, led to Facta's resignation, forcing the king to try to incorporate Mussolini into a government with five fascist ministries. However, Mussolini, in 1922, at the young age of thirty-nine, demanded to be prime minister and in the end the king granted him his wish. With only thirty-eight deputies, Mussolini was very dependent on deputies from other parties for his position but he was in no hurry to get democratic legitimacy. The fascists had come to power through a great degree of mass approbation coupled with thuggery. Public opinion, both in Italy and abroad, had not condoned this thuggery but was prepared to put up with it to prevent Italy becoming chaotic.

Mussolini now strutted on the European stage, his tactics being to consolidate his power by gaining concessions on the question of Fiume, the Dodecanese and Jubaland. Meetings at the highest level increased his prestige, especially as he was not averse to using his blackshirts as a backdrop for his activities. He had a gift for publicity and creating drama. Many thought he had great talent, even political genius, although Britain's foreign secretary, Lord Curzon, was not among them and refused to concede Jubaland.

Mussolini came to London and King George V went to Rome. Every attempt was made to keep Mussolini sweet. The Greeks talked with him over the Dodecanese without finding a solution. The Yugoslavs talked with him over Fiume with the same result until Mussolini threatened to use force over a strange diplomatic incident when five Italians were murdered in Albania and the Italians blamed the Greeks. This started an imbroglio of some complexity, which occupied several countries plus the League of Nations for several months. Mussolini threatened to leave the League and sent seventeen warships to Corfu. They attacked the city, causing several deaths and even more casualties. Britain was powerless to act and this show of force had a ripple effect. Yugoslavia agreed that Fiume become an Italian town, while Greece no longer questioned Italian occupation of the Dodecanese.

Mussolini now moved to gain democratic legitimacy and, in April 1924, there was a general election. The Fascist party became the largest with 260 deputies. With 116 other deputies in support, the fascists had 376 seats out of 575. The opposition had been routed. It did not make the fascists more conciliatory or their opponents on the left less vehemently critical. Matteotti, a persistent critic, attacked the way in which the election had been held, with endless violence and intimidation. The fascists did not like this criticism so they abducted and murdered Matteotti.

The scandal coincided with a great diplomatic victory. Ramsay Macdonald had become prime minister in Britain and his socialist government was pleased to disown the imperial pretensions of his predecessor and cede Jubaland to Italy. It was felt that such a gesture would keep Italy sweet in the international community, not realising that such naivety would bolster the dictator's pride to a dangerous level and would not satisfy his greed. Such success muted the fallout from Matteotti's murder, causing Mussolini much embarrassment. It was indicative, however, of the way in which he would rule Italy.

Chapter 16

The Changing World Scene

The World Scene

The League of Nations had become unrepresentative, with defection and exclusion, and the authority of supranationality had broken down. The nations of Europe were preoccupied with themselves. Germany under Hitler linked race with territory and wanted to unite all Germans into a Greater Germany. In the Far East there were similar worries as Japan wanted to dominate the region, one where the three great empires of Russia, China and Japan met, and a power struggle was emerging. With China seemingly weak, Japan felt that it was to its advantage to use force and invade the country; however, it was more circumspect with Russia, despite coveting some of its territory. Although there were some serious military encounters, it was more of a sparring match that neither side wanted to degenerate into a major war.

The Occupation of the Rhineland

Germany was not a great power in 1935 and Hitler knew it. Its armed forces were weak and its economy, although burgeoning, was still in a state of recovery from the shocks of hyperinflation and depression. During 1935, Hitler made conciliatory speeches, talking of peace and the acceptance of disputed frontiers. Some things were going his way, such as the Saar plebiscite, which was overwhelmingly favourable to Germany.

Thus, in Hitler's speech to the Reichstag on 21 May there was a certain generosity of spirit as he acknowledged Alsace and Lorraine as being French territory, accepted Poland as a nation and said that Germany would not interfere with Austria and would not be guilty of an Anschluss. He showed animosity towards the League of Nations, which Germany would not re-join until the military clauses of the Versailles Treaty had been abandoned, although he said he would respect the Locarno Treaty. He also spoke of his desire for disarmament but also asked for the German navy, which had been scuttled at Scapa Flow, to grow but be limited to 35 per cent of the British navy.

To a Europe still scarred by the memory of war, these were glad tidings from a statesman calling for peace, while the offer to limit the German navy struck a chord with the British. This ignored the fact that Hitler had already sidestepped a military clause of the Versailles Treaty by announcing a massive increase in the size of Germany's army, which deeply worried the French. However, as a major sea power, Britain not as worried, feeling that Germany was entitled to a small navy. It was Hitler's view, expressed in *Mein Kampf*, that it was ridiculous to rival Britain as a naval power and that this had been the kaiser's biggest mistake.

This speech was a tour de force of some profundity. If Hitler had kept his word he would have been revered as a great statesman and the saviour of Germany. However, among all this was a warning. He claimed that an element of insecurity had been inserted into the Locarno Treaty due to a pact between Russia and France, which both parties had signed but the French parliament had as yet not ratified. It was for the provision of mutual assistance if either nation was attacked, which, in private, Hitler was vehemently opposed to.

France had an able ambassador in Germany, André François-Poncet, who reported back on this opposition, adding that Hitler could use this as an excuse to occupy the demilitarised Rhineland. This had little impact in France, although he was right, as an invasion was being plotted and planned. However, Germany's generals were not enthusiastic, as they knew the weakness of their army, but Hitler pushed them on. If the Germans were opposed, they had a contingency plan to retreat. The French parliament ratified the Franco–Soviet Pact in February 1936, which gave Hitler his excuse. At dawn on 7 March four brigades of German troops marched over the Rhine bridges and occupied the demilitarised zone.

That day Hitler made a speech in his more familiar idiom, ranting about the injustice of Versailles, the Bolshevik menace and the Franco–Soviet Pact, which according to him invalidated the Locarno Treaty. The French and British were taken aback – François-Poncet's warning had been ignored. The French had a hundred divisions, not all instantly available but such a preponderance of power that the Germans could not compete. Chief of the General Staff General Maurice Gamelin was passive, although the French government was prepared to act. All Gamelin did was to assemble thirteen divisions, which if given the order could have bundled the Germans out of the Rhineland.

Even Hitler was holding his breath, describing the 48 hours after the march into the Rhineland as the most nerve-wracking of his life. The French foreign minister, Pierre-Étienne Flandin, flew to London to garner support, even though by the terms of the treaty France was entitled to take military action and Britain was duty bound to offer assistance. However, Britain failed to recognise the significance of the moment, the defining moment that would lead inexorably to war.

It was also a defining moment for Hitler because he had psychologically gained the ascendancy over his cautious generals. He had kept a cool nerve, his will had prevailed and he had gained his people's admiration. Until he panicked in Norway in 1940, having to be rescued by General Alfred Jodl, he would enjoy uninterrupted success. All his gambles succeeded, which to a politician in his forties fed his conceit and a belief in his destiny. He was too young to recognise the impotence of power and that success can bring its own nemesis, even though it may not be immediate.

The importance of the Rhineland lay in it being a defensive barrier against France and Belgium. Germany needed to protect itself against any attack from the west and started building fortifications. When these were completed, Hitler would turn his bullying diplomacy to the east and take parts of the old Austro-Hungarian Empire. To Hitler, the Austrian, this was part of Germany's sphere of influence that should be subject to German suzerainty. However, he had to be careful to get Mussolini's approval, as the Italians regarded parts of the Austrian empire as being in Italy's sphere of influence.

At this time Mussolini was busy with his adventure in Abyssinia. France and Britain were applying sanctions but these were partial and ineffective. An oil embargo would have crippled Italy but the French allowed supplies to reach that country. Sanctions were in the name of the League of Nations and Hitler observed their ineffectiveness. He also watched and courted Mussolini. Having spoken with forked tongue about Austria, which he wanted as a part of Germany, he also wanted Italy to be stretched and preoccupied with Abyssinia, so its concerns with Austria would be lessened. Hitler's objectives were clear.

Nuremberg Rallies and the 1936 Olympic Games

The humiliation of losing the Great War cut deep into the German psyche. Before the war, in many spheres Germany was seen as the most creative nation and, in what the Germans considered the most important sphere, the military, it had come to grief in the Great War. Through war Germany had made the Austro-Hungarian Empire subservient but it had not conquered. It had also made France subservient, which the French did not acknowledge, but Alsace and Lorraine were incorporated into the German Reich and France was impoverished. With military defeat, Germany lost its self-esteem and it was this that Hitler was determined to regain.

The Nuremberg rallies were a means to this end. Tens of thousands gathered at Nuremberg to praise their leaders and to hear the Nazi philosophy explained. With Nazi uniforms and banners, the assembled mass proclaimed their unity and cohesiveness. The *Volk* had come together. The Olympic Games had the same objective and had spectacular organisation. Hitler was hoping that his Aryan Germans would be consistently triumphant but in this he was disappointed. Talented Jews were excluded from the German team and the star of the Games was the black athlete, Jesse Owens of the United States.

The Memoirs of Lloyd George

Roosevelt and Hitler came to power to solve the problems of the depression and, in their different ways, they were successful. In France and Britain, democratic politicians muddled through but there was not much success. The outstanding minds were not in power, with one of them, Lloyd George, ageing, although he was still an MP and active in the political process. His opinion was sought, as he was still influential and his powers were acknowledged to be only slightly diminished. Although not a writer like Churchill, he was adept at manipulating words and linking them into phrases. He decided to stand back from active politics and dictate his war memoirs, together with the subsequent peace settlement.

The circumstance that hit Lloyd George was war, the greatest, most widespread war that the human race had by then experienced. Prior to that he had demonstrated that he was a politician of the highest rank, with measures that introduced the welfare state and mitigated the worst effects of capitalism. When war came, he responded magnificently as minister of munitions from June 1915 to July 1916. This was a recently created department that took powers from the War Office, dealing with industry and the creation and improvement of weapons.

At this time there was a shell crisis in every belligerent nation as people realised that this was an artillery war and the supply of shells was crucial. The shell was a complex artefact, which for simplicity can be divided into three parts: the casing, the filling and the fuse. The casing needed precision so that it could be fitted into guns, the filling consisted of materials that were often potentially lethal and had to be produced in large quantities, while the fuses needed technological precision. A variety of factories had to be formed quickly.

So successful was Lloyd George and his ministry that they increased the production of shells by eight times in the year to the start of the Battle of the Somme. This very real achievement led him to quote three German sources, who all pointed out that the Somme was the muddy grave of the German army because its leadership, training and flair had been negated by the industrial might of Britain. Lloyd George, not without reason, cites this as a great success story for the Ministry of Munitions. It could also be cited as a justification for the Battle of the Somme but he is less than charitable to the generals who waged the battle.

By the time he left the ministry, he claimed with justification that it was as well run as any in the government. He can also claim that he was responsible for technological innovations, especially with the development of the tank and, on a simpler level, the Stokes mortar. The War Office was sceptical about the latter, so Lloyd George's ministry took it over and it became a potent weapon in trench warfare. It was not sophisticated but consisted of a long tube with a fuse mechanism that could propel an inserted bomb a few hundred yards. It was effective and was used until the war's end.

After the Ministry of Munitions, Lloyd George went to the War Office for five months until he became prime minster. Having diminished the power of the War Office in his former ministry, he was greeted with suspicion and came face to face with the army mind, which acted in well-defined parameters. Lloyd George's mercurial genius made the generals take a defensive position.

The trouble with Lloyd George, and it is a mild character defect, was that he was unsympathetic to those who did not succumb to the charm of his genius. He manoeuvred people with words and the charm of his personality, a gift that could antagonise the military mind, as his intelligent reasoning might move the goalposts in an argument that may or may not be justified.

This was the root cause of the dissension between Lloyd George and Haig, which plagues his memoirs. Lloyd George as a politician and statesman was working on a higher plane than Haig. To describe Lloyd George as a great man, which he was, is a far higher accolade than the same description for Haig, which he also deserved. Haig was merely commander-in-chief of the British army on the Western Front during a great war; Lloyd George was prime minister of Great Britain and its empire, so responsible for all its wars and the well-being of its peoples. Nevertheless, he did not regard Haig as a great man and in his memoirs shows a lack of charity, which is disturbing because it was over fifteen years after the events described, Haig was dead and there was a lack of perspective in Lloyd George's judgement. Churchill discussed the problem in *The World Crisis*, in light of the retreat of March 1918 when the Allied forces were in trouble, under the heading 'Where the Blame Lies':

> We may however attempt a provisional judgment. If Haig had not consumed his armies at Passchendaele, or at least he had been content to stop that offensive in September, he would have commanded (without any addition to the drafts actually sent him from England, in the winter) sufficient reserves on March 21st to enable him to sustain the threatened front. But for the horror which Passchendaele inspired in the prime minister and the war cabinet, he would no doubt have been supplied with very much larger reinforcements. If, notwithstanding Passchendaele, the war cabinet had reinforced him as they should have done, the front could still have been held on March 21st.
>
> The responsibility for the causes which led to the British inadequacy of numbers is shared between general headquarters and the war cabinet. By constitutional doctrine, the greatest responsibility rests upon the war cabinet, who failed to make their commander conform to their convictions on a question which far transcended the military or technical sphere, and who also failed to do full justice to the Army because of their disagreement with the Commander-in-Chief. In view, however of the preponderance of military influence in time of war, and the serious dangers of a collision between the soldiers and the politicians, a very considerable burden must be borne by the British Headquarters.[22]

Even with hindsight, Churchill was unsure about and worried by the complexities of the period between July 1917 and April 1918. Lloyd George was different. His mind was seared by the losses of the Battle of Third Ypres. No one can deny that the bloodletting of the attrition battles was frightful and had affected the behaviour of all combatant nations. The Russians folded, the French almost gave up fighting, the Italians were nearly knocked out of the war, the Austro-Hungarians became weaker and had to be propped up by the Germans, the Turks virtually gave up in the west and went east into the Caucasus.

This left the British and the Germans, both profoundly affected by the Somme and Third Ypres. The Germans were shattered by the superiority of men and material at both these battles and, although they held on, they were being ground down. What saved them was the Russian armistice, which temporarily resolved the manpower crisis but not sufficiently to knock Italy out of the war or to split the British and French and send the former back to their island.

The battles of attrition are reasonably well recorded by history but, by the end of 1917, war had begun to change. By the middle of 1918 the effects of external events such as the blockade and the influenza epidemic were being felt. It was very difficult for historians to quantify the effect of these two events, with the latter hardly mentioned in Lloyd George's memoirs. Likewise, the effect of air superiority, which was very influential in the last year of the war, is barely talked of. Britain's air superiority was probably the most important factor in stopping the German offensive in the spring of 1918 and in establishing the ascendancy of the Hundred Days, but this is just opinion. The last year of the war is poorly served by history, which the memoirs reflect, with their over-emphasis on the battles of attrition.

It is true that Lloyd George's memoirs were provoked by the publication of books by Haig supporters but the circumstance of war had distorted Lloyd George's vision. From the Nivelle offensive, when he sided with the French leaders and tried to undermine Haig; to Passchendaele, when he supported Haig but would have been right to stop him in October; to the German offensive, when he denied Haig the manpower he wanted; to the Hundred Days, when he did not believe a breakthrough was possible, Lloyd George was always off balance. Haig had one great advantage in that the king and the Conservatives always supported him.

When Lloyd George wanted to get rid of Haig, he had to contend with the Conservative politicians who had put him in power. The tragedy of Lloyd George was that he had reached the pinnacle of political power but had unhinged his political position. He was not part of the Conservatives, although they kept him in power; he had only a rump of supporters within the Liberals, having split the party; and he had no significant link with the new force, the Labour party.

Lloyd George was a great premier but his political demise was of his own making, which he did not help by his cynicism about money, politics and the aristocracy. In 1912 he had to be protected in the share-dealing Marconi scandal, then after the war he tried to fund his political party by the selling of honours. This got out of hand and caused him grief. Having lost his party and his roots, he was unable to use his genius to modify the great socialist political heresy of the twentieth century.

The United States never succumbed to the great socialist heresy, which in its plausibility seduced so many able minds. The United States had its trade unions, which were sometimes very militant and anti-capitalist, but even with the depression the cardinal ideas of socialism had only a small following, which gave that nation an enormous advantage throughout the twentieth century.

Lloyd George was the creator of the welfare state in Britain but was not interested in the doctrinaire aspects of socialism. His chief endeavour during the 1920s was to appeal to the British public as a moderate left-of-centre leader, but his economic policies were rejected. His energies then turned to his memoirs, which centred on the war. The sacrifices that had been made seared into his consciousness and distorted his judgements on men and affairs. By the time he had completed his memoirs in 1936 there was the likelihood of another war; however, these memoirs suggested that he would hate the sacrifice that would be made and would try to avoid it at any cost.

How to Win Friends and Influence People – Dale Carnegie

This book, published in 1936, has sold tens of millions of copies. It is still in print and in some bookshops is so popular that it is a requirement that it be always kept in stock. It is a simple, homespun, folksy book but it is also hard, wise and sophisticated in its simplicity. It is, above all, a product of the American way of life. It had an oral genesis of over twenty years. Dale Carnegie came from poor farming stock in Missouri and he roamed the country by way of the railroad, working and trying to find his destiny. He started off in sales, tried acting, then linked himself to a great new industry and became a car salesman. None of these provided satisfaction, so he became a teacher, although not a mainstream teacher purveying a traditional subject. He asked the YMCA schools in New York to allow him to teach public speaking, something they had already tried to teach and failed. He persuaded them to allow him to go ahead but they refused to pay him the $2 nightly fee, although agreed to let him take a commission on sales and a percentage of the profits.

Within three years Carnegie was making $30 a night. Out of this came a book, *Public Speaking and Influencing Men in Business*, and his courses were spreading to other cities in the United States and Europe. He was oiling the wheels of the great business and professional corporations as they boomed and then went into depression and came out again. He taught people how to bond with their peers, how to lead, how to compete and fruitfully share endeavour, how to enhance an acquaintance's life and thereby enhance one's own. It all started as a short talk, which developed into a lecture of an hour and a half, then with development and refinement became a book in 1936.

It is in four parts, each with a simple and prosaic heading: 'Fundamental Techniques in Handling People', 'Six Ways to Make People Like You', 'How to Win People to Your Way of Thinking' and 'Be a Leader: How to Change People Without Giving Offence or Arousing Resentment'. Within these headings are several chapters, the last of which is entitled, 'Making People Glad to Do What You Want', in which Carnegie cites three examples involving Woodrow Wilson, two favourable, one unfavourable.

The first favourable example is when President Wilson asked his friend, Colonel Edward House, to go to Europe to try to broker peace during the Great War. Wilson bypassed Secretary of State William Jennings Bryan, who was a strong believer in peace and deeply wanted to be associated with such diplomacy. House finessed this deftly by telling Bryan that the president thought it unwise for anyone to do this officially and that if he went it would attract a good deal of attention and would question his purpose. Bryan was soothed by feeling too important for the job and that it should be initiated at a lower level. In the second illustration, William McAdoo recalls Wilson's invitation to become a member of his cabinet, couched in terms of McAdoo doing him a favour, which he found very flattering.

Then Dale Carnegie has a go, as the following quotation highlights:

> Unfortunately, Wilson didn't always employ such tact. If he had, history might have been different. For example, Wilson didn't make the Senate and the Republican party happy by entering the United States in the League of Nations. Wilson refused to take such prominent Republican leaders as Elihu Root or Charles Evans Hughes or Henry Cabot Lodge to the peace conference with him. Instead, he took along unknown men from his own party. He snubbed the Republicans, refused to let them feel that the League was their idea as well as his, refused to let them have a finger in the pie; and, as a result of this crude handling of human relations, wrecked his own career, ruined his health,

shortened his life, caused America to stay out of the League, and altered the history of the world.[23]

Carnegie was not writing a history book. He is steeped in history but this is a book on personal relationships. Some of the statements in this short paragraph are contentious and even his assertion that Wilson's lack of a relationship with the Republican grandees, certainly a contributory cause, was not the major cause of the rejection. Yet Carnegie was right in that Wilson had not found enough allies to support the League of Nations and it was a failure in personal relationships. It was not how Roosevelt would have acted.

How to Win Friends and Influence People is not a great work of literature. It is not badly written but does not employ great felicity of language, more the language of competent journalism, yet over seven decades it has struck a chord that is deep and resonant. In an indirect way it encapsulates the morality of capitalism. The business of the United States is business, then add a little bit of politics because that also helps business. His audience was essentially businessmen and professional people.

Carnegie's book is profound and essentially American in the self-help tradition. It embraces that great clause in the American constitutions, the pursuit of happiness, which always looks odd in a constitution, especially to European eyes. The book is about being happy and at peace with oneself and to make your business associate happy too because, if they are in that frame of mind, they are more likely to agree with you. Do not get mad with your antagonist, understand what has motivated their actions and realise they may have reason.

There were two famous Americans who one could say represented the spirit of the book but whose fame would transcend it: Franklin D. Roosevelt and Dwight D. Eisenhower. They were passionate men with a benign equilibrium, having an essential decency and believing that the other members of the human race shared these qualities. Sometimes they were fooled because there were people in high places of great talent who could obliterate these qualities, but they would give unity of purpose to a great nation and an army.

The Spanish Civil War

In July 1936, civil war started in Spain and within two years incorporated most of the horrors of the larger conflict to come. Spain had become a republic in 1931 and the 1936 election result was not dissimilar to that of France – a Popular Front coalition of socialists, radicals and communists held power.

Their mandate was legitimate but there was deep dissatisfaction on the right, which triggered rebellion. The right was not particularly strong, the apparatus of the state was not in its hands and it was divided.

The main forces were in the Sahara under an emerging leader, General Francisco Franco, and another strong force in the north-west of Spain. Neither had much in the way of arms and it quickly became a fight to win the friendship of other nations and get arms from them. Mussolini saw an advantage in supporting the fascists and was soon supplying arms, while Hitler saw an advantage in trying out the Luftwaffe's combat worthiness, receiving mineral rights as a quid pro quo, which would aid Germany's rearmament.

With its government of similar ideology, one would have thought that France would rush to help the Spanish government but Leon Blum went to London to review the matter and decided on a joint policy of non-intervention, a policy based on the hope that the rebellion would burn itself out. With the Soviet Union helping the Popular Front, this was unlikely to happen without strong diplomacy, which Britain and France were unable to provide.

The war escalated by degrees. At first, the Popular Front held all the advantages. The fascists were in pockets and were defeated in Madrid and Barcelona, while the navy, believed to support the fascists, now sided with the government after a revolt. If the navy could blockade the Sahara-based troops and prevent them getting to the mainland, the government would probably win. Franco acknowledged this dilemma and started using transport aircraft to fly in his troops. These carried only twenty at a time, so it took time for him to build up a force of a few thousand on the mainland. There was also little cohesion between the fascist forces. The Carlists of Navarre and Pamplona had a great leader in General José Sanjurjo, who had much more appeal than the prosaic Franco, but he soon lost his life in a plane crash. His successor, General Emilio Mola, was not as successful in building up his strength and following. Within a few months, Italy and Germany were dealing directly with Franco, while Mola was receiving arms via him, virtually ceding leadership of the right.

Franco was ruthless and had a philosophy of, if he lost, everything including his life and family would be lost; if he won, it did not much matter what he did as time would heal the suffering. Perhaps history has justified him. He was helped because the communists were guilty of equally nefarious deeds. Franco's ruthlessness was similar to Hitler's but history abhors Hitler's deeds. Franco used Moroccan mercenaries against his fellow countrymen.

They looted, raped, pillaged, murdered and sexually mutilated their way from the south to Madrid, behaving in a vile and inhuman way, spreading the cancer of fear wherever they went and with their commander's approval.

There were only a few thousand of them, which was a problem. When they had captured Saravera, 400 miles into the interior, they were counter-attacked and realised they had vulnerable lines of communication. The next 80 miles to Maqueda was tougher going. Here Franco had a choice: should he press on and try to take Madrid or should he go to the rescue of the besieged garrison at Toledo? In the two weeks straddling September and October, he lost the initiative but linked up with Mola, while the fascist forces had control of territory stretching from the Pyrenees to the Mediterranean. If they regained the initiative and Madrid fell, then Spain would be theirs and the war would soon come to an end.

The attack on Madrid did not proceed with urgency and was certainly not the blitzkrieg that was to become the way to wage war. Optimistic voices and plans of celebration began in fascist circles but this was an army drilled in a colonial context that had not fought a war with modern weapons nor been opposed by them. With Russian help and an appeal to volunteers all over the world, the republicans started to get weapons and construct proper defences.

In November 1,900 men were ready for action and there were some Russian heavy tanks and fighter aircraft to confront German and Italian weaponry. German advisers were appalled at Franco's dilatory conduct, which led to the Germans forming a battle group, the Condor Legion. Republicans did not think they could resist this group of 12,000 men plus modern artillery, aircraft and transport. Nevertheless, the defenders held out and within the next week Franco faced defeat, before Italy came to his aid. His fear that the British navy might blockade Spain was not realised, and the central fact of the Spanish Civil War remained: the help that Germany and Italy gave was greater than that of the Russians, while France and Britain remained neutral.

Inexorably, Franco increased his authority. He had to be cunning because both the Carlists and the Falangists had leaders who were full of ambition. Mola, the Carlist general, was as ineffective as Franco at waging war and had trouble subduing the Basques. Before capturing a Basque city, he used the Germans and Italians to bomb them before the troops moved in.

This culminated on 26 April in the attack on the market town of Guernica. The republicans were retreating. It was market day, so the town was packed and about forty bombers with fighter escort did their worst. Basques claim that over 1,000 people were killed and the fascists followed up and captured the town. There were journalists present who reported the carnage, their reports galvanising public opinion all over the world. The fascists were on the defensive and, in explaining their actions, downgraded the damage done, blaming it on undisciplined mercenaries who had caused explosions within the town. None of these explanations convinced anybody and, rightly or wrongly, Guernica has become a symbol of terror bombing of a defenceless population, which Picasso reinforced in his famous painting.

Although Mola had ceded the ultimate authority of the right to Franco, he had ambitions of becoming the political leader, with Franco its figurehead. Mola was not hard right like Franco or the Falangists and was waiting for the chance to usurp him. But fate took a hand when Mola was killed in an air crash on 3 June 1937. From all reports, Franco showed no emotion, but from that time on he would not fly to the front.

The Carlists now had no significant leadership and Franco was the beneficiary. On the far right, the Falangists had a genius for squabbling and falling out with each other. They had a leader in Manuel Hedilla Larrey but could not unify the faction. Franco allowed them to squabble, took pleasure in their disunity and was only interested in subjugating them to his command. Hedilla was ambitious, had a working-class following but was guileless. By July Franco had seen enough and, sensing Hedilla's weakness, created charges of disloyalty that led to his arrest and a sentence of death. This was eventually commuted but Hedilla was finished and the Falange emasculated. Franco was in control.

By 1938 Franco had overwhelming material superiority. His objective was to wipe out the republicans, so he dispersed his effort all over the country. His main attack was on Catalonia, with a drive towards the Pyrenees and south towards Valencia. In the attack on Catalonia, he had approximately 100,000 troops, 200 tanks and 1,000 aircraft. This was too much for the republicans and, despite their brave fight, their fate was sealed.

Although the major powers of Europe had been involved, this was a Spanish war involving Spanish pride and preoccupations. Franco thanked Germany and Italy for their help but his Spanish pride felt the humiliation of having to ask for it. In maritime affairs, where Britain was involved, he was ruthless. The republicans were helped by controlling many ports and seaborne trade. The British had many registered ships helping the republicans in this trade and Franco bombed them with relish. Chamberlain was at the height of his appeasement period and did nothing. Churchill or Eden would not have been so accommodating. As it turned out, Spain was a volcano capable of no eruptions to harm the outside world. The Civil War was a peculiarly Spanish event.

Hitler's Ambitions

While Spain was fighting, central Europe was in ferment below the surface, while on the surface, Germany's power had increased through industrial activity, full employment and the production of armaments. Some of these products, such as aircraft, had been tried in Spain and not found wanting, but Hitler had been detached from this Civil War, although pleased by its result. There had been some real gains for Germany in terms of mineral concessions, which the Spaniards had used to pay for armaments, and Hitler felt he had an ideological ally who was still in his debt, so he looked for future favours.

Hitler, as usual, was preoccupied with forming an inclusive racial state of the German Aryan *Volk*. There were six million Germans in Austria precluded from joining Germany by the peace treaties of 1919; three million Germans in Czechoslovakia in an area commonly called the Sudetenland; and 350,000 in Danzig. To some not versed in history, it might seem reasonable that they be forged into one state, especially as they were, on the whole, contiguous with one another, although the fact that Danzig was not was another bone of contention. Yet, despite Austrians being undeniably German, they might well not become a part of Greater Germany, the Germans of Czechoslovakia had been part of an empire that consisted of many races, while Danzig was indisputably a German city with a Polish hinterland.

There were Nazi sympathisers in all these areas who used Nazi tactics to try to get their way. In July 1936 in Austria it came to the point where Chancellor Kurt Schuschnigg agreed that Nazi representatives should join the government. Schuschnigg, like Chamberlain and most reasonable men, thought that appeasement would lead to responsible behaviour; however, this was not the Nazi way.

Hitler, for various reasons, tried to control his supporters and to temper their often vile exuberance. He always said that he wanted power to evolve and, being an Austrian, he seemed to sense that it would effortlessly come his way. He was also careful not to offend his ally Mussolini. The Italians considered themselves the guarantors of Austrian independence and Hitler understood Mussolini's pride in this.

Austria

Schuschnigg had Arthur Seyss-Inquart, the leading Nazi, as a cabinet colleague. They had been friends since childhood but he was unable to get him to control the Nazis. An Austrian police raid on Nazi HQ found that the they had plans for an armed takeover of the country. It was known that Hitler was not involved in these plans, so Schuschnigg wanted him to denounce the instigators and bring them to heel. Schuschnigg talked to the German ambassador, Franz von Papen, who said he would try to arrange a meeting.

Austria was too weak a power to confront Germany but Schuschnigg thought that, as the legitimate ruler of a democratic state, he could count on the support of the democratic world if he revealed that illegitimate forces were trying to usurp him. As it happened, Germany was in a state of flux, with military, financial and diplomatic leaders being thrown out and replaced by Hitler's henchmen. Generals Fritsch and Blomberg, the military luminaries, were dismissed for sexual misdemeanours, whether valid or not; Ribbentrop replaced Von Neurath as foreign minister; Hjalmar Schacht, the financial wizard, went; while on a more mundane plane, the diplomats Hassell (Italy) and Von Papen were dismissed. They were all old guard – respectable, conservative and generally able.

Although dismissed, Von Papen visited Hitler to take his leave and told him of Schuschnigg's request for a meeting. Ever the opportunist, Hitler sent him back to Vienna and, on 12 February 1938, the meeting was held. Hitler, as was his norm in negotiations, immediately hit Schuschnigg with several requests, such as the integration of Austrian foreign and economic policy with that of Germany and that Seyss-Inquart should become minister of the interior, controlling the police. This was tantamount to Austria becoming part of Germany, so Schuschnigg stood his ground and requested that Hitler respect his constitutional position and repudiate the Nazi extremists' activities.

The British and Italians were also talking to each other. Mussolini always leaned towards Hitler, even though German and Italian interests did not always coincide, but his son-in-law and minister of foreign affairs, Galeazzo Ciano, and the ambassador in London, Dino Grandi, were more pro-British and fearful that if Austria succumbed then Italy would be indissolubly linked to Germany. Chamberlain, too, was sensitive to the Italian link and saw in it one way of restraining Hitler. His foreign secretary, Eden, was of a different opinion and did not like or trust the Italians. He wanted them out of Spain but Chamberlain wanted Italian friendship and was prepared to recognise Italian Abyssinia and form a partnership in the Mediterranean. This forced Eden to resign. What is more, Chamberlain indicated to the Italians that if Germany took Austria, he would be indignant but do nothing.

Schuschnigg, by this time, was resentful of the Nazis and of Hitler's verbal bullying. On 9 March 1930 he announced to the Austrian people that a plebiscite would take place in three days' time to decide whether Austria wanted to remain independent. This galvanised Hitler, who was determined not to be humiliated by a vote. On 11 March he closed the border between Germany and Austria and placed troops there. The French government was in disarray, Britain refused to take sides and Italy was no longer interested in protecting Austria's independence. Schuschnigg was alone, lost his nerve and cancelled the plebiscite. The Germans said that they had no confidence in Schuschnigg and wanted Seyss-Inquart to replace him. Schuschnigg resigned but the president held out against replacing him with Seyss-Inquart.

The Germans gave an ultimatum, Seyss-Inquart appointed himself chancellor and asked Hitler to restore order, but Hitler had already ordered his troops to march. He was fearful of Czech intervention and of Mussolini's reaction. The Czechs did nothing, while Mussolini told Hitler that Austria did not interest him. When Hitler heard this, he went into paeans of gratitude and spoke of an indissoluble bond with the Italian dictator. It was one of the few great bonds that Hitler retained. On 12 March self-appointed chancellor, Seyss-Inquart, asked that the invasion be stopped but Hitler was on a roll, euphoric with the cheers of his native land. He arrived in his home town of Linz, where he spoke to excited crowds. His address was a bombshell. Austria would no longer be an independent nation but a part of Greater Germany. A referendum was held on 10 April, at which 99 per cent of Greater Germany voted in support.

Czechoslovakia

Austria, in a sense, was easy, as it was a predominantly German nation. Czechoslovakia was more complex, with the Czechs, Slovaks and Germans having a racial integrity of their own. Hitler had appointed Heinlein as his representative in the Sudetenland with instructions to use the normal tactics of raising the ante every time a concession was made. This in the end makes a mockery of diplomacy, which involves goodwill and a desire for a modus vivendi acceptable to both sides. Hitler's idea of diplomacy was the use of the threat of force, then after capitulation, concessions might be made.

President Edvard Benes of Czechoslovakia was predominantly a skilled and experienced diplomat. At the end of the war he would claim credit for this as he surveyed Prague from his palace and reflected that this was the only unscathed city in central Europe. Diplomacy was his weapon but he also had the use of force in the form of thirty-four divisions and a high-powered armaments industry.

Czechoslovakia, at the time, was one of the richest nations in the world on a per capita basis and, although the population was small compared with Germany, it was capable of giving its neighbour a bloody nose. This was particularly true if it could persuade its allies, France and the Soviet Union, to offer protection. France had a strong alliance with Czechoslovakia and, if the French moved, it would trigger a pact with the Soviet Union, while Romania and Yugoslavia would come to Czechoslovakia's aid if Hungary moved against them. If Benes could use these alliances and link them together, he could survive Germany's predation; however, he had difficulty in putting resolution into his allies.

The key nation was France, with a new prime minister in Edouard Daladier and foreign minister in Georges Bonnet. The former had fought in the Great War and was not an appeaser by nature until he reminded himself of the horrors of that conflict, while the latter was an out and out appeaser who was horrified by the thought of war. Daladier led from the front but was reluctant to do anything unless backed by Britain. Chamberlain, with his foreign secretary, Lord Halifax, took the lead and initiated the policy of accepting that the Sudeten Germans had a legitimate grievance and that Hitler was a man of goodwill who desired peace and would see reason.

With France prevaricating and weak, the Soviet Union eager on the surface to support France but unknown if it came to the crunch, it was left to Britain. The British usually abstained from taking the lead in Continental affairs, so Chamberlain put pressure on Benes to come to some sort of arrangement with the Sudeten Germans, which meant making concessions. Benes, surprisingly to some, was prepared to do so, while the Sudetens demanded more and more. One seeming weakness was that Benes ignored the Soviet Union because he was fearful of communist influence on his nation.

On 20 May there was a panic, with the Czechs expecting a German attack, calling up reservists and manning the German frontier in preparation for an invasion, à la Austria. This raised Czech morale but Hitler was incensed and was forced to announce that he had only peaceful intentions, which was not his style. At this stage Hitler respected the power of France and was not going to attack Czechoslovakia if France came to its aid. The Luftwaffe was still weak and there was only a small component available to defend German air space in the west, while the Wehrmacht had only a couple of divisions to oppose the eighty assembled on the French side of the border.

Nevertheless, the temperature was rising and Hitler was goaded. He saw

Greater Germany as heir to the Austro-Hungarian Empire, which meant that there was no room for an independent Czechoslovakia. Benes was cunning; he wanted to show the British mediators and the world that Hitler and his minions had overreached themselves. On 4 September he asked the Sudeten leaders to write down their terms, which meant they could no longer raise the ante, but they refused. Then Benes wrote his terms, which were generous, but again they were unacceptable. The result was that public opinion turned in countries such as Britain, which had been sympathetic to the Sudetens, and Hitler was seen in his true colours of a power-hungry dictator who bullied his neighbours.

Munich

On 8 September French premier Daladier was for war if Germany marched. However, on 13 September the Council of Ministers only supported him by six votes to four and he backed down. Two days later Chamberlain flew to Munich and saw Hitler at Berchtesgaden. Chamberlain still believed Hitler to be a reasonable man who wanted peace, a hard bargainer but someone who would acknowledge realpolitik. This was monumental naivety. Chamberlain was a decent man who saw the Sudeten question from Germany's point of view and was willing to help it reach a reasonable settlement. This was more or less what he told Hitler and, understandably, he purred but gave nothing in return.

Chamberlain abhorred the thought of war and wanted to prevent it at all costs. It was British policy not to support France in confronting Germany. Without France's resolution, the Soviet Union would pull out and Germany would win by default. However, Chamberlain did have one difficulty, because Britain led its empire and within it were independent countries that were not convinced that Britain should go to war. This does not condone his policy of appeasement because his diplomacy was fundamentally flawed. Meanwhile, Hitler also did not have a free diplomatic run. The Poles wanted Tesin, which could easily be ceded, but the Hungarians wanted the whole of Slovakia.

On Chamberlain's return from Berchtesgaden, he had Hitler's agreement that there would be no war, that problems would be resolved peaceably and that the Sudetenland would revert to German sovereignty. Chamberlain sold this to his cabinet. He had more trouble with Daladier, who had the perspicacity to recognise that the Sudetenland was not going to satisfy Hitler, only the dismemberment of Czechoslovakia. Daladier recognised that it would be a major diplomatic defeat if, having recognised the Sudetenland as

German, it led to the dismemberment of Czechoslovakia. Because of this he asked for a British guarantee of support to use force if this happened. It was the crucial agreement that led inexorably to outright war.

On 26 September Hitler announced that he would occupy the Sudetenland on 1 October. There was now a groundswell of sympathy for the Czechs. There was no doubt that they were the fall guys, with other powers deciding their destiny. When Britain and France presented Czechoslovakia with an ultimatum after it had rejected proposals, the Czechs concurred, only for the Germans to reject these proposals. So the diplomatic shenanigans went on, with Anglo–French despair causing them to turn to Mussolini as an intermediary. He arranged a meeting at Munich, which four of the five European powers attended, the Soviet Union being excluded. Moreover, the Czechs were excluded from the conference hall and had to wait in an ante room.

The Munich agreement, with the Sudetenland ceded to Germany, was presented to Czechoslovakia as a fait accompli and, after perfunctory consultations with the Soviet Union, was accepted. Chamberlain, however, went further and linked the agreement with the Anglo–German Naval Agreement as symbols of the two nations not wanting to go to war and that consultation would be the method used to resolve differences. He was delighted about Munich and, when welcomed by ecstatic crowds at Downing Street, he talked about peace with honour and peace in our time.

Munich was a tragedy, although a tragedy in many parts. Perhaps its greatest misfortune was to expose the fallacy of President Wilson's idealism in his concept of self-determination. Germans in the Sudetenland were given the right to reunite with the Germans of the German nation. This did a disservice to the Czecho-Slovak nation, which was like most nations, a mixture of races.

Chapter 17

Developments in the Far East

Japan Develops Manchuria

The development of Manchuria over the next few years produced an economic miracle. In seven years Japan's population increased by 250 per cent. The Japanese proclaimed an 'open door' policy of investment but successfully hindered any major foreign initiatives. Their energy and money poured into Manchuria and the road mileage was doubled, airfields built, telecommunications developed, the railways updated and extended, and the banking system rationalised. The country was covered in forests and the timber industry grew. Gold, iron ore and coal mines were opened and many of the raw materials that Japan lacked were in abundance. This was a cornucopia and the Japanese reaped the benefits.

With this business creativity came a darker side. The British had introduced opium into China in the early part of the previous century, against the Chinese government's wishes, and it had proved very popular. It was in itself a relatively mild drug, more addictive than tobacco but not greatly so, and certainly not proscribed by law in those days. However, its derivatives in pure form, heroin and morphine, were extremely dangerous and it was with these derivatives that the Japanese set out to corrupt the local population in Manchuria and beyond. They gave subsidies to opium poppy growers far in excess of the subsidies for those who grew food, then when the production of poppies rocketed, they cut the price as they were the monopoly purchasing power.

It is estimated that in 1937 Japan was producing 90 per cent of the illicit white drugs in the world. The League of Nations condemned the trade and the Japanese leaders promised reforms; however, the revenues climbed from $47 million in 1937 to $71 million in 1938, then to $90 million by 1939. With Japan's textile and armament industries expanding at home and Manchukuo feeding the exchequer, the economy was booming.

The Triumph of Chiang Kai-Shek

With the final defeat of the Kiangsi Soviet in October 1934, the communists had to retreat. Harassed by the nationalists, they fought their way through blockades and skirmished their way to the west of China, near Tibet, and from there they marched to the mountainous region of Shensi in the north-west. Some 90,000 started out on this 6,000-mile odyssey known as 'The Long March' but only 20,000 arrived at their destination. Here they had some security and could regroup. Such a small rabble did not seem much of a threat but natural selection had created powerful strong-willed leaders who believed in themselves and whose philosophy would reach out to the Chinese people.

Chiang's ambition of uniting China was seemingly achieved when his overt enemies retreated; however, he still had to win the hearts and minds of the people, create prosperity and maintain law and order. His army, his real power base, was becoming better trained and armed. The Germans had been training them since 1927 and had sent many distinguished officers to China. They inculcated a more disciplined approach so, in places, the former rabble were turned into a smartly attired and well-drilled cadre.

The Germans were not doing this for nothing, as 60 per cent of the country's arms exports were going to China, bolstering the German arms industry. As Germany was developing increasingly deep relations with Japan, this trade was not to Japan's benefit but, paradoxically, even after the China Incident and war between the two nations, the trade increased and was not officially stopped until April 1938, when it went underground.

Chiang had many problems and trials in uniting the nation. The Japanese were pressing from the north in a surreptitious way. They took Jehol and, with the signing of the Tanggu Truce with China in May 1933, a large 5,000-square-mile demilitarised zone was formed, which resulted in the Chinese retiring from Tientsin, the major port for Peking. Chiang was appeasing Japan for the pursuit of unity in China. The Japanese interfered in this buffer zone by encouraging autonomy among racial groups. They wanted north China to be as weak as possible as they felt vulnerable sandwiched between the Russians and the Chinese, fearing their collusion. Japan's diplomatic efforts were geared to an Asian Monroe Doctrine, whereby China and Japan would cooperate to minimise European and American influence in Asia.

Chiang's problems came to a head in December 1936. Chang Hsueh-Liang, who had been driven out of Manchuria, was still a roving warlord with an army of 170,000 allied to Chiang, who was trying to contain the communists in Shensi. They were blockading them but it was tedious work and two of his divisions were infiltrated and subsequently defected to the communists. Chang started talking to the communists, who were not particularly aggressive, so he and Zhou Enlai agreed that they should be fighting Japan, not arguing between themselves. Chang went to Chiang to report these views but he would not change his policy. The Japanese were to be appeased, not attacked, and China needed to be unified. Chang, known as the Young Marshal, returned to his HQ.

In December 1936 Chiang visited Chang. Chiang, who usually had good intelligence, knew the perils of disaffected troops and travelled with a bodyguard but, on this occasion, he had misread the situation. Manchurian officers rebelled, captured Chiang and held him hostage, demanding that the Kuomintang army march against the Japanese. Chiang behaved with great courage, as there is no doubt Chang was prepared to kill him.

The reason why Chang reprieved him is not absolutely clear but it is thought that Zhou Enlai, under Soviet pressure, was influential. It has been suggested that the Soviets wanted Chiang in power as a unifying force for China against Japan's imperialism. To kill Chiang might have created chaos, while the communists were hoping to be left alone in Shensi. Chang, in the end, gave himself up and received a sentence of ten years' imprisonment, which was soon to be commuted to a free pardon. Chiang's policy and intransigence continued until July 1937, when the Japanese threat consumed north China.

Revolution in Japan – 1936

In 1936 Japan also suffered a major revolt. There were two policy groups within the army, one of which was the Kodoha, which regarded itself as the new Samurai that would begin a new imperial order. Its followers believed in imperial glory and the omnipotence of the emperor but wanted to remove his advisers and transform his court. They hated the new world of democracy, parliament, the civil service and big business. In foreign policy, they wanted to confront and defeat Russia in Asia, while retaining good relations with their Asian kinsmen in China.

The other group was pejoratively called the Toseiha, or Control Faction.

It rejected the Kodoha's ultra-conservative features and did not like the militant attitude to the Soviet Union, considering it a step too far. Those in the Toseiha wanted to consolidate Japan's power in Manchukuo but were just as militant in the long term, wanting modernisation of the army and the financial means to do it, as a prelude to total war, whereby the resources of the state were geared to conquest.

Assassination and attempted coups were nothing new in Japan but the one in February 1936 was more substantial and worrying than anything that had gone before. It was very much a Tokyo uprising and the conspirators were junior officers from the best regiments stationed there. Their objective was to murder the leading members of the cabinet and Emperor Hirohito's main advisers and courtiers. They would then tell the emperor who they wanted in the new cabinet. Their initial success was to seize the police HQ, the Home Affairs Ministry and the War Ministry. The death toll was not as great as they had wished, as senior figures fled and hid, but the emperor was outraged at the death of his advisers and vowed revenge.

The war minister, Lieutenant General Shigeru Honjo, seemed unable to act decisively, perhaps feeling an ambivalence about his position and those around him, but Hirohito was decisive and threatened to lead his Imperial Guards against the rebels. The cabinet tried to resign but Hirohito would not have it until the rebels had been defeated. This shocked the rebels, who thought they were winning and had shown increasing naivety in the handling of the situation. They had made no appeal to public opinion nor captured and used the radio station. Meanwhile, the emperor had shown that he was not just a figurehead but a resolute opponent. The rebels now intimated that they were prepared to climb down if General Miyaki Shami was appointed prime minister. This was not acceptable. If the rebels were going to win, they had to broaden their base of support.

The general public in Tokyo was startled and then bemused and apathetic. Outside Tokyo the coup had hardly been noticed. If it were to succeed, it certainly needed the navy's help but there were influential moderates in the navy who were appalled at the murder of senior naval figures in the cabinet. Forty ships came into Tokyo Bay and landed marines, whose duty was to protect the imperial court. The rebels now recognised that they were beaten and sent word that they would commit suicide if ordered to do so by an imperial messenger. Hirohito, with great common sense, replied that suicide was for them to decide. Two did kill themselves, 124 of the principal rebels were prosecuted and seventeen shot, with many of the others given prison sentences.

The rebellion, however, was complicated and there were many implicated, including the emperor's brother, Prince Chichibu, the war minister and several business leaders. As such, it was an attempt to change regime by force rather than by the use of the ballot box, even though an election was taking place at the same time. The culprits' trials revealed the split loyalties of Japan's ruling class, as many who had initiated the conflagration also helped stop it. Some influential people who were implicated escaped without a reprimand.

The China Incident 1937

The outbreak of war between China and Japan is attributed to an event that was in itself trivial. In the vicinity of Lugouqiao, or the Marco Polo Bridge, near Peking, there were training grounds used by the garrisons that guarded the legations in Peking. A Japanese garrison of 550 marched to the training grounds, rifle fire was heard from the Chinese garrison of 15,000 nearby and a Japanese soldier disappeared. The Japanese appealed to the mayor of Peking and went in search of the soldier, asking permission to enter Wanping.

It turned out that the soldier had been searching for sexual diversion and returned a couple of hours later. The Japanese had by this time confronted the Chinese at Wanping and tempers flared into fighting. Both sides called up reserves for what was only minor skirmish. The Chinese did not realise how vulnerable the Japanese felt, for their North China Garrison was only an infantry brigade, but the Kuomintang had learned that it had to be hostile to the Japanese or its support in the region would wither. Although there were hotheads on both sides, the leaders did not want an escalation to war.

The next day Chiang sent four divisions into the buffer zone, which was meant to be demilitarised. The Japanese cabinet was unified and did everything in its power to stop an escalation to war, sending Hashimoto to Peking to try to sort out the trouble. Although the cabinet had mobilised three divisions, this was precautionary and they did not embark. On 9 July a hot-headed Japanese commander sent his battalion into battle but was defeated. On 16 July Chiang renounced the demilitarised zone, which greatly increased Japanese feelings of insecurity, but their policy was still to avoid war. Towards the end of the month incidents increased and were not favourable to Japan, culminating on 25 July in 300 Japanese soldiers, who were returning to their legation in Peking, becoming trapped and the Chinese firing on them, killing many. Surprisingly, those who survived were allowed to seek safety. Three days later the Japanese retaliated with escalating ferocity. Chiang, having received favours from the communists, realised that only an anti-Japan stance would hold hope for the unification of the north and south of China; however, he was not keen on total war.

In early August the Japanese cabinet decided to send an expeditionary force to protect its property and allow civilians to depart. This infuriated China and increased the temperature. On 9 August a Chinese sentry in Shanghai shot two Japanese, which triggered a war in that city. Garrisons were reinforced and air forces went into action. This was the first contested air war since 1918, as other actions such as Guernica had been unopposed. Japan had a numerical superiority of 3,000 aircraft to China's and there was little doubt about the result. However, it was a bruising encounter, both on land and in the air, with the Japanese reaching the Shanghai hinterland in early November.

Japanese troops were now pouring into China and, with disciplined panache and fanatical cruelty, they exposed the poor quality of the German-trained Chinese cadres. From Shanghai, the Japanese moved towards Nanking, about 200 miles away on the Yangtze river. The river curved around the town, forming a backdrop to a three-pronged attack from Shanghai: in the north, the attack followed the railway; in the centre, there was a direct attack across land and lakes; and in the south, the town of Wuhu was to be captured, thus stopping any supplies to Nanking by railway.

Nanking, as the capital, had a large mandarinate living there but, in November, most were ordered to leave and go to the cities of Changsha, Hankow and Chungking. In their place came 90,000 troops, who prepared the defences. They constructed a mile-wide battle zone outside the city walls, resulting in great destruction of property and increased homelessness, but it showed that the Kuomintang meant business.

However, when the test came, the Kuomintang failed. With ammunition and provisions for a five-month siege, the city fell in four days. Chiang left with an air corps before the battle, which allowed the Japanese to bomb with impunity and give intelligence to the army.

The Chinese could not concede this advantage. Their communication systems were in disarray, there were difficulties in exchanges between Mandarin and Cantonese speakers and there was a mixture of troops, some of whom were so inexperienced that they had not fired a bullet, while the experienced were exhausted by the retreat from Shanghai. With these deficiencies came chaos. The Japanese cohesiveness and control of the air enabled them to split the Chinese into small units and deal with them one by one. At midday on 11 December Chiang ordered his commander, Tang, to leave, an order that he questioned and decided to disobey. The next day it was repeated and Tang heard that the Japanese navy was clearing the Yangtze of mines and was threatening his line of retreat.

The Rape of Nanking

Victory was one thing but what happened next tarred Japan's army with disgrace and led inexorably to its defeat eight years later. It never learned to consolidate its victories into something acceptable to the vanquished. On 9 December 1937 the victorious Japanese dropped leaflets by air imparting the usual merciful decencies of conquerors. They stated that no mercy would be given to those who resisted but there would be fairness to those uninvolved in the fighting and to soldiers who bore no malice. When it came to the crunch, there was the most awful massacre and outpouring of gratuitous animal vengeance, which involved the whole army and went on for weeks. Its ghastliness was in its calculated, premeditated perversion and cruelty. Children, women and the old were slaughtered indiscriminately with a fearful bloodlust. The slaughter of prisoners is understandable, if deplorable, but rape and torture showed an awful depravity.

The Japanese army watched displays of beheading, with fountains of blood projected into the air and the heads collected as trophies. When they became bored with that, they killed using bayonets, there was dismembering, disembowelling, people buried alive or covered in petrol and incinerated, while others were forced into an icy lake and used for target practice. And, as a special variation, some would be half buried and dogs set upon them to rip the entrails out of their bellies and eat them. Rape was carried out ubiquitously and suffered by all ages from the very young to the very old. Once the victim was of no more use, or the soldiers were exhausted, they killed them. Men were not immune from this lust, with public displays of sodomy rife. Again, killing was the norm and the terror did not subside for weeks.

The Japanese army was conditioned to kill. On the rampage from Shanghai to Nanking, soldiers torched villages and killed their inhabitants. The army had become a killing machine, exacerbated by the insecurity of the Japanese in China. They were conquerors, respected but despised, surrounded on all sides by millions of Chinese who grudgingly accepted their fiefdom, but there were millions of others who did not.

The Japanese had a problem: if a Chinese army surrendered in their tens of thousands, what were they to do with the captives? Lock them up and feed them? Set them free? Treat them as slaves and make them work? For the Japanese there was no sensible answer. These men were worthless in a country of abundant labour and little available work, they were an embarrassing surplus of humanity, which is why the order went out from the highest level to kill all prisoners. Who actually gave it is not known but the commander was the emperor's uncle, Prince Asaka.

Asaka was not a favourite of the emperor as he had sided with Prince Chichibu during the February 1936 army mutiny; however, he had been given command of the army in the field at the beginning of December 1937 when General Iwane Matsui, ill with tuberculosis, was given a general command over central China. Hirohito doubted Asaka's loyalty and wanted to put him to the test.

On 17 December Matsui was well enough to visit Nanking for a ceremonial march and victory celebration through the centre of the city. The Japanese army temporarily stopped its debauchery and lined the streets as the emperor was given a triple banzai, which reverberated around Nanking. Matsui, however, had become suspicious, as he found a conspiracy of silence as to what had happened in Nanking. When he made further inquiries and had some intimation of the awful crimes committed, he feared for future relations between Japan and China. Within a few days he returned to Shanghai and told an American correspondent that the Japanese army was probably the most undisciplined in the whole world. He also sent a message to Prince Asaka's chief of staff, condemning unlawful acts and underlining the need for discipline, especially because of Asaka's relationship to the emperor.

The world's press was shielded from these acts. Americans and Europeans in Nanking lived in a certain area, which became known as the Safety Zone. The Chinese flocked to it for protection, which saved tens of thousands of lives. Of the approximate figure of 500,000 left in Nanking on 13 December, probably more than half were killed but no one knows for sure. Information about what had happened at Nanking seeped out, although the heinous nature of the massacre was not really investigated until the war crimes trial after the war. With time, the imprint of its horror and its significance has grown.

It is necessary to put this loss of a quarter of a million people into context because it was soon to be greatly exceeded. The fighting continued along the arteries of communication, the canals, the rivers and the railways. China looked after its water and had 225,000 miles of canals. The rivers could be massive, such as the Yangtze with its great gorges, while the railways were prevalent along the coast and linked the big cities to each other, which was the area the Japanese were conquering.

To stop the Japanese advance, Chiang ordered the opening of the Yellow River dykes, which gratuitously led to the death of a million Chinese and failed to halt the enemy. Which is the greater crime, the Nanking Massacre or the opening of the dykes? Is a leader able to murder a million of his compatriots in the defence of his country and not receive the opprobrium of the world? There is no easy answer, except that life was a cheap commodity to China and Japan.

The flooding did not hold up the Japanese, who captured Canton in October, thus separating Hong Kong from its hinterland, although the Chinese put up a good defence at Hankow. The Japanese were now coming under pressure in that serious fighting broke out with the Russians at Changkufeng and, with a war on two fronts, the Japanese were the filling in the sandwich.

Chiang had decided on a grand strategic retreat of about 1,000 miles to Chungking. This created a kind of stalemate, with the Japanese occupied by the problems of administering their conquest and protecting their lines of communication. They had got most of what they wanted, the defeat of the Chinese navy giving them control of the coastline, the big cities, most of the railway system, and they had a stranglehold of Chinese trade routes. All that was left unconquered and in contact with the outside world was the old silk route through Russia, the interminable Burma Road, unusable during the rainy season, and the port of Haiphong in Indo-China, controlled by France but subject to Japan's control of the coast.

Nevertheless, Japan's control of China was never easy. It was undoubtedly powerful along the lines of communication but its writ was not strong in rural areas and the communists started to use guerrilla warfare. What Japan really wanted from China was recognition that it was the lord of Asia, that the long history of Chinese cultural hegemony over Asia was ended. Japan did not really want to rule China but to do business with it and to gain control in that way. To aspire to rule China meant that a great Japanese mandarinate would have to be formed, which was impossible. Japan therefore looked around for a Chinese puppet to do its will and the obvious person was Chiang; however, he refused unless the Japanese retired from China. The Japanese therefore put in place some figureheads, who did not appeal to the Chinese, and it was not until 1940 that they found a man of substance in Wang Jingwei, a former colleague of Chiang in the Kuomintang, who led the Chinese, subject to the stringent constraints of the Japanese.

Chapter 18

Nations Seeking Advantage

The Jews as Heroes

On 16 June 1904, in Dublin, James Joyce met and fell in love with Nora, who would one day become his wife. They were in no hurry to marry but from that moment they were emotionally and spiritually interlocked. They were both Roman Catholics and were the product of Roman Catholic Ireland, which for 900 years had been under the yoke of what had become Protestant England.

The Joyces soon exiled themselves from Ireland and, after living in various European cities, ended up in Trieste during the Great War. Trieste was a polyglot city of the Austro-Hungarian Empire situated on the Adriatic Sea. Here Joyce eked out a living teaching English while writing a masterpiece, *Ulysses*. War affected him as it affected everyone but it was not part of his art and he treated it as a temporary aberration of human behaviour. He concentrated on that day in Dublin when he had fallen in love and, within the framework of that, one day he created a hero, Leopold Bloom, the Jewish wanderer, and his wife Molly, the Jewish earth mother.

Ulysses is an intensely intellectual book that rejects the classical framework of previous centuries. It is so avant-garde that the avant-garde exalted it to be the greatest novel of the century but it was not as fashionable by the beginning of the twenty-first century. Although the book was striving for something new, it did have a classical framework.

The prosaic subject matter is battered into literature by using Homer's

Odyssey as a template. The philosophical background uses the ideas of Giambattista Vico, the eighteenth-century Italian philosopher, whose belief was that mankind was passing into the third stage of its development – from the polytheism of the *Odyssey*, to the monotheism of the current religions, to the stage where men and women take their destiny into their own hands. To do this, man must know his own nature and know how to communicate. Joyce had great gifts as a linguist and lived in the nuance and sound of many languages, both dead and alive. Words and sound had a life that was universal and he sought this universality within the framework of the English language.

The quintessential heroes of *Ulysses* are Dublin, in which Joyce, by choice, would never live again, and a Jew and Jewess celebrating their love in a prosaic, middle-aged way. The Jew is the alter ego of the other hero of the book, the Catholic Irishman, Stephen Dedalus, who is rooted in his city. One can identify Joyce with both. By implication, Bloom is not rooted, which is what appeals to Joyce. In his years of exile from Dublin he would live in 120 houses. Yet there was something strange in the Gentile, Joyce, who had rejected religion, finding heroes in the wandering Jew and his uxorious Jewish wife.

In many ways it is an irritating book and is difficult to read parts of it without a guide and an interpreter. It interweaves the prosaic existence of life with allusions to the literature and philosophy of previous centuries, together with the topography of Dublin, the everyday conversation of its inhabitants and the popular songs of the day. Added to this is the manipulation of language, because language, dead and alive, in all its prolific variety, dominates Joyce's mind and imagination. Here he seeks a universality, with sound the dominant factor. Whatever language we speak as a mother tongue, there is a universality of meaning through sound, and sound dominates meaning. The outcome was *Finnegans Wake*, an unreadable book that transcends any known language.

There is a chapter in *Ulysses* devoted to an Irish discussion on Shakespeare. Joyce was an Irish nationalist who tore himself away from his beloved Dublin and became a nationalist of the imagination when he went to live elsewhere. He wanted to see Ireland's greatness proclaimed through a great writer and wrote:

> Our young Irish bards, John Eglinton censured, have yet to create a figure which the world will set beside Saxon Shakespeare's Hamlet though I admire him, as old Ben did, on this side idolatry.[24]

The chapter is notable for the portrayal of what is known about Shakespeare's life. A mother and father, three male siblings and a sister, a wife, a daughter, and a son who died aged eleven. Shakespeare wrote *Hamlet*, which is discussed at length, a year after his father's death, with that tragedy leading to another, which in literature is immortal. We know little of Shakespeare's wife but on love he is immortal. Yet the prosaic fact is that the rough and tumble of sex led to marriage sans record:

> She put the comether on him, sweet and twentysix. The grey eyed goddess who bends over the boy Adonis, stooping to conquer, as prologue to the swelling act, is a boldfaced Stratford wench who tumbles in a cornfield a lover younger than herself.[25]

In Shakespeare's will he left Ann Hathaway his second-best bed, the implication of which is still subject to interpretation. Joyce understood how the artist is inspired, and his search for the prosaic facts of Shakespeare's life gives him a deeper insight, for *Ulysses* is about the prosaic facts woven artistically into a glorious fabric depicting a single day. In the end the supreme accolade is given to Shakespeare. In the words of John Eglinton, quoting Alexandre Dumas Senior: 'After God, Shakespeare has created most.'[26]

Laws Against the Jews

Legislative attacks on the Jews started immediately after the Nazis had taken control of Germany. Many Jews felt that the Nazis would modify their hatred with the responsibilities of power; however, they were deluded. The persecution would be incremental until the Nazis had finally been destroyed. From time to time there were signposts to this incremental racial assault. The Nuremberg Laws of 15 September 1935 were one example. These defined Reich citizenship, which did not include the Jews as they were not of German blood. Marriage and sex between Jew and Gentile was forbidden. The Jews were to be expunged from German life by the simple expedient of death and migration. Either would mean that the state could purloin their wealth, as with emigration they were only able to take the bare necessities.

By the time the Nuremberg Laws were introduced, 75,000 German Jews from just under 500,000 had emigrated. Being deprived of their rights and their livelihood, they had little option if they did not possess capital. They dispersed all over the world. Some went to other European countries, some to Britain and its empire, others to the United States, but the biggest exodus was to Palestine, which was under a British mandate. The reaction of the indigenous Arabs there was not encouraging. They resented the newcomers and within two years the influx of the despairing was reduced to a trickle.

If the Jews went east, as many did, especially to Poland, they found persecution awaiting them, not in such a forthright way but they had to endure potential suffering. The Jews in Poland, of whom there were between three and four million, could not forget the pogroms, so 10 per cent of their number had emigrated between 1921 and 1937.

The Nazis, heedless of virtue and genius, initiated the greatest banishment of talent that has ever been known. This was blind rage and, although a few exceptions were made, there was little consistency, as the case of Fritz Haber indicates. Haber was the originator of the synthesis of ammonia, which was used in the production of explosives and had enabled Germany to continue the war until the end of 1918. Maybe he was a spent creative force but there were men of genius, men of talent, men of great competence who were banished.

German universities contained a significant number of Jews, often from other countries, who had been attracted by the German genius. Now they left the country. John von Neumann, the mathematician, and Eugene Wigner went to Princeton. Edward Teller and later Otto Frisch went to Copenhagen to work with Niels Bohr. Wolfgang Pauli stayed in Switzerland. Rudolph Peierls remained in England. Leo Szilard thought he might like to work in India and was active in getting Jewish academics posts abroad but finally ended up in the United States. Britain was active in providing temporary appointments for talented émigrés and took on about a half of them but it was American money from the likes of the Rockefeller and other foundations that gradually drew many away from England. The diaspora of talent was immense.

The Cost of Broken Glass

Sometimes the Jews hit back. In 1926 in Paris a Jew killed the exiled Ukrainian nationalist leader, Symon Petliura, who was one of the main culprits responsible for the pogroms a few years earlier. In 1936 a Jewish medical student killed Hitler's personal representative in Switzerland. He gave himself up to the Swiss authorities as a martyr and received eighteen years imprisonment. But it was in November 1938 in Paris that the murder of the third secretary at the German embassy caused the greatest fracas. The perpetrator was a seventeen-year-old Jew who was incensed because his father had been deported with 10,000 others to Poland in a box car.

This incident was what the German leadership wanted and, in what they described as a spontaneous demonstration, a terrifying pogrom was started. Its agent was Reinhard Heydrich and documentary evidence after the war revealed how well it had been planned. Synagogues were to be burned to the ground but, when the fires were started, care had to be taken of German property. Jewish businesses, houses and flats could be destroyed but not looted, as loot would be for the state. As many Jews as possible, especially the wealthy, would be arrested, without overcrowding the prisons. From there they would be sent to concentration camps.

On the following day, Heydrich reported to Göring that 119 synagogues had been set on fire, another seventy-six completely destroyed, about 1,000 shops and houses destroyed, 20,000 Jews arrested, thirty-six killed and thirty-six seriously injured. Heydrich grossly underestimated the number killed. No one, however, was convicted of murder but there were some cases of rape and some members of the Nazi party were expelled for defiling themselves by having congress with a Jewess. The humiliation for the innocent Jews continued, with a fine of one billion marks for starting the uprising.

There was, however, another problem – a vast insurance claim. With the wilful destruction costing about twenty-five billion marks, several German insurance companies could become insolvent. Of course, they could refuse to pay but a lot of the property was owned by Gentiles and let to Jews. Moreover, German insurance was in an international market so, if they did not pay, confidence in German insurance would plummet. There was also the small problem of broken glass, which was everywhere, and estimated to cost five billion marks to replace. Most of the glass would have to be imported from abroad, thus increasing the strain on foreign exchange, which was a German economic weakness.

Göring chaired a meeting two days after the pogrom at which these facts were pointed out. He became annoyed with Heydrich, telling him that he ought to have killed 200 Jews instead of causing such destruction. This was recorded and shown to Göring after the war. He did not deny it but attributed it to excitement and bad temper and said it was not meant to be taken seriously. However, the insurance problem persisted. Göring's suggested solution was that the insurance companies should pay the Jews but that this money would then be confiscated and partially reimbursed to the insurance companies. This would, of course, only partially reduce the losses.

This meeting was the peacetime culmination of the attack on the Jews. It was decided to eliminate any Jewish influence on the German economy, with all assets being transferred to Aryans. Any money accruing from these forced sales would go into bonds, to which the Jews had the right to the interest but their capital would be lost. For the time being the question of whether the Jews should be excluded from schools and public places, be confined to ghettos and used as forced labour was left to a later decision. The true evil of the Nazi regime had therefore been established before war started.

The Soviet Union at the Centre of Affairs

War is not the natural state for most of mankind, although swift aggression has often been mankind's way to settle problems. Long drawn-out wars are not uncommon but short, sharp conflicts are more the norm. Hitler was a man who believed in such conflicts to resolve problems, as did the Japanese, who had done so well in this way against the Russians in 1904–05. Both believed that they could benefit from this approach to war and that they would remain unmolested by nations that took a longer view but were far from the action.

Munich was a disaster, not because France and Britain did not go to war but because they misread Hitler and thought they had a solution to Europe's ills. Both Germany and Japan were probing to gain advantage and the Soviet Union was at the fulcrum of these events, not Britain and France. The Soviets saw diplomatic advantage in linking with either antagonist, Greater Germany or the Franco–British axis, and being wooed by both. What the Soviet Union feared was for Germany, France and Britain to gang up on it. To the east, it was trying to contain Japan, which was also probing for advantage but was circumspect, as it had its hands full in China. Although Britain and France would declare war against Germany, it was the Soviet Union that held centre stage.

Japan and the Soviet Union

The borders of Manchuria and Mongolia, and of Manchuria and the Soviet Union were not clear cut. They were barren, inhospitable and useless unless mineral deposits were found or there was some strategic advantage. However, there were young men patrolling these borders who were bored and militant, and in the 1930s there were thousands of incidents recorded, mostly trivial.

However, in June and July 1937, an incident escalated that was not trivial. The Soviets landed on some small islands in the Amur river and imprisoned some Manchurian gold miners. There were also some Soviet gunboats firing at the Manchurian army. This brought the 1st Tokyo Division of the Kwantung army into the equation. It had been exiled to this dreary part of the planet because of misdemeanours in the 26 February 'incident' of 1936 but this had not cooled their ardour; diplomacy was not their way of doing things and they were spoiling for a fight.

The Soviets claimed that the territory was theirs and the general staff in Tokyo ordered the Japanese forces to hold back. This was difficult for the 1st Division as a Soviet gunboat was too tempting a target, so it was sunk. The result justified the action as the Soviets withdrew and the Japanese reoccupied the islands. This border dispute, the Amur River Incident, was merely an hors d'oeuvre to what was to follow.

Changkufeng – July to August 1938

Changkufeng is near the borders of Manchuria, the Soviet Union and Korea, 70 miles south-west of Vladivostok. The Japanese port of Rashin was 15 miles away in Korea, linked by railway to distant parts of Manchuria. Changkufeng is a mountain whose sovereignty had been in dispute for many years and it had the strategic advantage that it overlooked Rashin.

The Soviets were nervous at this time because Genrikh Lyushkov, the Soviet intelligence overlord in south-east Asia, had defected to Japan and it has been suggested that this was a reason that they occupied the mountain. The Korean part of the Japanese army was responsible for opposing this infiltration but the militant Kwantung army wanted a part of the action. The Korean soldiers watched and did little but the Kwantung army goaded them. Tokyo's policy was one of containment and, if it came to a fight, to go no further than reclaim what they considered theirs. As it happened, Japanese reconnaissance forces became involved in a battle and removed the Soviets from the heights, retaining the territory against the inevitable counter-attacks.

The Korean army in the area consisted of one division, as the other had been sent to China, and the division had to fight without tanks or aircraft, although it had good artillery support. It was an elite division, well led by an able general, but outnumbered by three to one, with the Soviets having over 120 aircraft, more than 200 tanks and even superiority in artillery.

The Japanese were not afraid of this manpower ratio; they considered that one Japanese was as good as three Russians and in infantry combat they were more than a match for the Soviets. But the Japanese suffered from the armoured and aerial might of the Soviets, even though it was poorly applied. Most of the fighting took place in 6 square miles of territory, with significant casualties. The Japanese lost 500 dead and had 1,000 wounded, while an estimate for the Soviets was about 1,200 killed and 4,000 wounded.

The outcome was interesting. Although the Japanese were close to their mainland, had a port nearby and a railway running to the front, their logistical system was poor. If the Soviets had persisted, they would have won the battle. As it was, they seemed prepared to accept the outcome but the Japanese knew how narrow the victory had been and felt that the Soviets would probably try again at some opportune moment.

In Japan there had been considerable tension between the emperor and his war minister, Seishiro Itagaki, and the army chief of staff, Prince Kanin, who had asked for permission to attack beyond the borders if that seemed reasonable; however, an angry Hirohito had refused. Despite the defection of its intelligence overlord, the Soviet Union still had a great advantage in that Richard Sorge was providing first-class material, which was believed. Japan now felt it wanted a diplomatic solution to these border disputes, which could so easily lead to its forces being sandwiched between China and Russia, so it yielded its gains on Changkufeng to give the Soviet Union a political victory.

Nomonhan Incident – May to September 1939

Nomonhan is a small mountain on the Mongolian–Manchurian border. Nearby is the Khalkhin-Gol river, which Japan recognised as the border, while the Soviet Union claimed the border was 16 miles to the east. Stalin was in confrontational mood and moving troops to the area, while the Kwantung army patrolled in its usual pugnacious way. Mongolian horsemen were the catalyst for this incident, as they moved into what Japan claimed as its territory, so the Japanese pushed them back to the river borders.

The Soviets retaliated by crossing the river and building bridges, which they defended. Then 2,000 Japanese confronted 1,500 Soviets, who had superior armour, fighting an inconclusive battle. However, the Japanese retreated in what they called a lateral advance, while the Soviets held their bridges and some territory across the river. Soviet air strikes deep into Japanese territory caused the Japanese to retaliate deep into Mongolia. The emperor and his high command disapproved and were this time obeyed.

Stalin had sacked the military loser of Changkufeng, Marshal Blyukher, and had him liquidated. He turned to General Georgy Zhukov, a protégé of Marshal Semyon Timoshenko. Zhukov had made his reputation in mobile warfare trials in the early 1930s. He had respect for Stalin and his despotic power but he was never craven and, on taking command, asked for and received superior forces. Border clashes continued until the end of June, sometimes more than skirmishes as, in one incident, a Japanese cavalry regiment was trapped and wiped out.

Soviet diplomatic pressure developed and they warned Tokyo of the potential conflagration. Tokyo took fright, a feeling that the Kwantung army did not share, ever eager for glory. The trouble was that the Soviets had carte blanche to bomb but the Japanese did not. They also had the advantage of intelligence. Richard Sorge was at his most accomplished in this conflict, providing excellent intelligence from three sources.

The first concerned Japan's aims and came from the top echelons of government. He reported that it was not Japan's intention to start a general war against the Soviet Union. A border clash would remain a border clash even though it involved several divisions. Japan, in the short term, had no intention of purloining Soviet territory. This was very useful information if correct and seemed to be backed up by Changkufeng. Secondly, information was relayed to Moscow about the strength of the Japanese forces and their logistical support from the South Manchurian Railway. Thirdly, there was information from agents on the spot about Japanese dispositions and strength.

Japan's forces had 15,000 men divided into thirteen infantry battalions, two tank regiments and one artillery regiment, covered by an air force of 180 planes. At this time, the Soviets were slightly below this strength, having 12,500 men, and although they had only twenty-three anti-tank weapons, there were 186 tanks and 266 armoured cars of superior quality to the Japanese.

Although the Soviets had been confrontational, it was the Kwantung army under General Kenkichi Ueda that became the aggressors. His war minister, Itagaki, who had been involved in the Manchurian Incident of 1931, encouraged him, and although Ueda had to clear his plans with the general staff in Tokyo, he felt he had the right as the man on the spot to decide tactics. The army's general staff, divining that he might act unilaterally, sent an officer to try to control matters but Ueda refused to be hamstrung and brought forward the date of his planned pre-emptive air strike. His air force attacked a Soviet base and returned triumphant, claiming the destruction of well over a hundred planes in the air and on the ground. The claims were probably a substantial exaggeration but there had been a triumph, which was also a clear case of insubordination and recognised as such by Ueda's HQ.

The emperor was infuriated, yet the Kwantung army refused to budge and stated that its soldiers were the people on the ground who knew what was happening and they should be entitled to make the decisions. More than anything it showed the power of the army in Japanese politics. Even when high-ranking generals were brought to book, they had protectors in high places who would fight to modify any penalties imposed so that the worst an errant general would get was a slap on the wrist, and not even that if he had been successful. In this case, all that was achieved was an agreement that Soviet air bases would not be attacked in the future.

At the beginning of July the Kwantung army marched and destroyed more than a hundred tanks in a fierce battle but was held and forced back after two days. There was another engagement when the Japanese crossed the Halha river, losing forty tanks, but the result was inconclusive. This was worrying to the Japanese as it became obvious that the Soviet tanks were better armoured and were resilient to their anti-tank guns, while the Japanese tanks were vulnerable. Any Soviet tanks destroyed was largely down to the individual bravery of Japanese soldiers, who would attack with grenades, often giving their own lives. Although Japanese valour was evident, it was not enough for a result. The Soviets realised their artillery superiority and the Japanese tried to get heavy guns to the battle zone to achieve parity.

The uninhibited Soviet air force now started raiding bases deep into Manchuria. This time the Kwantung army did try to get permission to retaliate but it was refused. Tokyo wanted the escalating battle to be stopped and summoned the chief of staff, General Rensuke Isogai, who argued fiercely against the refusal of permission. He was sent back to Manchuria with orders to stop the fighting pending a diplomatic solution. Such a solution would be tough and dictated by the Soviet Union, which had well-ordered logistical support and was building up its strength via the Trans-Siberian Railway.

Japan knew that there would soon be a substantial Soviet attack but was confident that it could be repulsed and now lifted the order forbidding the bombing of Soviet targets in Mongolia. This intelligence reached the Soviets, who started their attack in bad weather with low cloud before the Japanese air force could be effective. Due to poor visibility and lack of aerial intelligence, the Japanese were overwhelmed by superior forces. The Soviets had used three infantry divisions and five tank brigades, with two divisions in reserve. Within a week the Kwantung army was in retreat and had ceded any border territory that it might conceivably have claimed.

While this was happening, the German–Soviet Pact was signed. Both this pact and the Battle of Nomonhan were great tidal waves, whose surge influenced all the great powers in the world. Although Germany, Britain, France, Poland and the Soviet Union were involved in diplomacy of immense significance, the Soviet Union's involvement in the east put it at the fulcrum of world affairs. For the time being it had security in the east and was arranging territorial expansion in the west, which had enormous significance.

Life became more difficult for Japan. Its view of the world hinged on the link with Germany, and when Germany did a volte-face and made a pact with its traditional enemy, Japan had to reorientate itself. The Japanese government fell in late August because of the pact. Although the prime minister and the war minister were both generals approved by the general staff, their attitude was different. Prime Minister Prince Konoe was more belligerent, while the war minister, General Shonroku Hata, sought diplomatic solutions, which the situation required.

Japan needed stability and peace with the Soviet Union and Hata sought it. He was an interesting character, a participant in many of the great events of Japanese history of the past forty years. He had fought the Russians in the war of 1904–05, had helped establish diplomatic relations with the Russians in 1925 and had been commander-in-chief in China after the rape of Nanking. He understood what it was like to be engulfed by an enormous population with tenuous lines of communication. Moreover, as aide-de-camp to the emperor during the Battle of Nomonhan, he understood the emperor's reluctance to go to war and the folly of doing so.

It was a bad defeat, which the Kwantung army thought was only temporary. Defeated but defiant, it wanted another crack at the enemy and the means to defeat them. Its objective that autumn was to regain the initiative, then go to war with the Soviet Union in the spring. This was folly and, fortunately for the Japanese, they did not have the means to do very much, even when other divisions in Manchuria were summoned to help. World events had now diminished the Kwantung army's importance and its usefulness was purely in defending Manchuria. Its ability to attack was negligible until it was able to be re-equipped, which was not to be, and the insubordinate, arrogant army was to languish in an emasculated way and would never make another significant contribution.

The Battle of Nomonhan illustrated the defects and virtues of the Japanese army and its air wing. The army was brave and valorous to the point of fanaticism, with an air arm that was not particularly strong, artillery that was good but not outstanding, weak in tanks and armoured vehicles, and not outstanding in the gaining and use of intelligence. But it was an army that would learn quickly, its air arm would rapidly improve, as would its gathering and use of intelligence, but it would always remain weak in its use of armour. Although its instincts were to conquer eastern parts of the Soviet Union, the bloody nose it received at Nomonhan was a vivid experience and a major factor in Japan's ambitions to move southwards.

The Tientsin Incident

The influence of diplomacy was now in a crucial state on a worldwide basis and the East was not divided from the West. Tientsin was a treaty port with British and French concessions. The Japanese in north China resented these concessions and put pressure on the British and French to leave by isolating their territory, the hinterland of which they controlled. Britain retaliated by stating that if its concession were violated, it would send its fleet to the Far East and Japan and Britain would be at war. This would have been a far-reaching decision over what seemed a simple matter, but the British felt that any breach would be the end of the treaty port system, and their assets in China could not be defended. China was not a formal part of the British Empire but it contained a formidable trading asset to the British and the Chinese.

Although appeasement had been policy in the West, it was not policy in the East. Although Japan made life difficult in the concessions by only letting people in and out after being searched, the rigour of this varied during 1939 according to whom Tokyo put in charge. Public opinion had been roused in Tokyo, there were anti-British demonstrations and to many it gave much pleasure to tweak the nose of the mighty British Empire.

The Royal Navy, still the largest in the world, enforced the Pax Britannica with its allies, which allowed the trade routes of the oceans to remain unmolested. On the Chinese littoral this was not so, as the Japanese navy was in control, although this did not hamper British or American trade. The Royal Navy was run by competent men who found themselves in a dilemma. Before the formal war started, they realised that they had three enemies: Germany, Italy and Japan, and they prepared for war against all three. For the navy this meant defending the North Sea, the Mediterranean and the Far East.

For much of the 1930s, Lord Chatfield was first sea lord and he knew that the Royal Navy was stretched against three enemies, meaning there would have to be priorities. As he saw it, the North Sea fleet could be thinned and could link up with the French navy, which would also be useful in the Mediterranean; however, if the British had to fight all three enemies, Chatfield would sacrifice the Mediterranean and send a substantial part of the fleet to Singapore and the Far East. He joined the cabinet in 1938 to coordinate defence and his successors as first sea lord considered Egypt and the Suez

Canal just as important as Singapore and that the logistical problems of the latter were much greater.

Although the politicians talked about defending Tientsin, there was no question of fighting Japan. The quality of the Japanese navy in its own backyard was far too good and it would also have the advantage of air cover. No one knew at this time how important air cover was for ships but it was not discounted and more aircraft were sent to Malaya, although their quality was not impressive.

Britain badly needed a diplomatic solution to the impasse at Tientsin. In London there was obviously great consternation about a possible European war but Lord Halifax, the foreign secretary, was also preoccupied by the Far East and declared to the cabinet at the beginning of August that he was suffering great anxiety over Tientsin. Not only could the empire disintegrate if Japan went to war but the silver reserves of the Kuomintang government were held in Tientsin and its economy would be weakened if these were captured.

The whole matter came to a head in August 1939. The Royal Navy had new leadership. Admiral Sir Dudley Pound became first sea lord, with Admiral Tom Phillips as his deputy, and the former deputy, Admiral Cunningham, was sent to the Mediterranean. The latter was very much against too many resources going to the Far East. Phillips produced a paper on naval strategy, which was realistic. It made the statement that Britain could not have three fleets, that the home waters had to be fully defended, it was pointless sending a below-strength fleet to the East and that a choice had to be made between Singapore and the Mediterranean as circumstances dictated.

The resolution of the matter came when Japan also applied common sense. The Kwantung army's defeat at Nomonhan had rocked it, so it did not want to be opposed by China, the Soviet Union and Britain. Roosevelt had abrogated the Japan–US Treaty of Commerce and Navigation, which put Japan on the defensive, and the Nazi–Soviet pact caused total confusion. In this chaos, the government fell and Tientsin was relieved.

Czechoslovakia – February to March 1939

With the boundaries of Germany increased by the inclusion of the Sudetenland, observers thought that Hitler would be satisfied; however, he was cantankerous and hated Benes's diplomatic manoeuvrings. In particular, he was slighted by the pact that Czechoslovakia had with the Soviet Union and its constant insistence on sovereignty and independence. Hitler had fought in a great war with the Austro-Hungarian Empire intact and at no time in his memory had the Czechs or the Slovaks been independent. They had been members of the Hapsburg Empire and, while acknowledging the part that the Hungarians had played in that empire, Hitler saw Germany as the dominant part of it.

The Czechs, however, were an able people and they had forged a prosperous nation with which the majority of the Slovaks were ambivalent but reasonably happy as long as prosperity continued, although secession had its adherents. The Slovaks felt that they were in many respects subordinate to the Czechs and subject to a colonial structure of government. Bohemia and Moravia, with the great central European city of Prague, did dominate economically and, at times, the Czechs were less than diplomatic with the Slovaks. The historical background of Slovakia was different in that it had been part of the kingdom of Hungary. Part of it was disputed between the Slovaks and the Hungarians and, at Munich in 1938, a slice of Carpatho-Ukraine containing the two main towns reverted to Hungary, with Ruthenia (Western Ukraine) remaining with Czechoslovakia. The ethnic mix of Ruthenia was 500,000 of Slav extraction, who felt a racial and religious affinity with Ukraine, 100,000 Hungarians and 90,000 Jews. The Hungarians wanted to annex it and had to be stopped by the Germans.

In a certain sense, Czechoslovakia was a strange nation cobbled together out of the disasters of war. Around it were predators: Poland, Hungary and Germany. Hitler's strategy was to split the Czechs and the Slovaks, which was not especially difficult, but what the Slovaks did not want was German suzerainty over their affairs. This was a potential independent nation but they did not want German colonial administration to replace the relatively benign Czech version. This misunderstanding on the German part led to many inept advances to Slovak leaders, which got nowhere. No leader appeared who wished to take Slovakia into the German camp.

After Munich, Czechoslovakia had a new leader in President Emil Hácha. Altruistic for a politician, religious and scholarly by nature, he did not lust after power and was astounded by Hitler's use of it. Events determined the future of the nation, events that to Hitler were a balancing act and to Britain were a betrayal of trust and the final indication of Germany's bad faith.

Slovakia was the trigger. The Germans were intriguing but had little control over events that led to a Slovak government falling out with Prague and being dismissed. If chaos ensued, then the Czechs were prepared to march and restore order. This worried the Germans, who wanted the Czechs and Slovaks to stay apart and did not want the Hungarians to claim Slovakia if there was a power vacuum.

Hitler felt that he needed to act quickly and provide guarantees for the Slovak nation. Fearful that Czechoslovakia was disintegrating, Hácha went to Berlin to find out what Hitler wanted and, when bullied, caved in and allowed Hitler to march into Bohemia and form a protectorate. The Czechs provided no resistance and Hitler spent the night of 15 March in Prague, leaving the next day, never to return. This was a natural fiefdom to be taken for granted and the ethnic structure ignored.

The reaction in the West was one of open-mouthed amazement at this brash bit of national engineering. Anyone believing that Hitler should be appeased and that nations should give way so that ethnic groups could be united was shattered by what happened to the rump of Czechoslovakia. They were not interested in the fact that Czechoslovakia was a nation of dubious creation, questionable integrity and little legitimacy. All they saw was a rampant, powerful Germany enclose it in its maw and the settlement in central Europe arising from one of the most terrible wars in history come to naught.

Overnight, public opinion in Britain changed. The dominant emotion of the British public before these events was fear of war. The suffering of the Great War was uppermost in their minds and that was why they hailed Chamberlain when he returned from Munich with peace in our time, mistaken as it was. They craved peace but they were not a people who were craven, nor were they a people who eschewed justice. They felt that the victors of the Great War may have treated the defeated with a certain injustice and were prepared to make amends. This is what appeasement was about, an attempt to create a new and just equilibrium where the historical victors and vanquished could both flourish. The French were different in that they feared war more, with good reason, because of past sufferings and they were yet to experience a significant industrial resurgence.

The Germans, on the other hand, had also suffered, experiencing desperation and financial chaos until Hitler restored their optimism and drilled them into a coherence of his own making. The Germans implicitly trusted him to restore their self-esteem and greatness as a nation, so were prepared to accept war on a local, central European scale. There is little evidence that they wanted it on a grand scale but Hitler knew that he could take them there by degrees. What he did not understand was his effect on the French and British people, and he underestimated the leaders of those countries. He was contemptuous of them, with little justification except his own exalted conceit.

During six years of power, which had become greater and more dictatorial, Hitler had created an economic momentum that had not been checked or seriously questioned. He had created a nation of full employment, sustained by deficit financing, based on public works and armament production, and all the bills had yet to be paid. To the outside world, Germany appeared very prosperous and strong but this was deceptive. Undoubtedly its people felt renewed, even exhilarated, but real wealth and real strength take time to accumulate and it was no accident that Germany would evolve the concept of blitzkrieg in war. It had to go for the knockout blow, as it would be at a disadvantage at the end of a long fight.

Poland

Hitler knew what he wanted strategically but tactically he was an opportunist. When he mentioned to his allies that the opportune moment for war was 1943 or 1944, he meant it; however, he did not consider the momentum he had created. Until the dismemberment of Czechoslovakia he had savoured great diplomatic success. The self-esteem it engendered fed his conceit that he had genius as a statesman.

He was not yet fifty and had been in power for six and a half years. As a politician he was at the peak of his powers; as a statesman who would leave a coherent framework for the German people, he had not matured. A true statesperson understands the impotence of individual power, that true power resides in the institutions through which he or she operates and that legitimacy comes through these institutions and the people he or she rules. This is just as true of the dictator as the democrat, although the dictator usually tries to circumvent this by the coercion of a secret police.

As a statesman, Hitler was now going to badly overreach himself with one of the most cynical pacts in the history of diplomacy. He was eyeing Poland but his diplomacy was low key, with a certain amount of sabre-rattling in Danzig and shadow-boxing in the embassies. There was nothing of real significance, although he had taken the decision that Germany would acquire most of Poland and he was prepared to go to war to get it.

All the time that Hitler had been chancellor, invective had been aimed at their ideological opponents in the Soviet Union. Communism and fascism, in many ways bedfellows, engendered a hatred that admitted to nothing in common, a fact that had been endorsed in Spain, with great cruelty and lack of humanity on both sides. Yet Hitler sought the German–Soviet Pact, forestalling any link between the Western Allies and the Soviet Union, acclaiming it as his greatest diplomatic triumph. In a sense it was but, to his ideological allies of Italy, Spain and Japan, it created total confusion and would lead to repercussions that he had not foreseen.

Britain and France were dazed by the multifarious diplomatic problems of Poland. First there was Danzig, indisputably German with a Polish hinterland and Poland's gateway to the Baltic, and there was not much inclination to go to war over this. Second, there was Poland's relationship with its neighbours – predatory towards a bit of Slovakia, ambivalent towards Romania and totally distrustful of both Germany and Russia. Thirdly, there was the question as to whether the Poles would defend themselves if attacked. If they did it would trigger the alliance with Britain and France, but to what extent could they help? To Hitler and Stalin, the Western powers' position seemed weak.

France, Britain and the Soviet Union

The historical link between Russia and France was still strong and the French knew it was indispensable if war was to be waged against Germany. Negotiations began for an alliance and, on 11 August, an Anglo–French team arrived in Moscow. The French premier, Daladier, had instructed General Doumenc to obtain a result. The British side was led by Admiral Erne-Erle-Drax, who had no great prestige or status in the scheme of things but fully represented Chamberlain's view that if there was to be an agreement, it would be a purely military one, the negotiations, like all negotiations with the Soviets, would be protracted and difficult and, if there was hope of a more political agreement, a heavyweight politician could be sent to the Soviet Union. What Chamberlain wanted was to keep Germany on its toes with the threat of an effective alliance with the Soviet Union but his heart was not really in it. He was a politician alienated by ideology from the Soviets but he wanted to keep Germany in check and silence his domestic critics – the Labour party, Lloyd George and Churchill – all of whom advocated the Soviet alliance.

The Soviets, in turn, were ultra-suspicious that France and Britain might link up with Germany and were determined to keep these nations apart. Although the Soviet Union had defeated Japan in the East, no one was prepared to give much credit to this victory. The Anglo–French team was in the dark as to Soviet military capability, so concentrated on presenting a set of principles that did not impress Marshal Voroshilov, the Soviet head of mission.

Voroshilov demanded concrete proposals and outlined over a period of days what he meant by this. He then asked a series of questions. What did France and Britain want from the Soviet Union if France, Poland, Romania or Turkey were attacked? Would Poland allow the Soviets to fight the enemy on Polish soil? If France or Britain were attacked, would they expect Poland to fight at full strength? Would the Soviets be allowed to attack East Prussia as in the last war? If Romania were attacked, would Poland join with the Soviet Union in attacking the Germans? If the Soviet Union were attacked in the north, as feared, would it be acceptable for the Soviets to expect France and Britain to enter the war with Poland and the British and French fleets to link up with the Soviet fleet to try to control the Baltic?

All of this was politically charged and had the honourable old sea dog, Admiral Drax, completely at sea. The basic requirement was to get Poland to agree with the Soviet Union that under certain circumstances the Soviets would be allowed to fight on Polish soil or to use it as a place of transit. The Poles did not trust the Soviets, though. Despite the French and British imploring them to accept these conditions, they refused. There would be no Soviets on Polish territory and that was final. The French foreign minister, Georges Bonnet, desperate for an alliance, told Doumenc to lie to the Soviets but the British vetoed this proposal, which was just as well because it was not something that could be concealed for long, even though Soviet intelligence was not particularly strong in the West at this time.

The German–Soviet Pact

The Germans instinctively knew of the difficulties that France and Britain had with the Soviet Union but also knew that the Anti-Comintern Pact confronted the Soviet Union from east and west, a fact that had to be considered, as Japan, Germany's ally, had still not completed a peace treaty with the Soviet Union. Therefore, the Soviets wanted any agreement with Germany to have a structure and proceed by several steps. First, there would be a trade agreement, which would be followed by a non-aggression pact linked to a secret protocol. This last twist, with the emphasis on the word 'secret', would outline the division between Germany and the Soviet Union of various states that divided them. This activity was in the tradition of the most powerful monarchs of these parts and was nothing new.

The usual difficult, procrastinating negotiations continued. The Germans bartered knowledge, especially technical knowledge of armaments and shipbuilding. Meanwhile, the Soviets provided raw materials such as oil, minerals and food. This economic agreement was concluded on 20 August 1939, to the mutual satisfaction of both sides, and the Soviets wanted the non-aggression pact to be signed a week later on 27 August. This was rather late for the Führer, who pushed his ambassador to get an earlier agreement. Hitler had been fretting for days, worried that his timetable would be upset. There was less than a week to go before he wanted to attack Poland and the date was already in jeopardy. Communications via code and teleprinter took time and there was the bureaucracy to bypass as Hitler and Stalin were not in direct communication.

In fact, Stalin had never met a German politician, not even the ambassador, as he left the negotiation of foreign affairs to his henchmen. To someone of Hitler's impatient and mercurial temperament, it was insufferable. Already the Soviets had agreed to a non-aggression treaty and for Joachim von Ribbentrop, the German foreign minister, to go to Moscow, but Hitler was in a hurry and sent a message to Stalin that Ribbentrop be received no later than 23 August, to which Stalin agreed.

Ribbentrop and his entourage left for Moscow via Konigsberg, not knowing what to expect, fearing that he would be played off against the Anglo–French. He warned the Soviets that he would only stay for twenty-four hours and was there to make decisions. It was a gamble but the situation on the Polish frontier could not be held for long. Already the Danzig senate had swept the League of Nations aside and made Gauleiter Forster head of state, while the battleship *Schleswig-Holstein* was steaming towards the harbour at Danzig. The Soviets, on the other hand, were aware of British and French diplomatic efforts for a modus vivendi with Hitler. Even though they were aware of Hitler's warlike intentions, they feared an Anglo–Franco–German deal, which would pit them against the Soviets.

On 22 August Hitler held a military conference to prepare his commanders for war. He was still on a roll. Whenever he met opposition his will prevailed and he emphatically believed in his own star. He told his commanders that all depended on his existence because of his great political talents and authority. He did, however, acknowledge that all could be upset by his own mortality. Just as revealing was his belief in Il Duce, his greatest political ally from another country. Here too there was realism, as he pointed out that if something happened to Il Duce, the Italian alliance would be vulnerable as the king of Italy and his courtiers were opposed to him. He was disparaging of France and Britain, saying that they possessed no outstanding personality.

Hitler then told his commanders that this was the time to go to war, there was nothing to lose and much to gain. However, he then stated another reason for going to war: the German economic situation was such that the nation could not survive for more than a few years. This was the reality. The deficit financing on armaments, which had brought full employment, had to be paid for and Germany needed the fruits of conquest to do this.

This was the dynamic that would gear all Hitler's strategy throughout the war. He also realistically summed up the options of the Western nations if he invaded Poland. Any blockade would be ineffective because of resources coming from the east, an attack from the Maginot Line would be unlikely from France, while the Netherlands, Belgium and Switzerland would remain neutral. Hitler then said that he was relying on a short war and that Britain could also only survive a short war.

This was a long diatribe, which his commanders received in silence. After a break for lunch Hitler became more specific and talked about how the war would be conducted. Part of it was pure Hitler, with phrases that would ring with endless repetition in the ears of the military leaders in the years to come. The phrases rang out: iron determination, life-and-death struggle, it is not right that matters but victory, close your hearts to pity, act brutally, the stronger man is right, be steeled against all signs of compassion. The brutal warlord was out to impose his vision on the world.

Ribbentrop in Moscow

The greeting of Ribbentrop on 23 August was low key but the meeting was at the highest level. He was joined by Graf von der Schulenburg, the ambassador, while the Soviets were represented by Molotov and Stalin, the presence of the latter acknowledging the importance of the occasion.

Both sides accepted the principle of the non-aggression treaty but how it was to be presented proved more difficult. Ribbentrop tried to wrap up the package in diplomatese but Stalin scornfully dismissed this, saying that after six years of shovelling shit over each other, they could not start talking about eternal friendship. Stalin agreed that disputes should be settled by the friendly exchange of views and the pact should have a ten-year duration. This was seemingly straightforward but it was the secret protocol, which would define spheres of influence.

That was the real core of the meeting. Poland was to be divided up and the split would be by the rivers Narew, Vistula and San. Hitler asked for Lithuania and part of Latvia up to the river Dvina, including Riga, while the Soviet Union took the rest of Latvia, Estonia and part of Finland. This was not wholly acceptable to Stalin, as he wanted ice-free ports and asked for the whole of Latvia. This was outside Ribbentrop's remit and he had to seek Hitler's permission to cede this, which was granted. But Hitler insisted that the two nations were to be the only powers to have spheres of influence in the area.

The pact was concluded, the two great regional powers colluding in the obliteration of the sovereignty of smaller nations. Stalin was pleased. Hitler was ecstatic. Stalin's last words to Ribbentrop were that he took the pact seriously and he would guarantee his word of honour that the Soviet Union would not betray Germany. Ribbentrop was prosaically diplomatic. The Soviets, whatever their shortcomings, did take pacts seriously. Hitler did not, however, and he was gripped by a febrile euphoria, which his staff witnessed. He now thought the odds were against Britain and France making war over Poland and crowed, 'Now Europe is mine. The others can have Asia.'[27]

There is no doubt that Hitler had a genuine intuitive feel for a deal that served Germany's interests but he was blinkered about how other nations viewed the world. On the surface this was a pact that would virtually complete the process of Germany being the successor state to the Austro-Hungarian Empire. Most of the territories that the empire embraced, with Hungary being *sui generis*, were to be incorporated into Germany. Although it made a mockery of the settlement made after the Great War, there was a logic to it, just as the Soviets were claiming the territories of the tsarist empire.

To the rest of the world it was not like this. In case of Spain, an insignificant power impoverished by civil war but territorially significant. Franco, although ideologically allied to Hitler, would never trust him because of this alliance with the communists. Japan, having been locked in battle with the Soviets, was mortified by the link. To those in power in Japan, Germany was a great nation in the process of renewal, a nation to be emulated, a staunch ally that, through a secret protocol to the Anti-Comintern Pact, would not betray them. But Germany did betray Japan, to its surprise. A piqued Japanese journalist even revealed the plans for the partition of Poland but was not taken seriously.

Japan was in a delicate situation as it was negotiating for peace in the Far East, a process that had started on 20 July. The Soviet Union held the intelligence card and, while welcoming peace negotiations, was spinning them out and had in the meantime won an overwhelming victory. Japan was in a fix and knew it. The government fell on 28 August, to be succeeded by one that was more sympathetic to the Anglo–Americans, although it was still sympathetic to Germany and was awaiting the outcome of events. The immediate aim was peace with the Soviet Union, which Japan achieved in mid-September.

Britain's reaction was unequivocal but Hitler only partially believed this. Some historians believed that the Great War had happened by accident and few in power at that time believed that the various pacts between nations would lead to a general conflagration. Chamberlain wanted his position to be crystal clear and requested his ambassador to deliver a letter to Hitler, telling him that war was inevitable if he attacked Poland but that a solution could be reached by negotiation.

It was too late. The momentum for war was too great. Hitler asked himself what Britain could do for Poland and considered it negligible, as he was contemptuous of its leaders. British public opinion was, paradoxically, not in the least put out by this pact, which could have been hugely dangerous if Germany and the Soviet Union had decided to join forces against Britain. British instincts told them that the pact reeked of cynicism and was unrealistic. In a way, they enjoyed the discomfiture of communist sympathisers in their midst. To many intellectuals, communism embraced the ideological hope of the world, the creed that would overcome the wicked capitalist exploitation of the people. All through Western Europe there were communist parties thrown into disarray by this pact and for many idealists it was the end of the road.

France, on the other hand, was hard hit by the pact. Above all, it used the Soviet connection as the lynchpin of its foreign policy on the continent of Europe. Like the Japanese, the French felt betrayed and could not believe it was happening, so they tried to persuade Poland to be more amenable. The French than realised that they would have to honour their pledge to Poland, immediately ordering mobilisation to man the Maginot Line and to create the means for Britain and France to act in concert during the coming war.

Italy also felt betrayed. Foreign ministers Ciano and Ribbentrop had met in the middle of August, with Ciano's mission to prevent the outbreak of war. Ribbentrop's task was to tell him that war was necessary and inevitable. This was a change of policy as Hitler had always maintained that Germany would not be ready for war until 1943 or 1944, which suited Italy's timetable as its economy was weak and it was still recovering from its efforts in the Spanish Civil War.

Both Ciano and Ribbentrop knew the British, although Ciano's understanding was greater and he knew there would be a general European war if Poland was invaded. Ribbentrop discounted this and believed that Anglo–French hostility would stop short of a general war. If they did attack in the west, Ribbentrop believed they could be held and, once Poland had capitulated, they could be beaten. This view of the coming war helped Italy, which could remain neutral until such time as it wished to push for domination of the Mediterranean; however, Ciano felt that events were spinning out of control and that Italy was no longer a partner but a pawn in

Germany's power game. This feeling would lead to a series of unilateral actions by Italy in the next two years, which would not help the Axis.

The German–Soviet Pact caused insecurity in all the Balkan nations, even Turkey. Romania was one of the key Balkan nations because of its oilfields. The Soviet Union wanted Bessarabia, although it had a large German population. Germany wanted oil. Romania, after its experiences in the Great War, wanted to be left alone. The sympathies of Romania's ruling class were with France and Britain and they tried to remain neutral but were in a weak position.

Hitler's euphoria lasted only a few days. He felt he was in an unassailable position, his timetable was working perfectly and he would attack in the early hours of 26 August. He was slightly put out by Britain's indifference to his diplomatic coup but Italy's reaction hit him harder. Mussolini was under pressure from many in his cabinet, especially Ciano, to have nothing to do with a full-blown war. In essence, Italy pledged to support Germany in a localised conflict, otherwise it would remain neutral. Because of Italy's military and economic weakness, any future action would depend on German aid. The Italians were fearful that Anglo–French action would fall on Italy as much as Germany, a product of resourceful British diplomacy.

Receiving this information in the late afternoon of 25 August, Hitler was stopped in his tracks. After discussion with Ribbentrop, the orders went out at 7.30 p.m. to abort the next morning's attacks. Couriers raced around the borders of Poland rescinding orders but, inevitably, some incidents took place.

War

For another week, diplomacy was vital but attitudes were hardening. Hitler wanted war but he was also fearful of war. France and Britain had had enough of Hitler's confrontational diplomacy, while there were some who treated the dangerous German–Soviet Pact as a bit of hilarious opportunism that would not last. They were to be proved right but not before a lot of damage had been done. Britain and France felt that a stand had to be made. There would be no more conciliation, as the diplomacy of all take and no give, with the lack of mutual goodwill that is diplomacy's essential ingredient, had made life impossible. Hitler did not understand this. He was used to his implacable will being used to humble his opponents.

Amid all this diplomacy, there was one man of importance on the German side who fought for peace. Göring was an opportunist, a bully and a sybarite, but he loved life and he lived it to the full. He mediated with Britain via a Swedish industrialist, Birger Dahlerus, and the British treated this as a weak lifeline. However, Hitler rejected it as his nerve had been restored. On 1 September the Germans staged a mock battle on the frontier, with the German provocateurs dressed as Poles killing men wearing German uniforms, who had been sent to the frontier from concentration camps. It was an incident that triggered the Wehrmacht's move across the frontier.

It took two days for Britain, followed by France, to declare war on 3 September 1939. This really would be war but there was not much they could do to help Poland. Britain did not have its army on the Continent, so only France could act, and its mentality was defensive. But the die had been cast and, whatever happened in Poland, there would be war in the West. As such, it was to the Europeans the true start of the Second World War, although it could be said that Japan had already started it in 1937 in China and continued it in 1939 with the Soviet Union.

To Germany and the Soviet Union, however, this was not the beginning of the Second World War. They were trying to impose a solution on the nation of Poland. The Soviet Union, after neutralising Japan, wanted to regain influence over Finland by conquest, while Germany wanted a safe major port leading to the Atlantic, which only Norway could provide. These were just skirmishes in restarting the European war. The Second World War is a misnomer. The global war was yet to start.

Acknowledgments

Roger Chapman - For advice and encouragement.

Henrietta Browne - For help with IT

Louisa Keyworth of Lovell Johns - For production of maps.

Stephen Games of Envelope Books - For suggesting paperbacks.

Ivan Butler - For editing the books.

Samantha Martin and Amy Missin - For printing the books.

1. Joyce. J. 1922. *Ulysses.*
2. Axson, S. (1932). *Goethe Centenary Lectures. (Chapter V, 'Goethe and Shakespeare', quoting from Goethe's essay 'Literary Criticism' (1771)).*
3. Gandhi, M. (1948). *An Autobiography or The Story of My Experiments with Truth.*
4. Watson, A. (2019). *The Fortress: The Great Siege of Przemysl.*
5. A. Roberts. (2019). *Churchill: Walking with Destiny.*
6. J. Röhl. (2014). *Wilhelm II: Into the Abyss of War and Exile, 1900–1941.*
7. J. K. Galbraith. (2009). *The Great Crash of 1929.*
8. Somerville, D. (1992). *Monty: a Biography of Field Marshal Montgomery.*
9. Overy, R. (1984). *Goering: The Iron Man.*
10. Steyn, R. (2018). *Jan Smuts: Unafraid of Greatness.*
11. Asprey, R. (1965). *At Belleau Wood.*
12. Manchester, W. (1978). *American Caesar.*
13. Churchill, W. (1923). *The World Crisis. Vol.1.*
14. Sheffield, G. & Bourne, J. (2005). *The Haig Diaries 1914–1918.*
15. Keynes, J. (1919). *The World Crisis. Vol.1.*
16. Boadle, D. (1973). *Winston Churchill and the German Question in British Foreign Policy 1918–1922.*
17. Pasternak, B. 1957. *Doctor Zhivago.*
18. *Ibid.*
19. Churchill, W. (1923). *The World Crisis. Vol.1.*
20. Jünger, E. (1929). *Storm of Steel.*
21. Whitman, W. (1855). *Leaves of Grass.*
22. Churchill, W. (1923). *The World Crisis. Vol.1.*
23. Carnegie, D. (1936). *How to Win Friends and Influence People.*
24. Joyce, J. 1922. *Ulysses.*
25. *Ibid.*
26. *Ibid.*
27. Shiver, W. (1960). *The Rise and Fall of the Third Reich.*

Abdul Hamid, Sultan 34
Abyssinia 185, 234, 235, 268, 280
Adriatic Sea 137, 179, 185, 294
   coast 68
   Dalmatian coast 185
AEG 222
Aegean 72, 76, 191
armistice arranged to bury dead 76
Afghanistan 79
Africa 32, 113, 180, 185
Africa, North 79
Afrikaans 28
Afrikaners 27
aircraft 106, 131, 139, 140, 146, 207, 276, 277, 278, 279, 290, 300, 306
   Albatros D.III 107, 138
   Avro Lancaster 12
   Boeing B-39 Superfortress 12
   Douglas DC-3 Dakota 9
   Fokker/s 106, 107
   French technological breakthrough .. 106
   Gotha G.IV 134
      damage done to London 134
   Handley-Page V/1500 135
   Royal Aircraft Factory B.E.2c 107
   Royal Aircraft Factory S.E.5 138
   Sopwith Camel 138
   Sopwith Triplane 138
   SPAD planes 138
   statistics 17
   The air war develops (1917) 138
   Zeppelin balloons 107, 134
Albania 163, 189, 234, 265
Alexander II, Tsar 45
Alexandrovich, Michael 120
Alfonso, King 166
Allenby, Edmund 125, 194
Allies/Allied 7, 72, 74, 78, 80, 82, 83, 84, 87, 96, 105, 106, 111, 112, 113, 115, 120, 121, 123, 125, 129, 131, 136, 137, 140, 150, 153, 157, 160, 161, 163, 167, 168, 169, 170, 172, 175, 181, 184, 185, 187, 198, 203, 208, 214, 239, 271
   air supremacy 7
   Bretton Woods 10, 13
   create artificial port 8

   front 154
   General Reserve 176
   Supreme War Council 137, 138, 153, 175, 176
American/s 122, 129, 136, 150, 153, 155, 160, 167, 169, 172, 255, 261, 262, 292, 297, 305
   Civil War (1861–1865) 21, 24, 93
      Confederacy 24, 93
      Federal Army 24
   Distinguished Service Cross 163
   Distinguished Service Order 132
   idealism 25
   Medal of Honour 163
   Republican/s 230, 253, 255
Amman, Max 243
amphibious warfare 75, 81, 82
Amur River Incident 300
Anglo–German Naval Agreement 284
Anglo–Japanese Alliance 261
   1902 35
   1905 37
anti-aircraft guns 134
Anti-Comintern Pact 311, 314
anti-Semitism 57, 222, 243, 263
ANZAC (Australian and New Zealand Army Corps) 14, 76
Arabia 192
Arabs 164, 194, 297
Armenia 33, 191
Armenian/s 39, 79
   death toll (1915) 80
   Massacres, The 33, 39
      death toll 34
   persecution of (19th century) 34
   population figures 33
   Second Armenian Massacre 79
   treatment by Ottoman government 34
artillery 64, 68, 88, 92, 102, 104, 105, 106, 125, 126, 131, 133, 137, 138, 139, 145, 153, 154, 157, 158, 161, 162, 170, 171, 172, 174, 237, 240, 258, 270, 277, 300, 302
artillery, breech-loading 25
Aryan/s 240, 242, 269, 279, 299
Asaka, Prince 292

Asia Minor 189, 190, 191
  Smyrna 189, 190, 191
Asian Monroe Doctrine 286
Asquith, Herbert Henry 71, 74, 77, 115, 125
Atatürk, Kemal 188, 190, 191
Atlantic 72, 77, 95, 113, 161, 167, 317
Atlantic Charter 13
atomic bomb 13
  development of 9
Australia 14, 180, 186
Australian/s 131, 133, 140, 158, 193
Austria. 47, 56, 110, 136, 141, 164, 183, 184, 195, 212, 234, 267, 279, 280, 281
  Galicia 54, 55, 56, 60, 68
  Peace Conference, The 184
  Tyrol 185
  Vienna 8, 25, 57, 136, 184, 242, 280
Austrian/s 101, 114, 166, 182, 183, 268, 281
  number of military personnel defending border (1915) 70
Austro-Hungarian Empire 24, 39, 56, 68, 114, 119, 166, 175, 178, 179, 183, 219, 220, 221, 242, 268, 269, 283, 294, 306, 314
  disintegration 4, 169
  population growth (1890-1914) 31
Austro-Hungarian/s ... 4, 54, 60, 84, 87, 109, 111, 112, 114, 119, 137, 166, 170, 174, 181, 215, 272
  A-Staffel 54
  B-Staffel 54
  casualties in Galicia 61
  put out peace feelers (1915) 114
  retreat from Przemysl 64
Austro-Hungary 74, 229
Avanti 135
Axis 5, 316
Azerbaijan 79
  Baku 211
Baldwin, Stanley 224, 235
Balfour, Arthur 167, 168, 187, 193, 201
Balkans 6, 26, 33, 39, 47, 54, 61, 78, 164, 166, 173, 175, 229, 316
  Dobrudja 163
Ball, Captain Albert 139
Baltic 38, 93, 182, 201, 209, 212, 310
Bank of England 116, 225
Bank of the United States 254
Basques 277

Battle of Adowa 234
Battle of Britain 6
  inaccurate statistics 18
Battle of Broodseinde 131
Battle of Cambrai 138, 172, 228, 239
Battle of Cambrai, First 142
Battle of Caporetto 137, 141
  casualties & prisoners 137
  prisoners 141
Battle of Coronel 72
Battle of Crete
  perils of taking statistics too seriously 17
Battle of Dogger Bank 94, 99
  death toll 94
Battle of Jutland 96, 99, 227
  death toll 99
Battle of Kursk 7
Battle of Magenta 24
Battle of Neuve Chapelle 77, 83
Battle of Nomonhan 5, 303, 304, 306
Battle of Passchendaele 17, 131, 133, 142, 150, 228, 239, 271, 272
Battle of Poelcappelle 131
Battle of Polygon Wood 131
Battle of Port Arthur 36
Battle of Sarikamish
  Turkish casualties 79
Battle of Solferino 24
Battle of Tannenberg 57, 58, 60, 106, 230
Battle of the Bulge 9
Battle of the Falkland Islands 72
Battle of the Marne 58, 59, 227
Battle of the Marne, Second 156
Battle of the Masurian Lakes 60
  German casualties 60
Battle of the Menin Road Ridge 131
Battle of the Somme 4, 88, 102, 103, 107, 108, 111, 171, 227, 270, 272
  casualties 105
Battle of Tsushima 37
Battle of Verdun 4, 83, 84, 91, 102, 106, 108, 111, 139, 145, 171, 172, 173, 227
  victor 88
Battle of Ypres 63, 83, 132, 138, 139, 160, 172
  Belgian casualties 63
  British casualties 63
  French casulaties 63
  trench system established 63

Battle of Ypres, Third..... 129, 131, 133, 137, 150, 171, 271, 272, *See* Battle of Passchendaele
    casualties...132
Bavarian/s..155
Bay of Biscay..168
bayonet/s................................. 105, 162, 291
Beatty, David.......................................94, 98
Bedny, Demyan...217
Beevor, Anthony..17
Behr, Sofia...44
Belarus...182
Belgian/s...72
Belgium . 48, 74, 87, 110, 112, 113, 115, 117, 179, 180, 268, 313
    Antwerp......................9, 58, 72, 93, 113, 227
        Germans take..................................63
    Ardennes...91
    Brussels...63
    Dinant...91
    Gheluvelt...129
    Gheluvelt Plateau.................................131
    Langemarck
        German mass grave........................63
    Liège..51, 113
    Messines........................... 129, 131, 139
    Namur...51
    Roulers..129
    Ypres 103, 124, 129, 132, 142
Benes, Edvard................................ 281, 282
Bengal
    Japanese retreat..9
Bernstorff, Johann von 121, 122, 123
Bessarabia...316
Bethmann-Hollweg, Chancellor 84, 94, 109, 111, 112, 114, 115
Bible 42
    Luther translates to demotic German. 29
    Sermon on the Mount 42, 45
Bishop, Billy..139
Bismarck, Otto von 34, 40
Black Sea . 23, 26, 63, 75, 109, 110, 114, 202, 209
blitzkrieg 277, 309
blockade 92, 93, 94, 95, 98, 100, 128, 140, 169, 172, 196, 227, 272, 277, 313
Blomberg, Werner von 247, 280
Blum, Leon...276
Blyukher, Vasily..301

Boelcke, Oswald 107
Boer War (1899–1902).... 21, 27, 35, 43, 149
    Cape Province 27
    Natal..27
    Orange Free State 27
    peace...27
    Transvaal...27
Bohemia.................... 164, 183, 307, 308
Bohr, Niels 222, 297
Bolshevik/s 128, 144, 145, 179, 182, 189, 191, 201, 203, 205, 209, 210, 213, 241, 250, 257, 263, 267
    Curzon Line.................................182, 210
    secret police 205, 206, 209
    head of Petrograd Cheka assasinated
       206
    tsar murdered 206
Bolsheviks, Ekaterinburg.......................206
Bolshevism 193, 201, 230
Bonapartism 249
Bonepart, Napoleon.................................93
Bonnet, Georges.............................282, 311
Borotbists..214
Bosnia and Herzegovina 39
    Sarajevo...47, 110
Botha, Luis 28, 149
Boyle, Edward...77
Braun, Eva..245
Brazil...121
Briand, Aristide.......................................223
Britain.... 31, 32, 47, 61, 75, 87, 92, 108, 110, 113, 115, 121, 124, 136, 137, 149, 158, 164, 168, 170, 173, 180, 184, 188, 192, 195, 200, 214, 222, 223, 227, 231, 234, 235, 243, 252, 261, 263, 265, 268, 269, 270, 273, 278, 281, 282, 296, 297, 299, 303, 305, 306, 307, 310, 311, 314, 316, 317
England...................... 77, 134, 168, 297
    Cambridge.......................................116
        King's College........................116
        University 28
    Eton...116
    Folkestone..134
    Hartlepool... 93
    London 74, 76, 82, 92, 116, 144, 150, 197, 262, 268, 276, 306
        bombing of (1915)..................107
        underground stations 134

Manchester, University of 193
Scarborough 93
English Channel 98, 106, 113, 167
funds other nations war efforts (1916)
.... 117
Orkney Islands 168
Scapa Flow 196, 267
return to gold standard 225
Scotland
Firth of Forth 168
Glasgow 225
British.. 27, 73, 76, 77, 78, 79, 80, 84, 95, 97, 99, 103, 105, 106, 109, 112, 119, 129, 138, 140, 142, 149, 153, 156, 160, 163, 166, 167, 168, 169, 170, 171, 172, 196, 204, 229, 235, 261, 262, 267, 271, 272, 277, 280, 283, 285, 297, 305, 310, 312, 315
Air Board 74
codes
Germans penetrate 7
Conservative Party ... 73, 74, 77, 224, 272
economy (1920s) 223
Empire .. 10, 13, 14, 28, 42, 43, 149, 178, 188, 229, 305
Expeditionary Force 59, 63
Labour Party 272, 310
Ministry of Munitions 270
trawlers attacked by Russian fleet 36
Treasury 196
Victoria Cross 139
War Office 82, 270
British Air Force .... See Royal Flying Corps
British Army 135
29th Division 157
33rd Division 133
3rd Army 125
47th (London) Division 133
5th Army 129, 139, 153, 175
casualties at Le Cateau 52
great general retreat, WWI 52
Royal Scots Fusiliers 74
15th Division 74
9th Division 74
Warwickshires 132
Brockdorff-Rantzau, Ulrich von 195, 196
Brodrick, Joseph 254
Brooke, Alan 8
Brooke-Popham, Brigadier 139

brownshirt .... See SA
Bruning, Gustav 244
Bruning, Heinrich 232, 233, 234, 245
Brusilov Offensive 4, 89, 101, 102, 105, 108, 111, 114, 119, 227
Brusilov, Aleksey 101, 121, 209, 214, 215, 228
Budenny, Semyon 212
First Cavalry Army 212
Bukharin, Nikolai 248, 249, 250
Bukovina 102
Bulgaria 40, 64, 74, 163
armistice signed (1918) 163
Pleven 26
Russian & Turkish occupation 26
Shipka Pass 26
surrender 175
Vidin 26
Bulgarian/s 109
Christians, ethnic cleansing of 26
Bullitt, William 196
Bulow, Karl von 59
Burma 8, 9, 14
Japanese domination 8
Mandalay 9
Rangoon 9
Burmese National Army 9
Byelorussians 182
Byng, Julian 81, 142
Cadorna, Luigi 137
Caillaux, Joseph 138, 175
camouflage 170
Canada 14, 187
Canadian Corps 126, 142
Canadian/s 117, 133, 158
capitalism 225, 269, 275
Carlists 277, 278
Carnegie, Dale 274
How to Win Friends and Influence People 273, 275
Public Speaking and Influencing Men in Business 274
Carolina Islands 186
Carpathian/s 64, 102
Carpatho-Ukraine 307
Carranza, President Venustiano 122
Castel Gandolfo 232
Catherine the Great 30

Catholic 33, 181, 183, 231
  Bavaria 30
  Poles 56
Caucasian Army 207
Caucasus ... 6, 70, 79, 110, 114, 164, 189, 272
Central Powers 68, 79, 84, 96, 109, 110, 112, 120, 136, 137, 145, 147, 163, 167, 170, 189
  collapse 166
Chamberlain, Neville 278, 279, 280, 282, 283, 308, 310, 315
Chanak 75
Chang Hsueh-Liang 287
Charles, Emperor 166
Chatfield, Lord Ernle 305
Cheka ...... 205, *See* Bolshevik/s: secret police
Chertkov, Vladimir 45
Chiang Kai-Shek 256, 257, 258, 286, 289, 290, 292, 293
  Kuomintang, and the 256
  Triumph of 286
Chichibu, Prince 289, 292
Chile 128
China . 13, 15, 22, 33, 85, 113, 186, 187, 188, 256, 257, 259, 262, 266, 285, 286, 287, 289, 290, 291, 292, 293, 299, 300, 301, 304, 305, 306, 317
  Boxer Rebellion (1899-1901) 34
  Canton 256, 293
  Changkufeng 293, 300, 301, 302
    death toll of Japanese & Russians 301
  Changsha 290
  Changzhou 260
  Christian insurgency 21
  Christianity, entrance of 22
  Chungking 290, 293
  Great Wall 259
  Hankow 290, 293
  Jehol 260, 261, 286
  Kiangsi 257
  Liaotung Peninsula 33, 37
  Lugouqiao 289
  Manchuria 235
  Marco Polo Bridge 289
  Ming Dynasty 259
  Mukden 37, 260
  Nanjing .... *See* China:Nanking
  Nanking 290, 291, 292, 304
    Hong Xiuquan captures 22
  Peace Conference, The 187
  Peking 33, 35, 188, 286, 289
  Port Arthur 33
  Qing Dynasty 23
    fall of 38
    officers drastic response to the Manchus 22
  Rape of Nanking, The 291
    Safety Zone 292
  Shanghai 257, 290, 291, 292
    national peace conference 188
  Shantung peninsula 186, 187, 197
  Shensi 286
  The Long March 286
  Tientsin 286, 305, 306
  Tientsin Incident, The 305
  treaty with Japan (19th century) 33
  Tsingtao 186
  Wanping 289
  war with Japan 5
  Wuhu 290
  Yangtze 22, 290, 292
    chaos of civil war 22
China Incident, The (1937) 286, 289
Chinese ... 197, 256, 258, 259, 260, 261, 286, 289, 290, 293, 305
Civil War (1851–1864) 22
  British, French & Americans want trade 22
  death toll 23
chlorine gas .... 84, *See also* gas
Christ, Jesus 15
  Divinity of Christ 46
Christian/s 15, 33, 192, 194
  Alexandria massacre 26
Christianity 15, 23, 263
Church 16
  Sermon of the Mount 16
Churchill, Sir Winston 4, 5, 8, 11, 13, 70, 71, 72, 74, 77, 82, 112, 117, 129, 133, 147, 149, 167, 170, 171, 172, 193, 194, 201, 202, 224, 228, 235, 250, 253, 263, 269, 271, 278, 310
  as minister of air 140
  as minister of munitions 136
  demoted 73
  determines prime objective with Roosevelt 6
  Roosevelt meeting in Quebec 10

The World Crisis 226, 227, 230, 271
Ciano, Galeazzo 280, 315
Clausewitz, Carl von 89
Clemenceau, Georges 138, 153, 168, 174, 175, 176, 179, 181, 184, 185, 189, 190, 191, 194, 195, 197, 202
coal 31, 113, 181, 207, 285
Colard, Hermann von 57
Comintern 248
Commission of Inquiry 194
communism ... 5, 14, 179, 184, 206, 207, 210, 309, 315
Confucianism 22, 23
Confucius 22
Conrad von Hötzendorf, Franz 87
Constantine, King 163
Control Faction .... *See* Toseiha
Coolidge, Calvin 253
Cossack/s 207, 209, 211, 213
 cavalry 55
cotton 24, 93
Council of Four 180, 185, 189
Council of Ten 180, 186
Cox, James 252
Crimean War (1853–1856) 21, 23, 26
 Sebastopol 23
Croat/s 166, 185
Croix de Guerre 91
Crusades, the 192
Cuba 252
Cunard Line 95
Cunliffe, Lord 116
Cunningham, Andrew 306
Curzon, Lord George 190, 265
Czech/s 57, 65, 183, 204, 209, 281, 282, 284, 307, 308
 Legion 183, 206
Czechoslovakia 182, 183, 184, 224, 281, 282, 306, 309
 comes into being 166
 Peace Conference, The 183
 Prague 221, 281, 307
 Prague, University of 220
 Sudetenland 279, 281, 283, 306
D'Annunzio, Gabriele 185
d'Espèrey, Franchet 164, 175
d'Espèrey, Louis 52
Dahlerus, Birger 317
Daladier, Édouard 282, 283, 310

| 325

Daniels, Josephus 167
Dardanelles 34, 64, 70, 72, 73, 75, 76, 77, 81, 95, 110, 164, 170, 201, 227, 228
 Hellespont 82
Dardanelles Commission Report 74
Darwin, Charles 220
de Gaulle, Charles 11, 14, 91
 Croix de Guerre 91
de Robeck, John 73, 77, 81
Declaration of London 92
Dedalus, Stephen 295
democratic rights of individuals
 principle of 24
Denikin, Anton 203, 207, 212, 214
Denmark
 Copenhagen 297
Deutsche Luftstreitkräfte
 Albatros D.III 107, 138
 Fokker/s 106, 107
 Gotha G.IV 134
  damage done to London 134
 Jasta 4 140
 Zeppelin balloons 107, 134
Diaz, Armando 137
Dickens, Charles 46
disease 79
dogfights 106
Don Army 207
Dönitz, Karl 7
Douglas, Sholto 107
Doumenc, Joseph 310
Dreyse rifle 25
Duchy of Teschen 182
Dumas, Alexandre Senior 296
Dutch 28
 language 30
Dutch East Indies
 Japanese attack on 6
East Africa 14, 149
 Kenya–Tanganyika border 149
 loss of by Italians 6
 Tanganyika 149
East Africa, British 149
 Jubaland 136, 265
East Africa, German 113
East Prussia ... 11, 14, 47, 55, 56, 58, 64, 110, 114, 181, 311
 exodus caused by Russian conquest ... 56
 Königsberg 58

Eberhard von Mackensen, Frederick......109
Eckhardt, Heinrich von............................122
Eden, Anthony..10
Eglinton, John..295
Egypt.................. 6, 14, 26, 75, 192, 193, 305
 Alexandria....................................26, 235
 Cairo...147
 French & English financial support....26
 September 1882, battle of.....................27
Egyptian/s..193
 army revolt..26
Einstein, Albert................30, 220, 221, 222
 theory of relativity.............................220
Eisenhower, President Dwight D.....11, 275
El Alamein..6
Empty Quarter.......................................192
Entente Cordiale (1904)..........................40
Erich Maria Remarque
 All Quiet on the Western Front..............238
Erle-Erle-Drax, Admiral............... 310, 311
Estonia.. 208, 313
Evans Hughes, Charles..........................274
Evert, Alexei...101
extremism..233
Facta, Luigi..264
Falangists..................................... 277, 278
Falkenhayn, Erich von63, 64, 68, 83, 85, 87,
 102, 109, 112, 147
famine...154
fanaticism...................................... 188, 304
fascism..5, 309
Feisal, Hussein
 proclaimation......................................194
Ferdinand, Franz..............................47, 110
Finland............. 38, 201, 208, 226, 313, 317
Finns/Finnish..208
First World War (1914–1918)..4, 15, 21, 26,
 108, 149, 150
 Balkan Front.......................................163
 Belgian defences...................................51
 catalyst for war.....................................47
 commences..49
 Eastern Front...............64, 79, 170, 171
 economics of...4
 flu pandemic....................................4, 18
 geographics of..4
 Italian front111, 141, 166, 170, 172, 176,
 229
 ceasefire..167

Kosturino Pass.......................................163
Laon–Soissons line...............................157
Macedonian front.................................176
Meuse–Argonne area............................162
number of military personnel
 (Germany)..49
number of military personnel (Russia) 49
peace... 169, 173
Peace Conference, The............... 178, 180
rejection of peace..................................119
seeking peace (1916)................................4
stalemate (1916).......................................4
Western Front60, 68, 70, 74, 83, 88, 105,
 106, 108, 120, 121, 131, 138, 163,
 166, 170, 171, 175, 176, 183, 197,
 202, 229, 238, 239, 271
 British line/s................. 150, 154, 174
 Hindenburg Line..............................169
 Saint Quentin–Cambrai line.........169
Fisher, John.......................... 72, 75, 81, 167
 resignation..77
Fiume...185, 187
Flanders........................... 154, 157, 160, 172
Flanders fever............. *See* Spanish:influenza
Flandin, Pierre-Étienne.................235, 268
Flemish
 language..30
Flying Corps............. *See* Royal Flying Corps
Foch, Ferdinand....59, 63, 89, 138, 153, 157,
 160, 172, 174, 176, 195, 196, 197
Formosa..8, 9, 33
Forster, Gauleiter....................................312
France . 48, 61, 71, 72, 75, 77, 81, 82, 83, 87,
 102, 108, 110, 113, 115, 117, 119, 121,
 136, 137, 156, 158, 170, 173, 175, 179,
 180, 184, 187, 188, 189, 192, 194, 198,
 219, 222, 223, 229, 234, 235, 243, 262,
 267, 268, 269, 275, 276, 282, 283, 293,
 299, 303, 310, 311, 314, 315, 316, 317
 alliance with Russia (1892)..................40
Alsace........................... 115, 179, 266, 269
Alsace-Lorraine....................................112
Amiens......................... 52, 133, 153, 154
Ardennes..9, 51
Arras...153
Bar-le-Duc......................................87, 89
Bordeaux..136
Calais...8, 72, 125
Champagne......................................83, 91

Château-Thierry 155, 168
Chemin des Dames ... 125, 126, 154, 172, 175
Côte de Châtillon 162
Dunkirk 72
Fromelles 156
Hazebrouck
   British casualties 154
La Voie Sacrée 87
Le Cateau 52
Lille 133
Lorraine 51, 115, 179, 266, 269
Lys sector 154
Marne 59, 141, 154, 157, 160
Metz 9, 161
Meurthe 51
Meuse 59, 88
Mézières 169
Mons 132
Moselle 59
Neuve Chapelle 132
Normandy 8
   Allies land in 8
Oise 175
Paris 49, 58, 106, 112, 116, 134, 151, 154, 178, 190, 202, 297
   German retreat from, WWI 59
Picardy 83
Pyrenees 277, 278
Rheims 155, 157
Saint Nazaire 60
Saint Quentin 153
Saint-Mihiel 160, 162
Soissons 154
Somme 74, 83, 89, 119, 124, 132, 153, 156, 158, 160
St Gond 59
Vaux 88
Verdun 51, 74, 85, 160, 161, 168
   Fort Douaumont 87
   Fort Vaux 87
Versailles 153, 182, 197, 222
Vesle 154
Vimy 156
Vimy Ridge 126
Franco, Francisco 276, 277, 278, 314
François, Hermann 57
François-Poncet, André 267
Franco–Prussian War 21, 26, 49, 179, 202

Franco–Soviet Pact 267
French 73, 76, 80, 84, 92, 102, 105, 106, 112, 126, 129, 136, 138, 150, 160, 163, 166, 167, 171, 172, 173, 193, 229, 267, 269, 272, 281, 305, 308, 312, 315
   economy (1920s) 223
   franc 14
French Army
   10th Army 63
   1st Army 51
   2nd Army 51, 89
   33rd Infantry Regiment of Arras 91
   3rd Army 51
   4th Army 51, 52, 161
   5th Army 52, 59
      Guise 52
   6th Army 59
   Centre Army Group 89
French Navy
   Bouvet
      sinking of 75
French, John 63
Freyberg, Bernard 17
Freyberg, Paul 17
Frisch, Otto 297
Fritsch, Werner von 280
Frunze, Mikhail 249
Galicia 181, 182
Gallipoli 73, 74, 76, 80, 82, 193
   Anzac Cove 76, 80, 81, 82
   Cape Helles 76, 78, 80, 82
   death toll 78
   Sari Bair 81
   Suvla Bay 80, 81, 82
   triumph for Turkey 78
Gamelin, Maurice 268
Gandhi, Mahatma 42, 166
   & Smuts, Jan Christian 44
   & Tolstoy, Leo 46
   ahimsa 43
   brahmacharya 43
   on religion 43
   satyagraha 43
   upbringing 42
Garibaldi, Giuseppe 135
Garner, John 255
Garros, Roland 106
gas 77, 84, 125, 139, 144, 153, 154, 156, 162, 237

first gas attack 221
first gas attack of WWI 65
gas masks 125, 162
Geneva Naval Conference 261
genocide 80
George V, King 72, 149, 166, 265
George VI, King 14
Georges-Picot, François 113
Georgia 38
German Army ...*See* Imperial German Army
German Empire 93, 119
German Navy .... *See* Imperial German Navy
German/s .61, 76, 77, 84, 91, 93, 95, 97, 99, 103, 105, 106, 108, 112, 122, 126, 129, 131, 132, 136, 137, 138, 142, 157, 160, 168, 171, 173, 176, 181, 186, 195, 202, 204, 211, 219, 228, 230, 241, 243, 244, 266, 267, 268, 269, 270, 272, 277, 279, 281, 282, 286, 297,298, 307, 308, 309, 311, 312, 317
    aerial reconnaissance 51
    Anschluss 184, 267
    black market 129
    coal production 31
    codes 94, 122
        Britain uses computers to break 7
    death toll due to hunger 169
    economy (1920s) 223
    Embassy 95
    High German language 29
    influence in Mexico 122
    Iron Cross 17, 141, 145, 155
    Lebensraum 242, 244
    Low German language 29, 30
    National Socialist party 244
    Occupation of the Rhineland 266
    pilotless aircraft 8
    press, WWI 56
    Reichswehr 246
    Schlieffen Plan 41, 47, 49, 58, 59, 63
        demise of 59
    Volk 242
Germans Air Force .... *See* Deutsche Luftstreitkräfte
German–Soviet Pact 303, 309, 311, 316
Germany ... 28, 32, 54, 64, 72, 74, 78, 83, 84, 92, 99, 110, 113, 114, 115, 116, 120, 121, 122, 123, 128, 136, 140, 144, 145, 146, 149, 150, 155, 158, 163, 166, 167, 169, 170, 175, 178, 181, 183, 186, 195, 198, 199, 200, 201, 210, 212, 215, 219, 221, 222, 223, 227, 229, 233, 234, 235, 240, 243, 246, 257, 263, 266, 267, 268, 278, 279, 280, 281, 283, 286, 296, 297, 303, 304, 305, 306, 307, 310, 311, 314, 315, 316
    as a great power 29
    attacks Soviet Union (22 June 1941) 5
    Berchtesgaden 283
    Berlin 6, 25, 121, 135, 149, 233, 308
    bombing of 7
    Congress of 34
    University of 221
    captures Lvov (1915) 70
    Danube 26
    Darmstadt 146
    Dresden 164, 183
    Elbe 11
    formation of a nation 31
    Great Inflation, The 198
    Hamburg
        bombing of 7
        invasion of 10
    Lippe-Detmold 247
    Munich 146, 155, 240, 242, 283, 299, 307
    population growth (1870-1914) 31
    problem of reparations 4
    Regensburg 30
    Reichstag 40, 244, 246, 247, 266
    relations with Russia deteriorate (1890s) 40
    reperations bill 197
    Rhine 93, 174, 195
        crossing of 10
    Rhineland 113, 224, 267, 268
    Ruhr
        bombing of 7
        large surrender 10
    Saar 113
Gibraltar 235
Gladstone, William E. 26
    speech deploring Turkish behaviour ... 34
God 15, 166, 252
Goebbels, Joseph 244
Goethe, Johann W. von 15, 29
    Faust 30
    The Sorrows of Young Werther 30
Goltz, Colmar von der 79

Göring, Hermann 145, 146, 247, 298, 316
Gorky, Maxim 217, 252
Gough, Hubert 129, 131, 153, 154
Grandi, Dino 280
Great Britain .... See Britain
Great Depression, The 5, 231
Great War See First World War (1914–1918)
Greece 6, 64, 74, 163, 189, 234
   Athens 163, 189
   Corfu 163, 265
   Crete 6, 39
      Heraklion 17
      Maleme 17
   Dodecanese 136, 189, 265
   Galatas 17
   Lemnos 164
   Loukinia cemetery 17
   Rethymno 17
   Rhodes 136, 189
   Salonika 109, 163
   Thessalonica 163
Greek/s . 39, 75, 82, 189, 190, 191, 193, 265
Guadalcanal 12
Guam 8
gunboat/s 78, 300
   protect trade routes 23
   use of on the Yangtze 22
Gurkha/s 10
Guynemer, Georges 139
Haber, Fritz 221, 297
Hácha, President Emil 307, 308
Haig, Douglas . 104, 106, 129, 131, 135, 137, 151, 153, 160, 170, 172, 173, 174, 175, 176, 228, 270, 272
Haiti 252
Halifax, Lord Edward 282, 306
Hall, Reginald 122
Hamilton, Ian 76, 77, 81, 82, 171
Hammersley, Frederick 81
Hapsburg, House of. 54, 55, 56, 57, 60, 182, 183, 307
Harding, President Warren 252
Hashemite 193
Hassell, Ulrich von 280
Hata, Shonroku 304
Hathaway, Ann 296
Heavenly Kingdom .... See Taiping Heavenly Kingdom
Heligoland Bight 71, 93

| 329

Hemingway, Ernest 137
   Farewell to Arms 137
Henry Cabot Lodge 274
Hersing, Otto 77
Hess, Rudolph 243
Heydrich, Reinhard 298
Hindenburg Line 125, 161
Hindenburg, President Paul von . 58, 84, 87, 102, 109, 112, 244, 245, 246, 247
Hinduism 42
   Vedas 43
Hipper, Admiral 93
Hirohito, Emperor Michinomiya ... 258, 288, 292, 301
Hitler, Adolf 5, 8, 9, 11, 17, 155, 222, 224, 226, 232, 233, 234, 235, 240, 241, 244, 245, 246, 247, 251, 266, 267, 268, 269, 276, 280, 281, 282, 283, 297, 299, 306, 307, 308, 309, 311, 312, 313, 314, 315, 316
   ambitions 279
   First World War 155
   Iron Cross 155
   Landsberg prison 241
   Mein Kampf 226, 241, 242, 243, 267
   plans to bomb Britain into submission .6
   Rise to Power 244
   The Rise of Hitler 240
Hoare, Samuel 235
Hoare–Laval Plan 235
Hoffmann, Max 58
Hohenzollern dynasty 113
Holy Land 192
Holy Roman Empire 29, 30
Holy See 232, 233
Homer
   Odyssey 294
Hong Kong 293
Hong Xiuquan 22
Honjo, Shigeru 260, 288
Hoover, President Herbert 195, 226, 254
Hötzendorf, Franz Conrad von ... 54, 60, 64, 68
House, Edward 274
Hsueh-Liang, Chang 259
Huerta, President Victoriano 122
Hughes, Billy 187
Hundred Days 174, 175, 272
Hungarian/s 183, 283, 307

Hungary 47, 57, 68, 102, 164, 183, 184, 185, 234, 263, 282, 307, 314
- Budapest 64, 184
- independence 167
- Peace Conference, The 184
- Ruthenia 307
- Hussein, Abdullah 194
- proclaimation 194
- Hussein, Emir 193, 194
- Hussein, Feisal 193, 194
- hyperinflation 223, 266
- Il Duce .... See Mussolini, Benito
- Il Popolo d'Italia 135, 136
- Immelmann, Max 107
- Imperial Conference of Dominion Prime Ministers 149
- Imperial German Army
  - 14th Army 141
  - 1st Army 59
  - 2nd Army 59
  - 3rd Army 59
  - 5th Army 88, 146
  - 6th Army 51, 63
  - 7th Army 51
  - 8th Army 60
  - 9th Army 59
  - Alpenkorps 137, 141
  - Bavarian mountain division 137
  - casualties at Ypres 63
  - Condor Legion 277
  - II Corps 58
  - III Corps 58
  - North Western army 208
  - stormtrooper/s 139, 153, 154, 160
- Imperial German Navy
  - attempt to break Bristish supply lines ...6
  - *Blucher*
    - sinking of 94
  - *Breslau* 61, 72
  - *Goeben* 61, 72
  - High Seas Fleet 93, 96, 98, 107
  - *Seydlitz* 94, 99
  - U-boat/s. 7, 77, 94, 95, 96, 113, 125, 168
    - *U-21* 77
- Imperial Japanese Army
  - 1st Tokyo Division 300
  - Imperial Guards 288
  - North China Garrison 289
- Imperial Japanese Navy 9

- British built ships 36
- imperialism 180, 287
- income tax 117
- India 8, 14, 31, 37, 79, 166, 179, 180, 190, 192, 297
  - Gujarat 42
  - Kohima and Imphal
    - Japanese supply lines 8
  - India, British 42
  - Indian Empire 79
  - Indian National Army 63
- Indian Ocean 14, 113
- Indian/s 27
- Indo-China 293
  - Haiphong 293
- Industrial Revolution 31
- industrialisation 170
- influenza . 155, 156, 164, 165, 166, 202, 228, 239, 272
  - pandemic death toll 165
- International Monetary Fund (IMF) 13
- internationalism 135
- Iraq
  - Baghdad 79, 192, 194
  - Basra 39, 79, 192, 194
  - Ctesiphon 79
  - Faisal 164
  - Germans make no headway in 6
  - Kut-al-Amara 79
  - Mosul 80, 113, 192, 194
  - Tigris 79
- Ireland 199
  - Dublin 294, 295
  - rebellion 119
  - Kinsale 95
- Irish 81, 119
  - Catholic 253
  - independence 178
- Islam 188
  - Mecca 192
  - Medina 192
- Ismail Enver Pasha 76
- Isogai, Rensuke 303
- isolationists 12
- Israel
  - Beersheba 147
  - Jaffa 147
  - Jerusalem 125, 147, 192
  - the capture of 146

| 331

precursor to 193
Itagaki, Seishiro 301
Italian Empire 5
Italian/s 84, 120, 131, 137, 170, 185, 190, 232, 234, 235, 272, 277, 279, 280, 295, 316
   Fascist party 265
      formation 263
   National Executive of the Italian Socialist 135
   number of military personnel on Austrian border (1915) 70
Italy ... 30, 39, 54, 64, 68, 111, 112, 117, 136, 137, 168, 173, 175, 180, 184, 189, 190, 200, 215, 223, 229, 234, 235, 243, 263, 265, 272, 277, 278, 305, 309, 312, 315
   Bologna 263
   Emilia 263
   enters war (1915) 70, 111
   Ferrara 263
   Fiume 136, 265
   Forli 264
   Genoa 219
   Isonzo 137
   Longarone 141
   Milan 136, 263, 264
   Naples 264
   Peace Conference, The 185
   Piave 137
   Rapallo 219
   Ravenna 264
   Romagna 135, 264
   Rome 168, 233, 264
      the fall of 8
   San Remo 191
   Tagliamento 137
   Trentino 136
   Trieste 68, 136, 294
   Udine 136
Japan ... 21, 33, 113, 122, 123, 180, 185, 186, 187, 200, 222, 231, 235, 257, 258, 259, 261, 262, 266, 285, 286, 288, 289, 291, 292, 293, 300, 301, 302, 303, 305, 306, 309, 310, 311, 314, 317
   and the Soviet Union 299
   Iwo Jima 12
      casualties at 12
   Okinawa 12, 14
   Peace Conference, The 186

   racial equality clause 187
   rise of 34
   strikes Russian fleet at Seoul & Port Arthur (1904) 35
   Tokyo 260, 288, 300, 302, 303, 305
      Shidehara Policy 260
   Tokyo Bay 288
Japanese ... 187, 204, 256, 259, 260, 261, 285, 286, 289, 290, 291, 292, 293, 299, 300, 301, 302, 303, 304, 305, 314, 315
   Empire 14
   fanaticism 9
   Home Affairs Ministry 288
   imperial ambitions 35
   Kodoha (The Imperial Way) 287
   kokutai 12
   revolution (1936) 287, 289
   Russian ultimatum 35
   treaty with China (19th century) 33
   War Ministry 288
   war with China 5
Japanese Empire 260
Japan-Russia conflict
   death toll 37
   naval battle (1905) 37
Japan–US Treaty of Commerce and Navigation 306
Jaumann, Gustav 220
Jellicoe, John 99, 100
Jennings Bryan, William 274
Jew/s ... 10, 56, 182, 192, 193, 202, 209, 213, 222, 242, 244, 263, 269, 295, 298, 307
   Cost of Broken Glass, the 297
   Laws Against the 296
   Pale of Settlement 213
   persecution in Galicia, WWI 57
   pogroms death toll in Ukraine 213
Jewish 181, 213, 242, 243, 251, 263, 297
Jodl, Alfred 268
Joffre, Joseph 52, 58, 63, 83, 87, 89, 121, 124, 174
Jordan 192
Joseph, Emperor Franz 220
Joyce, James 294, 295, 296
   Finnegans Wake 295
   Ulysses 294, 295
Jünger, Ernst 238, 240
   Storm of Steel 237, 238
Kaas, Ludwig 233

Kamenev, Lev 206, 248, 249, 263
Kanin, Prince 301
Kemal, Mustafa 76, 78, 81
Kenya 185
   Lake Victoria 149
   Mombasa 149
   Nairobi 149
Kerensky, Alexander 121, 128, 206
Keyes, Roger 81
Keynes, John Maynard 10, 116, 117, 196, 198, 199, 225, 226
   A Treatise on Money 226
   The Applied Theory of Money 226
   The Economic Consequences 198
   The General Theory of Employment, Interest & Money 226
   The Pure Theory of Money 226
Khan, Genghis 251
Kiangsi Soviet 257, 286
Kippenberger, Howard K. 17
Kitchener, Lord Herbert 72, 76, 81
Kleiner, Alfred 220
Kluck, Alexander von 106
Knobelsdorf, Schmidt von 108
Kolchak, Alexander .203, 207, 208, 212, 216
   execution of 209
Konev, Ivan Stepanovich 12
Konoe, Prince 304
Koran 43
Korea 33, 36, 37, 161, 300
   Japan's army tested by Chinese army (1895) 33
   Rashin 300
Krosigk, Lutz von 247
Krupp 25
Krupp 420 ....51, 87
kulaks 211
Kun, Bela 263
Kuomintang 256, 257, 259, 287, 289, 290, 293, 306
Kurdish 192
Kurdistan 191
Kurds 80
   militia (1892) 34
   persecution of 34
Kuropatkin, Aleksey 101
Kut-al-Amara 110
   casualties 79

Kwantung Army 260, 300, 301, 302, 303, 304, 306
lachrymatory gas 84
landing barges 80
Lansdowne, Lord 115
Larrey, Manuel Hedilla 278
Lateran Treaty 232
Latvia 313
   Courland 112
Laval, Pierre 1. 234
Law, Bonar 82, 117
Lawrence of Arabia ..*See* Lawrence, Thomas Edward
Lawrence, Thomas Edward... 164, 180, 193, 194
League of Nations ..184, 186, 187, 188, 195, 199, 202, 219, 224, 230, 234, 235, 236, 252, 255, 262, 265, 266, 267, 268, 274, 285, 312
   formation of 5
Lebanese 194
Lebanon 194
   Beirut 192, 194
Lee-Enfield rifles 52
Legion of Honour 139
LeMay, Curtis 13
lend-lease 10
Lenin, Vladimir 128, 144, 145, 182, 205, 206, 208, 210, 211, 212, 213, 248, 249, 252
   13th Party Congress letter 249
   attempted assasination 206
   death 248
Leninism 248
Les Cicognes 139
Lettow-Vorbeck, Paul Emil von 149
Libya 6, 39
Lithuania 112, 313
   Memel 182
   Vilna (Vilnius) 181, 182
Lithuanian/s 55, 181
Little Russians of Ukraine, The 207
Lloyd George, David..17, 74, 115, 116, 117, 125, 126, 129, 136, 137, 138, 150, 153, 172, 173, 174, 175, 176, 180, 181, 182, 184, 189, 190, 191, 193, 194, 195, 196, 197, 201, 202, 219, 228, 269, 270, 271, 273, 310
   Memoirs of 269, 272, 273

welfare state 273
Locarno Treaty 267
Loerzer, Bruno 145
London Times 221
Lord Salisbury 34
Ludendorff, Erich 58, 60, 64, 84, 87, 102, 109, 112, 131, 153, 154, 156, 157, 160, 165, 229, 241
  Liège & Namur 51
  resignation (1918) 169
Ludwig of Bavaria, Crown Prince 30
Ludwig, King 155
Luftwaffe 6, 8, 146, 153, 276, 282
Lusitania
  death toll 95
  sinking of 95
Luther, Martin 29, 30
  abdication (1848) 30
Luxemburg, Rosa 263
Lvov, Prince Georgy 121, 203
Lytton Report, The 262
Lytton, Lord Edward 262
Lyushkov, Genrikh 300
MacArthur, Douglas 7, 8, 161, 162
Macdonald, Ramsay 223, 265
Macedonia 163
Macmillan, Harold 117
Mai-Maevsky, Vladimir 207
Majestic
  sinking of 78
Makarov, Nikolay Y. 36
Makhno, Nestor 207, 213
malaria 149
Malaya 8, 14, 306
  Japanese attack on 5
Malta 6, 194, 235
Malthus, Thomas R. 31
Manchukuo 261, 288
Manchuria 259, 261, 287, 299, 300, 303, 304
  Japan develops 285
  Taku Forts 23
Manchurian Incident, The 259, 260, 262, 302
Manchurian/Manchus.. 21, 22, 36, 256, 259, 260, 261
  South Manchurian Railway 302
Mandelstam, Osip 217
Mangin, Charles 89, 157
Manila 9

| 333

Mannock, Mike 140
Mariana Islands 12, 186
Marshall Islands 186
Marshall, George 163
Marx, Karl 135
Marxism 243, 257
Masaryk, Thomas 183
Matsui, Iwane 292
Matteotti, Giacomo 263, 265
Mauretania 95
McAdoo, William 274
McCrae John
  In Flanders Fields 176
McCudden, Jimmy 140
McKenna, Reginald 116
Mediterranean 40, 77, 78, 114, 189, 235, 277, 305, 306, 315
Mediterranean Sea 6
Mehmed V, Sultan 39
Mehmet VI, Sultan 188
Menshevik/s 128, 210
Mesopotamia 79, 113, 164, 189, 192, 194
Mexican/s 122
Mexico 122, 167
Middle East 32, 112, 113, 146, 153, 164, 175, 189, 192, 194
  modern warfare arrives 77
Midway Island 6
Mikoyan, Anastas 211
militarism 47
Minami, Jiro 260
minefields 73
minesweeper/s 75, 82, 124
Mitchell, Billy 162
Mitteleuropa 113, 115
Model, Walther 10
Mola, Emilio 276, 277, 278
Molotov, Vyacheslav 250, 313
Moltke, Helmuth von 58, 63, 85
Monash, John 131
Mongolia 33, 299, 301, 303
Mongolian/s 301
Monro, Charles 82
Montagu, Edwin 116
Montenegro 39
Montgomery, Bernard 8, 10, 11, 132, 133
Moravia 307
Morgenthau Jr., Henry 10
Moroccan 276

Muslim/s 15, 27, 33, 39, 190, 192, 194
  persecution of Bulgarian Christians 26
Mussolini, Benito 5, 135, 185, 232, 234, 235, 263, 264, 265, 268, 276, 279, 280, 281, 284, 316
  discharged 136
Namibia.............................. 145
Nanking Massacre........... *See* China:Rape of Nanking
Napoleon Bonaparte 21, 30
Napoleon III, Emperor.................... 25
Napoleonic army
  attacked by the Prussians (1870).......... 25
Narrows 72, 73, 77, 82
  great attack on (1915) 75
Nasmith, Eric 77
Natal Indian Congress................... 43
national socialism..................... 232
nationalism.. 33, 39, 119, 120, 186, 190, 210, 214, 223
nationalists 181, 209, 213
Native Americans........................ 21
  herded into reservations 25
Nazi/s 244, 245, 246, 247, 269, 279, 280, 296, 298
  HQ
    Austrian police raid 279
    Party................................ 233
    sympathisers......................... 279
    Youth................................ 233
Nelson, Horatio 92
Nernst, Walther......................... 221
Netherlands 93, 313
  Arnhem 9
  Rotterdam 93
Neumann, John von 297
Neurath, Konstantin von 247, 280
New Guinea............................. 14
  US air supremacy....................... 7
New York Times....................... 253
New Zealand 14, 180
Nicholas II, Tsar....................38, 56
Nicholas of the Stavka, Grand Duke 53
Night of the Long Knives................ 234
Nimitz, Chester William................ 7, 8
Nivelle, Robert .. 89, 121, 124, 126, 175, 272
NKVD 217
Nomonhan Incident.................... 301
North America 121

North Sea...... 36, 41, 71, 77, 93, 94, 98, 100, 124, 137, 168, 305
  Dogger Bank 93
Northcliffe press....................... 82
Norway 268, 317
Norwegian............................167, 168
Nuremberg Laws, The 296
Nuremberg Rallies..................... 269
oil 6, 7, 39, 128, 189, 192, 194, 211, 235, 268, 311
  replacing coal........................ 32
Old Testament......................... 42
Olympic Games (1936) 269
Operation Overlord...................... 8
Opium Wars.........................22, 285
Orlando, Vittorio..................... 185
Orthodox Church..................... 231
Oseen, Carl.......................... 222
Ottoman Empire .. 15, 23, 26, 33, 34, 39, 61, 72, 79, 112, 115, 119, 164, 166, 188, 192, 219
  break-up of 4, 39
  disintegrates 164
  German influence 40
  Khedive 26
  Macedonia war 39
  Peace Conference, The............... 188
  Thrace 189
Ottoman/s 120, 188
  Armenians........................... 80
Owens, Jesse 269
Pacelli, Eugenio............. 231, 232, 233
Pacific.............72, 113, 180, 186, 231
Page, William....................... 123
Painlevé, Paul...................... 125
Palestine.. 113, 146, 164, 171, 192, 193, 194, 263, 297
  Gaza 147
Papen, Franz von............. 232, 246, 247, 280
paratrooper/s........................ 10
  German tradegy at Battle of Crete 17
  significance of use.................. 10
Pasha, Osman......................... 26
Pasternak, Boris..................215, 217
  Doctor Zhivago 215
  Nobel Prize........................ 217
patriotism.........................170, 244
Patton, George S............. 9, 10, 11, 162
Pauli, Wolfgang..................... 297

Pax Britannica 305
Peierls, Rudolph 297
percussion fuses 25
Pericles 189
Pershing, John ..122, 153, 161, 162, 163, 165
Persia 79, 192, 201
Persian Empire 33
Persian Gulf 113
Pescadores, the 33
Pétain, Philippe 87, 88, 89, 131, 151, 153, 157, 172, 173, 174, 176
Peter the Great 208
Petliura, Symon 209, 213, 297
Petrograd .... *See* Russia:St Petersburg
Philippines 8, 9, 14
   invasion of 9
   Japanese attack on 5
Phillips, Tom 306
Picasso, Pablo 278
pillboxes 131, 162
Pilsudski, Josef 181, 182, 209
Pius XI, Pope 231, 234
Planck, Max 220
plantocracy 24
Plumer, Hubert 129, 131, 133
pogroms 243
   Jewish death toll in Ukraine 213
Pohl, Hugo, von 96
Poincaré, President Raymond 89, 138
Poland ... 11, 14, 38, 112, 114, 115, 145, 180, 183, 201, 209, 224, 267, 297, 298, 303, 307, 309, 310, 313, 314, 315, 317
   Cracow 64
   creation of a sovereign state 179, 180
   Danzig 181, 219, 279, 309, 312
   independent 166
   Lodz 64
   Lublin 61
   Narew 313
   Peace Conference, The 180
   Przemysl 64
   Saar 181
   San 313
   seeks independence 114
   Silesia 114, 181, 219
   Upper Silesia 181, 196
   Vistula 57, 65, 181, 313
   Warsaw 64, 182, 210, 212

| 335

Poles/Polish 57, 114, 180, 181, 209, 212, 213, 214, 243, 283, 311, 312, 317
   Blunting of Polish Ambitions, The ... 209
Potemkin
   mutiny on 38
Pound, Dudley 306
Pour Le Mérite 141, 146
press 77, 99, 244, 292
   underground 250
Princeton 297
Prittwitz, Maximilian von 57
Promised Land 192
propaganda 244
   Entente about Germany 55
Protestant 181, 183
Prussia 24, 25, 29
   Alsace & Lorraine, annexation of 25
   Austro-Hungarians, conflict with (1866) 25
   Coulmiers, small French victory at 25
   Konigsberg 14
   Paris, seige of 25
   Sedan (1870) 25
Prussian Academy of Sciences 221
Pu-Yi, Emporer 261
railway/s 32, 33, 54, 60, 65, 83, 93, 104, 113, 127, 128, 157, 160, 164, 181, 189, 197, 203, 205, 207, 208, 211, 259, 285, 290, 293, 300
   Baghdad railway 39, 40
   importance to Germany in WWI 49
   influence in Russian-Japanese war 37
   transformation of war 25
Rashadiye 61
Rathenau, Walther 222
Raubal, Geli
   suicide 245
Rawlinson, Henry 81, 174
reconnaissance 106, 132, 162, 171, 300
Red Army 204, 207, 208, 209, 212, 213, 214, 215, 249, 257, 258
   10th Army 60
   11th Army 102
   1st Army 60
   2nd Army 60
   7th Army 102
   8th Army 102
   9th Army 102
   army class fissures, WWI 52

as invading army 55
attack on East Prussia 55
cavalry a supply nightmare 70
invasion of East Prussia 57
march into Manchuria 35
mobilisation on 24 July 1914 47
Red Guards 144
Reich Concordat 231
Reijiro, Wakatsuki 260
Remarque, Erich Maria
   All Quiet on the Western Front 237
Rennenkampf, Paul von 57
reparations 113, 189, 196, 197, 198, 199, 219
Repington, Charles 77
respirators 84
Ribbentrop, Joachim von 280, 312, 314, 315
   Ribbentrop in Moscow 313
Richthofen, Manfred von 140, 146
Richthofen's Circus 140, 146
Robertson, William .. 125, 137, 175, 176, 228
Rockefeller 297
Rolls-Royce 71
Roman Catholic Church 232, 294
Romania 26, 39, 64, 74, 87, 102, 109, 111, 112, 115, 141, 163, 184, 201, 282, 310, 316
   Bucharest 109
   Gagesti 141
   joins the Allies 109
   Monnet Costa 141
   Monte Matagar 141
   Transylvania 102, 109, 112, 184
Romanian/s 167
Romanovs 13, 46
Rommel, Erwin 8, 137, 141
   first sees action 140
Room 40 .... 122, 123
Roosevelt, President Franklin D. 5, 8, 13, 167, 168, 226, 252, 254, 255, 269, 275, 306
   and North Africa 6
   Churchill meeting in Quebec 10
   determines prime objective with Churchill 6
   mine barrier of Norwegian waters 167
   Newport scandal 253
   poliomyelitis virus 253
   visits England (1918) 168
Roosevelt, President Theodore 37, 123, 167

Root, Elihu 274
Royal Air Force (RAF) 7, 150, 171
   beginning of the 135
Royal Flying Corps .. 107, 125, 135, 138, 139
   Avro Lancaster 12
   Handley-Page V/1500 135
   Royal Aircraft Factory B.E.2c 107
   Royal Aircraft Factory S.E.5 138
   Sopwith Camel 138
   Sopwith Triplane 138
Royal Navy 37, 71, 75, 93, 96, 135, 235, 262, 305, 306
   E. 11 77
   E. 14 77
   Grand Fleet 99
   Lion 94
Rozhestvensky, Zinovy P. 37
Russia .. 26, 44, 61, 64, 74, 75, 77, 78, 79, 82, 102, 108, 110, 114, 116, 117, 120, 123, 126, 127, 129, 145, 147, 150, 163, 166, 167, 170, 173, 181, 189, 191, 193, 196, 200, 210, 213, 215, 217, 219, 222, 224, 229, 241, 263, 266, 267, 293, 301, 310
   agreement with Turkey 40
   alliance with France (1892) 40
   Archangel 202, 204
   Burma Road 293
   Chinese granted rights in Korea 33
   collapse of Capitalism 126
   Communist party 263
   cultural flowering 32
   Duma 38
   Ekaterinburg 206
   Ekaterinoslav 207
   famine death toll 251
   insurrection 127
   Konigsberg 312
   Kremlin 217, 249
   Kursk 207, 212
   Leningrad 250
   martial law (1918) 204
   massacre at Winter Palace in St Petersburg (1905) 38
   Moscow 127, 144, 202, 205, 207, 208, 209, 211, 212, 213, 214, 216, 249, 310, 312
      Germans ignore 6
   Nizhniy Novgorod 207
   Omsk 204, 208

Orel 205, 207, 208, 209, 212
Orenburg 203
Pale of Settlement 213
Perm 211
persuades Britian to come to aid (1915) 70
political vacuum appears 120
population growth (1890-1914) 31
promise to France, WWI 54
Rostov 207
Samara 45
Second Soviet Congress 206
Serbia
    Irkutsk 209
Siberia 203, 211
    Tobolsk 206
St Petersburg .38, 45, 127, 144, 183, 202, 205, 208, 211, 212, 248
Stalingrad 6, 7, 207
Tauride 214
territorial power of 32
Tsaritsyn .... 211, *See* Russia:Stalingrad
Tula 207
Ufa 203
Vladivostok 33, 36, 183, 202, 209, 300
Volga 45, 203, 204, 207, 211
Voronezh 207, 208
war with Poland 4
Yuryatin 216
Russian Empire 23, 25, 33, 79, 119, 178, 202, 204
cracks begin to appear (1915) 70
Russian/s 71, 72, 84, 112, 131, 173, 183, 207, 209, 219, 231, 243, 250, 272, 277, 286, 293, 299, 300, 304
    casualties in Galicia 61
    civil war 4, 166
    economy, WWI 53
    New Economic Policy 249
    Orthodox Church 15, 33, 45, 46, 56
    retreat to the San 68
    revolution 38, 144, 201, 202, 203, 207
        casualties 202
        lumpenproletariat brigade 205
        Reds and Terror, The 204, 206
    Revolutionary Military Council 249
    Stavka, the 53
Russo–Turkish War 26
Ruthenes 55, 56, 57, 167

SA (*Sturmabteilung*) 240, 244, 245, 246
Sahara 276
Saionji, Prince 186
Saipan 8, 12
Salonika 75
Samsonov, Alexander 57
San Remo Treaty 191
Sanders, Liman von 76, 81
Sanjurjo, José 276
Saud, Ibn 194
Saudi Arabia 192
    formation of 194
    Hejaz 194
Sazonov, Sergey 80
Scandinavia 93
Schacht, Hjalmar 280
Scheer, Reinhard 96, 98, 100
Schlachtstaffein (Schlastas) 138, 139
Schleicher, Kurt von 246
Schleswig-Holstein 312
Schulenburg, Graf von der 313
Schuschnigg, Kurt 279, 280
schwerpunkt 170
Sea of Marmara 76, 77, 78, 82, 202
Second World War 4, 173, 227
    Archangel–Astrakhan line 5
    Maginot Line 315
Sedan 163
Selassie, Emperor Haile 235
Serb/s 110, 112, 163, 166
Serbia 39, 54, 72, 114, 117, 163
    Belgrade 164
    Ferdinand, Franz 47
Seyss-Inquart, Arthur 279, 280, 281
Shakespeare, William 15, 30, 46, 295
    Hamlet 296
    King Lear 44
Shami, Miyaki 288
Shaposhnikov, Boris 9
Sherman, William 24
Sicily
    invasion of 6
Singapore 305, 306
Skoda 68
Slav/Slavic 65, 114, 243
Slim, William 9
Slovak/s 183, 281, 307
Slovakia 283, 307, 310
    Bratislava 184

Slovenes 166
Slovenia 184
   Isonzo 120, 131
Smith, Adam 225
   An Inquiry into the Nature and Causes of the Wealth of Nations 225
Smith, Al 253, 254, 255
Smith-Dorrien, Horace 106
smoke shells 144, 153, 154
Smuts, Jan Christian 15, 28, 44, 46, 135, 149, 196
   & Gandhi, Mahatma 44
socialism 32, 135, 169, 214, 232, 273
Socialist 128
Solomon Islands
   U.S. want control at Guadalcanal 7
Somalia 185
Somaliland, British 235
Sorge, Richard 301, 302
South Africa 14, 28, 37, 42, 149, 180
   sugar plantations 43
   Transvaal 44
South African/s 149, 196
South Manchurian Railway 37
Soviet Union ... 6, 14, 15, 209, 215, 224, 235, 252, 262, 276, 282, 283, 288, 300, 301, 302, 303, 304, 306, 309, 310, 311, 314, 316, 317
   at the Centre of Affairs 299
   GPU 250
   Moscow Soviet 248
   Slav line, the 14, 15
Soviet/s ... 287, 299, 301, 302, 303, 310, 312, 314
   learn to retreat 6
Spain 276, 279, 280, 309, 314
   Barcelona 276
   Catalonia 278
   Guernica 277, 290
   Madrid 276, 277
   Maqueda 277
   Pyrenees 277, 278
   Saravera 277
   Toledo 277
   Valencia 278
Spanish
   Carlists of Navarre and Pamplona 276
   Civil War 275, 277, 278, 279, 315
   influenza

     origination of 156
Popular Front 275, 276
war between fascism and communism. 5
Speer, Albert 7
Stalin, Joseph 5, 6, 11, 210, 211, 212, 213, 217, 232, 241, 248, 249, 250, 251, 301, 310, 312, 313, 314
   14th Party Congress 249
   appendicitis 212
   The Rise of 248
Stalinism 252
starvation 228
Steyr 68
Stimson, Henry L 13, 262
Stokes mortar 270
Stopford, Frederick 81
Straits of Gibraltar 77
Strasser, Gregor 246
Stresemann, Gustav 223, 244
submarine warfare 78, 82, 87, 92, 94, 95, 96, 98, 115, 117, 120, 122, 124, 167
Sudetens 183, 282
Suez Canal 27, 37, 39, 113, 188, 192, 193, 194, 306
sui generis 314
Sukhomlinov, Vladimir 53
Sultan Oman 61
Sumatra 8
Sverdlov, Yakov 212
Sweden 122
Swedish 122
Swiss 297
Switzerland 183, 221, 297, 313
   Geneva 235
   Swiss border 161
   Zürich university 220
Sykes, Sir Mark 113
Sykes–Picot Agreement . 113, 164, 189, 192, 194
Syria 80, 113, 192, 193, 194
   Damascus 125, 164, 192, 193
   Germans make no headway in 6
Szilard, Leo 297
Taft, Howard 95
Taiping Heavenly Kingdom
   formation of 22
   keen to capture Shanghai 22
   Taiping rebels embrace Christianity 22

Taiping Rebellion.........*See* Chinese:Civil War (1851–1864)
Taiwan .... *See* Formosa
Talaat, Mehmed 80
Tanaka, Kakuei 259
Tanggu Truce 286
tank/s 73, 136, 138, 142, 144, 158, 160, 161, 169, 170, 171, 174, 176, 208, 237, 239, 270, 277, 278, 300, 302, 303, 304
   Churchill funds first tanks 73
   first major tank attack........................ 105
   Renault 162
Tanzania
   Dar-es-Salaam 149
   Lake Tanganyika 149
   Moshi 149
Tao-Lin, Chang... 259
telegraph/telegram 122, 123
   transformation of war 25
Teller, Edward 297
Thalmann, Ernst 245
The Great War See Churchill, Sir Winston:*The World Crisis*
Tibet... 286
Timoshenko, Semyon 301
Tinian 8
Tirpitz, Alfred von.................................. 40, 95
Tolstoy, Leo 15
   & Gandhi, Mahatma............................ 46
   Anna Karenina...................................... 44
   as a soldier 44
   death 44, 46
   final years 46
   secret police 45
   sexual appetite 44
   views on Christianity 45
   War and Peace....................................... 44
   What I Believe 45
   Yasnaya Polyana 44
Tolstoyans 46
Tories ....*See* British:Conservative Party
torpedo/torpedoes 77, 95
Toseiha 287
Townsend, Charles... 79
trade .. 74, 78, 82, 92, 93, 110, 116, 198, 286, 305
Transjordan 194
Trans-Siberian Railway 36, 38, 183, 202, 203, 216, 303

| 339

work started on (1891) 33
Treaty of Brest-Litovsk.. 144, 179, 189, 197, 230, 243
Treaty of Locarno 223, 231
Treaty of London 112, 136, 185
Treaty of Rapallo 219, 220, 222
Treaty of Riga 182, 210
Treaty of Sevres 191
Treaty of Versailles. 195, 196, 197, 199, 219, 223, 234, 267
   Germany sinks its own fleet............. 196
   Polish–Russian border 210
Treaty of Washington 231
trench/es ...64, 73, 81, 83, 91, 102, 103, 119, 142, 145, 150, 155, 158, 171, 187, 238
   French mutiny 126
Trenchard, Hugh 107, 135, 138, 139, 171
Triple Alliance 114
Triple Entente. 40, 48, 61, 62, 110, 111, 112, 115
   declare war on Ottoman Empire 63
Triumph
   sinking of 78
Trotsky, Leon . 145, 204, 206, 207, 208, 209, 210, 211, 212, 248, 249, 250, 263
   12th Party Congress 248
Truman, Harry 11
Tunisia
   surrender of 350,000 soldiers 6
Turk/Turkish.. 39, 70, 72, 74, 76, 77, 79, 80, 81, 82, 110, 147, 174, 190, 191, 229, 272
   driven out of Europe (1912) 40
   front 65
   navel losses 78
   navy
      British built ships 40
   parliament, opening of (1908) 39
   racial ambitions 79
Turkey 15, 26, 33, 48, 61, 72, 74, 77, 82, 109, 110, 114, 120, 145, 164, 170, 173, 178, 185, 188, 191, 192, 194, 197, 201, 229, 310, 316
   Anatolia... 191
   Ankara 191
   Bulair 82
   Cape Helles
      stalemate 81
   Constantinople 40, 70, 72, 74, 75, 77, 78, 82, 110, 164, 189, 191, 214

Istanbul
  British & French consult sultan 27
  surrenders 164
Turkish Empire 146
typhus 202, 204
Udet, Ernst 146
Ueda, Kenkichi 302
Uhlans 60
Ukraine .. 7, 87, 145, 164, 182, 204, 208, 209, 211, 213, 214, 307
  Crimea 7, 214
  Donbass 207
  Kharkov 207
  Kiev 208, 209, 212, 214
  Lemberg 102
  Lvov 212
  Odessa 38, 208
Ukrainian/s 55, 182, 207, 209, 213, 214, 231, 243, 297
  nationalists 57
unconditional surrender
  development of 24
Uniate Church 56
United Nations 13
  setting up of 11
United States 14, 15, 32, 87, 92, 96, 111, 115, 117, 122, 123, 124, 137, 156, 168, 169, 178, 179, 180, 181, 185, 186, 188, 192, 199, 203, 219, 222, 224, 225, 226, 229, 231, 235, 252, 261, 269, 273, 275, 296, 297
  begins to become world's great financial power 117
  California 186
  Camp Devens 164
  Chicago 255
  Congress 187
  Democrat/s 254
  Democratic Party 11
  economy (1920s) 222
  enters the war (1917) 121
  Federal Reserve 225
  Federal Reserve Board 117
  Missouri 273
  New York 253, 273
  Pearl Harbor 5
    aerial torpedoes 5
  Republican/s 254
  Supreme Court 256

Texas 123
Washington 122
United States Air Force
  Boeing B-39 Superfortress 12
  Douglas DC-3 Dakota 9
United States Army
  29th Division 76
  42nd Division 161
    casualties (July 1918) 161
  88th Division 165
United States Navy 7
universal reserve currency 13
Urals 15
Valhalla 30
Valkyries 30
Van Deventer 149
Vansittart, Robert 235
Vatican 234
Venizelos, Eleftherios 163, 189, 190, 191
Vico, Giambattista 295
Villa, Pancho 122
Volga 6
Volk 269, 279
Völkischer Beobacter 240
Voroshilov, Kliment 211, 249, 310
Wang Jingwei 293
Wehrmacht 5, 6, 7, 9, 282, 317
  Von Manstein, Erich 7
Weimar system 244
Weizmann, Chaim 193, 222
Wemyss, Rosslyn 81
West Africa 14, 121
  Allied invasion of 6
West Africa, German 28, 145
Western Approaches 96, 98
Weygand, Maxime 138, 174
wheat 70, 75
White Russians 191, 202, 204, 207, 208, 209, 212, 213, 214, 215, 216
  arms from the Allies 203
  End for the Whites, The 213
White Star 95
White, Harry Dexter 10
Whitman, Walt
  Leaves of Grass 256
Wigner, Eugene 297
Wilhelm II, Kaiser 40
Wilhelm, Crown Prince 88, 108, 146
Wilhelm, Kaiser 39, 93

Willmer, Wilhelm 81
Wilson, Henry 137, 175, 176
Wilson, President Woodrow 95, 115, 117,
   122, 123, 138, 166, 167, 178, 181, 184,
   185, 186, 187, 188, 189, 190, 194, 195,
   199, 200, 202, 203, 230, 236, 252, 255,
   262, 274, 284
   asks Germany for unconditional
      surrender (1918) 169
   Fourteen Points 179, 187, 195
   wireless 98, 107, 121, 133, 206
Witte, Sergei 38
World Bank 13
world's reserve currency 10
Wrangel, Baron Peter 207

| 341

Wrangel, Peter 214
Yagoda, Genrikh 217
Yalta 11
Yudenich, Nikolai 208, 212
Yugoslavia 6, 185, 234, 265, 282
   provisional government 166
Yugoslavs 183
Zeng Guofan 23
Zhou Enlai 287
Zhukov, Georgy 9, 12, 301
Zimmermann, Arthur 122, 124
Zinoviev, Grigory 248, 249, 263
Zionism 193, 263
Zulu Rebellion (1906) 43

BIBLIOGRAPHY

A Bridge Too Far – Cornelius Ryan Hamish Hamilton
Achtung Panzer – Heinz Guderian Arms & Armour 1992
Africa Corps at War – George Forty Ian Allan 1978
Albert Speer – Gitta Sereny Macmillan 1995
African Trilogy – Alan Morehead. Cassell 1998
A Genius for War – Carlo d'Este Harper Collins 1996
A German Officer in Occupied Paris – Ernst Junger Columbia 2018
A History of South Africa – Frank Welsh. Harper Collins 1998
A History of the Indians of the United States – Angela Debo. University of Oklahoma Press 1970
Aircraft of the 2WW – Philip Jarrett Putnam 1997
Air Crew – Bruce Lewis. Orion Books 1997
Alanbroke – David Fraser Collins 1983
Alex – Nigel Nicolson W&N 1973
All Quiet on the Western Front – Erich Remarque Folio Society 1994
A Full Life – Brian Horrocks Collins 1960
A Matter of Honour – Philip Mason. Jonathan Cape 1974
An Autobiography – M K Gandhi Penguin 1982
A Peoples Tragedy. 2 Russian Revolution – Orlando Figes. Jonathan Cape 1996
Architect of Victory. Douglas Haig – Walter Reid Birlinn Ltd 2006
Armageddon – Max Hastings Macmillan 2004
Articles of War – Spectator Collins 1989
A Study of History – Arnold Toynbee. OUP 1972
An Autobiography – M K Gandhi, translated from Gujerati by Mahadev Desai. Penguin books 1982.
At Dawn We Slept – Gordon Prange Penguin 1982
At Hitler's Side – Nicholas von Below Greenhill Books 2001
Asquith – Roy Jenkins Collins 1964
A Writer at War – Vasily Grossman Harvill Press 2005
Autumn in the Heavenly Kingdom – Stephen Platt. Random House 2012. Penguin 2000
A World at Arms – Gerhard L Weinberg CUP 1994

B17 Flying Fortress – Jeffrey Ethell Motorbooks International 1995
Barbarossa Derailed – David Glantz Helion & Co 2012

Battles Lost and Won – Hanson Baldwin Robson Books 2000
Battle of Britain – Len Deighton Jonathan Cape 1980
Battle of Britain illustrated – Paul Jacobs, Robert Lightsey. McGraw-Hill 2003
Battle of Britain myth and reality – Richard Overy. Penguin 2000
Battle of Wits – Stephen Budiansky. Penguin 2000
Berlin – Antony Beevor Penguin 2002
Behind Enemy Lines – T Macpherson
Berlin to Baghdad Express – Sean McMeekin Penguin 2010
Berlin Diaries – Marie Vassiltchikov Chatto & Windus 1985
Berlin Diary – William L Shirer. Hamish Hamilton 1941
Bernard Freyberg VC – Paul Freyberg. Hodder and Stoughton 1991
Beyond the Chindwin Bernard Fergusson 1971
Blenheim Summer – Alastair Panton Penguin 2018
Blitzkrieg – Len Deighton. Jonathan Cape 1979
Blood Lands – Timothy Snyder Bodley Head 2010
Blood Tears and Folly – Len Deighton. Jonathan Cape 1993
Bomber Command – Max Hastings Max Joseph 1987
Bomber Command War Diaries– Martin Middlebrook C Everitt Midland Publishing 1994
Bomber Harris – Henry Probert Greenhill Books 2001 Bomber Harris - Dudley Saward Cassell 1984
Bombers – Brian Johnson, H Cozens Thames Methuen 1984
Britain's Army in the 20th Century – Field Marshal Lord Carver. Macmillan 1998
Britain's Greatest Defeat – Alan Warren Hambledon 2002
British Intelligence in the Second World War – F H Hinsley and others. HM Stationery Office 1979
Burma – Louis Allen J M Dent 1984
Burma 1942 – J Grant & K Tamayana Tampi Press 1999

Cambridge Minds – Ed by Richard Mason. CUP 1994
Castles of Steel – Robert K Massie. Jonathan Cape 2004
Catch 22 – Joseph Heller Jonathan Cape 1962
China's Last Empire – The Great Qing – William T Rowe. Harvard University Press 2012.
China's War with Japan – Rana Metter Penguin 2013
Charles de Gaulle – Don Cook Seckers & Warburg 1984

The Globalisation of War, Vol. 1
Chronology of WW2 – E Davidson D Manning Cassell 1999
Churchill as War Leader – Richard Lamb 1991
Churchill A Life – Martin Gilbert. Heinemann 1991
Churchill and De Gaulle - Francois Kersaudy Collins 1981
Churchill – John Charmley Hodder& Stoughton 1993
Churchill – Roy Jenkins. Macmillan 2001
Churchill – Walking with Destiny – Andrew Roberts. Penguin 2018
Churchill and Hitler – John Strawson Constable 1997
Churchill's War Memoirs – Cassell 1948
Cunningham – John Winton John Murray 1998
Curzon – David Gilmour Macmillan 1994
Climate of Treason – Andrew Boyle Hutchinson 1979
Commander-in-Chief – Eric Larrabee. Andre Deutsch 1987
Convoy – Martin Middlebrook Penguin 1978
Coral Sea Midway & Submarine – Samuel Morison Little Brown 1949
Counterfeit Spies – Nigel West Little Brown 1998
Crete – Anthony Beevor. Penguin 1991 Das Boot – L Gunther Bucheim Cassell 1999

Day of the Bomb – Dan Kurzman W&N 1986
Defeat in the West – Milton Shulman Pan Books 1998
Defeat into Victory – FM Viscount Slim Folio Society 2017
De Gaulle – Bernard Ledwidge W&N 1982
De Gaulle – Andrew Shennan Longmans 1993
D Day – Antony Beevor Penguin 2010
D Day – Warren Tute Sidgwick & Jackson 1974
De Gaulle The Rebel 1890 – 1944 – Jean Lacouture. Collins Harvill
Diaries & Letters 1939 – 45 Harold Nicolson William Collins 1967
Donitz – Peter Padfield Harper & Row 1984 1990
Douglas Haig – Ed Sheffield & Bourne W&N 2005
Douglas Haig – Walter Reid Birlinn 2006
Dresden – Frederick Taylor Bloomsbury 2001
Dresden – Sinclair McKay Penguin 2020
Dynamo – Andy Dougan Fourth Estate 2001
Dr Zhivago – Boris Pasternak. Wm Collins 1958

Eastern Front – J&L Erickson Carlton 2001
Eastern Front Combat – Ed Hans Wigers Stackpole Books 2008

Einstein – his life and universe Simon & Schuster 2007
Empires in World History – Jane Burbank & Frederick Cooper. Princeton University Press 2010
Empire. How Britain made the modern world – Niall Ferguson. Allen Lane 2003
Enigma – Hugh Sebag Montefiore W&N 2000
Europe – Norman Davies. OUP 1996
Europe since 1870 – James Joll. Weidenfeld and Nicolson 1973
Economic Consequences of the Peace – J Maynard Keynes

Failure of a Mission - Neville Henderson Hodder & Stoughton 1940
Far Eastern File – Peter Elphick Hodder & Stoughton 1997
The Fall of Berlin – A Read & D Fisher Pimlico 1992
FDR -Ted Morgan. Grafton Books 1985
FD Roosevelt – Joseph Alsop. Thames & Hudson 1982
Fighter – Len Deighton Jonathan Cape 1977
Fighter Command – David Oliver. Harper Collins 2000
Final Solution – David Ceserani Macmillan 2016
Fire in the Night – J Bierman & C Smith Macmillan 1999
First Nations – First hand – Cameron Fleet editor. Chartwell Books 1997
First World War Atlas – Martin Gilbert. Weidenfeld & Nicolson 1970
Flu – Gina Kolata. Farrar Strauss & Geroux 1991
Forgotten Armies – C Bayly T Harper Allen Lane 2004
Forgotten Victory – Gary Sheffield. Headline Book Publishing 2001
Forgotten Voices of the Great War – Max Arthur. Ebury Press 2002
Franco – Paul Preston. Fontana 1995

Gallipoli – Alan Morehead. Hamish Hamilton illustrated 1973.
Gallipoli – Richard van Emden, Stephen Chambers. Bloomsbury Publishing 2015
Gandhi – Rajmohan Gandhi. Haus Publishing 2007
Gazala 1942 – Ken Ford Osprey 2008
German Army Handbook – James Lucas Sutton 1998
Germania – Simon Winder. Picador 2010
Germany 1918 – 1990 The Divided Nation – Mary Fulbrook. Fontana 1991
Germany and the Second World War. Research Institute for Military History – Freiburg 1991
Germany Hitler & WW2 – Gerhard Weinberg CUP 1995

Germany's Invasion Plans - Bodleian Library
Goring – David Irving. Macmillan 1989
Goebbels – David Irving Focal Point 1996
Goebbels – Mastermind of the Third Reich – David Irving. Parfora UK Ltd 1996
Goebbels – The Life of Joseph Goebbels – Ralph George Reuth Constable 1993
Guy Gibson – Richard Morris Viking 1994

Haig's Command – Daniel Winter. Viking 1991
Hall of Mirrors – David Sinclair. Century 2001
Hess Hitler & Churchill – Peter Padfield Icon Books 2013
Hess The Fuehrer's Disciple – Peter Padfield London 1991
Hirohito – Herbert Bix Harper Collins 2000
Hirohito's War – Francis Pike Bloomsbury 2016
History of the First World War – B H Liddell Hart. Faber & Faber 1930
History of the Second WW – Liddell Hart Cassall 1970
Hitler – Ian Kershaw Vols 1&2 1998 &2000
Hitler – Joachim Fest W&N 1974
Hitler – Norman Stone. Hodder and Stoughton 1980
Hitler – hubris – 1889 – 1936 – Ian Kershaw. Allen Lane 1998
Hitler & Stalin – Alan Bullock Harper Collins
Hitler's Mediterranean Gamble – Douglas Porch W&N 2004
Hitler's Table Talk Ed M Bormann OUP 1953
Hitler's U Boat War 1939 - 42 Clay Blair W&N 1997
Hitler's U Boat War 1943 – 45 Clay Blair 1999
Hitler's War – Heinz Magenheimer Arms & Armour 1998
History of the Russian Revolution – Leon Trotsky Pathfinder 1960
Hitler's War – Germany's Key Strategic Decisions 1940 – 1943 – Heinz Magenheimer. Arms and Armour 1998
Hitler – Volker Ulrich Bodley Head 2020
Hitler's Army – Command Magazine
Hitler & Stalin – parallel lives – Alan Bullock. Harper Collins 1991
Hitler's Generals – Ed Corelli Barnet Phoenix 1989
Horror in the East – Laurence Rees Constable 2002
How to win Friends and Influence People – Dale Carnegie
How it Happened World War 1 – ed Jon E Lewis. Constable & Robins 2003

How War Came – Donald Watt Heinemann 1989

Ideas & Opinions – Albert Einstein. Crown Publishers 1954
I Flew for the Fuehrer – Heinz Knoke Cassell 2003
Ike – Piers Brendon Seckers & Warburg 1987
Inventing Japan – Ian Buruma W&N 2003
Images of War – The Luftwaffe in WW11 – Francis Crosby. Pen & Sword 2005
Industry & Air Power – Sebastian Ritchie. Frank Cass 1997
In Flanders Fields – Leon Wolff Penguin 1979
In Search of Churchill – Martin Gilbert Harper Collins 1994
Inside Hitler's Headquarters 1939 – 45 – General Walter Warlimont. Presidio Press 1962
Inside the Centre - Ray Monk Jonathan Cape 2012
Inside the Center – the life of J Robert Oppenheimer Jonathan Cape 2012
Interrogations – Richard Overy Penguin 2002

James Joyce – W Y Tindall. Charles Scribner 1960
James Joyce and the Making of Ulysses – Frank Budgen. Indiana University Press 1960
Jane's Naval History of World War 11 – Bernard Ireland. Harper Collins 1998
Jan Smuts – Unafraid of Greatness – Richard Steyn Jonathan Ball 2015

Keynes The Return of the Master - Robert Skidelsky. Allen Lane 2009
Kharkov 1942 – David Glantz Ian Allan 1998
Knight's Cross – David Fraser Harper Collins 1993
Koba the Dread – Martin Amis Jonathan Cape 2002
Kursk – Geoffrey Jukes Ballantine Books 1969

Lenin on the Train – Catherine Merridale. Allen Lane 2016
Leningrad – Anna Reid Bloomsbury 1954
Lloyd George & Churchill Richard Toye Macmillan 2007
Luftwaffe – Williamson Murray Chartwell 1986

Macmillan – Alastair Horne Macmillan 1988
Manstein – Mungo Melvin Phoenix 2010
Masters and Commanders – Andrew Roberts Allen Lane 2006

The Globalisation of War, Vol. 1
Mein Kampf – Adolph Hitler. Translation 1969
MI6 – Nigel West W&N 1983
MI6 – Keith Jeffery Bloomsbury 2010
Miracle of Deliverance – Stephen Harper Sidgwick & Jackson 1985
Memoirs of Hope – Charles de Gaulle W&N 1971
Military Errors in WW2 – Kenneth Mackesy Arms and Armour 1983
Molotov's Magic Lantern – Rachel Polowsky Faber 2010
Moral Combat – Michael Burleigh Harper Press 2011
Mountbatten – Philip Ziegler Collins 1985
Monty – Nigel Hamilton Hamish Hamilton 1981
Mussolini – Jasper Ridley. Constable 1997

Natasha's Dance – Orlando Figes. Allen Lane 2002
Naval History of World War 2 – Bernard Ireland Harper Collins 1995
Nemesis – Max Hastings Harper Collins 2007
Nazi Germany – Klaus Fischer Constable 1995
Nazi Germany at War - -Martin Kitchen Longman 1995
Never Give In – Winston Churchill Pimlico 2004
Nomonhan – John Colvin. Quartet Books 1999
North American Indians – George Catlin. Abridged edition Folio Society 2009
Nuremberg – Joseph Persico Allison & Busby 1995
Nuremberg Raid – Martin Middlebrook Allen Lane 1973
1914 – Virginia Greenlaw Pushkin Press 2013goo
1914– 18. The History of the First World War – David Stevenson. Allen Lane 2004
1918. A Very British Victory – Peter Hart. Weidenfield and Nicolson

Old Soldiers Never Die -The Life of Douglas MacArthur – Geoffrey Perrett. Andre Deutsch 1996
Official Secrets – Richard Breetman Penguin 1998
Orde Wingate – Trevor Royle W&N 1995
Overlord – Max Hastings Michael Joseph 1984

Pacific Fury – Peter Thompson Randdom House 2008
Panzer Leader – Heinz Guderian. Michael Joseph 1952
Park – Vincent George. Methuen 1984
Pearl Harbor – Gordon Prange Penguin 1986

Peacemakers – Margaret McMillan John Murray 2001
Peenemunde Raid – Martin Middlebrook Allen Lane 1982
Petain – Charles Williams Little Brown 2005
Penguin History of Economics – Roger Backhouse. Penguin Books 2009
Prisoners of Hope – Michael Calvert Jonathan Cape 1952

Quartered Safe Out Here – George Fraser Harper Collins 1995

Racing for the Bomb – Robert Morris Steerforth Press 2002
Radar – Werner Haupt Schiffer Military History 1995
Rape of Nanking – Iris Chang. Penguin Books 1998
Red Army Tank Commander – Vasily Bryukhov Pen& Sword 2013
Resistance – memoirs of occupied France – Agnes Humbert. Bloomsbury 2008
Resistance – MRD Foot Eyre Methuen 1976
Reflections – Charles Farrell Pentland Press 2000
Ring of Steel – Alexander Watson. Penguin Books 2015
Road to Victory – Martin Gilbert Heinnemann 1986
Road of Bones – Fergal Keane Harper Press 2010
Rome 44 – Raleigh Trevelyan Secker & Warburg 1983
Royal Air Force 1918 – Ed C Cole William Kimber 1968
Royal Air Force, 1939 – 45 – Denis Richards, Hilary Saunders. HMSO 1974
Royal Flying Corps WW1 Ralph Barker 1982
Russia – Antony Beevor W&N 2022
Russia – Martin Sixsmith. Ebury Publishing 2011
Russia's War – Richard Overy Penguin 1998

Salerno 43 – Hickey Smith Coronet 1983
Second World War – Peter Calvocoressi, Guy Wint and John Pritchard. Viking 1989
Second World War – Martin Gilbert W&N 1989
The Secret War Against Hitler – William Casey
Siege of Leningrad 1941-44 – David Glantz Brown Partworks 2001
Six Armies in Normandy – John Keegan Cape 1982
Singapore – Peter Elphick Coronet 1995
Singapore Burning – Colin Smith Penguin 2005
Six Minutes in May – Nicholas Shakespeare. Harvill Secker 2017

The Globalisation of War, Vol. 1

Soldaten – Sonke Neitzel Harold Wilzer Simom & Schuster 2012
Soldiers of the Night – David Schoenbrun Hale 1981
Sonya's Report – Ruth Warner Chatto & Windus 1991
Spitfire – Portrait of a Legend - Leo McKinstry.
Spitfire – Jonathan Glancy Arms and Armour 2007
Spitfire Ace – M Davidson J Taylor Macmillan 1988
Spitfire – the Combat History – Robert Jackson. Airlife Publishing 1995
Stalin – Dmitri Volkogarou W&N 1991
Stalin – Edward Radzinscharles Scribneerky. Hodder and Stoughton 1996
Stalin – Isaac Deutscher. Penguin Books 1990
Stalin – a time for judgement – Jonathan Lewis, Philip Whitehead. Methuen 1990
Stalin – Man and Ruler – Robert H McNeal. Macmillan 1988
Stalin – S Sebag Montefiore W&N 2003
Stalin – Triumph and Tragedy – Dmitri Kozunov. Weidenfeld and Nicolson 1991
Stalin – Waiting for Hitler 1928 – 41 – Stephen Kotkin. Allen Lane 2017
Stalin – Walter Laqueur Charles Scribner 1990
Stalin's Generals – Ed Harold Shukman Phoenix 1993
Storm of Steel – Ernst Junger Penguin 1961
Supreme Gallantry – Tony Spooner John Murray 1996
Suite Francaise – Irene Nemirovsky. Chatto and Windus 2006
Sword of Honour Trilogy – Evelyn Waugh

The 900 Days – Harrison Salisbury Harper Row 1969
Tail End Charlies – T Bennett J Nicoll Penguin 2004
Tales by Japanese Soldiers – K Tamayana J Nunnelly Cassell 2000
Tank – Patrick Wright Faber & Faber 2000
Tanks – George Forty. Osprey 1995
Tempestuous Journey – Lloyd George his life and times - Frank Owen. Hutchinson 1954
Thanks for the Memory – Laddie Lucas. Stanley Paul 1989
The American Magic – Donald Lewin Farrar Strauss 1982
The Armies of Rommel – George Forty Arms & Armour 1997
The Army Air Forces in WW2 – Ed W Craven J Cater 7vols Univ of Chicago 1955
Army Group Center – C Latham A Stobbs Sutton Publishing 1996
The Art of War – Sun Tzu – trans Richard Sawyer. Westview Press 1994

The Audit of War – Corelli Barnet Pan 2001
The Battle for History – John Keegan Hutchinson 1995
The Battle for Spain – Anthony Beevor. Weidenfeld and Nicolson 2006
The Battle of Bretton Woods – Benn Steil Princeton University 2013
The Battle of Britain– Richard Hough & Dean Richards. Hodder and Stoughton 1989
The Battle of Britain – Richard Overy Penguin 2000
The Battle of Hamburg – Martin Middlebrook Viking 1980
The Battle of the Bulge – Charles MacDonald W&N 1984
The Berlin Raids – Martin Middlebrook Allen Lane 1988
The Big Three – Churchill Roosevelt and Stalin-Robin Edmonds. Hamilton 1991
The Boer War – Thomas Pakenham. Weidenfeld and Nicolson 1979
The Bomber War - Robin Neillands. John Murray 2001
The Bombing War – Richard Overy Allen Lane 2013
The Burma Campaign – Frank McLynn Vintage 2011
The Burning Tigris – Peter Balahean Heinemann 2003
The Case of Richard Sorge – G Sorry. Chatto & Windus 1966
The Chief – Douglas Haig and the British Army – Gary Sheffield. Aurum Press 2011
The Churchillians – John Colville W&N 1981
The Cruel Sea – Nicholas Monsarrat Penguin 1954
The Dam Busters – Jonathan Falconer Sutton Publishing 2003
The Damned and the Dead – Frank Ellis Univ of Kansas 1953
The Decision to use the Atomic Bomb – Gar Alperovitz Simon & Schuster 1995
The Desert Generals – Corelli Barnett. Allen & Unwin 1983
The Desert War 1940-1942 – Imperial War Book – Adrian Gilbert. Sidgwick & Jackson 1992
The Dictators – Richard Overy. Penguin 2004
The Dynasties of China – Bamber Gascoigne. Constable and Robinson 2003
The Earth is Weeping – Peter Cozzens. Atlantic Books 2017
The Eastern Front – Erickson Carlton 2001
The Eastern Front photographs
The Eastern Front 1914-17 – Norman Stone. Hodder and Stoughton 1975
The End – Ian Kershaw Allen Lane 2011
The Face of Battle – John Keegan. Jonathan Cape 1976

The Fall of France – Julian Jackson OUP 2003
The Fall of the Ottomans 1914-20 – Eugene Rogan. Penguin 2015
The First World War – Michael Howard OUP 2002
The First World War an illustrated history – A J P Taylor. Penguin 1966
The First World War an illustrated history – John Keegan. Hutchinson 2001
The First World War – a new illustrated history – Hew Strachan. Simon and Schuster 2003
The First World War – the outbreak, events and aftermath – Keith Robbins OUP 1985
The French Defeat of 1940 – Reassessments – Ed Joel Blatt. Berghahn Books 1998
The Fringes of Power 1939-55 – John Colville. Hodder and Stoughton 1985
The Gales of Europe – Serlin Plokhy Penguin 2015
The German Defeat in the East – Samuel Mitcham Jnr Stackpole Books 2001
The German Economy at War – John Milward Athlone Press 1965
The German War – Nicholas Stargalt Bodley Head 2015
The Great Crash 1929 – JK Galbraith Bodley Head 2015
The Great War – Winston Churchill. George Newnes 1933
The Great War – John Terraine. Hutchinson 1965
The Great War and Modern Memory – Paul Fussell OUP 1975
The Guns at Last Light – Rick Atkinson Little Brown 2013
The History of the Russian Revolution – Leon Trotsky. Anchor Foundation 1980
The Hitler of History – John Lukacs Phoenix 2000
The Hitler Options – Kenneth Mackesy Greenhill 1995
The Indian Army – Charles Chevenix Trench. Thames & Hudson 1988
The Killing Spies – Simon Read Spellmount 2008
The Lancaster – Norman Franks Arms & Armour 1994
The Lancaster Story – Peter Jacobs Cassell 1996
The Last Battle – Cornelius Ryan Collins 1966
The Last Great Frenchman – Charles Williams. Little Brown 1993
The Life of Tolstoy – Aylmer Maude. OUP 1957The Luftwaffe 1933 – 45
The Luftwaffe 1933-45. Williamson Murray 1986
The Making of the Atomic Bomb - Richard Rhodes. Simon & Schuster 1986
The Memoirs – Lord Chandos Bodley Head 1962
The Memoirs – Lord Ismay Heinemann 1960

The Naked and the Dead – Norman Mailer Harper Perrennial 2006
The Near East – Arthur Cotterell. C Hurst 2017
The Ottoman Endgame – Sean McMeekin. Penguin 2015
The Oxford History of the British Empire – 4 volumes
The Origins of Empire – Nicholas Canny OUP 1998
The Eighteenth Century – P J Marshall OUP 1998
The Nineteenth Century – Andrew Porter OUP 1999
The Twentieth Century – J M Brown, W R Louis OUP 1999
The Royal Air Force – Michael Armitage. Cassell 1993
The Royal Air Force 1939 – 1945 – Chas Bowyer. Ian Allam 1984
The Hardest Victory – Denis Richards Hodder & Stough
The Holocaust – Martin Gilbert Collins 1986
The Origins of the First World War – Ed H Koch Macmillan 1984
The Pacific – Hugh Ambrose Canongate 2011
The Peacemakers – Margaret MacMillan. John Murray 2014
The Pity of War – Niall Ferguson Penguin 1998
The Rise and Fall of the Third Reich 4 vols – William L Shirer. Simon & Schuster 1959
The Royal Air Force – C Bowyer Pen & Sword 1996
The Royal Flying Corps in World War 1 – Ralph Barker Constable and Robinson 1995
The Road to Berlin – John Erickson W&N 1975
The Road to Stalingrad – John Erickson W&N 1983
The Road Past Mandalay - John Masters Michael Joseph 1961
The Road to Verdun – Ian Ousby. Jonathan Cape 2002
The Russian Civil Wars 1916-26 – Jonathan D Smale C Hunt 2015
The Schweinfurt – Regensburg Mission – Martin Middlebrook Penguin 1985
The Secret War Against Hitler – William Casey Simon and Schuster 1989
The Second World War – AJP Taylor Penguin 1976
The Second World War – Anthony Beevor. Weidenfeld and Nicolson 2012
The Second World War – John Keegan Pimlico 1997
The Second World War - Several Osprey 2018
The Second World War Atlas – Martin Gilbert W&N 1970
The Siege of Leningrad – David Glantz Spellmount 2001
The Somme – Peter Barton. Constable 2006
The Southern Front – Big Series Time Life Books
The SS – Gordon Williamson Sidgwick & Jackson 1994

The Globalisation of War, Vol. 1
The Struggle for Europe – Chester Wilmot Wandeworth Editions 1997
The Struggle for Mastery in Europe 1848-1918 – A J P Taylor OUP 1954 Profile
The Tank Rider - Eugeni Bessonov Greenhill 2003
The Third Reich – Richard Evans Allen Lane 2008
The Third Reich – K Hildebrand 1979
The Third Reich – Michael Burleigh Harper Collins 2000
The Times History of War – Ed by Ian Drury. Harper Collins 2000
The Unforgettable Army – Michael Hickey Spellmount 1998
The Ultimate Enemy – Wesley Warkm OUP 1985
The Viking Atlas of World War II – John Pimlott Penguin 1995
The Wages of Destruction – Alan Tooze Allen Lane 2006
The War Against Germany - US Pictorial Brassey 1999
The War Against Japan Vol 2 – Several Editors HMSO 1958
The War Against Japan Vol 1 – Several Editors HMSO 1957
The War at Sea 4 vols – SWRoskill HMSO 1954 – 61
The War for the Seas – Evan Maudsley Yale 2019
The War that Ended Peace – Margaret Mitchell Profile 2011
The War the Infantry Knew – JC Dunn
Tobruk – Frank Harrison Arms & Armour 1996
To Hell and Back – Ian Kershaw Penguin 2015
To Lose a Battle - Alastair Horne Macmillan 1969
Tolstoy – Rosamund Bartlett. Profile Books 2010
Truman – David McCullough Simon Schuster 1992
Truman – Roy Jenkins Collins 1986
Through German Eyes – the British and the Somme 1916
The Unfree French David – Life under the Occupation – Richard Vinen. Allen Lane 2006
The War 1939 – 45 – D Flower & J Reeves Cape
The War at Sea – John Winton. Random House 1967
The War at Sea – Captain S W Roskill. H M Stationery Office 1954
The War Diaries – Weary Dunlop Viking 1986
The War that ended Peace – Margaret Macmillan. Profile Books 2013
The Western Front – Richard Holmes. BBC Worldwide 1999
Time to Kill – Ed. P Addison, A Calder Pimlico 1997
Tumult in the Clouds War in the Air 1914-18 – Nigel Steel and Peter Hart. Hodder& Stoughton 1997

Ulysses – James Joyce. Bodley Head 1960
Ulysses with annotations – Sam Stote. Alma Classics 2012
Universal Man – Richard Davenport William

Verdun – Ian Ousby Jonathan Cape 2002
Victory Denied – Dudley Saward Bachan & Enright

Wages of Guilt – Ian Buruma Farrar Strauss 1994
War at Sea – Nathan Miller Scribner 1995
War Diaries – Alanbroke Phoenix 2001
War Diaries – Harold Macmillan Macmillan 1984
War Memoirs – David Lloyd George. Odhams 2 vols 1930's
War Beneath the Sea – Peter Padfield 1995
Warsaw 1920 – Adam Zamoyski. Harper Collins 2008
What Soldiers Do – Mary Roberts University of Chicago 2013
What Stalin Knew – David Murphy Yale 2005
Where Fate Leads – Harry Howarth Ross Anderson 1983
Why the Allies Won – Richard Overy Jonathan Cape 1995
Winston & Clementine – Richard Hough Bantam Press 1990
Winston Churchill – Lord Moran Constable 1986
With our backs to the Wall – David Stevenson Penguin 2012
With Rommel in the Desert – Heinz Schmidt Constable 1997
With the Jocks – Peter White Sutton Publishing 2001
World War One – a short history – Norman Stone. Allen Lane 2003
World War 1 – Ed Jon Lewis Constable 2003